The Mystery of Analytical

This book provides an exploration of the clinical practice of psychoanalysis and analytical psychology. It explores the ways psychoanalysts and other clinicians are taught to evade direct emotional connections with their patients. Sullivan, suggesting that relatedness is the basis of emotional health, examines the universal struggle between socially oriented energies that struggle toward truth and narcissistic impulses that push us to take refuge in lies. She maintains that, rather than making interpretations, it is the clinician's capacity to bring relatedness to the clinical encounter which is the crucial factor.

Examining the work of both Jung and Bion, Sullivan draws on the overlap between their ideas on the psyche and the nature of the unconscious. The book uses clinical examples to examine the implications that these perspectives have for the practising therapist.

Specific areas of discussion include:

- the creative unconscious
- the structure of narcissism
- transformation in analytic work.

New modes of listening and relating that deepen analytic work and greatly facilitate transformative changes are described in easy-to-follow language that will help the therapist to find new approaches to a wide range of patients. *The Mystery of Analytical Work* will be of interest to Jungians, psychoanalysts and all those with an interest in analytic work.

Barbara Stevens Sullivan is a Jungian analyst in private practice in Oakland, California and a training analyst member of the C.G. Jung Institute of San Francisco, where she is on the teaching faculty. She has previously written *Psychotherapy Grounded in the Feminine Principle* (Chiron Publications, 1989) and two novels.

The Mystery of Analytical Work

Weavings from Jung and Bion

Barbara Stevens Sullivan

Routledge
Taylor & Francis Group

LONDON AND NEW YORK

First published 2010
by Routledge
27 Church Road, Hove, East Sussex BN3 2FA

Simultaneously published in the USA and Canada
by Routledge
711 Third Avenue, New York NY 10017

*Routledge is an imprint of the Taylor & Francis Group,
an informa business*

© 2010 Barbara Stevens Sullivan

Typeset in Times by
RefineCatch Limited, Bungay, Suffolk

Paperback cover design by Andrew Ward

British Library Cataloguing in Publication Data
A catalogue record for this book is available from the British Library

Library of Congress Cataloging-in-Publication Data
Sullivan, Barbara Stevens, 1943–
   The mystery of analytical work : weavings from Jung and Bion /
Barbara Stevens Sullivan.
      p. cm.
   ISBN 978–0–415–54775–8 (hbk.) – ISBN 978–0–415–54776–5 (pbk.)
   1. Psychoanalysis.   2. Jung, C. G. (Carl Gustav), 1875–1961.
   3. Bion, Wilfred R. (Wilfred Ruprecht), 1897–1979.   I. Title.
   RC506.S837 2010
   616.89'17–dc22   2009019146

ISBN: 978–0–415–54775–8 (hbk)
ISBN: 978–0–415–54776–5 (pbk)

Contents

Acknowledgments

Many people supported me and contributed to the birth of this book. I learned a great deal about the analytic orientation presented in this book from Lynda Schmidt and Neville Symington. Each of them listened to me in ways that enabled me to find enough of my truth to imagine I could articulate it in a way that might be of interest to others. The third person whose attention and emotional holding made this book possible by making my development possible is my husband, Mark, without whom I would simply be a different person.

I have a few friends whose devotion and availability provide sustenance for my creative efforts. In the middle of my work on this project, I almost despaired of pulling together the whole vision I sensed in inchoate form, almost out of reach. Beth Barmack, Hilde Burton, Marjorie Nathanson, Ruth Palmer, Tom Richardson and Dorothy Witt had faith in me and provided me with emotional support through my work. Without the web of their friendship to hold me, I would not have been able to stay with this project to completion.

Beth Barmack, John Beebe, James Grotstein, Candy Siegle, Neville Symington, Dorothy Witt and Bryan Wittine all read the manuscript in a semi-finished form and their feedback helped me to work through a variety of difficulties I had not recognized on my own.

Finally, and most of all, I want to acknowledge the anonymous patients who so generously trusted me with their souls, especially those very brave individuals who gave me permission to use material from our work in this book. My students, from many seminars in San Francisco and Berkeley, also were invaluable aides in the development of my thought.

To all these people, a heartfelt thank you.

Chapter 1

Beginning with relatedness

The growth process, like the person within whom it is operating, is a mystery that can never be fully explained. This book is my attempt to think about that mystery, partly by circling around it and examining it from different vantage points and partly by exploring how analysts[1] can impact it constructively. Much of the literature focuses on what the clinician can say to affect the patient. Here I will present a perspective that radically questions the centrality of the therapist's interpretations or comments.[2] The analyst's feeling and thinking and being turn out to be much more important than what she says to the patient (although her feelings and thoughts will obviously affect what she says).

Her first job is to open herself to receive the fullness of the patient. She seeks an ever-evolving knowledge of who this person is. One central focus of this book, therefore, is the listening process. How can the therapist hear what the patient, outside his own awareness, is trying to tell her? As we shall explore, there is not a great deal of useful advice to be had about exactly what the analyst should *do* in her work (where "doing" means "speaking," rather than "listening"), but a lot can be said about how to listen to and receive the patient. A profound listening process brings significantly expanded understanding. The clinician's new level of comprehension can help her to find creative approaches to each unique situation that she faces – approaches that may involve very few interpretations. In fact, much of what clinicians say in trying to follow the instructions of their training is counterproductive. For example, patients can secretly experience interpretations that are made by good-hearted and well-meaning therapists as attacks, criticisms or triumphant humiliations. There are ways the practitioner can understand sooner rather

---

1 I use the words "therapy/therapist" and "analysis/analyst" interchangeably. This reflects my belief that patients come for healing – for therapy – rather than simply for knowledge about themselves, the goal of analysis. But, as I will qualify later in this chapter, my subject is depth therapeutic work rather than any of the many other procedures that are also called "therapy," some of which are undoubtedly helpful, too.

2 Analysts from the interpersonal school centered in the William Allison White Institute in New York have also offered critiques of an interpretation-centered focus.

than later how the patient is hearing her, so that she can change her behavior in felicitous ways. Too often, the kinds of interpretations that the literature advises, in addition to being experienced as subtle criticisms of himself by the patient, actually undermine nascent positive developments. A different understanding of the psyche's natural growth process can minimize the potential for these unfortunate developments.

The literature's advice radically neglects relatedness. There have been many ideas about what kinds of interpretations are helpful, and the vast majority of them do nod in the direction of emotional connectedness by mentioning the importance of a comment's "timing." Sometimes, theoreticians have even tried to provide formulas for timing, perhaps suggesting as a guide that an interpretation should include only material that the patient has brought into *this* session. A guideline such as this one is not bad – it minimizes the potential for the patient's feeling misunderstood or confused. But the cumbersome nature of such guidelines highlights the fact that theories of therapeutic technique fail to explicitly address the primary role of relatedness in therapeutic work and emotional health.

A related approach (which should optimally be taken toward all other human beings, not simply those with whom one is in relationship) requires that one holds in mind both one's own and the other's point of view, neither dropping nor privileging either. (If someone holds only the *other's* perspective in mind, she is merged rather than related and is left with as flat a picture as if she saw only her own point of view. If someone has only her own viewpoint through which to see the world, colloquial speech calls her "narcissistic.") In relationships with severe power inequalities, like therapy or family life, the more vulnerable person's needs will frequently trump the other's if the dominant member is compassionately related. But even as she puts her own feelings aside, a related therapist (as contrasted with one who is following the rules in an unrelated manner) will be aware of them. When her patient is hateful the therapist will not *only* know about the wounds that push the patient into demeaning or scornful behavior; she will also feel some hurt and therefore at least some anger in response, even though she will typically not express this.

Relatedness, both inner and outer, is the basis of emotional health. Psychological health implies the ability to coordinate behavior with reality, again both inner and outer. In fact, these two basic realities mirror each other. People treat others in ways they internalized from their childhood relationships, and they treat themselves the way they treat others. The inner world develops as a replica of the infant's outer world and when he becomes an adult that infant will gravitate to outer situations that replicate those initial relational templates as they have been modified and developed in the course of his development. If consonant outer situations cannot be found, people behave in ways that create them, no matter how painful the result may be. When the patient is caught in a masochistic orientation to the world, he will call up his therapist's sadistic potentials; when he takes a scornfully contemptuous attitude toward the other, his therapist is apt to feel inferior no matter what her more ordinary way of being may be.

Although we shall explore the ways that neither outer nor inner reality can ever be *known*, two perspectives on the obscure situation provide a kind of binocular vision that brings depth to the picture. The ability to hold multiple points of view offers the individual choices about his behavior and prevents him from being flung into compulsive action. As long as I am seeing only through the eyes of my limited conscious self, I have no choice; I can only go after whatever it is I want. I will not remember the needs or wishes of other parts of myself any more than I will be able to notice the other people who will be affected by my behavior. In order to have a choice there has to be more than one possible path to choose from. The ability to hold one's conscious wish in mind and to study it with some detachment depends on being able to imagine other perspectives as equally valuable. This is the basic building block of relatedness, whether to oneself or to others: the ability to hold in mind differing perspectives.

But no one is ever "related" or "unrelated." We all contain a related side and an unrelated side, which are always in conflict with each other. To the extent that someone is able to be related, he will be able to imagine other ways of seeing his situation than his own; he will want one thing and at the same time remember the parts of himself that want something else; he will notice the other people who will be affected by his choices and their perspectives will moderate his own. As we shall explore, the extent to which someone can stay related will be determined by the degree to which he feels safe. To the degree that he feels endangered, he will be thrown back into an unrelated stance where all that matters is *his* need, *his* safety.

The world of depth psychology is a little over one hundred years old. Our emotional depths are so terrifying that psychologists have historically armed themselves thoroughly with theories and techniques that keep the patient at such a distance as to prevent our awareness of these dangers. *The patient* is being analyzed; the therapist or healer may seek a *training* analysis, but does not, of course, need a *therapeutic* one; when the patient quits prematurely or otherwise rejects or abandons the therapist, supervisory discussion often centers exclusively on the patient's neurotic conflicts, ignoring whatever inadequacies in the therapist might have triggered the breach. We are only beginning to recognize the inherent insecurities in our work. The fundamental threat of the inner world that we explore calls up deeply unrelated energies which have been important in shaping our field. Let us look at a thumbnail description of the effective action of analysis written by the research psychoanalyst Peter Gay. This description appeared over twenty years ago, and the field has certainly developed since then, but Gay's description tells us something about the obstacles of our history that we still need to overcome.

[T]he psychoanalytic situation is a dialogue. The analyst, though largely a silent partner, offers interpretations that the analysand presumably could not have reached on his own ... While the patient, swollen with grandiosity or bowed down with guilt feelings, distorts the world and his place in it, the analyst, neither praising nor condemning but tersely pointing out what the analysand is really saying, provides a therapeutic glimpse of reality. What is perhaps even more important ... is that the analyst – relatively anonymous and attentively passive – offers himself as a kind of screen onto which the analysand projects his passions, his love and hate, affection and animosity, hope and anxiety. This transference, on which so much of the curative work ... depends, is by definition a transaction between two human beings.

(Gay, 1988, p. 97)

Although Gay calls this a "transaction between two human beings," the analyst he describes does not seem real. In Gay's image, the patient, "swollen with grandiosity or bowed down with guilt feelings," is a full human being, with unknown and messy tangles running through his depths. (Though this person is in a most pathetic condition.) The other is "anonymous and attentively passive." He has not brought *his* depths into the consulting room. He has no unconscious conflicts of his own and can therefore hear exactly what is said. He points out "reality" – being in the privileged position of knowing what that is while his patient is confused. He knows what his analysand is "really" saying, as though the patient's unconscious intent is unidimensional and definitively ascertainable while his conscious intent is irrelevant, not "real." Only the opaque surface of this attentive listener touches the befuddled patient. The analyst's *words*, rather than his tone, communicate his message to the patient, who is no more stirred by his analyst's depths than the analyst is by his patient's. It is a very long step from this sterile image to the messy realities of real consulting rooms.

Clinical training may tell us what the therapeutic relationship *should* be like, but in practice the transference relationship develops between two people who are both present and fully participating, even when they are trying to withhold themselves or to block each other out. We can never leave our depths at home. They always muddy the waters, communicating things we do not know we know to people who do not know what they are learning even as their deeper selves store away these new understandings in parts of themselves they know nothing or little about. Furthermore, a relationship, even between a mother and a newborn or a therapist and patient, is an *inter*dependent experience, although one person may be much more helpless and out-of-control than the other. After all, the analyst needs the patient if she is to be an analyst and the patient needs the analyst if he is to be a patient. A relationship can never be fully dissected; it branches out in infinite directions into the unknowable inner reaches of each participant's soul. Like the growth process, a relationship will always include some mystery, highlighting our vulnerability to the inner or outer realities that we can never be sure we understand.

All schools of depth psychology know that the transference relationship lies at the heart of the work, but there is a stunning tendency to attend inadequately (if at all) to the quality of the therapist's back-and-forth responsiveness – to her relatedness. Yet this is obviously the most powerful way that the therapist influences the nature of the clinical relationship. The initial fantasy was that the therapist could behave in such a neutral way that the patient's inner situation would be the only factor to color the developing bond. We now know that no comment or silence can ever be simply neutral. As we will explore, human beings live in an emotional river at all times and the patient will have feelings about whatever the clinician says or fails to say. Caught in the legacy embodied in Peter Gay's distorted description of the therapeutic relationship, training programs have tended to imagine that there can be a standard approach for the therapist. When the patient asks the practitioner to vary some ordinary aspect of this "correct" approach the dominant theoretical tendency often seems to value the clinician maintaining the proper stance rather than opening herself to curiosity. Why does this patient want to sit up or lie down today instead of continuing in his previous position? What would it mean to accede to his request that his therapist stop taking notes? Would it open the door to an unraveling frame to agree to do phone hours while he is on vacation or would it maintain a fragile tie in the best way that can be managed right now? Analysts even less than psychotherapists are not encouraged to weigh requests in a related manner; more commonly, they are encouraged to maintain the "correct" position regardless of the patient's wishes.

Certainly, it is crucial to hold the analytic frame,[3] and equally important for the therapist not to get caught in polite, socially appropriate ways of relating. The analytic frame provides the therapist with the one escape valve for her own anti-related energies. "It's time to stop," she may say, or "You haven't paid me for last month." As she holds the frame here, she is *not* swayed by how the patient is going to experience her demand: you have to pay me, you get only the minutes you paid for, you even have to pay for that hour you missed. Winnicott (1947) suggested that this was the outlet for the therapist's hate. To my mind, the issue is more an outlet for the therapist's selfishness. Although even when the analyst's stance must be painful for the patient, there are related and unrelated ways of communicating that. It frequently seems as though "experts" judge the *un*related response to be more

---

3 When I refer to the "frame," I am talking about the ordinary fixed frame of analysis: a consistent time and place of meeting, a consistent fee, a firm cancellation policy, a commitment to confidentiality and privacy as well as a promise to work with the patient until he is ready to end the work. Although none of these elements can ever be perfectly adhered to, it is possible for the therapist to try to do so.

"analytic" than one that tries to let the patient know that he has been heard and understood even if his request cannot be granted.

Recently, I attended a psychoanalytic conference at which a senior analyst presented several clinical hours to an eminent visiting psychoanalyst. In one of the hours he described, the patient came into the hour, her third analytic hour of the week, saying that she was exhausted, manifestly by the previous two days at her work. All she could imagine just now, she said, was going home and pulling the covers over her head. Throughout the hour, the analyst spoke to his patient about her inability to use him effectively for help. When the visiting expert questioned the presenter's rather hammering line of interpretation, the presenter explained that as a Kleinian he tried to interpret the patient's central anxiety. In this case, he added, since he judged that that anxiety was centered in the transference, he was interpreting it there. I was struck with the way the analyst's theoretical training trumped his human relatedness. He could not hear, apparently, the patient's statement: the previous two hours had used her up; she had nothing left to work with. He could not respond to *her*. His training told him to interpret the central anxiety and even though the patient was telling him quite clearly (though unconsciously) that she could not hear anything, he needed to keep talking. This particular analyst's training told him to interpret the central anxiety; another analyst's training tells him to interpret the genetic roots of the current difficulty or the archetypal meanings of an image that arises in the hour. The problem is not a Kleinian problem; it is a human problem. It is frightening to be with another person without some kind of professional armor to protect us.

We shall explore the central role of relatedness in emotional health in Chapters 4 and 5, when we look at the structural and dynamic aspects of our anti-related energies. Here, let me just note that people are attachment-seeking creatures from birth on. We all know that infants need to be met by caretakers who can recognize their needs and adapt to them. (After a short time, of course, this adaptation needs to be something less than a hundred per cent, but for a very long time it must be tilted in favor of the more helpless member of the dyad.) A self-centered me-me-me approach to others and to life is not only frowned upon by society; it is also a pathological perspective that indicates the presence of emotional wounding. But a related approach is a vulnerable one, while a selfish stance offers the illusion of safety. Holding one's own perspective along with the other's means accepting a world in which the ground upon which one stands is never reliable. If *I* remember/believe/perceive such-and-such while *you* say thus-and-such, a related response will be suffused with unknowing. I cannot take refuge in the assumption that *my* eyes see clearly while yours are clouded. (If ten of us see one thing and the eleventh another, probably the general perception is reliable, but even this is not always true.) A related approach is dangerous; taking a selfish stance is like living inside a fortress. If I know what is out there because *my* eyes do not distort, I am safe and secure. *You* may be crazy, but I am not.

Thus it is not surprising that faced with the terrifying depths of the psyche and told to contain those depths and transform them, therapists hang onto their theoretical instructions as though they were life preservers. It is dangerous to face the suffering patient as one person to another, where both of us are subject to confusion and error, and the therapist's "mental health" is not presumed superior at any given moment. Plain relatedness seems too simple, although this assessment is a defense against the reality: it is harder for a clinician to sit with a patient and share his distress than to imagine that she can zap away his pain with transformative interpretations. To sit still and hear the patient's pain means to recognize that emotional pain like the patient's can overcome her, too. It also means accepting that in the face of pain the practitioner is helpless to *do* anything to make it go away. It is much more comfortable to hang onto a theoretical bible and to imagine herself strong, capable and mentally healthy, healing her disturbed and needy patient.

At the heart of this book is my attempt to raise therapists' consciousness about the nature and importance of relatedness. It is widely accepted in the depth theoretical world that the self exists only in relationship. Winnicott (1952) suggested that in the absence of a mother, there is no such thing as an infant. As we shall explore in the pages of this book, the human being cannot think or feel (the prerequisite for the self's existence) in isolation. The self exists only in relationship and the self varies from one relationship to another. I am a different person with my husband than I am with my best friend or my daughter or any given patient. There is no "me" in isolation. The quality of each relationship structures who it is possible for me to be. The quality of the therapeutic relationship determines how much the patient will be able to grow inside its container. We certainly know that the quality of the parent's bond with his or her child is infinitely more important than what bedtime she sets or the age at which she allows her daughter to wear make-up. The teacher who adjusts her way of being to accommodate her student's idiosyncratic learning style will be much more successful in facilitating his intellectual development than will the teacher who approaches all her students in one standard way. Why should it be such a leap to recognize that the quality of the analytic bond rather than some standardized analytic approach is the most important element in psychotherapy, too?

My dictionary (Gove, 1993) defines "relate" and "relatedness" in rather solipsistic terms. "Relate" is "to be in relationship" or "to have meaningful social relationships." "Relatedness" is "the state or character of being related" or "a particular manner of being related or of being constituted by relations." These self-referential definitions indicate how elusive and subtle these terms are, for they refer to something as fundamental for the psyche as air or water is for the body. The definition of "related" is slightly more suggestive: "having relationship," "allied by kindred," or "having similar properties." It is the last phrase that evokes a taste of the dangerous aspect of being related: if my patient and I have "similar properties," it implies that emotional fissures and wounds exist in *me* as well as in him. Inside or outside the analytic situation, a related approach opens one to the other's pain and stirs one's own. Relatedness hurts. And then it nourishes. First the pain of embodied existence is experienced and then the compassionate atmosphere of relatedness assuages the pain. But often the looming danger of the pain thrusts aside the healthy related energies and constellates the narcissistic anti-related forces of the psyche.

The etymology of "relate" is also interesting. It comes from the Latin *relatus*, from *re-* ("back, again") and *latus*, the past participle of *ferre* ("to bear"), thus meaning "carried or borne back." In a parallel fashion, *relationem*, the source of "relation," means "a bringing back, restoring." "Relationship," then, implies that two substances have been brought back together after being separated, as though the relationships that we form with strangers are actually connections that existed once before. I believe that this particular etymology developed from the fact that when we are in relationship to another, parts of ourselves that we have lost touch with are carried back into connection with us. And if we add to this the Greek *talantos* ("suffering, bearing"), which is also connected to the Latin *latus*, we have the implication that a relationship with another arouses suffering – intense emotional distress – for it brings us face to face with aspects of ourselves that we have disowned.

Although "relatedness" rests on sensitivity to the other's subjective experience, in therapeutic work it does not imply attempting to create a "nice" experience for the other, especially since the other's *unconscious* immediate experience must be included in the analyst's understanding of the present. But an attempt to adapt to the other's experience in the most related way possible is a most important dimension of the practitioner's approach. In the unique container of the therapeutic relationship a "loving" approach will lead to behaviors that might seem quite *un*loving in other situations. But when a related therapist behaves in ways that her patient finds disturbing, she tries to soften that, to speak to it, at least to hold in her awareness the central importance of the patient's distress. Too often the more depth-oriented the clinician's training, the less it concerns itself with this dimension and the more it values clinical behavior that adheres to the particular school's theoretical orientation. Behavior that accommodates itself to this peculiar patient's receptive channels may be criticized as "unanalytic" instead of being analyzed. How is the therapist's unusual behavior impacting *this* person's process at this singular moment? While the same behavior might often cover up or avoid something difficult, perhaps just now it is opening up something that needs attention.

In this book, I explore a variety of points of view concerning the nature of the psyche, how it processes emotional experience and how it develops. My central focus is on using whatever understanding we can muster to enhance the clinician's effectiveness in the consulting room. Because the most fundamental determinant of the patient's capacity to use his analyst constructively is the quality of their relationship, one core question that this book asks is, "what makes the therapeutic relationship therapeutic?" Here, I am suggesting that it is the degree to which the clinical relationship is permeated with relatedness. The analyst, of course, is only half the equation; how related she is able to be will depend on how related her patient can be as well as on her own capacities. What does relatedness look like in the analytic consulting room and how might it differ from social relatedness? Can we approach our patients therapeutically without forgetting everything that we know about how to approach people with the compassion and respect from which love can develop?

The first section of this book looks at the nature of the human psyche. What hunches can we develop about the unconscious, the foundation on which everything else rests, given that we can never have direct access to it? Remembering that unprocessed emotions destroy the possibility of rational thought, what can we say about how the psyche processes emotions? What underlying templates structure the emotional woundedness we each carry and how does the tension play out between someone's healthy, growing side and her resistant, injured aspect? Developing ideas about these issues provides a ground from which we can approach our patients in a related fashion. In the second section of the book, we will look explicitly at how these understandings will guide us in interacting with our patients.

In the early years of this century, while on vacation in Costa Rica, I read *A Pattern of Madness* (1983) by Neville Symington. I had, of course, been working on myself in various ways, so that Symington's ideas fell on fertile ground – I was ready for them. Reading the book burst open my psyche in a way I had never imagined a book could. This supposedly intellectual experience set in motion a fruitful train of development that has led me to a new level of integration in my work. From Symington's inspired work on narcissism, I was drawn into the work of W. R. Bion, a British psychoanalyst, whose perspective informed Symington's. Bion's utterly original point of view has now strongly influenced my thinking. If I could summarize Bion's creative perspective, I would say that he has helped me to see that people are verbs rather than nouns.[4] Reality is a verb; truth is a verb. Like the universe, every object, living or non-living, is in constant motion, both developing and deteriorating all the time. Bion communicates an ability to swim in the new order that his work illuminates, an ability to keep one's head above water in an endlessly mysterious and always shifting world. Who I am changes from moment to moment; my history is unknowable and my understanding of it

4 I am indebted to my husband, Mark Sullivan, Ph.D., for this overarching conceptualization of Bion's intuitive sense of the nature of existence.

moves from one version to another as I develop and find new vantage points from which to view it. The other is similarly volatile. We must find new ways to think about what any of our realities consist of, for every "fact" we know is at most an approximation of reality. Perhaps we can be certain of the year in which the Boston Massacre occurred. But how it was triggered, what emotional or material elements "caused" it we can never know in any definitive sense. Everything and everyone is always moving and changing. We will explore many aspects of this radical perspective in the following pages, seeking to imagine how it impacts our work with individual patients.

One element of that exploration involves my attempt to integrate Bion's point of view with that of C.G. Jung, for the two men share a deeply congruent vision of the nature of the psyche and of reality. Like Bion, Jung describes a largely fluid universe, where the laws of science, the facts of history or politics, and most especially the human beings working to understand them, can never be known in any definitive sense. Instead, exploring reality becomes endlessly fascinating; mysteries proliferate, opening new lines of investigation rather than leading to firm solutions or understandings. Bion's work grounds Jung's in the clinical situation, for although Jung wrote a great deal about psychology, he wrote very little about psychotherapy, and his most valuable work on the analytic situation (1946) is hard to understand. Just as Bion's work expands the reach of Jung's, Jung's perspective illuminates Bion, making this impenetrable writer more comprehensible. Finally, taking a stance that is developed from integrating the philosophical outlooks of both men opens up the clinical situation dramatically. The clinician's capacity to hear is greatly enhanced and new implications and levels in the patient's material are revealed, thus expanding the therapist's capacity for relatedness. And, of course, these two geniuses had differences. Often their differences can fertilize our thinking about the analytic or therapeutic situation.

In this book I develop a clinical perspective based on my understanding of psychological growth. In the fifty-minute hour, the therapist is under constant pressure to respond to the patient's distress, even if that distress lies well under the surface. Two personalities come together in a first hour and "an emotional storm" ensues (Bion, 1979). We know that the patient is caught in an emotional storm; if he were not, he would not have called a therapist. We also know, though we are often tempted to forget, that the therapist or analyst, no matter how "thoroughly analyzed" (whatever that might mean), is also tossed about inside by tempests that she knows less about than she likes to imagine. We have all seen our colleagues behave in startling ways. If we are honest with ourselves, we must know about clinical choices of our own, perhaps choices taken with considerable thought, which proved in retrospect to have been imbued with, even dominated by, unconsciousness, sometimes of a wondrously creative nature, but also sometimes destructive. These "choices" that prove on reflection to have been determined by forces outside the therapist's awareness can manifest as transformative interpretations that the therapist did not know she had, or as obviously problematic enactments, or in subtle and unconscious ways: a murmured "umm" at exactly the right moment versus silence when that "umm" is needed; an intuitive understanding of the patient's emotional state based on no obvious data versus the acceptance of a patient's decision when a question is called for. We know so little about what we know and what we feel at any moment! Truly, it is as though the therapist is called upon to perform brain surgery during a double earthquake where one of the earthquakes' epicenters is in his own core.

No one is immune to severe distortions in his or her ability to think. All therapists and analysts make serious mistakes in any therapeutic venture. The issue must be seen not as an attempt to achieve perfection in technique, but rather as a continuous struggle to work with one's errors, to turn dross into gold. It is widely accepted in the world of depth therapy that the patient (a category that always includes the patient inside the therapist as well as the outer patient) grows through two kinds of experiences. In one kind, the therapist functions well, in the other she functions reparatively vis-à-vis situations in which she functioned badly. Following Winnicott (1965), we call this "good-enough" treatment. It is the best available.

Just as we must accept the fact that our clinical thinking must be distorted by inner emotional upheavals about which we have only glimmers of awareness, in writing this book about how to approach clinical work, I must begin by acknowledging that my ideas have been shaped by pressures outside my awareness as well as by conscious considerations. Nothing I say should be taken to imply that I am describing the "right" way to approach the work. I am describing my thoughts about how to approach the work. Each clinician must work out his or her own thoughts, and if thoughts of mine are helpful to a reader in sorting out what he or she thinks, that is all I can hope for. I would take that as definitely good enough.

And beyond this *caveat*, what I am describing is *my* approach. It is a reflection of who I am, and each therapist must be him- or herself. Beyond any question of technique looms the issue of being authentically oneself. As Jung emphasized, the person of the analyst, rather than his technique, is the core issue. An emphasis on the *person* of the analyst is a crucial counterweight to the therapist's yearning for "rules" to support herself in the turbulent sea of the consulting room. But it is a distortion of this good idea to imagine that the person of the therapist alone, regardless of technical competence, is enough. While I can describe only my approach to the work, I do hope that my thinking will be relevant to others. While there is certainly no *right* way, there are ways that are, if not simply wrong, deeply problematic.[5] I hope that the perspective I offer on how to think about what we do will help others to decide what *they* think.

5 Freud (1912) makes this same point in his papers on technique.

As I noted above, the most important element of the work is the one that gets the least attention in the literature: the nature of the bond between patient and therapist. Jung (1946) comments that love plays the crucial part in the transference relationship and we all know that love never arrives on demand. In the ordinary course of therapeutic work, love *is* constellated between the two individuals (although for many decades the literature seemed to want to destroy the analyst's capacity to experience her own love and it repeatedly warned her not to believe that the patient's affection was "real"). But sometimes love refuses to appear. We cannot control love, but even when some form of *dis*like has taken over, it is possible to demand devotion from ourselves. When that devotion fails to give rise to love – or even affection – it is possible to continue to devotedly attend to the patient while focusing our curiosity on the missing element. "Why am I not feeling love for this person?" the therapist must ask herself. "What is the blockage in him, what is the blockage in me? What is going on here that I feel revulsion – or indifference or disdain – instead of loving concern?"

It has been noted that people rarely say that their analyst's brilliant interpretations are what mattered to them in their analyses; the patient's focus is usually on the quality of the emotional relationship, and when a patient considers his therapy successful, the biggest element in that assessment is almost always the feeling of having been cared for and accepted in all his messy imperfection. Psychotherapy outcome studies consistently fail to find a correlation between the therapist's theoretical perspective and the impact of the therapy; what does affect whether the work prospers or founders is the quality of the relationship (Blatt, 2007). There is nothing surprising about this. In every other situation a person's growth depends on the way he is being held by the other. The parent who tells her children to do as she says, not as she does, will never find her attempts successful. The child may not do as she does – he may even do the opposite of what she does – but he will certainly not do as she says. Most measures of emotional "health" attend to the person's ability to establish successful relationships – at work, but most especially at home. Does it not seem strange that the analytic literature hardly mentions the importance of the quality of the therapeutic bond? A great deal of attention is devoted to interpreting the transference but nourishing the relationship goes largely unmentioned.[6]

My previous book, *Psychotherapy Grounded in the Feminine Principle*

---

6 Even the fact that we continue to talk about "the transference" is symptomatic of this problem. We know now that transference is present in all relationships and that the "chemistry" between analyst and patient is crucial in the viability of their relationship, but we continue to call the therapeutic relationship a transference relationship as though it is primarily distorted and unreal. We do this to protect ourselves from a bald recognition of the fact that while transferences from the past are always present, therapist and patient know each other on the most personal of levels and care about the real other person in passionate (though not necessarily positive) ways.

(1989), focused on the non-interpretive aspects of the work – on the therapist's holding capacity. I believe that its concentration on the feeling dimension is what made it popular with therapists, who had read so many books and articles on how to interpret or how to analyze dynamics, finding nothing about what they *knew* had mattered to them as patients or about what their own patients clearly valued. I described in that book the way object relations thinkers had turned drive theory on its head. Where drive theory explains relationships on the basis of how they serve the basic bodily drives ("I love her because she will continue to be available sexually"), relational theories describe the way that people *use* biological pleasures *in order to* form and maintain loving connections ("I want to have sex with her as a way to express my love for her"). In drive theory's largely outmoded approach, the clinical hope is that insight will enable the patient to extend his conscious control over his instinctual impulses. Relational theories hope to expand and deepen the patient's capacity for emotionally intimate relationships, perhaps by nourishing his ability to be emotionally intimate with himself.

While the importance of the transference relationship was rapidly recognized in the early days of the twentieth century, drive theory *per se* did not explain much about where this powerful tie had come from. Although psychoanalysts quickly came to see that the patient's pressured quest for a new parent or lover *could be interpreted* to constructive ends, they had no way to imagine that something constructive in the patient's psyche was calling up his needy, demanding infantile self. The transference was seen as a resistance that could be put to good ends but it arose because the patient wanted to refuse the burdens of adulthood. And there was no way to imagine a central importance for a loving connection since the therapy's outcome depended on conscious insight rather than on unconscious shifts in the deep structure of the patient's psyche.

In relational therapies,[7] on the other hand, it is easy to explain the centrality of the therapeutic relationship. From this later perspective, our interpersonal experiences have laid down templates inside us that structure how we can relate to others. In the therapeutic situation a relationship arises between patient and analyst that is similar to and also different from the patient's childhood bonds. The two people combine in what Jung (e.g. 1946) called a "chemical combination" that affects both of them (to different degrees). As the relationship evolves and develops, interpersonal patterns arise between the two people that are new to both of them, although these patterns have roots in both people's historical experiences. These new ways of being with each other open up new ways to understand themselves and the other. An over-simplified description of the effective action of therapy would

---

7 Relational theorists include Winnicott, Sullivan, Rogers, Greenberg, Mitchell, Ogden, and Ferro as well as Jung. They span an enormous spectrum of (often contradictory) ideas.

describe the patient as gradually introjecting new patterns of relatedness, changing the basic templates in his psyche. He then carries these new patterns into his outer life.

In my previous book, I suggested that what Joseph Campbell (1949) calls "the monomyth" structures the unfolding therapeutic process of any successful analysis. This monomyth, the skeleton of the universal hero myth, describes the way the hero is called to accomplish some feat. In analysis, this feat is the healing of the suffering hero's soul. The myth shows the hero first preparing for the journey, a preparation that may be portrayed in an analytic patient's dream as a purification. In psychotherapy, this "purification" calls the patient to take up a new attitude. He must submit to a mysterious process that cannot be explained fully and renounce the goal of triumphing over himself. He must let go of the narcissistic attempt to perfect himself and must shoulder the more soulful goal of becoming his true self, something that includes his weaknesses and inadequacies as well as his strengths. This new attitude can never be fully accepted – there will always be power strivings, too – but when the patient yields to the therapeutic relationship's demands on his heart, he has begun his descent. The monomyth's hero descends into the underworld – the modern patient dreams of being threatened in an urban ghetto or of being lost in a subway. The hero encounters dangerous forces with which he contends. In a myth this might be a hydra; in a fairy tale, a wicked witch; in contemporary dreams we find Nazi pursuers or a mind-altering drug slipped into a cocktail. There is an ultimate ordeal that the hero accomplishes, followed by a return to the ordinary world, bringing up the treasure he has attained to share with his family, his tribe, the human race. In analysis, this final trial is the renunciation of the infantile transference. This might be marked by a dream in which a victim is sacrificed (imaging the end of the patient's identification with the victim role) or by a conscious shift in which the patient takes up an attitude that accepts his legitimate suffering rather than attempting to overcome it.

Looking at the work of six psychoanalysts, three Jungians and three neo-Freudians,[8] I showed how they all describe the analytic process as tracing the monomyth's basic pattern. The patient sheds his adapted, appropriate persona and regresses to a more infantile level of development where he connects with what Balint (1968) called his "basic fault." Therapist and patient become a couple, something larger than the sum of the two, creating what Jung (1946) called the "conjunction," the Barangers and Mom (1983) called a "field" and Ogden (writing in 1994, after my previous book) called "the analytic third." Although each of these terms has its own flavor, they all refer to an experience of interpersonal confusion in which an image or affect that arises "inside" one person may express an aspect of the other's subjectivity more

---

8 The analysts are Carl Jung, Donald Sandner, Sylvia Brinton Perera, D. W. Winnicott, Michael
   Balint and Heinz Kohut.

clearly than it does his own. The therapist–patient pair has left the ordinary world and descended to a place with unknown laws that operate in unpredictable and disorienting ways. This central stage of the work – the hero's descent and his endeavors in the underworld – is described by Jung (1946) as a situation "enveloped in a kind of fog" where the couple find themselves in "an impenetrable chaos. . . . The elusive, deceptive, ever-changing content [i.e. the combined unconscious of the two individuals] that possesses the patient like a demon now flits about from patient to doctor . . ." (para 383). At this time "the patient is at a loss to know where his personality begins or ends. It is like passing through the valley of the shadow . . ." (para 399).

If the analyst can allow this pattern to develop, she will be lost and frightened, too, unable to know where *her* personality begins or ends. The inner pressure to interrupt the unfolding descent is as powerful in the clinician as it is in the patient, so that the work of holding the container and the process rather than disrupting it is constantly threatened from within the therapist's psyche as well as from the patient's resistances. Each person is caught in an unconscious struggle, with energies that impel them toward the emotional unraveling that brings them closer and closer to understanding the truth of who they each are versus energies that push each of them to close off the process in order to hang onto their cherished fictions about themselves. Perhaps gradually but perhaps rather suddenly, the patient's complexes relax their grip and he returns to what Campbell (op. cit.) calls "the upper world," where the two members of the couple begin to sort themselves out and to return to the fantasy of a Newtonian universe ordered by elegantly simple laws. As I suggested twenty years ago, this basic pattern of emotional growth is innate in the human psyche and the analyst's core job is to hold and support this process that is *trying to happen*, guided and impelled by the unconscious drive to development and healing.

In 1989, when *Psychotherapy Grounded in the Feminine Principle* first appeared, the literature's focus on interpretation was almost unchallenged. It is certainly still central, but there are now some prominent analysts who are developing images of "interpretations" that include many non-interpretive remarks. Antonino Ferro (2002), an Italian psychoanalyst, is especially interesting. He talks of "weak interpretations," meaning comments that stay within the metaphor that the patient's psyche is unconsciously creating. Thus, a statement like, "Oh, that teacher is being *so* dominating," is called a "weak interpretation," rather than an empathic, mirroring comment because the analyst is silently thinking about how the patient might be experiencing him as domineering. If we saved the word "interpretation" to refer only to interventions that attempt to directly tell the patient something about himself or about the analytic couple, we might see that interpretations are less centrally important than has been thought. Many analytic thinkers today recognize the need to respect the therapeutic or analytic process that Campbell's monomyth pictures. It is this inherent process that carries the work to a successful conclusion; unless it is constellated[9] the best interpretations in the world will do no good. With it, interpretations that are experienced unconsciously as persecutory or that are objectively inaccurate may do little damage. When the process is *not* spontaneously constellated, the clinician's attention needs to turn to whatever the blockage might be. A healing transference relationship emerges from this innate growth process and it is the process that counts.

The basic structure of most therapeutic hours traces a mini-monomyth: the patient leaves the ordinary world outside the consulting room; his psyche unravels and he descends to an inner underworld, filled with surprising and frightening affects and thoughts that he needs to grapple with. The therapist watches, unconsciously drawn into the patient's depths as an emotional participant. She watches his associations and his non-verbal behaviors; she watches her own reverie in all its imagistic, verbal, emotional and physical aspects. Feeling cold, or remembering a personal dream or a painful experience from childhood, are part of the field, brought up by the relational situation of the moment, especially by the patient's immediate unconscious emotional situation. By protecting and maintaining the therapeutic container, the clinician supports the uncoiling of the patient's psyche; her interventions should most centrally focus on facilitating that unwrapping. She tries to feel into the patient by feeling into the field created by the two of them. Sometimes she will make a real interpretation, but often the analyst's focus must be on trying to adjust her way of being with the patient, working to accommodate the distresses she is hearing, both directly from the patient and indirectly from her own unconscious psyche. The analyst works to change *herself* to meet the patient's needs, not to change him.[10] The patient must always be accepted for who he is now, for only by beginning where he is can he grow. The therapist wants, above all, to stay related, which always begins with working to know what the patient's experience is: his basic experience of aliveness, his experience of this particular moment.

Much of my thinking in 1989 describes, in more primitive form, the thinking I will develop in more detail in this new book. The therapist must begin not by knowing, but by not-knowing. One of her most central tasks is to champion the *reality* of the non-material psyche that is "all in one's head." Our hope for the re-born patient is that he *not* be "normal." We are each peculiar if we are real, with our own surprising pattern of twists and turns, talents and vulnerabilities, our personal warts and wounds. The therapist tries

9 "Constellate" is frequently used in Jungian discourse to describe the way an interaction or a situation can call forth in an individual a particular energic pattern with set emotional and behavioral responses. As in: "being with an older, autocratic man constellates her father complex."

10 In the earlier example (see p. 6) of the analyst who needed to follow his own theories about healing rather than hearing his patient's inability to operate psychologically the way his theories said she should, we can see how easy it is for someone *not* to be able to change himself to meet his patient's needs.

to see her patient's inner reality and to reflect it back to him so that he can see it and believe in it. She wants to stick up for the value of suffering in a culture that asks us to get over it and get on with it. By being with the patient instead of trying to *do* something to him, the practitioner lives her acceptance of his pain, allowing his suffering to do its work of powering the engine of development. By providing the patient with a container within which he can face increasing quantities of his legitimate suffering, the impulsion to growth and wholeness that operates in each of us is supported.

Let me end this summary of those aspects of my 1989 thinking that still seem relevant today by quoting the dream that marked the beginning of my personal shift from an Apollonian stance of perfection and cure to the softer and less certain values of wholeness, inclusion and uncertainty:

> *I am talking with my stepfather, a dream figure who resembles my analyst. I am finishing high school and preparing to go to college where I hope to study nursing. I want to go to Barnyard (sic) College, which is run by the Sisters of Mercy and Hope. My stepfather, whom I deeply love and whose approval I intensely seek, tells me I'm too smart to be a nurse, I should go to medical school and become a doctor. With some faint tremors of regret I agree to go to Harvard Medical School.*

When I woke from the dream I felt how very much I wanted to be a nurse, someone who would *be* with suffering people and cradle them through their griefs rather than someone who would operate on them without connecting with their souls. Twenty-odd years later, I look back on the dream and on the book I wrote describing the psychotherapeutic approach that seemed then to be congruent with that dream's desire, and many of my old ideas still seem fresh and exciting to me, as though they are new ideas that my contemporary immersion in the conjunction of Bion's and Jung's work has illuminated and deepened. (Of course there were ideas in that old book that now seem dated to me and I have not described *those* here.) But it is only now that I am able to articulate relatedness as the central issue in psychological health. The danger of relatedness and the inherent emotional resistances that pull us away from it into the safety of narcissism now seem clear enough for me to begin to explore them. It is enormously difficult to take a receptive stance that rejects mastery and dominance and that centers itself in unknowing, confusion, faith and patience. Our Western culture puts powerful demands on each of us to be right rather than wrong, on top of things rather than lost, and to cure rather than accept someone in his messy, wounded imperfection. On a personal level, I continue to struggle to live this attitude of unknowing rather than being caught in our culture's dominant ideology of triumph. On a more collective level, I would hope that there are enough therapists trying to escape the tentacles of the *Diagnostic and Statistical Manual of Mental Disorders* and of managed care to be interested in exploring the poverty of those perspectives that seek to dominate reality. We need to find ways to swim in the murky waters of our lostness rather than getting out of the water to live in the dry desert of certainty.

Beyond this, in this book I will look at some of the areas that I neglected twenty years ago. As I stated then, there is no formula for emotional health; there are as many paths to wholeness as there are people. But I now see that no path to wholeness exists outside of interpersonal relationships and that every path to health brings the individual to a related stance to life. The form my relatedness takes may be very different to the form that yours takes, but when anyone is able to be related, it always includes an awareness of her own emotional experience as well as the other's. (As we shall explore, "the other" may as well be an inner other as an outer one.) This fundamental fact of human nature has been articulated in many ways through history. One suggestive fact is the Western belief that God is love. Although organized religion may seem to have been anything but loving historically, its theory points us in this very positive direction. God is love: relatedness is the supreme value, the highest good.

While this statement seems very simple, there are many inner forces that mobilize against the vulnerability of relatedness. (Hence, the actual history of organized religion, a history so at odds with "Christian" virtues.) Bion's work on thinking enables us to identify deficits in seeing and hearing and thinking; he helps us see how these failures are rooted in an inability to process the powerful emotions stirred in deep relationships. All human beings' thinking fails – not infrequently – so one aspect of the therapeutic venture's focus involves an attempt to recognize both the patient's and the analyst's failures in thinking – failures that underlie the two people's difficulties in getting related to each other. At the same time, therapy must grow both people's capacity to digest the powerful emotions aroused by the analytic situation, thus enabling them to think more and react mindlessly less. By considering how difficult it is for anyone to digest emotions, I hope to offer the practitioner a way to recognize disturbances in her patient's mental processes (as opposed to his choices or behaviors) and to understand the roots of these disturbances. We can conceptualize these micro-level disturbances in ways that make it easier to recognize them when we see them – certainly in others, perhaps also in ourselves – and then to change our posture in ways that enable the distortions to be approached. Recognizing troubled thinking can at least help the analyst to avoid getting caught in the patient's false unconscious axioms. And to the extent that the patient can be helped to expand his capacity to think and to diminish his area of reactivity, he will be freer to choose his behavior in ways that foster his expression of who he really is; he will be freed to grow into his true shape.

Recognizing the power of the analytic field that is created by the two members of the analytic pair leads us to realize that what the analyst is *thinking* impacts the field. It is not simply what she says. The field contains *all* of each person – his or her unconscious depths, overt comments and unspoken, secret thoughts. In 1989 all I could say was that the analyst's holding of the patient allows the patient to grow, just as watering a seed allows its genetic possibilities to emerge. But if we take Jung's understanding of the deep unconscious and integrate it with Bion's work on "O,"[11] we can develop a framework that supports the analyst's holding of the patient with a structure for deepening our understanding of what is happening inside that holding. This book offers the clinician a framework that can hold *her* as she holds her patient, a framework that enriches the analytic field by enriching the analyst's mind.

This book is concerned less with the dimension of holding and more with the question of how to listen and to understand what we hear. As my analytic identity has developed over the past twenty years, I have become increasingly aware of the way that a focus on "holding" can bleed seamlessly into an identification on the therapist's part with a parental role. Subtle forms of reassurance or advice may become prominent, depriving the patient of the space to experience *all* of himself. The therapist who imagines that she is re-parenting the patient will be unable to remain neutral; she will have a personal stake in his "improvement," she will try to "help" him. This will exert an unconscious pressure on him to screen out his darker aspects. When the analyst's central focus is on listening, she becomes much quieter and, paradoxically, her silent receptivity will provide a stronger and larger holding container for the patient.

When the therapist's listening leads her to believe that she understands something meaningful, she can say something about it. There is no way to prescribe *what* she should say in response to her new understanding, but the patient is impacted by the *entirety* of the clinician. How she understands what she hears fundamentally impacts the atmosphere that she creates, and the atmosphere that sustains the analyst and the patient makes all the difference in the world. We will explore many aspects of the listening and understanding process in the course of this work.

When the analyst speaks, interrupting the patient's associations or thinking, her comment is usually considered in terms of its cognitive content, but the driest interpretation also carries extensive feeling information. The music of the therapist's voice may be more important than the content; the aspect of the interpretation that makes the patient feel seen and understood may be more salient than whatever leads the patient to see something he had not understood before. One thing that happens in any reasonable therapy is that the patient, on a regular basis, spends forty-five or fifty minutes in the presence of someone who is devoting all of her conscious energy to understanding him. The therapist's stance is as non-judgmental as possible (for her); she is

---

11 Bion's "O" is roughly equivalent to the universe of Jung's archetypes. See p. 38 for an
   extended discussion of "O."

hoping to be fond of her patient; she tries to see things through his eyes. The individual whose mother made a similar attempt in his infancy is very fortunate indeed. I do not think that after infancy one can encounter a sustained attempt of this kind anywhere except in therapy (and, of course, sometimes not even there). We have no way to measure the impact of this devoted attention, but intuitively it would seem to be enormous. But because it is subtle – the air we breathe rather than something we *do* – the literature neglects it. In talking about how to listen and to think about what we hear, I (like others) am trying to describe a way the clinician can position herself to maximize her capacity to see the patient empathically.

Many of the ideas that I discuss derive from Bion's theories. Just as the approach I describe here is mine and cannot be swallowed whole and regurgitated in another therapist's consulting room, so the Bion I present here is my Bion. He is a difficult writer, notoriously dense and obscure. I have read most of his clinical writing, as well as several books that attempt to present his clinical ideas in succinct and comprehensible form. Joan and Neville Symington (1996) have written the most comprehensible summary of Bion; Grinberg, Sor and Bianchedi (1977) have also done a solid job of explaining his work. James Grotstein (2007) most recently summarized Bion's thinking in a subtle and far-reaching exploration of the implications of his concepts. Each of these authors has studied Bion for much longer than I have and they might be considered "experts,"[12] but their "translations" of his obscure ideas into English do not always agree with each other. For example, the "Language of Achievement" is a term that Bion introduces in *Attention and Interpretation* (1970). Grotstein considers it one of Bion's central ideas and defines it as non-verbal emotional communication like the understanding that passes between mother and infant; the Symingtons do not discuss the term at all, implying that they certainly do not consider it a *central* idea; and Grinberg *et al.*, define it as symbolic language, contrasted with the concrete language of psychotic thinking. (In the latter case, a name represents the outer object itself rather than the individual's personal sense of the object.) After chewing up most of my cuticles in my own attempt to imagine what Bion meant, I decided that he was referring to comments that express knowledge that has been gained through emotional experiences as contrasted with statements that come from expert opinions or from deductive intellectual activity. Is one of these understandings "right?" Perhaps each of these translations describes the same thing from different vantage points, each noting a different implication of Bion's pithy formulation.

I do not believe that trying to understand what Bion "really" meant is the

---

12 Although I presented a paper recently at a Bion conference in San Francisco, and the moderator asked for a show of hands as to how many people were new to Bion's thinking, how many were fairly familiar with his work and how many considered themselves experts. No one, including any of the presenters, dared to call him- or herself an "expert."

issue. He says repeatedly throughout his work that he is not trying to tell the reader what he thinks; he wants to plant seeds that will lead the *reader* to think his or her own creative thoughts. My goal is not to describe Bion's thinking; it is to describe what his thinking means to me and how it has impacted my own perspective. He himself uses his concepts in varying ways: what "K" means in *Learning from Experience* (1962) seems to be somewhat different from what it means in *Attention and Interpretation* (1970). I think that Bion would be the first to tell us that what he meant is not important; what matters is what *we* mean. What any person means at any given moment will (hopefully) be different from what he or she meant yesterday or will mean tomorrow. I use concepts that Bion developed in ways that may differ from how he uses them. Do not use this book as a guide to Bion! It is simply a statement of my current perspective, and I use Bion's ideas in my own way.

Reading Bion has been an exciting experience for me. When I was a younger woman, Jung[13] held the same numinous quality for me, and Symington's book on narcissism had some of that impact, too. Bion and Jung, like Freud and Klein, were great psychological geniuses who upended old paradigms in their explorations of the psyche. Symington, also an exceptionally insightful interpreter of the depths, has understood and mapped the core pathology of our time, narcissism, the anti-related attitude, and in so doing has shed light on some widespread blind spots in our understanding of ourselves and of our patients. His work also illuminates the depth psychological field's neglect of relatedness and its strange approval of narcissistic behavior by the analyst. We will explore the pervasive influence of narcissism in mental illness and in psychoanalysis in Chapter 4, where we study the structural dimension of anti-related energies. Reading Bion's or Jung's *oeuvre* or Symington's *Pattern of Madness* gives me the feeling of being in the presence of someone who sees deeply into the fundamental layers of the psyche, into the places where madness and transformation slip in and out of each other's arms. All these books are difficult, at least partly because of the depth of the unconscious layers they describe.

Generally, these books share another quality. They circle around and around their topics rather than developing a linear argument that moves from A to B to C. Symington, in his introduction, asks the reader to read his book twice. He is describing, he says, a single thought, but in order to do so, he has split up his idea into parts; only when the entire book has been read can its beginning be truly understood. Neither Bion nor Jung offers us this kind of

---

13 Virtually everything I say here about Bion applies also to Jung. He is also a difficult writer and an obscure one. He understands the psyche from an imagistic perspective, relying on a profusion of converging mythic images to describe its nature and its growth. Some people find this poetry natural, but many of us must work very hard to become fluent in his language. I use his ideas, like Bion's, in my own way, emphasizing the aspects that seem valuable and passing over those that seem dated or distorted to me.

helpful advice, but everything they wrote profits from more than one reading and much of their work requires at least two to grant the reader even a modicum of understanding. I do not think this book requires two readings; my talent seems to lie in presenting complex ideas in simple language and I am not a genius in any sense at all. But I have faltered in organizing my ideas because many of them inform such a wide variety of issues. They do not go from A to B to C because neither the psyche nor the work proceeds in that way.

What is analysis?

But before we begin, it seems important to try my hand at describing what I think depth-oriented clinical work – analysis – is. At times, definitions that seem simply silly have been offered, as though lying on a couch rather than sitting in a chair or coming four times a week rather than three is the determining factor. For a procedure that explicitly seeks meaning and substance in the psyche, definitions that avoid dealing with meaning and substance make no sense. But nothing I can say will capture the infinitely proliferating issues that come up in any analytic venture. On the one hand, the analyst or therapist is consistently enjoined not to fall into enactments with her patient; on the other, enactments are ubiquitous and the couple's work disentangling and sorting out an enactment is often the most dramatically transformative work. But still: the therapist should try not to enact unconsidered patterns with her patient. I am presenting here my idea of the stance an analyst should strive for. An attempt to take *any* stance will always fail some of the time; working through analytic failures is the most fertile process that occurs in clinical work.

A person consults a therapist or an analyst because he is subjectively caught in emotional distress. The two individuals spend their first forty-five or fifty minutes together deciding whether they believe that talking with one another has the potential to bring the patient emotional relief; if they do feel sufficiently sanguine about that possibility, they set up a regular schedule of appointments and proceed to develop a relationship with one another based on the verbal and non-verbal aspects of the conversations that occur between them. The resulting relationship may be based on relatedness, or it may be deeply imbued with anti-related energies. The most fundamental goal of working with the transference is the transformation of anti-related strivings into relatedness. One of the major ways that the therapist approaches this is by noticing and working with her own anti-related energies as they are constellated in this particular dyad. While words, rather than actions, must remain the only form of interaction in analytic work, offering the patient a cup of tea or a glass of water, shaking his or her hand and similar minor non-verbal forms of connection do not determine whether or not what is occurring is analysis: the individual practitioner works out his or her own preferences in these areas.

Neither frequency nor posture nor the practitioner's certificates and memberships determines whether a given therapeutic relationship is analysis. There are two areas that reflect what I consider to be the basic issues.

Taking a symbolic attitude

A symbolic attitude means that the therapist holds the patient's communications in the way a dream is held. "I saw this guy treating his little boy as though he was an amusing toy instead of a person," does not primarily refer to the father and child the patient saw on the subway. It is an image that the patient has taken from his daily life to express something about the way he treats himself, the way he feels treated by other important people in his life, and also about the experience he is having at this moment in his relationship with his therapist or analyst. But in this imaginary example we do not know what his image means about the therapeutic interaction. Perhaps he is unconsciously feeling that he is treating his therapist like a thing; perhaps he feels objectified by the therapist; perhaps he is asking the therapist for help in recognizing his membership in the human race. We need to sense the emotional currents that seem to be present at the moment that the image comes to mind in order to have a solid hunch about what it might mean to the patient. Communications that refer to important people in the patient's outer life do truly refer to his experiences in his interpersonal relationships but they are *also* symbolic images that describe the patient's inner world and that capture something about the way he experiences himself in relation to his therapist in the immediate moment. His experience of his analyst can as easily be accurate as distorted. Perhaps the analyst *is* thinking about him as a thing rather than as a person.

When the therapist falls into listening concretely to the "facts" that her patient is telling her, the question is whether she can bring herself back to a symbolic attitude in a reasonable length of time. Participating with the patient in the most personal and sensitive layers of his development, all therapists get swept into the manifest emotional meaning of the patient's stories. This is a *necessary* connection to the patient's life even though it also pulls the therapist away from symbolic thinking. We certainly do not want to rid ourselves of concern for the patient's objective outer situation; we want to make space also to wonder, sooner rather than later, about the story's symbolic meaning in the moment.

Another way to think about this asks, "What is the practitioner's attitude toward symptoms?" Does she focus on trying to rid the patient of his symptoms or on trying to hear what the symptom is telling the suffering individual; can she wonder about the implications and meanings contained within the painful symptom? A symbolic attitude asks that we not get caught in the illusory concreteness of life and that we remember that nothing is "only this;" everything is this *and* that and maybe something else again, implying infinite levels that can never be fully plumbed.

Yet another way to think about the question asks, "Is the analyst/therapist trying to accompany and understand the patient rather than to help her?" The patient wants to be "helped" and the clinician has undoubtedly chosen this work out of a conscious wish to help people. But as the beginner therapist matures and learns more about how people develop, he will come to see that people grow when they are seen and accepted *as they are* (Sullivan, 1989). The woman whose violent attempt to force her child into this or that shape may frighten or horrify the therapist, causing him to try to "help" her become a better parent. But until the terrors that are impelling the mother into a destructive posture have been recognized, accepted and patiently held by her therapist, the mother will not be able to make a consistent change. It may look, on the surface, as though the therapist's advice helps the parent, but I believe this is deceptive. The therapist's advice can be taken in only if the therapist compassionately holds the mother's distress, *even if he is only partly aware* of the emotional pressures he unconsciously accepts. In other words, if, in objective reality, the therapist's advice is discharging his not fully conscious horror, it is extremely unlikely to have any positive impact; if, on the other hand, the therapist truly holds his distress and empathically understands the mother's pain, child-raising advice that is really just advice may be helpful. But improving the patient's parenting skills will never be the core focus of a depth perspective. The analytic task is to help the person to become as much of herself as is possible. The analyst's job is to get to know the patient, a task that can never be completed. As we shall see, when we imagine that we "know" someone, we have closed off the space to continue to be curious about that person's infinite depths, with all their surprising and unmappable twists and turns. Getting to know him, on the other hand, an endless process that supports the therapist's curiosity, is *the* job of the depth therapist. As this process unfolds, the frighteningly difficult mother of our example will inevitably become a better parent because we treat others as we treat ourselves. If the patient can take up the therapist's curious and compassionate attitude toward her, she will be able to open herself to her children and to other intimates, as well.

This core attitude was articulated by Winnicott (1971) when he described analysis as a long-term giving back to the patient what he has brought. Advice is not called for because the depth therapist is not trying to "cure" the patient; she does not assume that there exists a desirable shape into which people should be molded. Rather, she assumes that this particular person has a natural shape, which is unique to him, that he needs to spend his life becoming. This does not actually mean that we give up all thought of emotional health. As I indicated above, by focusing on her own capacity for relatedness vis-à-vis this particular patient, the therapist is working to create a healing relationship with him. To the extent that this relationship develops, the archetypal process of emotional growth that I outlined above will be set in motion and the patient will grow. The patient will move in the direction of becoming all of himself and will develop more of an ability to choose what to do with the truth of who he is. We have nothing to say about who we *are*, but it is possible to have a great deal of say about how we behave. So Winnicott's attempt is to reflect back to the patient who he is today, without judgment about what he wants to do with that.

A concrete example of this stance imagines a patient who typically discharges emotional tension by shopping. In this situation, the therapist may be tempted to tell the patient that his behavior is not good for his growth. "A lot of painful stuff has been uncovered this hour," she might say, "and it would be good if you could resist discharging your distress by shopping and instead stay with your pain." This is an anti-analytic comment. Speaking in an accepting manner about the anti-growth energies that grip the patient is an entirely different animal. "I think that this painful material might be hard for you to bear after you leave me and are all alone. And I'm remembering that we talked about the way you sometimes go shopping when you're in pain. Do you think you'll be tempted to run away from your distress when you leave me today?" is a very different comment. The practitioner is not telling the patient how to behave, she is wondering if he can notice a link that has been discussed before. If the link has not been made before, this may be an opportunity to make it: "I can see how painful this new material is for you. Sometimes I have the impression that you turn to shopping to soothe yourself when you're in pain. Do you think there might be a link there? Maybe we could together pay attention to how you will manage your pain when you leave here." How could the therapist *not* want to help her patient? But the patient will not grow through the therapist's attempt to cure him; he will grow if a spark of curiosity about himself can be ignited.

Many therapists and analysts might disagree with this perspective. Many practitioners orient more centrally to being helpful rather than to understanding. In my opinion, attempts to help will inevitably limit the clinician's capacity to receive the fullness of the patient in this moment. In order to grow, we need the space to be destructive and to learn from our mistakes. An affair that destroys a marriage need not be "a mistake." If the individual can learn from it and grow, it may prove to be a constructive step in development. Certainly an affair is not the best possible way to end a marriage, but sometimes the marriage needs to end and it may be the only possible way out for this person at this time. Knowledge can be passed on, but wisdom must be earned anew by each individual; and wisdom emerges from reflecting on our errors, not from being helped to do things the "right" way.

The relationship is central

Although I do not differentiate in this work between "therapy" and "analysis," it is important to distinguish between depth and surface orientations. In addition to the symbolic attitude that seeks always to glimpse what lies under the surface and to include that in any understanding of the situation, an analytic point of view will be centered in a recognition that the interpersonal relationship between practitioner and patient is *the* core container for the patient's development. A contemporary understanding of the therapeutic relationship begins by recognizing that we do not *exist* as unitary selves. In working to know my patient, I must begin by knowing myself. But such knowing does not imply a fixed understanding developed in the past. Thomas Ogden's (1994) "analytic third" describes the "us:" the unconscious life that patient and analyst share. Patient and therapist each hopes to find more of themselves than existed before the work began. As the practitioner works to know the "us" that has been born in this unique therapeutic relationship and to get herself sorted out from it, she begins to develop ideas about who her patient might be.

This implies that the analyst holds the transference relationship in mind as much of the time as is possible. This focus has little to do with what the practitioner should *say* to the patient. When a comment on the relationship has the potential to bring the two people emotionally closer, a comment is called for. But often the issue will be for the therapist to find ways to approach her patient in a more related way that does *not* include telling the patient what the problem is. It can be difficult to keep a firm grasp of the centrality of the relationship in therapeutic situations that do not allow the therapist to talk much about it. But no matter what else is happening and no matter what the manifest content of the conversation may be, an emotional experience of the interpersonal relationship evolves at every moment. It seems intuitively inescapable that that emotional experience impacts the patient more power-fully than any cognitive content being discussed. Symbolic listening is one stance that helps the analyst imagine what the patient's emotional experience might be. *Internal* symbolic listening that fosters recognizing her own emotional experience similarly helps the analyst imagine what the patient is working on at the moment.

The analyst must try to take responsibility for her own feelings. This means that she will not immediately decide that her emotional state falls under the rubric of "syntonic countertransference" (Fordham, 1978) – a subjective state brought up inside the therapist in direct response to the patient's internal psychological structures. If I feel envious of my patient, it may be that I am replicating his mother's envious attitude (a syntonic countertrans-ference reaction), but my relationship to my own envy will also impact what happens with envy in this clinical relationship. The therapist must take a humble attitude, working to open herself to whatever emotional currents are stirred inside her rather than attempting to deny them, and to use what-ever understanding of her subjective state she can muster in intuiting her patient's subjective state. The practitioner has to try to contain her needs, her personal distress, her judgments, holding an awareness of her feelings in consciousness without discharging them into action. It is never possible to do so perfectly. It may not even be possible to do it very well. We hope to manage it well enough.

The therapist wants to stay curious about the impact of her behavior on the patient rather than getting caught in trying to behave "correctly." Can she recognize her "errors" without getting thrown into frightened attempts to undo them and take away their impact? Can she be curious about the ways she makes "mistakes" and remember that everything always goes wrong, including her own efforts? People do not grow in sterile containers with perfect analysts; they grow in messy human relationships, with analysts who try their best to do right by their patients but whose best must frequently consist of reparative efforts vis-à-vis the difficulties they have created.

A depth perspective recognizes that analysis is a mutual endeavor. Whether it helps the patient to become more of himself and to live a fuller, richer life depends on mysterious factors that we can only hold as hunches. In the transference relationship, each person is both growing and resisting growth in ways that neither one can ever hope to pin down definitively. The depths of the developmental process are infinitely mysterious; the rest of this book circumambulates that mystery, exploring it from one perspective after another.

Part I

Theoretical considerations

Chapter 2

The creative unconscious and the Self

Before we can think about how the therapist might approach the clinical situation, we need to explore the nature of the human psyche's depths. Freud's original sense of the unconscious focused on its function as a storehouse for fundamental instincts of sex and aggression. It began as the id, a seething cauldron of biologically based urges that the person learns to repress. Analysis worked to explore the war between the rational individual, who wanted to be civilized and appropriate, and his unconscious, which wanted to pull him into a maelstrom of sexual and aggressive behavior. In this early model, the finite aspects of the unconscious were emphasized; it was a repository of repressed material that the analyst's interpretations would exhume. The original optimistic goal of analysis imagined the possibility of emptying the unconscious by becoming fully aware of one's instinctual urges. Conscious awareness was supposed to allow the person to sublimate unwanted passions into constructive channels. This very early understanding of the unconscious no longer reflects any depth therapist's theories.

Rather than believing the unconscious is bounded and finite, many depth psychological thinkers now follow Bion's lead in conceiving of it as infinite in nature. Contemporary analysts struggle against their wishes for perfection and try to renounce "completion" as the goal of analysis or of life. Bion said:

> The domain of personality is so extensive that it cannot be investigated with thoroughness. ... [A]djectives like 'complete' or 'full' have no place in qualifying 'analysis'. The more nearly thorough the investigation, the clearer it becomes that however prolonged a psycho-analysis may be it represents only the start of an investigation. It stimulates growth of the domain it investigates ...
>
> (Bion, 1970, p. 69)

The domain investigated by analysis is the area of the infinite unknown, the unconscious. Jung images its boundless nature with a metaphor that describes the conscious "I"[1] as an island in the sea of the unconscious (1946, para 366). As the area of consciousness grows, the shoreline of the island gets larger; a greater stretch of the infinite unknown is contacted by one's finite consciousness. Similarly, Bion's (1970) statement that attending to the unknown stimulates its growth renders meaningless his conclusion that the proportion of the known to the unknown is smaller during an analysis than at its conclusion. The proportion of any finite known, like consciousness, to any infinitely vast unknown, like the "unconscious," always approaches zero in mathematical terms. It can never be larger. Psychologically, the notion is meaningless; consciousness is limited while the realm of the unconscious is infinite. The unknown reaches of our inner reality always stretch out forever.

Just as Bion spoke of the impossibility of a complete or full analysis, Jung spoke of wholeness as the goal of analysis or development rather than perfection, explicitly recognizing that "wholeness" is no more achievable than perfection. We are never complete; the unconscious seems to enlarge rather than shrink as we connect with it, it is never emptied. Speaking in the metaphors of alchemy, Jung emphasized that "the goal [of wholeness] is important only as an idea; the essential thing is the *opus* [the work] which leads to the goal: *that* is the goal of a lifetime" (1946, para 400, emphasis in original). The goal of life is the lifelong attempt to become more and more of oneself by fully living life but any hope of completing the work must be renounced.

As psychoanalysis developed over the last half of the twentieth century and into the twenty-first, it increasingly recognized the constructive as well as the destructive currents in this infinite and unmappable unconscious. The unconscious does not *only* deny, repress, undo and split off. It also points out, brings up, pulls together. A "Freudian" slip can be seen as breaking into consciousness because the urge in question is so strong that the repression barrier cannot hold against it, but this characterization sees nothing hopeful in the slip. The psyche also slips in helpful attempts to make the person more whole. A patient calls me by the name of a detested supervisor or a disrespected colleague. While the patient's psyche is embarrassing or frightening her, it is more fundamentally trying to help her take up the negative feelings that would give her relationship with me depth and substance. It is not only that unwanted feelings have broken through; it is also that if they are welcomed, they will enrich her and bring her to greater substance at the same time as they enrich our work and help me to grow, too.

Jung's concept of the collective unconscious and Bion's concept of "O" represent two perspectives on the infinite creative wellspring of life. Each

---

1   Throughout this book, to whatever extent possible, I avoid technical language that distances the reader from the experiences being described. Thus, I call the subjective sense of "this is me," the "I" rather than using a technical term.

of them tried to map a psyche that they both spoke of as volatile and nonmaterial in nature. Although their emphases differ, their resulting images of the psyche prove highly compatible. They offer us a sense of mystery rather than certainty, of an ever-shifting potential reality that can never be known. In this chapter, I will explore the two concepts, O and the collective unconscious, and try to show the underlying congruence as well as the differences between them. Both Jung and Bion ultimately rejected Freud's logical positivism[2] as they attempted to investigate the ungraspable mystery of the psyche. A generation apart, they both trained as medical doctors and initially approached the work from a traditional scientific perspective, in which concrete data, experiments and facts were the arbiters of conclusions. But as these two geniuses burrowed more and more deeply into the intangible reality of the psyche they each came to realize that its study required a different approach from that of the body.

The later decades of Jung's life found him increasingly compelled by ancient alchemical texts. He postulated that alchemists unconsciously projected their psyches into the matter they worked with. The gold they sought was the modern analytic patient's hope: the inner transformation of *themselves*, a conclusion he arrived at from noticing that the alchemists' formulas could not have described literal processes. A formula might instruct the worker to begin with the menstruum of a whore, to seal it in an impenetrable container, to bury it in the deepest, darkest sea until it became dry and, by desiccation, sandy and black. This kind of instruction cannot be followed in concrete reality; we can understand it only as a projection of the alchemist's psyche into the matter he worked with. Jung's many volumes exploring alchemical processes and imagery are based on the idea that alchemy is a way to look at the phenomenology of the psyche's growth process. By studying the unconscious imagery of that growth process in the alchemists' alien culture and comparing it with the way people develop in our own, Jung hoped to describe the universal form of psychological development.

But the bizarre quality of the texts that Jung relied on was reflected in his work. As he tried to interpret the invisible, nonmaterial psychological processes enveloping the alchemists, he began to sound like an alchemist himself. His standing in the mainstream psychological world, already prejudiced by the bitterness of his break with Freud, was further compromised by the increasingly mystical flavor of his work.

Bion was twenty years younger than Jung, and although we know that he had some interest in Jung,[3] he almost never cites him in his work. He, too, began with what appears to be an attempt to be rigorous and "scientific" in

---

2 The school of philosophy that tried to bring the methodology and precision of mathematics to philosophy – in this case, to psychology.
3 Since he took his patient, Samuel Beckett, to hear Jung's Tavistock lectures (Grotstein, 2007).

the stereotypical sense of the word.[4] He was analyzed by Melanie Klein and joined the Kleinian group. His early analytic work on psychosis and thinking (by which he meant the processing of emotional experience) preserves a respectably "sensible" tone and perspective. It has a flavor that pervades much of the Kleinian literature, in which speculative ideas about unconscious phantasies and processes are presented as though they were concrete facts. But by the mid 1960s, in *Transformations* (1965) and *Attention and Interpretation* (1970), mystery begins to permeate his work. He focuses more and more on unknowability and explicitly challenges logical positivism's rejection of metaphysics. "Logicians," he wrote, "tend to believe that logical rigour is a *sine qua non*. Hence complete neglect of Newton's theological and mystical preoccupations as if they had no part in the genesis of, for instance, *Opticks*" (1965, p. 109, n. 2). Bion's fate has been a milder version of Jung's: many psychoanalysts who value his early work on groups and psychosis neglect and even disdain his later more mystical work.

Unique among writers, Bion does not try to communicate *his* thinking to the reader. His ideas come in obscure telegraphic descriptions and he says repeatedly that he does not want the reader to absorb his thinking; he wants the reader to *use* his thinking in the construction of her own ideas. He offers very few case descriptions, asking the reader to provide her own. He created "unsaturated"[5] concepts such as "L," "H," "K" and "O," preferring to leave the mystery *in* rather than to explain and rationalize it.

To understand the gulf between Freud's perspective and either Jung's or Bion's we need to understand the axioms that underpin the men's perspectives. Freud was a materialist where Jung and Bion both tried to hold both materialist and idealist perspectives equally in mind. I am not talking about "materialism" as we use the word in ordinary conversation. We all grew up immersed in materialist theories. The issue has nothing to do with acquisitive greed. Materialism is a philosophical system that contrasts with idealism which, again, has nothing to do with our ordinary notions of "idealistic"

---

4 I refer here to the popular image of the scientist, performing controlled experiments on measurable data, an image based in the hard sciences. In fact, a scientific approach must begin with the nature of the area under investigation and must decide what the most fruitful way of studying *that* area will be. No one has been able to imagine, for example, a way to study the meaning of dreams via controlled experiments. This does not mean that the meaning of dreams cannot be investigated in a scientific spirit.

5 Bion talks of "saturated" or "unsaturated" interpretations and terms. "Love" would be a saturated term, for it is surrounded by a cloud of implications that the listener or speaker has absorbed over the course of her life; "L" is unsaturated: it is a neutral symbol with no meanings from the listener's past to obscure its current meaning. Similarly, a saturated interpretation spells out exactly what it means: "You are associating to your daughter's tummy ache because you are finding it hard to digest my words." An unsaturated interpretation leaves the patient free to fill in its meaning in his own way: "Oh, tummy aches are so painful," is unsaturated. The patient can choose to hear the analyst as referring only to his child's pain or the empathy may cause the patient to think about the pain that *he* is in at this moment.

values. Idealism posits the mind or some other nonmaterial spiritual reality as the foundation of the sensual world. The religious idea that God created the world by thinking it into existence, animating humanity by blowing His breath into the clay Adam, is a familiar idealist perspective. "I think therefore I am" is another. In its most extreme form, the thinking itself is believed to bring the body into existence. The materialist, on the other hand, says, "I know that I exist because I can see and touch and smell my body; this tangible body – with its brain and neuronal network – is what allows me to think." Our culture's unquestioned acceptance of a materialist perspective distorts what any of us are able to think, just as our psychological theories distort what we are able to see. We know that previous ages have all been seriously flawed in their understandings of reality. Why should we imagine that at this particular moment in history, human beings are suddenly getting it right?

As we shall see, the sight of one's material body, its feel and its smell, are actually all nonmaterial psychological factors. We may understand these factors as based on messages received and interpreted by the material brain, but that understanding, too, comes from the psyche's interpretation of data. It is not possible to contact the material world directly. Everything is filtered through the intangible psyche.

At this time in the United States, a materialistic approach to the psyche is ascendant. Neurons, synapses, genes, biochemistry: these are the respected points of psychological intervention. The mainstream press scoffs at the "outmoded" approach of psychoanalysis; medication and "evidence-based" brief cognitive behavioral therapies are seen as the gold standard of treatment by such media outlets as the *Science Times* section of *The New York Times*. This approach is based on an axiomatic belief that sees the material world as the "real" world. It sees the psyche first as *dependent on* rather than *interdependent with* the body; and second as "imaginary." There is no way to test the assumption of matter's primacy. No one would disagree that electrical and chemical activity in the brain can cause depression, or that chemical intervention can alleviate it. (Although many psychotherapists might question the idea that the chemicals can "cure" depression.) But there are infinite examples of situations in which an emotionally distressing event (a phone call announcing a death, perhaps) causes the electrical and chemical activity in the brain that accompanies emotional upheaval. Freud, the founder of psychoanalysis, was immersed in a materialist philosophical outlook. The body is the first cause. The ephemeral psyche is a reaction to the body's distress rather than a primary reality of its own.

The primacy of the psyche

Jung and Bion both begin with the psyche itself. They each saw the psyche and the body as a unit, two sides of one coin, neither side dominant. Both note the fact that all we actually have are psychic data: our knowledge of outer reality, though it feels so compellingly "real," is actually a subjective experience that has been deduced from the mental signals being processed in our brains. Freud's basic perspective is compatible with the current intellectual fashion; the approaches of Jung and Bion are fundamentally out of step with the prevailing world view.

Familiarity with Jung's work makes reading Bion a startling experience. It is as though Bion has taken Jung's vision of the depths of the individual psyche and translated it into the two-person clinical situation. Jung's interest was not analytic work *per se*; he was compelled by the psyche and its numinous depths. As a young man, he worked with schizophrenics in a psychiatric hospital, developing an ability to understand the symbolism of their dreams and fantasies. He responded to their phantasmagorical creations in symbolic language that created a dialogue between himself and the patient's unconscious psyche (although in many of these cases the "unconscious" had taken over the individual and become the persona with which he or she met the world). But after close to ten years of this work, he began to focus on outpatient work with less profoundly disturbed individuals. The astounding imagery that had gripped him in his work with psychotics continued to compel his attention as he worked with neurotic patients. The imagery of the unconscious brought him to the study of mythology and eventually alchemy, where parallels to an individual dream's symbolism of can be found.

Jung wanted to help heal psychic wounds, but he did not like the regressive engagements of the dependent transference, so he devised ways that people could work on their own with the symbolic products of their depths. He wanted to help patients out of the worst of their neurotic difficulties and teach them how to continue to grow on their own. For him, patients were unique carriers of the human archetype; he expected and encouraged them to join him in the marvelous adventure of exploring the unpredictable and creative way the universal psyche manifested in their individual lives. He believed, correctly in many cases, that their mutual exploration would be healing, and that by continuing the work on their own, people's healing would be solidified. But the psyche itself, especially in its universal aspects, rather than its personal healing was his central interest. His one profound study of the analytic interaction, *The Psychology of the Transference*, is a masterpiece of prescient insight, describing as far back as 1946 the intersubjective foundation of the therapeutic experience. But the monograph was based, I believe, on his experience of digging himself out of the emotional breakdown that followed his rupture with Freud, and he does not seem to have been very interested in attending to the same level of the work with his patients. Bion, on the other hand, focused almost exclusively on the clinical situation itself, studying the way the patient's and analyst's psyches appear in that infinitely mysterious, interpenetrating two-person mix-up (Balint, 1968). Putting together the insights of these two geniuses – Jung's vision of the nature of the deep unconscious and of the psychic processes unleashed by it, along with Bion's perspective on the way those processes manifest and unfold in the consulting room – greatly broadens one's view of the situation.

Repeatedly, Bion says that the psyche is a nonmaterial "thing" and cannot be approached the way the body can be. Discussing the divergence between medicine and analysis, he writes:

> Suppose the patient complained not of physical but of mental pain; no one doubts the existence of anxiety or sees any incongruity in seeking help to cure it. . . . The point that demonstrates the divergence most clearly is that the physician is dependent on realization of sensuous experience [i.e. experience that comes through the five senses] in contrast with the psycho-analyst whose dependence is on experience that is not sensuous. The physician can see and touch and smell. The realizations [elements, emotional experiences] with which a psycho-analyst deals cannot be seen or touched; anxiety has no shape or colour, smell or sound.
>
> (1970, pp. 6–7)

Our language – the psyche as a "thing" – distorts reality for it is based on the nature of the outer world. We might see bodily sequelae of anxiety: sweaty palms, agitated movements, and so on. But the anxiety itself is something that can be picked up only intuitively through "vibes." The unconscious is frequently described as though it were a place; yet it has no tangible substance. The collective unconscious "contains" human nature but the word, calling up cups or boxes, misleads. Saturated with the Enlightenment's perspective, we must stretch to remember the powerful *reality* of the intangible psyche.

Jung repeatedly emphasizes that the analyst's job is to hold firmly in mind the reality of the psyche. This is the symbolic attitude.

> [T]he unconscious of man . . . mirrors the totality of the world. . . . Looked at from the standpoint of the conscious, this world is the reality and that the reflex. But the reflex is just as living and real, just as big and complicated. There is even the standpoint that the external world is a reflex of the unconscious. . . . The whole East [believes that] what we say is reality is just a sort of degenerate phantasmagoria which they call the veil of Maya. That is Plato's idea . . .
>
> (Jung, 1984, p. 447)

The philosophically idealistic point of view that Jung and Bion take is the depth psychological perspective. No matter how steeped in it one may be, one loses it repeatedly. As we shall explore in detail in the next chapter, the analyst strives to listen symbolically to his patient's associations, to follow the psyche's movement as it uses one outer situation after another to paint a picture of itself struggling with its complexes as they are activated at this moment. But sometimes the analyst falls into the concrete meaning of the patient's story. Indeed, the concrete meaning is real, *too*, and often to ignore it would be an abandonment of the patient. But to lose the symbolic meaning – to fall *into* the concrete – is to drop the patient at the crucial level of his soul.[6]

"O"

Bion and Jung both struggled to approach the mystery of an intangible inner universe. Bion postulates a primary reality called "O" that is roughly equivalent to what Jung called "the collective unconscious," the infinite container of the archetypes. As many writers have noted, Bion's work is opaque. I will offer here *my* use of Bion's concept O. I read him as using the term in a variety of ways. O is difficult to discuss because it is infinite, and in order to explore it, the limited human mind must divide O into finite – or at least less infinite – segments. In the next few pages, I talk of the O of an individual or of the analytic couple or of the session, as though these aspects of O can be compartmentalized. Although O is an indivisible realm that underlies all of reality, Bion also talks about the drama in the consulting room as "the intersection of an evolving O with another evolving O" (1970, p. 118) as though each individual is an evolving O. If we imagine O as one continuous membrane, my O and your O as well as the O of the earth and the solar system are all aspects of this membrane. We are all related to each other and to every element of existence; our fates are intertwined in ways we cannot hope to comprehend in any fullness; we are all part of one great O. O cannot be pinned down; my discussion is intended to convey a *feeling* for O, not a definitive mapping of it.

The domain of O has been explored by philosophers and mystics under titles like the Absolute, Ultimate Reality or Ultimate Truth, the Ground of Being, God or the godhead. O is the world of Plato's ideal forms, Kant's things-in-themselves, Bion's pre-conceptions, Klein's inborn phantasies and Jung's archetypes. O speaks to the infinite ocean of truths excluded from our conscious view of reality. It lies beneath[7] the unconscious capacities that

---

6 The secular reader may have difficulty with this word. "Psyche" is the Greek word for "soul." "Mind" is a much narrower and chillier concept that implies, for most people, thinking; generally (in our culture) we picture the mind as residing in the brain or the head. My thesaurus (Chapman, 1992) suggests the following synonyms for "soul:" passion, heart, interior, life force, person, essence, inner nature, particularity, individual and psyche. In using "soul" I do not intend to imply anything about immortality, God or any religious issue.

7 Although "beneath" implies matter. We do not have a language that can do justice to the psyche's reality. Our language defines experience in terms of space and time; the unconscious seems to be timeless in its outlook, easily mixing together the past, the present and the future, and, as we have seen, it does not exist in space.

make life livable, like α (alpha) function[8] or ego defenses. Milton (1968), in *Paradise Lost*, speaks of "the void and formless infinite:" Bion offers Milton's words as a description of O.

But Bion's use of the term is fluid and somewhat shifting. It is a symbol, not a sign. A symbol, Jung says, stands for something that is "beyond all conceivable explanations. . . . [It expresses] an as yet unknown and incomprehensible fact of a . . . psychological nature. . . . An expression that stands for a known thing remains a mere sign" (Jung, 1971, paras 815–17). The essence of O is its unknowability. We cannot wrap our minds around its fullness; like one's personal nonexistence, it is unimaginable. The collective unconscious shares this inconceivable quality, but Jung and his descendants focused more on its finite manifestations than on its infinite mystery, so Bion's work on O deepens a Jungian understanding of the nature of the archetypal foundation.

Here are some "definitions" of O that Bion offers in *Attention and Inter-pretation* (1970):

O is "the experience (thing-in-itself)" (p. 4). The phrase "thing-in-itself" means the thing as it exists, without having been filtered through a human psyche, something clearly unknowable for the human mind (psyche). In this definition, O is my experience in its pure form, outside my mind's understanding or representation of it.

O is "represented by terms such as ultimate reality, absolute truth, the godhead, the infinite, the thing-in-itself. O does not fall in the domain of knowledge or learning save incidentally; it can be 'become' [sic], but it cannot be 'known' " (p. 26). One can intuit the infinite truth behind a given finite reality by settling into the experience of the immediate moment, but one can never *know* that truth in the sense that we can know the times tables or the history of the succession of the English kings. When Bion says that O can be "become" he means that one can sense the essential nature of the current experience by opening oneself to it. After this, the mind can try to articulate what was experienced, but this articulation can never do full justice to the entirety of the experience. The idea is not that someone can "become" O *as such*; we can only "become" the O of this moment. Antonino Ferro has described this in simpler terms (2002): When the analyst is "in O," her central experience is of being empathically connected to the patient – we could say, "through the heart." He contrasts this with the situation in which the analyst is connected to the patient through the mind, trying to understand the meaning of the patient's associations. Here, the reader can perhaps feel Ferro's attempt to bring relatedness into the picture, but because the human connection between analyst and patient has been so severely ignored in most of the literature, he does not have a way to simply say this. He has to cloak his point

---

8 α function is the function that controls symbolization. We will explore it in depth in the next chapter.

in technical language – using an abstruse term like "O" – in order to make it respectable in the analytic world.

Bion's definition continues: "It is darkness and formlessness but it enters the domain K when it has evolved to a point where it can be known through knowledge gained by experience . . . its existence is conjectured phenomenologically" (p. 26). The "domain K" is that aspect of the universe or of one's life experience that one can hope to get to know by interacting with it in an open and receptive frame of mind. Here, Bion is emphasizing that he is not talking about book learning, which will never reveal O. We sense O by sinking into our experience and letting it absorb us until we can intuit the intangible fundamental reality that is making itself known through our lived experience. This will not lead us to know O. What we can hope for is a sense of the leading edge of O as it evolves into material existence. Bion reiterates in *Attention and Interpretation* (1970) that it is not important for the reader to try to understand the text she is reading; what matters is that she recognize what he is talking about through an intuitive apprehension of the O of the book, an apprehension of the essential truth he is trying to convey with his imperfect and limited words. This kind of "aha!" moment – Oh! That's what he means! – while reading or doing clinical work will reveal the meaning and value of his concepts. Then the reader will *know* what he means from her own experience. (This very typical Bionian instruction, of course, means that different readers will take away at least somewhat different understandings of his meaning as they make it theirs.) Only knowledge that comes from lived experience can bring a reliable sense of the nature of O. We cannot prove the existence of O. It is a theory; we conjecture its existence from the phenomena with which we have immediate contact: "O [is] the unknown and unknowable. . . . Every Object known or knowable by man, including himself, must be an evolution of O" (p. 27).

O is "the absolute truth in and of any object . . ." (p. 30). "In any object, material or immaterial, resides the unknowable ultimate reality, the 'thing-in-itself.' Objects have emanations or emergent qualities or evolving characteristics that impinge upon the human personality as phenomena. . . . [T]hey differ from the ultimate reality" (p. 87). With one turn of phrase after another, he tries to convey a sense – it is not possible to give a simple "definition" – of what he is talking about. He wants to open Western eyes to the notion of a nonmaterial, spiritual reality standing behind the concrete world. Like the unconscious, this reality is not confined in space or time. It has no tangible substance, and just as night-time dreams can image past, present *or future* possibilities, the world of O includes all of time.[9] The outer and inner realities we know about emerge from this ineffable universe. Perhaps the Big Bang exploded from this nonmaterial ground of being: from "nothing."

---

9 Bion talks about O's nonmaterial quality, but I am not aware of him talking about its timelessness.

The Platonic theory of Forms and the Christian dogma of the Incarnation imply absolute essence which I wish to postulate as a universal quality of phenomena such as 'panic', 'anxiety', 'fear', 'love'. In brief, I use O to represent this central feature of every situation that the psycho-analyst has to meet.

(1970, p. 89)

The Christian dogma of the Incarnation states that the godhead – something scientific Westerners might think of as "the Big Bang" or the energy of the living universe while Eastern mystics might think of it as the Ground of Being or Ultimate Source – took the finite form of Jesus of Nazareth. In naming the godhead "absolute essence," Bion is saying that this is the stuff of emotional experiences like anxiety or love. In the clinical situation, Bion suggests that every emotional reality the analyst encounters has evolved – developed – from O.

Bion is using a myth – the Christian myth in this case – to describe the nature of the psyche. Freud rejected religion as superstitious, and suggested that it would disappear when people had become sufficiently conscious to live rational lives. Rather than dismissing religion for its obvious irrationality, both Bion and Jung investigated it as a projection of the psyche's nature. Where Jung uses the word "god" in analyzing the meaning of religious imagery, repeating not infrequently that he is not talking about a hypothetical outer reality but about a demonstrable *inner* reality, Bion invents the neutral term "O." It is easy to imagine while reading Jung that he did believe in the outer existence of some god-like consciousness, even though he says over and over that he is not offering *any* statement regarding the issue of god's objective existence. Bion never sounds as though he believes in god; he believes in O.

In Bion's model, inner reality precedes outer. The phenomena we ordinarily call "reality," whether outer or inner, are emanations from O, which is the primary reality, ineffable and unknowable in nature. He even suggests that geometry, which we imagine is based in the points, lines and shapes of the outer world, first emerged from the attempt to understand the shapes of inner, imaginal space (Bion, 1965, p. 105; 1970, p. 10).

The mature Bion did not divide the psyche into conscious and unconscious. His focus was on the finite versus the infinite. What psychoanalysts designate by "the unconscious" includes both finite and infinite aspects but the infinite must always be unconscious because the finite human mind cannot grasp infinity. The mind cannot help asking, "What about infinity plus one?" All the terms that Bion uses to describe O, the primary reality, are infinite terms: The Absolute, Ultimate Truth, etc. This is the fundamental layer of the psyche, shared by all of us, personal to no one but foundational for all.

Begin by thinking about the O of an individual, the *un*conscious ground of being, Milton's "formless infinite," before images have evolved from it. This endless expanse holds the human given, the entirety of human potential, overlapping a great deal with the animal given, and with the givens of life itself. As we shall see, this is the universe of Jung's archetypes. Each individual is an evolution of that ocean of human possibilities, just as each tree is an evolution of the archetype/ideal form/thing-in-itself of trees. This person is shorter or taller, he or she is smarter or slower, more or less musical/graceful/mathematical, all within certain limits that set the range of our species.

There is also a personal O for each of us, a formless infinite of *me* that has not yet emerged, my particular given, lying in a narrower strip of the human possibility, but no less infinite for that. Our materialist culture would call this "the genetic givens of the personality;" more mystical cultures might think in terms of the soul or some other nonmaterial carrier of the person's nature. Interacting with my diet, my genes will cause my bones to evolve into a particular skeleton. My psyche's potentials are similar but harder to define or measure. Each of us is born with a temperament that tends toward sweetness or acidity, softness or hardness, more or less relatedness, lovingness, penetrability. Many psychoanalysts, following Winnicott (1960), posit the existence of a "true self" and a "false self," implicitly suggesting that the "true" self develops from an inborn underlying reality. This reality, this unknowable O, is the inner universe from which the person evolves. No matter how substantial one becomes, there is always endlessly greater depth and breadth yet to be discovered.

We can think about the O of an individual (either patient or analyst) in yet more specific terms. At any moment there is an inner reality that one knows much less than everything about. This is a fundamental understanding of depth psychologists. The boring patient is skating over terrifying material; the rageful patient is defending against an experience of his vulnerability. The analyst forgets to return a call, chats with a patient or gives advice, finds herself unable to concentrate, struggles with narcolepsy, offers this interpretation rather than that one. Every lapse and every choice is determined by many factors that lie outside one's awareness. The finite details of these factors emerge from O, the elemental truth of who one *is*, an essence that can never be known, no matter how many detailed aspects of it are grasped.

Although O is ultimately unknowable, we sense its nature because it presses against us, constantly forcing us to interact with it. Our knowledge of O is restricted to hunches partly because its infinitude is always fluid, never fixed. When an interpretation comes together in a practitioner's mind, it is because the patterns that she has been sitting with have taken a firm-enough shape to be intuited. But at this point Bion suggests that he expects "the rigidity conferred by the formulation to be resisted by the fluidity of O represented by the formulation" (1970, p. 85). As soon as you try to nail down some aspect of O by articulating it, the reality you are trying to nail down slips away. It is like a drop of mercury, always slithering out of your grasp. O is constantly evolving into the world of lived experience. We glimpse its contours for a moment but as we begin to sense its shape, it shifts and changes. (And, of course, to talk of its "shape" is a metaphor; O exists outside the world of space and time.)

The extremity of Bion's perspective is emphasized by his noting that the patient the therapist takes into the consulting room is someone she has never met before, even if she has seen him only yesterday. To believe that you *know* the person you are seeing is oxymoronic if the goal of each session is to *get* to know some unknown aspect of the constantly evolving person who walks in. The therapist's belief that she knows her patient is "intended to prevent emergence of an unknown, incoherent, formless void and an associated sense of persecution by the elements of an evolving O" (ibid., p. 52). Bion is not suggesting that O holds only terrible and fearsome material, but O is *unknown* and for that reason, on initial contact it is terrifying. The unknowable nature of reality is what terrifies, not the reality itself, which can as well be positive as negative once it is known. Behind the fixed, mapable world, where my husband or child is someone whose behavior I can (at least to some extent) predict, lies an ephemeral reality, always in motion, growing or contracting, so that the person who I "know" can always surprise me with unknown aspects of his or her self. These surprises may be deeply disturbing and the fantasy of familiarity protects us from the anxiety that the situation constellates.

Bion's position here is too extreme, but it is useful in that it helps the practitioner to compensate for her tendency to rely on The Known regarding her patient. As we shall explore throughout the book, but especially in Part II, the section on clinical work, there is a constant danger that the therapist will cling to previously developed understandings and will blind herself to startling new elements that do not fit neatly into those old "knowns;" Bion's suggestion that we try to meet a *new* person in each hour is helpful. But it does leave out something central about relatedness. Each hour, I go toward the waiting room to take in my waiting patient with a unique feeling. On a recent day at work, I noticed myself feeling something positive as I turned toward each hour, since (on that day) I saw one person after another whom I like and enjoy being with. We could call that positive feeling "liking," but it was a different feeling in each case. I can work to empty my mind of particular memories or concepts that relate to Carol or Mike or Sandra so as to be available to receive the particular shape each of them takes today. But surely something is missing if I do not remember my *bond* with each of them. It is provocative to talk about seeing the familiar patient as someone new; it helps us to remember that the patient is not a noun, he is a verb. But we do not want to forget the relationship we have forged together, often in circumstances that have been painful and difficult for both members of the couple.

Jung talks of the always shifting quality of the unconscious by personifying it as the Spirit Mercurius, following the imagery of various fairy tales (e.g. Grimm's "The Spirit in the Bottle"), folk myths and alchemical texts. He describes how

> [t]he elusive, deceptive, ever-changing content that possesses the patient
> like a demon now flits about from patient to doctor and, as the third
> party in the alliance, continues its game, sometimes impish and teasing,
> sometimes really diabolical. The alchemists aptly personified it as the wily
> god of revelation, Hermes or Mercurius. . . . [I]t would be an altogether
> unjustifiable suppression of the truth were I to confine myself to the
> negative description of Mercurius' impish drolleries, his inexhaustible
> invention, his insinuations, his intriguing ideas and schemes, his ambiva-
> lence and – often – his unmistakable malice. He is also capable of the
> exact opposite . . . the highest spiritual qualities.
>
> (Jung, 1946, para 384)

The impossibility of nailing down any understanding of the infinite unconscious, of O, is clear in this passage. The way that Jung personifies that
unknowable infinity as a pagan god gives it a noticeably different flavor from
Bion's O; I will explore that difference in more detail when I discuss Jung's
understanding of the Self.

O cannot be understood rationally; it is apprehended by an act of faith.
Faith is the mindset brought to the work by the analyst who takes her stand in
the fluid reality of O, working to disengage from the fixed, material world and
to become a conduit that can receive messages from an ever-shifting, ultimate
truth. The facts of the patient's history or the diagnostic category into which
he has been sorted are of no relevance here. Knowledge – of the patient's
history, for example – when held in mind, is a defense against the unpredictable and unknowable O. An act of faith is needed to approach something that
is unconscious and unknown, perhaps because it has not yet happened; the
individual needs faith in her eventual ability to intuit the O of the moment.
Faith is the state of mind that is receptive to O, the source of what we call
"reality." Bion's apparent atheism is in no sense hard-headed; he believes in a
spiritual reality underlying all the world, O.

Faith is also the basis for the analyst's opening herself to the patient in a
related manner rather than working to preserve her professional authority
and dignity. The latter stance is deeply *un*related. It is as though the clinician
can say (non-verbally), "I am an expert who has been analyzed and you are a
troubled person who knows very little indeed about the workings of your
mind." Or she can say, "We are two troubled people here, both subject to
suffering, neither of us knowing much about what is going on. I have some
expertise in the human psyche and you have some expertise in your own
psyche. Let's combine our perspectives and see what we can sort out." I am
not making a plea for an egalitarian approach. The two individuals' roles are
very different; there is a severe power differential that must be accepted by
both. But a related approach brings an open mind to the table. If the two
people are in trouble in one way or another (a formulation that covers virtually every moment of the work), the therapist must be as curious (almost

always silently) about her own difficulties and blindnesses as she is about the patient's. She can take this stance because she has faith that between the two of them they will make some sense of the situation. Faith that she, for all her confusion and not knowing and helplessness, will be good enough to contribute enough to the mix to be valuable for the patient's development. Faith that she can grow enough to meet her patient's need.

The collective unconscious

The concept O is highly compatible with Jung's notion of the collective unconscious, the archetypal given of the human mind; it is related to his theories of the Self which describe the way O presses toward what Bion called "evolution" into the world of conscious experience. Jung defines archetypes (the contents of the collective unconscious) as pre-existing inherited forms but, he goes on to say, they are "*forms without content*, representing merely the possibility of a certain type of perception and action" (1936/37, para 99, emphasis in original). They are "the unconscious images of the instincts themselves . . . *patterns of instinctual behavior* (ibid., para 91, emphasis in original). The archetype's "form . . . might perhaps be compared to the axial system of a crystal, which, as it were, preforms the crystalline structure in the mother liquid, although it has no material existence of its own" (Jung, 1938, para 155). Although Jung and his descendants have written a great deal about the nature of various archetypes, what is discussed in work like von Franz's many volumes analyzing the archetypal imagery of fairy tales (e.g. 1974) or in Edinger's various attempts to explicate Jung's work (e.g. 1996) is not the indescribable archetype *as such* but the no-longer-empty form that has been filled in with "the material of conscious experience" (Jung, 1938, para 155).

The archetypes are not fixed entities. We cannot say how many archetypes there are. The concept simply asserts that "our imagination, perception, and thinking are . . . influenced by inborn and universally present formal elements" (1936/37, para 92). Jung named certain common archetypes (or archetypal images) like the Mother, the Child, the Wise Old Man, but for our purposes here, rather than thinking of archetypes as discrete entities, it is more helpful to think about the inborn archetypal world as a fluid universe where archetypes that may or may not be named merge into each other and constellate our fundamental reactions to human life. This substrate of the mind "contains" – again the word is misleading – patterns of behavior, perception and experience in an unformed state.

> We call the unconscious 'nothing,' and yet it is a reality *in potentia*. The thought we shall think, the deed we shall do, even the fate we shall lament tomorrow, all lie unconscious in our today. . . . The unconscious has a Janus-face: on one side its contents point back to a preconscious, prehistoric world of instinct, while on the other side it potentially anticipates

the future – precisely because of the instinctive readiness for action of the factors that determine man's fate.

(Jung, 1939, para 498)

These factors are the archetypes. They are

[r]eally perfectly indescribable, . . . perfectly empty, but capable of assimilating a certain kind of material of tremendous variation, yet always pointing to a certain archetypal quality. For instance, the archetype of a house, a hut, a cave or a temple. These are all very different, but it doesn't matter by which name you call them, because all these names or concepts are merely attributes of the underlying thing, which is really indescribable.

(Jung, 1984, p. 525)

Bion talks of a primordial mind that parallels the "survival of parts of our ancestry like the branchial cleft, signs of a kind of fish anatomy, or a vestigial tail" (2000, p. 247). An unnamed seminar participant asks him if what he is talking about is similar to Jung's concept of archetypes and he replies, "I think he was talking about the same thing. There exists some fundamental mind, something that seems to remain unaltered in us all" (ibid.).

If we think about the archetypal image of the Mother, say, the concept postulates that the infant is born with an expectation of a relationship with a female parental figure, of a breast and milk, although these factors that the infant "expects" have no form until he meets them in outer reality. But the archetype is activated in the mother as well as in the infant. Each culture builds on the archetypal given to create a broad form of relatedness that structures how the mother initiates her relationship to her child and then, ultimately, how the child relates to her over the life of their relationship. Each particular mother in interaction with her child will find her unique realization of both the archetypal and the cultural given for the role of "Mother."

There are as many archetypes as there are typical situations in life. . . . When a situation occurs which corresponds to a given archetype, that archetype becomes activated and a compulsiveness appears, which, like an instinctual drive, gains its way against all reason and will.

(Jung, 1959, para 99)

Freud's "Oedipal Complex," for example, is hypothesized as a universal dilemma of human existence. We see signs of it in all the situations where a person feels inside or outside of the boundaries of a given group or dyad. Jung calls this sort of universal life problem that every human being must navigate "archetypal."

How, we might ask, can Jung's universe of pre-existing forms be equivalent to Bion's "formless infinite?" Although Bion talks frequently about the formlessness of O, he also describes O as the universe of things-in-themselves made up of the "absolute essence" implied in "the Platonic theory of Forms" (1970, see p. 41). If we can avoid fixating on the contradictory uses of the word "forms," we can readily see that both men are talking about the same area. In fact, Jung describes Plato's Forms as "a philosophical version of [the archetypes]" (1960, para 388). Bion is more straightforwardly mystical than Jung dared to be. He seems to posit O as a spiritual background to empirical reality, something that Jung never implies. Bion indicates, however, that his idea of "empirical reality" is actually a *psychological* factor. He sounds as though he is, for example, concerned with a house, but more centrally he is describing what lies behind *a human experience* of a house. The person has an experience of a particular house; behind that emotional perception stands the Platonic Form of House which is the thing-in-itself, the archetype of House. If we remember that before the person begins to experience the outer world, the collective unconscious is made up of a matrix that has no content, consisting of potential "images" that shape the person's perception even though they are as yet "perfectly empty," we have as good a description of O as a Bionian could produce. The collective unconscious feels like a narrower concept than O because it so clearly refers to the human psyche, rather than to all of reality. But this is a question of emphasis rather than of substance. Bion uses O primarily to describe the immaterial source of the emotional experiences that analysis concerns itself with; Jacobi, one of Jung's most important students, calls the collective unconscious "an inner correspondence to the world as a whole" (1959, p. 60). The concepts bleed into each other.

All of human life is structured by the unknowable archetypes that determine human nature. The collective unconscious is a hypothetical concept that attempts to explain the constancy of our species across cultures and time. In talking, for example, about a contemporary dream image that he amplifies with an ancient Egyptian text, Jung asks

> [w]hat connection is there between your particular dream and the pyramids? – the two seem incommensurable. Yet you might find a close parallel to your dream in an Egyptian text containing the same symbols . . . and you think: that is Egypt and this is my dream and it is foolish to compare the two, there is nothing in common. *But the scribe who produced that text was a human being, in most respects exactly like yourself – hair, two eyes, a nose, two ears and hands, the same natural functions, he was happy, sad, loved, was born and died. . . .* Primitive tribes are moved by the same emotions as we are. . . . [O]ur unconscious speaks a language which is almost international.
>
> (1984, p. 70, emphasis added)

Postulating a collective unconscious is a way of saying that there is such a thing as "human nature" and that it is relatively timeless. Jacobi (op. cit.)

suggests that we cannot ask when archetypes developed. They are a feature of organic life and came into existence along with it.

Although Jung did not explore it, one aspect of his theory reflects a contemporary Bionian perspective that does not see "the unconscious" as a storeroom or even as an infinite well of material just like the material of consciousness except for its *un*consciousness. Both O and the collective unconscious describe an infinite universe whose nature, by definition, we can never know. The energy emanating from this source takes comprehensible forms when it enters consciousness; all we can know of its unconscious nature is that it must be different (Jung, 1971, para 838). O or the collective unconscious is the boundless universe reflected in Plato's cave that we perceive darkly, flickering behind the sensual world of outer reality. We might call this "the deepest unconscious" in a sort of shorthand, but any noun is necessarily inadequate to describe it.

We shall explore Bion's conception of the dreaming process in the next chapter. He presents it as an ongoing, lifelong transformation of emotional experiences into symbolic forms capable of generating new meanings and directions for the person. His theory emphasizes the impossibility of *having* the totality of one's life experience. One's emotional life is always more extensive than one can bear, there will always be potential aspects of the self that are unknown and missing, not exactly residing in "the unconscious" but not yet included in the conscious experience of the self. Instead of a musty storeroom of elements consciousness has rejected, the unconscious has become "a world of possibilities which will never end, which are always in the process of evolution and transformation" (Andrade de Azevedo, 2000, p. 85).

This is the unconscious that Jung describes in all his work, even the work predating his break with Freud. The creative unconscious is like the sea, yielding "an endless and self-replenishing abundance of living creatures, a wealth beyond our fathoming" (1946, para 366). He talks of

> the baffling symbolism of things that are still in the unconscious where things are existent and nonexistent . . . things are yea and nay, good and bad, black and white. . . . It cannot be both, but it may be either. . . . This is not really a new discovery. The Gnostics had that idea and expressed it as Pleroma, a state of fullness where the pairs of opposites . . . are together, then when they 'become', it is either day or night. In the state of 'promise' before they become they are nonexistent, there is neither white nor black, good nor bad.
>
> (Jung, 1984, p. 131)

This is a timeless "place" where everything that has been or will be *is*, a universe where the dead and the unborn are as real and alive as the living (op. cit., para 529). As I described above, the unconscious can be personified as Mercurius and appears in dreams and fantasies as fundamentally dualistic, a "fiend, monster, beast, and at the same time panacea," the infinite wisdom of God, the holy spirit that oversees the unfolding of one's aliveness (ibid., para 389).

Jung is almost never credited by them, but contemporary psychoanalysts, influenced by Bion, have developed an image of the unconscious remarkably congruent with Jung's. It has become

> . . . an organic entity . . . a dwelling that is inhabited by indivisible *numinous presences, phantoms, demons*, or *spirits* who constitute the permanent cast of an ongoing unconscious dramatic series in repertory, otherwise known as *phantasies*, that highlight and play our ontological themes from the 'dailies' of our normal lives in a veritable cinematographic 'mixing room.'
>
> (Grotstein, 2004a, p. 101, emphasis in original)

Rather than a storeroom for ugly junk, the unconscious is understood as "a form of dynamic mental activity which permeates our life and is sustained by our emotional experiences" (Andrade de Azevedo, 2000, p. 86). Instead of an image of consciousness absorbing and rendering harmless the unconscious poison that interferes with its operation, we picture "consciousness [as] continually widened through the confrontation with previously unconscious contents . . ." (Jung, 1916, para 193). Although Jung did not use the word "infinite," describing the unconscious instead as "indefinitely large" (1950a, para 634), his images are infinite in nature. In his mature work, Bion spoke of the infinite because "the unconscious" sounds like a bounded place that could, at least in theory, be thoroughly explored.

Jung describes a sensible, rational patient, a businessman who lives in the "real" world.

> Suddenly he finds himself in the unconscious, where everything is up and down, to and fro, with the most contradictory impulses and opinions. . . . He is lost . . . and he cannot understand that this peculiar experience is the main thing. . . . In the unconscious he must submit to . . . a sort of torture. One day you think you have come to a clear decision, the next day it is gone. You feel like a fool and curse it until you learn that this thing is pairs of opposites, and you are not the opposite. If you learn that, you have got your lesson.
>
> (1984, p. 149)

The finite "I" must separate itself out from the infinite psyche that Jung called "the unconscious." In working at this impossible task, the individual can come to know, for example, her greed or lust or hate. She can take responsibility for managing inner forces by recognizing that we small individuals are not responsible for their *existence* any more than we are responsible for the winds or the tides. As long as someone imagines that she *is* the forces that swirl around inside, pushing her hither and yon, she is at their mercy. To whatever extent these ruthless life energies are recognized, the individual will be filled with shame. By gaining some perspective on the infinite inner depths, and recognizing their objective rather than subjective nature, she begins to know who she is.

The Self

Freud's unconscious is a chaotic mass of energy struggling to satisfy its primal, body-based urges. Its blind, uncoordinated goal is what Freud called "pleasure:" a state of non-stimulation and rest that is similar to the perfect peace of nirvana. Jung's unconscious, on the other hand, is centrally powered by an *intentional* – mindful and coordinated – energic force that strives for much more than instinctual satisfaction. He calls this force "the Self."[10] The Self is concerned with the most spiritually developed aspects of our lives as well as with our instinctual needs – and with everything in between. Jung talks of dreams, for example, as *attempts* on the part of the unconscious to "penetrate the conscious," to "impress the conscious with the unconscious point of view" (1984, p. 524). The unconscious, organized and guided by the Self, is not blind; it is trying to balance and complete the person. In case examples Jung describes the ways given individuals' dreams try to complete them by balancing their one-sided, conscious impulses with the feelings of other parts of themselves, even when what is at issue are relatively quotidian choices and attitudes.

James Grotstein talks about "the cosmic indifference of O" (2007). The Self is an archetypal energic force that works to bring the individual into a personal relationship to O. A Jungian perspective suggests that each particular form that existence can take – each person, each rock, each living creature – is a part of the harmonious whole of the universe, of O. The "cosmic indifference of O" turns into O as a wholeness that we are each part of. Just as each kidney cell in our bodies is a part of an integrated organism, each of us is an element of O. While the body as a whole has no particular concern for any given cell, every cell does its work, living and dying in harmony with the rhythms of the whole. The concept of the Self suggests that behind O's apparent cosmic indifference lies an interdependent harmony

10 There is much disagreement in the Jungian world about whether or not to capitalize "self." When it refers to the subjective sense of "me-ness" it is never capitalized; when it refers to the organizing center of the psyche it often is capitalized in English. Since Jung wrote in German, where all nouns are capitalized, he did not deal with this issue. The editors of the *Collected Works* decided not to capitalize the big self/Self, but the tendency in English has increasingly been to do so. As we shall see, the little self shades ultimately into the big self/Self so that sometimes deciding whether or not to capitalize the word can be difficult. To make the distinction as well as it can be made, however, I will capitalize the big self/Self.

that we can never understand or map. Each of us is an infinitesimal but meaningful part of the whole.

All psychoanalysts struggle to articulate a concept of "the self." Jung's idea is central to his understanding of the psyche and its mysteries. It is difficult to grasp, partly because it is quite different from mainstream psychoanalytic notions. He defines the ego – what I am calling the "I" – simply as consciousness. The Jungian ego is similar to most psychoanalytic notions of the self[11] – it is the waking sense of "me." The Self, on the other hand, is

> [t]he union of the conscious mind . . . with the unconscious. . . . The [S]elf . . . is both ego [the "I"] and non-ego, subjective and objective, individual and collective. It is the "uniting symbol" which epitomizes the total union of opposites. As such . . . it can only be expressed by means of symbols.
>
> (Jung, 1946, para 474)

Because it is *organized* by the Self, the Jungian unconscious has a different flavor from O. O is impersonal and implacable; no intentionality is hypothesized for it. It is an unrelated force. The person against whom it impinges struggles to know and to not-know about it. Its power arrives by virtue of its Truth. For Jung, on the other hand, the mystery of ultimate reality is mediated by the Self that intentionally presses the person to become the individual – the self – she truly is. Again it is the *truth* of who she is that overwhelms the attempt of consciousness to be the person she wants to be, but rather than the truth being blind, Jung conceives of the psyche as centrally impelled by an energy that attempts to meet the truth and to press the conscious person to bow down to it. It is certainly easy to imagine the evolutionary advantage that would be conferred by attempting to meet the truth rather than trying to avoid it, although it is also easy to imagine that denying the truth of a situation (in the way that young people, for example, believe themselves immortal) may sometimes offer the advantage. Both of these human impulses, to know and to not-know, are needed. (In Chapter 5 we will explore these conflicting urges in more detail.)

When we include the Self in our understanding, we see that the unconscious psyche is *related* to the person. It suggests an inborn relational energy that structures our connection with ourselves. This innate human energy underlies our need for relatedness. When therapists ignore this need, the good food that they have to offer their patients is inadequately processed; it may be indigestible.

---

11 Heinz Kohut and Massud Kahn are exceptions. They each talk at times of a self that seems similar to Jung's Self. Kohut talks of the fundamental impossibility of defining the self since all we can know are its manifestations, and Kahn states that we can know the self only through the symbols which image the self at the same time as they construct it.

Since consciousness is so much smaller than the infinite depths on which it rests, the Self, the center and circumference of our energic aliveness, has an unknowable quality, a sense of otherness. Encompassing the infinite reaches of our wholeness, the Self "hits consciousness unexpectedly, like lightning. ... It thrusts the "I" aside and makes room for a supraordinate factor, the totality of a person . . ." (Jung, 1950b, para 541). In its energic aspect, the Self channels the life energy animating and guiding us, rarely in accord with our conscious wishes. It is never what "I" planned or chose. It is a surprise, at least partly unwelcome because it confronts the individual so forcefully with his smallness in the face of Nature, both inner and outer. The Self overturns our plans, it disrupts us. It forces us into connection with our aliveness; its activity requires submission to the power of the life force. The Self humbles, even humiliates, the person. The relationship of the Self to the individual parallels in some ways the optimal therapist's relatedness with her patient. She is not nice, she is not easy to be with, but she never loses track of the impact she is having on the patient's emotional subjectivity.

It is, perhaps, easy to see why the Self has been projected out as God or the gods. A sense of the experience of the Self is captured in Saint Paul's expression, "Not I, not I, but Christ in me." It is the small, still, inner voice that Isaiah described as the voice of God. A secular person would call it the voice of her conscience (not to be confused with a judging superego). Remember here that one of Bion's definitions of O is God or the godhead. It has been suggested that when Bion used the term "God," he meant something different from what Jung meant by the term, but I would disagree with that perspective. I believe that both men used the term not to refer to an external *being* who created and who guides the universe, but as a *concept* or *symbol* that captures a human psychological experience which is inexpressible in any finite or exact description. Possibly, they disagreed on whether or not a unified being that could be called "God" exists in outer reality, but I do not know of either man publicly discussing his subjective belief in this regard. What Jung does say, over and over, is that he is *not* talking about the validity or falsity of religious beliefs, he is describing the psychological meaning of humanity's religious beliefs. Bion, who called the idea of heaven, for example, "preposterous" (1970, p. 100), sounds more skeptical about theological ideas than Jung does; while a different feeling is aroused in reading the two men, their ideas are actually similar.

When a therapy or analysis is working, the Self is constellated – it is activated and the activity of its energy is felt. We follow the activity of the Self when we follow the meanderings of an individual's emotional life. The Self is found in all the despised emotions that people would like to amputate: shame, neediness, dependency, hopeless yearnings, "foolish" hopes and fears. The Self cannot be thought of as *consisting* of our emotions, but our emotions trace the path that the Self is taking; they are the Self's attempt to capture our attention and to tell us the truth of who we are.

Typically, the Self is projected onto the therapist, whom the patient begins to see as larger than human, dazzlingly impressive or frightening. In an effective therapeutic process the Self seizes hold of the conscious patient and demands recognition and precedence. Sometimes, when a difficult decision looms, the Self will clearly be the architect of a dream: Allison wanted to end her analysis just at the point where it was beginning to take hold of her. She was in imminent danger of being gripped by her attachment to me and by the analytic process in a way that would certainly threaten her autonomy. Rather than challenging Allison's wish to flee analysis, I said that her wish was an important idea; perhaps we could have a consultation from her dreams. In the next hour she brought in a dream that consisted only of an authoritative voice saying, "Stay right there." (A week or two later, of course, she had "forgotten" the dream and raised the idea of terminating again, but the idea of abandoning the work had lost its potency. The impulse faded away and she allowed herself to be pulled down into a powerful transformative process that lasted for years.)

Recognition of the activity of the Self conflicts with the narcissism that we will explore in Chapters 4 and 5. A universal complex of psychopathology permeates our contemporary civilization in a way that elevates narcissism to a desirable state and blinds us to its pathology. (As we shall see, this fundamental complex has been the source of psychoanalysis' unrelated approaches.) We are urged to "take care of ourselves" rather than to orient toward others; it is seen as a sign of health if someone can indulge himself with luxury items rather than trying to strike a balance between his (inherently infinite) greed and the needs of people outside his immediate family.[12] Enormous "Christian" churches have grown up around a gospel that centers itself in the notion that virtue will lead to wealth, perhaps of enormous proportions, and that mansions and luxurious cars demonstrate the owner's righteousness. Jung believed that the innate energy of the Self opposes this tendency and presses the individual to include his capacity for concern, his love, his ultimate values – to be related – in his choices.

Our culture emphasizes an illusory potency of the "I." Just *do* it, Nike urges us; where there's a will there's a way. Thirty days to a slimmer you, to a more forceful or effective or more confident you. Jung's notion of the Self stresses the fact that I may not be *able* to do "it" regardless of my attempts to focus my willpower on the aspects of myself that I would like to change. Saint Paul's reference to "Christ in me" sounds positive; Christ (in a Christian world, at least) would seem to depict a desired and reliable loving inner force that would be welcomed. But confrontation with the fact that one is not the master of her own house is invariably unwelcome. The person may *decide*, for

---

12 As we shall see in Chapter 4, the person who can *never* orient to himself is actually a different form of the person who *always* orients to himself. Either approach emerges from a narcissistic character organization.

example, to become an extravert but an inherent shyness will trip her up and force her to acknowledge the introversion that is her true nature, regardless of her conscious wishes for herself. She will not initially thank the god-within that forces her to be who she is, although ultimately she may be very grateful indeed for this energy pushing her to become all of herself even when her initial conscious take on that all-ness is negative.

Cognitive behavioral therapy (CBT), much more highly regarded these days in the United States than psychoanalysis, formalizes the idea that a person can work with his conscious attitudes to become the person he wants to be, supposedly bypassing the inner depths of the psyche whether we image those depths as an expression of the Self or as O. Short-term CBT may prove effective in changing neatly bounded symptoms in the unusual cases where discrete difficulties present in someone with a solid, mature "I." Longer-term CBT can foster deeper change, just as *any* therapeutic approach can, but analytic therapists would conceive of that change as rooted in the unconscious depths of the interpersonal relationship between patient and therapist rather than in the therapist's techniques or theories. The therapeutic process constellates the Self in the therapist, the patient and the couple. That activated Self organizes the unfolding of fundamental life energies that bring about qualitative changes in each person's psyche. The one element that research consistently shows to be crucial in determining psychotherapy outcomes is the quality of the "therapeutic alliance" – the relationship (Blatt, 2007). Who the therapist *is*, the kinds of unconscious attitudes that permeate her presence with her patient, and the chemistry between the two members of the couple prove to be the most important factors determining outcomes because these are the factors that reflect the movement of the Self as it mediates the underlying O of the experience.

Where psychoanalysts have historically focused – to our great advantage – on the technical competence of the analyst, Jung and his followers have paid more attention to elements less measurable than technique, to factors that reflect the depths of the individual practitioner's development. In the intensity of an effective therapy or analysis, where the transference is constellated and the practitioner is pulled into the maelstrom of unconscious material coming up not only in the patient but in herself as well, a

> genuine participation, going right beyond professional routine, is absolutely imperative, unless of course the doctor prefers to jeopardize the whole proceeding by evading his own problems, which are becoming more and more insistent. The doctor must go to the limits of his subjective possibilities, otherwise the patient will be unable to follow suit.
>
> (Jung, 1946, para 400)

Jung's repeated insistence on the fact that the analytic instrument reflects the entirety of the practitioner's psyche, rather than her conscious, technical choices led him to suggest that the primary requirement for becoming an analyst must be the individual's analysis, not her intellectual training. Freud immediately concurred. But sometimes psychodynamic training programs can unconsciously gloss over that eternally ambiguous, uncontrollable standard for a trainee's effectiveness and get caught instead in the nicely bounded issues presented by intellectual mastery of great texts. Jungians may look more to different texts and even areas (amplification of symbols, for example) than do other psychoanalysts, but any human being yearns for the certainty of intellectual mastery as the key to the work, because the depths of the emotional engagement can only be profoundly ambiguous and thus beyond the practitioner's control.

As the infinite expanse of O evolves, it presses to be known about, even though it never can be *known*, because it *is* the true reality with which the person is struggling. The notion of the Self suggests that the energy governing the individual's aliveness can be personified; this energy works actively to bring the person toward the truth of her experience. This personification is consonant with the natural language of dreams that image our subjective reality as conflicts between various inner figures. Jung describes the psyche's drive to realize its truth, its separate individuality, and its interpersonal, communal interconnectedness (e.g. Jung, 1963, para 778) as a struggle between the Self demanding realization in the individual's lived experience, and the "I," tied to his limiting internal objects, a little self that resists the pain and disorientation of change. Rooted outside of consciousness, the intentional Self seeks to compensate the "I"'s tendency toward a one-sided view of itself since, comprising the totality of the psyche and including all of human inheritance that links us to each other, its view is far broader than that of our puny consciousness. The Self personifies "a totality and unity in which the opposites are united" and it appears in dreams or fantasies in the figure of an exceptional person "such as a king, hero, prophet, saviour, etc." (Jung, 1971, para 790). The hero or prophet might seem perfect rather than someone who contains the opposites, but he is beyond the ordinary individual: he has something like a bird's eye view of the situation. He can see the hidden mysteries of the current predicament rather than just the little piece before his nose.

The psyche images the Self as governing or attempting to govern the "I" in line with a broader plan of some kind – whether one for the direction of the internal "nation," for a new and improved moral order, or for the realization of a desired and difficult new accomplishment. This understanding of the Self led Jung to focus on the unfolding of the unconscious – what Bion called the evolution of O – as an intentional process.

Bion talks about the "I" "winning" something from O. Jung's language more commonly pictures the "I" as giving in to something that demands inclusion in consciousness. Jung's perspective brings in awe in its awesome and awful aspects. It led him to conceive of the life cycle as one in which the conscious person must take a heroic stance in the first part of life in order to establish herself in the world but must yield in the second half of life to the inborn thrust from the Self that says, "*this* is who you are." The energy of the Self can be personified as the God of Job; it undermines the person's narcissistic sense of potency, ultimately by forcing her to grapple with infirmity and death.

Jung's theory offers a conceptual system for understanding the individual's driven search for the truth, even though an encounter with the truth is, virtually by definition, destabilizing and unwelcome. Through this concept Jung discusses the creativity of the unconscious. His unconscious does not blindly seek selfish gratification; it is fueled by the psychological organism's quest for wholeness, a much broader instinctual drive than an urge toward sexual or aggressive release. Jung conceived of this search for wholeness as reflecting *the* fundamental psychological impulse. The Self makes O more personal and more numinous or divine, both at once. It is personal in its concern for the individual who is carrying it and divine in its far-greater-than-human potency.

The Self is an ordering and orienting principle within the psyche. In the Hebrew Bible, it is personified as God, and the supportive function of the Self is often described in the psalms:

> My help comes from the Lord,
>   maker of heaven and earth.
> He will not let your foot give way;
>   Your guardian will not slumber.
>   (Psalm 121: 2–3)

But the Self is also a *dis*ordering principle that works against outmoded or inflexible ways of being. This is the God of thunder and wrath, who unleashed the flood and the Babylonian exile. Jung spoke of both aspects of the Self less than two years before his death, when he described his belief in "God:"

> When I say that I don't need to believe in God because I "know," I mean I know of the existence of God-images in general and in particular. I know it is a matter of a universal experience and, in so far as I am no exception, I know that I have such experience also, which I call God. It is the experience of my will over against another and very often stronger will, crossing my path often with seemingly disastrous results, putting strange ideas into my head and maneuvering my fate sometimes into most undesirable corners or giving it unexpected favourable twists, outside my knowledge and my intention. The strange force against or for my conscious tendencies is well known to me. . . . But why should you call this something "God"? [someone might ask; I would answer]: "Why not?" It has always been called "God".
>
>   (Jung, 1959b, pp. 522–3)

In my opinion, this is exactly why it is *not* helpful to call this force "God:" the proper noun "God" is imbued with meanings that profoundly differ from Jung's dark and wary attitude toward "God." Jung's *psychological* writing about "God" as a projection of the Self makes it possible to recognize the value of his description of the God image rather than being alienated by his religious tone.

Although, at first glance, it is puzzling why Jung would call this inner force "the Self." Rather than finding it easy, or even, as we shall see, desirable, to identify with this powerful energy of aliveness, we find it alien, not-I rather than "I." To discover the Self means to discover the fact that *I* am not in charge. In this form, it is a painful experience. It is unconsciously familiar to us, however, and has generated the slang term "headshrinker." The "I" gives up its inflation as it matures; it comes down to earth and recognizes its limitation and smallness rather than taking as its own the awesome power of the greater psyche. It is not the "I" that steers the ship. Something far greater than "I" determines the authentic nature of who I am and therefore the course of my life. As the individual becomes more of herself, her "I" becomes smaller and humbler at the same time as she acquires depth and substance.

The concept of the collective unconscious and the archetypes provides a container for thinking about the fact that just as the individual's breathing is both a personal act and something common not only to all mankind but to all higher life forms, so the psyche is both personal and much greater than the individual, connecting her to all of humanity and to life itself. The Self

> is brighter and darker than the ego, and accordingly confronts it with problems which it would like to avoid. Either one's moral courage fails, or one's insight, or both, until in the end fate decides. . . . You have become the victim of a decision made over your head or in defiance of the heart. From this we can see the numinous power of the [S]elf. . . . For this reason *the experience of the [S]elf is always a defeat for the ["I"]*.
>
> (Jung, 1963, para 778, emphasis in original)

One way to think about the Self grabbing the reins from the hands of the "I," is to recognize that something we could call "human nature" is stronger than any conscious wish we might have about who we want to be. Sometimes we see this in someone who is trying to be perfect – always good and kind and loving. Here, the Self trips up the person repeatedly, leading her to behave in less than perfect ways and confronting her with her humanness. In other cases, an individual's psychopathic behavior can cause the Self to pull her into enactments that lead to her downfall. Rather than thinking of these enactments as expressions of the person's "stupidity," a Jungian perspective suggests that the depths of her own psyche, in some cases at least, have engineered the experience in which her lack of a moral compass is unconsciously compensated by her humanness – her union with the human race and the human inheritance – a humanness that includes concern for the Other as well as herself.

Jung and Bion both interpret myths (i.e. religious stories) as projections of humanity's fundamental inner drama. Bion says that the Christian myth "represent[s] a pattern to which the human personality would be found to approximate" (1970, p. 115). Jung suggests that Christ represents the Self/the self: a unique individual living in time (the self) and an eternal form that transcends any one person's life or personality (the Self). Translating the myth into psychological terms, Jung says:

> Instead of using the term God you say "unconscious," instead of Christ "[Self/]self," instead of incarnation "integration of the unconscious," instead of salvation or redemption "individuation," instead of crucifixion or sacrifice on the Cross "realization of . . . 'wholeness' ".
>
> (1958, para 1,664)

It is important to notice in this quotation Jung's sense of the pain involved in approaching a realization of one's wholeness. It is an experience of crucifixion, of being torn between the wish to remain the familiar, acceptable person the individual knows as "himself," and the Self's pressure to take in the strange and despised elements of his authentic wholeness that he would prefer to leave out. As he absorbs these new aspects of himself, he may come to value them highly, but initially their unfamiliarity makes them unwelcome.

The Self embodies the totality of the infinite energy of the unconscious. It is the center, the circumference, and the wholeness of the psyche, a paradoxical entity that can be expressed only symbolically for it makes no rational "sense." One way to describe the central goal of the Self is to think of it as incarnation – to be held and lived in the experience of the self. Over and over Jung emphasizes that the impulses arising inside the individual must be understood as objective forces to be related to rather than dominated. While these impulses are shaped by our personal experiences, the core strivings are universal in nature, even when their particular form is individual. But the impulses themselves are not "mine;" "I" am the victim of the impulses, "I" belong to them. It is my responsibility to contain and work with the impulses that arise within me, but they are more realistically conceived of as other than mine. We cannot alter our natures and while we may be able to suppress some aspects of ourselves, what has been suppressed will pop up in some other place, in an altered form, and then it will be filled with hostility to the "I" that has tried to deny it its rightful existence. We are not responsible for the contents of the Self in the form they manifest in the personal self; we are responsible for what we *do* with those contents but not for their existence.

This theory of the Self offers a vivid confirmation of the fundamental need for relatedness in the therapeutic situation. The basic goal of the Self is to force the conscious person into relationship with his larger self. *The central aim of the Self is to foster relatedness.* It works to insist that all the different tendencies inside the self, tendencies that our dreams image as different individuals, are given a seat at the table. "I" am no more privileged than the flailing infant or the cold-blooded scientist who live inside me. The job of the "I" is to make room for and to respect *all* of the impulses that push against it. The Self approaches the "I" in an imperious manner, but its goal is an inner society that operates in a related manner. Its demanding approach to the "I" can be seen as validating the analyst's need to maintain the analytic frame even when it seems to break her patient's heart; its goal – the mutually respectful atmosphere of a well-functioning committee – supports the contention that maintaining the frame in a deeply related way is crucial.

The Self and the self

Let me return to the puzzle I referred to above: why does Jung call this awesome power that the psyche images as God the "Self?" It is so different from the subjective experience we know about, the sense of being "me," an experience of wholeness that, as depth psychologists, we know to be illusory.

When the patient has gone far enough in working with her shadow[13] – the disowned parts of herself that she finds unacceptable – she begins to experience something objective about herself. The "I" would like to be kind and loving but sometimes the person feels or behaves in a cruel and hateful manner. As she takes in one experience after another of her true nature, two things begin to develop. In this example, the "I" will become kinder and more loving in its behavior as it grows aware of its cruel and hateful impulses. And the person will suffer as she begins to realize who she really is. The growing expansion of consciousness

> reveals a unity which nevertheless is – or was – a diversity. No longer the earlier ego with its make-believes and artificial contrivances, but another, 'objective' ego, which for this reason is better called the 'self.' No longer a mere selection of suitable fictions, but a string of hard facts, which together make up the cross we all have to carry or the fate we ourselves are.
>
> (Jung, 1946, para 400)

As the "I" expands and deepens, the individual's sense of me-ness moves increasingly in line with the person her intimates see her to be. The CEO of

---

13 As I will emphasize throughout this work, the individual finds his shadow unacceptable, but this does not imply that the qualities he disowns would generally be considered negative. People push away the aspects of themselves that do not fit with their particular self images. Sometimes those images are negative, leading the person to deny qualities that most of us would consider objectively "good."

the large corporation begins to see herself more the way her secretary or her husband or her child does and less the way that the admiring reporter from *Fortune* magazine might. Her personal self – the little self – feels smaller, although as she takes in her shadow, she actually becomes more substantial. The suffering involved is great.

Rosemary Gordon (1985) suggests that there are three selves. First, there is a primary self, the infant at birth. The newborn state is one of undifferentiated wholeness that has the same relationship to the developed person that the original fertilized egg has to the complicated, ready-to-be-born baby that grows from it. Just as that egg contains the infant in implicate form, the primary self contains the person who will ultimately develop from it. The development of the differentiated self has been described by the Jungian analyst Michael Fordham (1978) as a repeating process of deintegration (a pleasant state of formlessness rather than the terrifying state of disintegration) and reintegration. The primary self, the initial state of wholeness, deintegrates. It comes apart or falls into pieces, perhaps first in the experience of being born. It then reintegrates into an experience of being that the infant begins to know as him or her "self." Out of these comings-apart and comings-together grow an increasingly differentiated psychological organism. This spiraling process that begins at birth (or perhaps before) and that continues through the life cycle is similar to Bion's understanding of the PS $\leftrightarrow$ D[14] sequence, which we shall explore in the next chapter.

Then there is what Gordon calls the little self, the subjective sense of "this is who I am," or "this is all of me." The solidity and structure of this self depends primarily on the infant's experiences with his or her primary caretaker(s). When these experiences are good enough, the person has a foundation that enables him to interact well enough with the big Self I have been describing. This interaction creates a developing self that can integrate its ever-evolving O into an ever-expanding sense of me-ness. Jung suggests that the Self, as a kind of "*a priori* existent out of which the ego evolves," is a kind of prefiguration of the "I" or the self. This speaks to the fact that "[i]t is not I who create myself, rather I happen to myself" (Jung, 1940/1954, para 391). We shall look at this relationship between the Self and the self in more detail in the pages that follow, when we will look at the concept and operation of the ego-Self axis (Edinger, 1972).

Finally, Gordon calls the Self that I described above – Jung's metapsychological concept that refers to the whole of the objective psyche – the "big self."

As I indicated above, we know intellectually that the subjective "self" we experience as "me" is incomplete. It is not, actually, "me;" it is *part* of "me."

---

14 The term "PS" comes from the paranoid-schizoid position and "D" refers to the depressive position, although in the symbol PS $\leftrightarrow$ D, the letters have a somewhat different meaning from Klein's positions.

On a day to-day-basis, as well as over a life span, the subjective experience changes. We see in analysis or therapy a repeating experience of, "This is me," followed by, "Oh! *This* is me, too." The subjective self falls into various moods that can dramatically shift the person's sense of who he is. Some days the individual may feel like a good, strong person, worthy and valuable; on other days he feels weak, fragile, inferior, ugly, inadequate. Many experiences seem like "me." Gordon suggests that

> [T]he more an individual recognizes the cohesion and interrelatedness of his several selves, the closer does he approach an experience of the big self [the Self]. And this is increased further if he can also get a feel of those little selves that seem diametrically opposed, alien or even distasteful to those he can experience and recognize as his. In other words, his capacity to be in ever better and closer touch with more and more aspects of his shadow puts him also in better and closer touch with the big self.
>
> (Gordon, 1985, p. 266)

Most of our patients are working early in this process, so experiences of the Self (as opposed to the self) are unlikely, but the Self may appear in a dream as an intimation of the ultimate goal of development. Penny, a patient who I will describe in Chapter 4, felt for many years that she didn't *have* a self. She felt shapeless and lacked a sense of herself as a unique individual moving through various moods and experiences but with some underlying continuity. At a point in the therapy where an elementary sense of having a self was beginning to appear, she dreamed that she was given the gift of an oblong ceramic dish of great beauty with a perfectly round ebony stone in its center. In the dream, she recognized the gift as being precious, although after she woke she had no sense of why it should be so.

The perfectly round ebony stone is a symbol of the Self that could midwife the birth of a personal self for Penny. It is a relatively indestructible unity that seems to be the antithesis of the biological processes of change, decay, and death. Cirlot (1962) says that the stone symbolizes "unity and strength" (p. 299) and notes that in primitive times people commonly worshiped stones. There is a black meteorite in the Kaaba in Mecca that remains a holy object of Muslim worship and there was a Black Stone of Pessinus that was believed in the ancient world to be an incarnation of the Great Mother. Genesis 28:22 states, "And this stone that I have set up for a standing pillar shall become a house of God" (Fox, 1983), implying that God lives inside the stone or that the stone holds God. And then there is the alchemical *lapis*, the stone that represented the goal of the work, the turning of the base human being into a golden vessel of God or the Self. In her dream, Penny is receiving the gift of the Self, a gift that would also give her a particular incarnation of the Self – her self – but the waking Penny could not understand why the gift had seemed so precious.

At a later point in the individuation process than Penny had been at at the time of her dream, I had a dream that imaged the Self. Because I was farther along in my development, my conscious self – my "I" – was able to experience the dream image more fully than she had been able to and the image became my touchstone for the meaning of life. In my dream, my first analyst, the person who had helped me to develop the solid sense of being a self that Penny still lacked, appeared. In outer reality, Dr. X had died quite suddenly some years earlier (well after the termination of my analysis). In the dream I was amazed and excited to see him:

> *"Oh, Dr. X," I said, "you've come back from the dead! Tell me: what is death like?" I knew that he possessed the secret of the fundamental mystery of life and that he could reveal it to me. In response to my question, Dr. X gestured broadly to the left and the dream became an image of the universe, an infinitely vast, utterly dark expanse, filled with brilliant nebulae and swirling galaxies of tremendous beauty. I was overcome with awe.*

In waking life, I do not believe that "I" will exist after the death of my body, and even though Dr. X appears here as himself – he is in his "I" – I would not understand the dream as describing an unconscious aspect of myself that believes in or yearns for an afterlife. I was young when I began my work with Dr. X, and I projected the Self onto him in the way only an undeveloped person can. He seemed infinitely wise and self-contained, and I did not consciously remark on my belief in his omniscience. Without thinking about it, I believed that he understood everything about me, and that our mutual process, where I associated for most of the hour and he occasionally offered a profound and revelatory comment, was something I needed to do for my own good, not something he required if he was to come to know me. Although I had long since revised this naïve image of my analyst, in my infantile psyche he continued to exist in this God-like form. His return in the dream is a function of his much-larger-than-human meaning in my psyche, not a comment on something a mere person like myself could expect.

In his appearance as a messenger from god (described by my secular self as the universe), Dr. X shows me an image of eternity that is directly defined as a human experience after – or beyond – earthly life. It is an image of infinity, of the endless archetypal unconscious that includes all of creation, an image of everything that exists. The swirling galaxies mark it as *alive*. The totality and completeness of this picture is the Self. A Bionian would, I think, call it O. It is as though Dr. X was telling me that when we are not caught in outer reality – in the limited four-dimensional world we know about – we become the infinite.

A patient named Peter told me that he had read an article about black holes in a popular magazine. As he talked about it, he felt dwarfed by the enormity of the universe and his infinitesimal place in that immensity. He felt distressed and angry, but as he talked he abruptly felt his point of view shift and instead of feeling insignificant he had a sudden rush of amazement and felt awestruck by this infinite universe *of which he was a part*. As we age and leave behind the tasks of young and middle adulthood – when we have lived enough of the arc of our career to begin to glimpse its end and have watched the children that we parented disperse into the world to form new families – we need to loosen our identification with our own existence and orient more toward the wholeness of our tribe, of the human family, of the Earth; in Peter's case, of the universe.

As various contradictory experiences of the little self are gathered into an increasingly substantial sense of a personal self, Gordon suggests that the individual comes closer to a feeling of rapport with the big Self. As a person knows a greater expanse of himself, he begins to connect with the essential human experience via his personal version of it. This is what Peter felt in the moment that he identified more with the universe than with his little self. "The closer [the person] can get to a feeling of rapport with [the Self], the greater, deeper and the wider is likely to become his capacity for understanding and compassion both of others and of himself" (Gordon, 1985, p. 267). As one aspect after another of the shadow is taken into the person's sense of himself, he begins to truly recognize that selfishness and arrogance and psychopathy do not belong to *others* – these are parts of him, too. The individual dreams of a jaguar, a moonscape, a bug. We *say* that every image in a dream is a part of the dreamer, but to truly take that in means to recognize not only that all things human belong to every human being, but that all of creation exists in the tiny organism trapped in such a finite slice of time and space. I am "just me," an infinitesimal grain in all of the universe, but the little, personal self is more than a mirror of the infinite outer world; it actually contains it, just as each fractal is (at least roughly) identical in form (but not in size) to the whole irregular geometric body from which it sprang. Gordon describes the goal of this process as recognizing the fact that the individual "is a singular, unique and responsible being, and yet, at the same time, just a particle in the universe" (ibid., p. 270). I would go further and say that the tiny particle that each person is *reflects* the universe. And just as chaos theory tells us that the flutter of a butterfly in Brazil can cause a typhoon in the Far East, the development of each person, each tiny particle of the whole, *impacts* the universe as a whole. The growth and development of each of us enhance the whole, while our destructive, anti-growth currents impoverish it.

The relationship between the "I" and the Self

The Jungian analyst Edward Edinger (1972) has done extensive work on the relationship between the "I" and the Self. The primary self of the newborn exists in a state of merger with the Self – with what Jungians call the archetypal psyche and psychoanalysts think of as the instinctual psyche. This is the identification that spawns the omnipotent defenses of infancy that Melanie Klein taught us so much about, the belief that I can destroy you with my feces or my urine, for example, which mutates as we get older into the fantasy that my rage can destroy my analyst or that I can work out my life autonomously, without the help of others. In the infant's experience of herself as merged with the Self, she feels all-powerful.

As she grows, ordinary daily experiences begin to undermine this sense of omnipotence, and the baby's "I" begins to separate from the Self. This development has two aspects: the "I" and the Self begin to be differentiated; the "I" and the Self develop a relationship that Edinger (ibid.) called "the ego-Self axis." As the baby painfully renounces her omnipotence, "a kind of unhealing psychic wound is created. . . . [She] is exiled from paradise" (ibid., p. 12).

These two processes of differentiation and developing connectedness continue throughout the life span. The "I" can never become completely distinct from the Self; some inflation of the "I" is universal. One hopes, as one ages, to develop an increasing handle on one's omnipotence, but it never disappears. And inflation, we must remember, has positive as well as negative aspects. Without some inflation, no one could ever write a book, for example, for the notion that the book I write is needed in this book-flooded world is surely an inflated idea. But inflation can also be destructive and painful. I will examine its destructive qualities in Chapter 4, where we will look at the archetypal anti-related complex and the omnipotent defenses that the "I"'s merger with the Self maintain. Inflation is also painful, because when one is inflated one is frequently headed for a crash landing ("pride goeth before a fall"). In therapy or analysis we hope that a soft landing can be provided through the practitioner's compassionate containment.

A relationship between the "I" and the Self is different from a merger of the two, and is crucial for the developing person of any age. The ego-Self axis is a theoretical construct expressing that relationship. When the axis is injured – when the "I"'s capacity for relatedness is compromised – the connection between consciousness and the infinite unconscious, O, is impaired. The "I" is cut off from its instinctual roots, its creativity, its basic aliveness. Throughout the life cycle, the Self is experienced mainly in projection. This is especially true in childhood, when the parents carry the Self for the baby and growing child, so that experiences of not being accepted or understood are equivalent to feeling rejected by God or the universe rather than understood for what they are: the failings of limited human beings.

As I mentioned above, in psychotherapy or analysis, the Self is typically projected onto the practitioner, who is felt to be much larger than life. Jung described this process using a series of medieval woodcuts to trace the typical development and resolution of the transference relationship. These pictures show a king and queen meeting, undressing and descending together into a bath. There they unite in sexual intercourse, fuse into one person with two heads, and die. Their one soul ascends to heaven and a healing dew rains down upon the corpse. Now the soul returns and the individual is reborn as a hermaphrodite in a picture replete with symbols of wholeness. Jung interprets the king and queen as symbols of the analyst's "I," of the patient's "I," and of each person's unconscious self. The archetypal, larger-than-"I" nature of this drama is emphasized by the use of a king and a queen, rather than ordinary citizens. Jung described the unfolding of this drama – of the trans-ference relationship – as one in which six relationships are informing and mirroring each other: The "I" of the analyst and the "I" of the patient are related on a conscious level; the two people's unconscious psyches are also interacting with each other; each person's "I" is dynamically connected to his or her own unconscious and to the other's unconscious as well. This complex interconnection fosters the growth of both patient and analyst.

The therapist's acceptance and cherishment can feel like a return to Para-dise for the patient, and the therapeutic hours commonly feel as though they are the center of her week, providing "a rejuvenating contact with life which conveys a sense of hope and optimism" (Edinger, 1972, p. 40) because a strong connection between the "I" and the Self gives the person a feeling of "energy, interest, meaning and purpose" (ibid., p. 43).

Feelings of despair and hopelessness that, when severe, may bring the per-son to suicide or murder, can be thought of as injuries to the ego-Self axis. These feelings of meaningless emptiness, however, when they do not send the "I" into nihilistic enactments, also set the stage for a subjective encounter with the Self. In religious texts, the encounter with God occurs in the desert or the wilderness, when the person has exhausted her own resources and given up hope. Saint John of the Cross's "dark night of the soul," which preceded his encounter with God, is an example, as is Jesus's or Saint John the Baptist's sojourns in the desert. Martin Luther spoke of this when he said, "When a man believes himself to be utterly lost, light breaks" (quoted in Bainton, 1950, p. 83). We consistently see this in therapeutic work. The patient enters therapy when he feels at a hopeless impasse with life, "at the end of his rope," he might say. In our inflated, individualistic culture, it is always a last resort to ask for help. As he feels welcomed and cherished by his therapist, the transference becomes established and light breaks over him. He feels some-thing that religious texts would call blessed. His therapist seems to be the very best ever and his connection with her comes to feel magically potent, as though it could heal all his pain and suffering. In the transference relation-ship, where the practitioner is carrying the Self, the injured ego-Self axis is being repaired.

Both O and the Self function in the analyst, in the patient and, most especially, between the two, in the couple. Both of these concepts evoke a sense of a nonmaterial psychic force that *surrounds* the person rather than being "inside" her. Both Bion and Jung become vague in their descriptions of

O or the Self in the sense that these concepts seem to be both inside and outside of the individual. O is the absolute truth of any object, whether inner or outer, the thing-in-itself unmediated by the human psyche. The Self is typically felt to be equivalent to the world or the universe. Remember the dream in which Dr. X showed me an image of the living universe as our fate after death – our fate beyond the finite world of time and place we know in outer reality. I described it as an image of the Self. Here I want to note that this human experience of the Self, where it is felt to be the whole of the world or the universe, offers a model of psychic reality that can support the fact of empathic intuition. If "my" psyche is a force field surrounding me, I can imagine it mingling with the other's psyche, fostering the unconscious communication on which the analytic process depends.

"My" psyche is a fundamentally inaccurate concept. "I" belong to "my" psyche, it does not belong to me. In the psyche's own understanding of itself, presented to us in our nightly dreams, the psyche surrounds me and I am subject to its laws rather than vice versa. Bion says that the Oedipal myth and "the elements that in the Christian religion touch on paternity and sonship both have a configuration suggesting an underlying group of which these elements are representative. I have used the sign O to denote this 'ultimate reality' " (1970, p. 81). In other words, Bion asserts that a particular "configuration" – a given pattern of human relatedness and emotion – expresses itself in the two myths. These "underlying configurations" are what Jung called "archetypes." The two concepts seem identical to me.

Truth and lies

O is the Absolute Truth of any situation; the Self pushes the person both to give up soothing lies about himself and to recognize who he really is – to get related to himself. But human beings, as we all know, evade true relatedness and lie to themselves extensively. We all work, at least some of the time, to *not* know ourselves. Before we can explore the universal human conflict between the wish to get to know our true reality, in all its interdependent aspects, and the wish not to know about our smallness and helplessness, we have to understand how the thinking process works. How does someone recognize his or her true experience and what factors facilitate honestly facing into oneself rather than pretending to be the person one expects or wants to be? In the next chapter, we will examine Bion's understanding of the thinking process, and in Chapters 4 and 5 we will return to explore the conflict between related and unrelated aspects of ourselves that plays out in each of our souls.

Chapter 3

The work of life

The 2003 movie *The Weeping Camel* tells the story of a camel in Mongolia who gives birth to a colt after a difficult labor that lasts several days. The mother rejects the colt, moving deliberately away from it when the baby tries to approach, despite the attempts of the camel's caretaker to encourage her to nurse. The family that owns the camel conducts a religious ritual that focuses on the ways man plunders the earth. The participants demonstrate remorse for their greed in order to summon the good spirits who keep the world's harmony intact. The camel continues to reject her colt. The family then sends its two young boys to a relatively distant town to fetch a musician. When the musician arrives he plays a mournful melody on a cello-like instrument while the woman caretaker brings the mother camel toward the musician. The caretaker, accompanied by the musical instrument, sings a mournful song while lovingly stroking the camel's neck.

A familiar living creature is holding and soothing a distressed creature of another species with the kindness of her voice. Many minutes go by as the woman patiently sings and strokes the camel. A short distance away, the herd of camels stares immobile, not even chewing their cuds, mesmerized by the unfolding drama. Slowly the mother camel's eyes fill with tears. She is re-presented with her colt and allows it to nurse. The tears increase. They spill out of her eyes. Soon the camel's face is drenched. Slowly the music winds down. Now the mother and baby bond in an ordinary camel way.

We have no way to know what happened inside the mother camel's psyche,[1] but I will speculate about the emotional experiences that led the camel to reject and then accept her baby: the trauma of the lengthy birth was literally unbearable for the mother. She could not endure the emotions the experience

---

1 An objection may be raised to the idea of a camel's psyche. The idea that animals other than humans do not experience emotions seems as misguided as the idea that they do not think. It seems likely that their emotional range is less extensive and complicated than is ours, just as their capacity to think is less complex, but to imagine that the human psyche sprung full-blown from nothing rather than evolving from something that is present in other mammals is to endorse creationism rather than evolution.

generated in her. She could not process them or hold them, her only recourse being to flee from them. One way to flee from one's own emotions is to avoid contact with anything that will trigger them, in this case the baby that caused his mother's suffering. The trauma of the labor and birth broke the mother camel's connection with her instinctual nature.

When the musician's music surrounded the Mongolian family's world, including all its flocks and its herds, he provided the woman herder with a form that could hold *her* as she, with her voice and her touch, held the camel. The woman's kindness, sympathy and patience are palpable for the human watcher; the camel, I hypothesize, experienced these qualities, too, and they held her in a way that enabled her to grieve her trauma rather than compulsively fleeing from it. As the emotional pain was experienced – something we call "working through" in psychotherapy – the mother's maternal instincts could reassert themselves and she was able to welcome her baby rather than rejecting it.

Experiencing emotional life

Bion's work on dreaming focuses on how human beings process emotional experience. Raw sensations of life, saturated with unformed protoemotional energies, assault us at every moment. At first, these are neuronal impulses traveling to the brain. How does the mind turn this raw data into something thinkable and feel-able? Bion (1962) calls this fundamental process "α (alpha) function" and I would suggest that it accomplishes a task that all higher mammals (and perhaps other creatures, too) must accomplish. The camel's story appears to demonstrate first a breakdown in α function and then, through the support of its handler, a strengthening of the camel's α function that enabled her to process the raw emotions of the very difficult birth – to grieve.

Bion's theory is revolutionary. It focuses on the ways the individual fails to *have* his emotional experiences rather than the ways the person defends against knowing about them. This theory describes a hypothetical inner "apparatus" that we must have in order to handle emotional life, an apparatus that develops throughout the life cycle, hopefully toward increasing levels of robustness, but never attains perfect reliability. The implication of Bion's work is that the universal psychological difficulty revolves around the task of *experiencing* life rather than that of *knowing the truth* of one's experience. His theory leads to a different perspective on the curative factors in psychotherapy or analysis. A Bionian perspective, especially as it has been developed by Antonino Ferro, a contemporary Italian analyst, hypothesizes that therapeutic work aims for an increased capacity to *be* oneself rather than for increased knowledge *about* oneself. This suggests that we ought to imagine the therapeutic relationship and the therapist/analyst's job in a fundamentally new way.

While the repressed unconscious still exists as a basic understanding of the psyche, its position has radically shifted. Where Freud initially saw this once-conscious deposit as *the* unconscious, Bion demotes it to a position similar to Jung's understanding of the personal unconscious, where the "acquisitions of personal life, everything forgotten, repressed, subliminally perceived, thought, felt" (Jung, 1971, para 842) are preserved. The repressed unconscious is a finite concept, quite different from O or the collective unconscious, the endless universe of life's potentials. For Bion, the repressed level contains aspects of the individual that she once experienced before relegating them to oblivion. The repressed, no matter how extensive, contrasts with the infinite expanse of truth that remains unexperienced and unthinkable for the person.

Processing emotional experience

We have no direct contact with reality. The world presents itself to us through the medium of our psyches as an *emotional* experience. Different witnesses to an event "see" a wide range of "facts;" it is common in life for two people to be absolutely certain that different things were said or done in a previous meeting between them, even when the incident was not obviously emotionally charged. Historically, analysts have imagined that their memories are more reliable than those of their patients, assuming that they are less emotionally entangled in the material or that they, having been analyzed, are "healthier" and less subject to distortion than their patients. Freud (1914) suggested that when a disagreement exists regarding what was said, the analyst can almost always be shown to be right. But how can that be? In the absence of a recording, the analyst can advance logical reasons for his point of view, and the patient, in a dependent and vulnerable position, may well accede to the analyst's certainty and be convinced (or at least give in). But imagining that the claim of correctness "proves" the validity of the analyst's memory is self-serving indeed. The ubiquity of differing memories, even when the events in question seem to be neutral, must lead us to recognize that all human beings, including analysts, regularly distort reality. In fact, reality itself, viewed from this perspective, turns out to be something we can never pin down with any certainty.

This state of affairs reflects the fact that our experiences are always emotional in nature. We have no direct contact with the outer world. Although the desk I am sitting at may feel compellingly solid and "real," I cannot actually see the *desk*.

> We can make only the dimmest theoretical guesses about the nature of matter. . . . The wave-movements or solar emanations which meet my eye are translated by my perception into light. It is my mind . . . that gives the world colour and sound. . . . [T]here is . . . nothing that is directly

experienced except the mind itself. Everything is mediated through the mind, translated, filtered, allegorized, twisted, even falsified by it.

(Jung, 1926, para 623)

Contemporary work on perception has shown that only a small percentage of what we "see" comes from light waves processed by the brain; much more than half of "sight" consists of memories with which the mind makes sense of visual patterns deciphered by the brain. All information about the world comes through the psyche, where it is interpreted and shaped. Experience begins as an avalanche of sensory data flooding the brain, at the same moment that an inchoate emotional state occurs. I do not see a desk *qua* desk; I see a desk that means something to me. It looks ugly or pleasing, it calls up positive or negative memories of that desk and of other desks, of paperwork, artwork or computer tasks. The thing-in-itself that is a desk is inherently unknowable by me. I can only hope to know my personal experience of the thing-in-relation-to-me.

Initially, the raw sensory–emotional experience is unmentalized. A feeling of well-being may be accompanied by the ripple of a breeze on the skin, the pressure of a layer of sand caught beneath one's bathing suit, a faint itching from yesterday's flea bite, a drop of coolness from a trickle of sweat running down one's chest, to cite only a small number of the skin sensations that are inundating the brain along with the visual, aural, olfactory and gustatory sensations that saturate the protoemotional experience of the moment. Bion called this sort of pixel of unsymbolized experience a β (beta) element and described its nature by imagining the infant's experience of hunger. The baby experiences a "bad breast" – a breast that is not there – and the mother presents him with a literal breast that he begins to suck on. This flesh-and-blood breast (or bottle)

> is indistinguishable from a "thought" but the "thought" is dependent on the existence of an object that is actually put into the mouth. . . . The breast, the thing in itself, is indistinguishable from an idea in the mind. . . . [Taking this] object compounded of emotional experience and thing-in-itself the two being as yet undifferentiated . . . we have arrived at an object very closely resembling a β element. The realization [i.e. the outer event] and the representation of it in the mind have not been differentiated.
>
> (Bion, 1962, pp. 57–8)

The infant's "thought" is not *about* a breast; it *is* a breast, and this is problematic for two reasons. First, useful thinking must be capable of taking place in the absence of the experiences being reflected upon. A "thought" that can exist only in the presence of the concrete outer object being considered is not useful for thinking about breasts that satisfy and soothe or breasts that reject, abandon, and refuse to nourish. Second, the infant's emotional experience of the breast and the breast-*qua*-breast are not differentiated. This kind of "thought" does not develop any sense of self for the baby. There *is* no self in the experience: there is a *breast* that is good, not an "*I*" having an experience. One of Bion's fundamental questions was to wonder how this bit of unthinkable experience, which he called a β element, gets processed by the unconscious psyche and symbolized, turned into something that can be reflected upon in its absence, and that can function to build a person with an emotional life separate from and related to other beings (or things) about whom or for which he or she has feelings.

The β element itself is not psychologically useful in any way. In this pre-alphabetized state, it cannot be used for emotional growth. The sensory elements must be unconsciously culled, for they are far too vast and disorganized to be experienced directly; the emotional aspect of the moment, equally disorganized and perhaps equally vast, is in a wordless (unsymbolized) state. When the emotions in question are painful, it is easy to see that some sort of unconscious psychological work must be done to make them thinkable,[2] but this is also true of positive affects. Love or joy, like loss or fear, can be too much to hold and can propel one into unconscious discharging activity. Bion's hypothetical α function (alphabetization) turns β elements into α elements: integrated atoms of sensory–emotional experience that have been symbolized and taken in as parts of the person's developing self. These elements can be stored and used by the psyche in any of the psychological activities (like thinking, feeling, dreaming, or remembering) that constitute emotional work. Instead of positing a breast as an absolute object, the α element, by symbolizing the breast, creates a self with an emotional relationship to it; the breast itself will always be unknowable because we have no access to an objective reality that exists beyond our psyches. When the infant symbolizes his experience – probably with an image, certainly not with a word – it becomes thinkable. He can dream about it or remember it, call up the idea of the-breast-as-it-means-something-to-me in its absence.

An α element is the product of a union between the body's experience and the psyche's. When one's α function is strong enough to handle the β elements in question, they are transformed into α elements that are unconscious and unknowable but that are mostly imagined as pictographs (although other senses can also form these elemental symbolic bits). Instead of a concrete outer fact or thing – Kant's "thing-in-itself" – an element that is the building block of symbols emerges, the thing-as-I-see-it. Jungians call this kind of union (here, between the body and the psyche) a *coniunctio*. It is the first step toward the larger unions that heal the macro-splits in the psyche that we call

---

2 Bion's notion of "thinking" is quite different from Jung's. Jung uses the word in its ordinary sense of manipulating and developing ideas; Bion uses it to refer to any psychological processing of experience, including what Jung and colloquial English talk about as "feeling."

emotional wounds. This first union of bodily and emotional experience gives form to the previously wordless, imageless and therefore unthinkable raw state of experience. The individual takes possession of his experience; it becomes *his* because he has developed a *relationship* with it. Over and over, as we look at one piece of psychological theory after another, we find that the foundation of growth and development is relatedness.

Although Bion describes the process of transforming β elements into α elements as the first step in the development of thoughts, this is clearly not something the individual thinks about consciously. It is a completely unconscious thinking process to which we have no direct access. Although Jung did not explore the origins of the psyche's dreaming capacity, he describes the process of creating α elements and building symbols from them:

> [The unconscious] mentality is an instinctive one; . . . it does not 'think'. . . . It simply creates an image that answers to the conscious situation. This image contains as much thought as feeling, and is anything rather than a product of rationalistic reflections. Such an image would be better described as an artist's vision.
>
> (1953, para 289)

But Jung did not ask *how* these images are created and he does not seem to have reflected on the cases where people do *not* create unconscious images of their conscious experience. He took the process to be instinctual and universal, innate rather than learned.

Unprocessed by α function, the protoemotional aspect of β elements will be unconsciously discharged. In the most hopeful scenario, this will mean giving the experience to another via projective identification in the hope that the other will have sufficient α function to process the β elements in question and to return them to the overwhelmed individual in a thinkable form. In the hope, in other words, that the recipient will be capable of a related response.

Alternatively, β elements may be discharged into the body in psychogenic illnesses, pains, mannerisms and tics; or they may fling the person into the behaviors we call acting out, behaviors that possess him rather than being chosen by him. Failing discharge, the β elements will lodge in the unconscious as a foreign body, an indigestible splinter of experience stuck in an emotional limbo. Winnicott (1949) is talking about this kind of β element when he suggests that in trauma the individual "memorizes" the overwhelming (unthinkable) experience, where "memorize" is not a conscious act but a way of preserving the experience in its raw, unthinkable form in the depths of the psyche. The individual is unconsciously hoping that he will someday find a sufficiently related partner to hold him emotionally in a way that will enable him finally to have the experience – to suffer it instead of preserving it in cold storage, where it pushes him into behavioral patterns that he cannot think about but can only succumb to.

In Jung's theory, these indigestible splinters of emotional experience agglutinate into complexes. Complexes are internal dramas that play out repetitively in the person's interpersonal relationships. The shape of one's complexes is laid down in childhood, where patterns of relating continually repeat themselves in indigestible ways. A parent, for example, is habitually tantalizing and unpredictable. The child cannot bear the inescapable torment that his helplessness exposes him to and so he not-notices and not-remembers the parent's behavior. Rather than thinking of his non-memory as something – like repression, say – that he has *done*, Bion's theory suggests that there is something he *failed* to do (due to lack of ability); his failure leaves the emotional experience of being tantalized in the un-remember-able state that we call dissociation.

Jung's complex theory describes the state that Bion is homing in on. When one is "in a complex," one is possessed by an inner emotional reality that one knows little or nothing about. The complex-ridden individual may feel intense and urgent emotions like desperation that speak primarily to his fear of the inner reality he is fleeing from. Or he may simply be making choices that seem most felicitous to him while observers think these choices foolish or self-destructive. Returning to the child whose tantalizing parent tormented him in ways he could not process: he will be impelled into interpersonal relationships where he is either tantalizing or tantalized, living out the interpersonal pattern that he cannot experience, failing to recognize the nature of that pattern as he enacts it. On the one hand, he may promise much more than he can deliver. He may rationalize his behavior as necessary in the cut-throat world of reality or he may simply change his mind and not-notice his repeating pattern. On the other hand, he may find himself attracted to people who seem poised to give so much more than they actually do – tantalizing people will look *so* attractive and their unreliable nature will be a surprise every time it expresses itself.

The hopeful perspective here is that the individual endlessly repeats his trauma in a search for someone who can help him to process it, first of all by helping him to experience it. Often psychotherapy or analysis will enable him to have his experience, although that positive development may be misunderstood as growing from his newfound understandings rather than from the increased capacity to bear his suffering that has developed from his introjecting the relatedness that he and his therapist have managed to create. Alternatively, the interpersonal relationships of ordinary life may foster the expansion of a person's capacity to have his emotional responses rather than those responses having him. But Jung never asked the question of what is missing inside us when we fail to work through the painful experiences of our lives, when we swallow them whole and preserve them in unconscious complexes. What are the inner "tools" the individual needs to process his experience, the tools the complex-ridden person lacks or lacked? Some people are much more capable of digesting their experiences than others. What skills enable them to succeed?

As early as 1914 Freud referred to the centrality of this psychological task of making life experienceable. For the analyst

> remembering . . . – reproduction in the *psychical* field – is the aim to which he adheres. . . . He is prepared for a perpetual struggle with his patient to keep in the psychical sphere all the impulses which the patient would like to direct into the motor sphere; and he celebrates it as a triumph for the treatment if he can bring it about that something that the patient wishes to discharge in action is disposed of through the work of remembering.
>
> (1914, p. 153, emphasis added)

Alpha elements

Before describing the apparatus that turns β elements into α elements, let us look at the nature of α elements: what are the earliest thinkable elements that the complex-ridden person has failed to construct? I imagine α elements taking aspects of the sensory experience and imbuing them with the emotional meaning of the moment. For example, imagine that a father shows his daughter his new black car. Perhaps the child is thrilled by the father's elation. Assuming an adequate α function to process this moment, the girl may unconsciously create an α element consisting of a child's-eye view of the car glistening in the sun, an image pervaded by her emotion. But perhaps in the child's experience of the idealized father's elation, she has her first experience of his vulnerability and need. The objectively shiny new car, imbued with the girl's grief, may register as densely black, funereal, dull. Or some other object – a mangy, feral cat slinking from under the car, for example – may capture the feeling of the moment for the child and be unconsciously elaborated into an α element. Such images (the glistening car or the mangy cat) are α elements not because they perceive the outer situation "correctly" or "incorrectly," but because they capture the child's authentic experience and create an image of it that she can relate to.

Having taken this initial step, the child can now dream about her experience and thus begin to process either the elation that she felt at her father's joy or the distress she felt at contacting his vulnerability. If her α function is inadequate to the task of creating symbols that will enable her to process her emotions, she may jump about disruptively, or whine annoyingly about some unrelated complaint or about a tummy ache, or fall into a fight with a sibling. This sort of discharging behavior can reflect an inability to process the positive emotion in question (here, the thrill of her father's elation) just as easily as a negative emotion. Strong feelings are always hard to bear.

In health, the psyche constantly produces α elements to image the emotional experience of the moment. But while the concept of "health" is of theoretical importance, it is crucial to remember that no living human being can ever attain "health." We are all imperfect creatures, injured by the painful experiences life inevitably brings and limited in our ability to process them. Even the shattered, institutionalized psychotic must have some remnant of α function working in his psyche, and even the most developed and intact individual's α function will fail at some points. When α function fails massively – because the trauma of an event or an ongoing situation overwhelms the person or because her own hatred or envy has been stimulated and she has attacked her α function to avoid experiencing these destructive emotions – the therapist hears "of inanimate objects, and even of places, when we would normally expect to hear of people" (Bion, 1962, p. 9). Again we see that health requires a relationship with ourselves and that emotional disturbance is characterized by an anti-related approach that attacks an element of the self (α function) thereby injuring the person's ability to relate to others.

At the end of this chapter I will present the case of Gertrude, a woman whose α function was severely limited when I first met her. In an early dream, I was imaged as Kaiser Hospital, the center of an enormous health care network, rather than as a person. Bion suggests that the question here is the extent to which one can suffer distress versus the extent to which one evades that suffering – the extent to which one can relate to his distress. Every human being experiences emotional pain, but the attitude he is able to take toward his pain determines whether or not he is able to suffer. Bion (1970) suggests that suffering follows when we recognize that pain is intrinsic to embodied life and therefore accept it when it appears rather than working to avoid it. The energy of the Enlightenment, in which human beings attempt to understand the universe and to use their understanding to improve their material lives, fosters an attitude of avoidance of emotional pain. We can conquer smallpox, we can fly faster than the speed of sound, we can repair birth defects *in utero*, even rearrange the genetic code of the fetus. Surely we can transcend pain! Pain becomes a symptom of failure rather than a natural element of life.

Jung called neurosis the avoidance of legitimate suffering. To the extent that a person can humble herself and recognize that every human situation involves pain, she will suffer. Suffering is a necessary ingredient for psychological growth. Instead of railing against fate – how can *this* be happening to *me*? – the person accepts that "this" is simply the particular form that his or her suffering is taking at this point in life. If her husband had not betrayed her, she or one of her children would be ill, or she would fail to achieve something she really wants. *Something* always causes pain. According to Bion, the "decision" to suffer pain rather than to protest or discharge it is the crucial "choice" we face at every moment of our lives. We will examine the nature of these unconscious choices in detail in Chapter 4. Often, we have nothing to say about these choices but they form our character structure (our complexes), brick by brick.

The infant (or adult) begins with what Bion (1962, 1963, 1965, 1970) called a pre-conception (sic). A pre-conception is a prejudice that prevents the person from seeing or hearing what is objectively happening at the same time as it *facilitates* perceiving the objective happening by providing the person with a structure within which to hold it. Initially pre-conceptions are the inborn templates that Plato described as the true reality in his metaphor of the cave. (Life experience also creates pre-conceptions which facilitate our making sense of the light waves being recorded in our brains. These pre-conceptions distort how the brain interprets the data it receives at the same time as they enable it to interpret that data meaningfully.) These inborn pre-conceptions, whether present at birth or constellated in the course of ordinary emotional development,[3] are the same as Jung's archetypes. The infant begins with a pre-conception about what the world "should" provide – a loving, responsive mother, for example. But a real mother, no matter how loving, can never be perfectly responsive and at any given moment the infant, child or adult must struggle with an emotional reality that does *not* fit its pre-conceptions.

At this point Bion's "choice" is presented: will the individual discharge the unpleasant experience – the β element – of the distressing event or can he hold an awareness of reality alongside his unmet expectation and feel his disappointment. Will he say, for example, "I didn't really care about that" or will he feel his emotional distress and admit that he did care. If he can hold his pain, he will be "in process of α function and the production of α-elements" (Bion, 1962, p. 103). If he cannot, his experience will not be alphabetized (transformed from β into α) and will remain a mass of meaningless, emotion-laden sensations. It is most meaningful to think about these two responses as different possibilities for the same person under more or less stress. In one situation he can feel, "When X did that I felt hurt," but under too much stress he must fall back on, "X is a bad person who did an evil thing."

β elements can only be evacuated. The infant may evacuate his too-intense emotional experience by crying, thrashing about, urinating or defecating, drooling, and so on. Positive emotions can be as hard to hold as negative ones. We see the difficulty with positive emotions most easily if we think about a toddler or young child who becomes uncontrollably wild when excited. The adult may jiggle his leg or bite his nails, develop a backache or become constipated, quit his job or leave his wife. He may also smile or frown, a physical movement that will be misinterpreted by his companion if it is assumed to image his authentic feeling. Even a verbal statement may represent "an evacuatory muscular movement" rather than an expression of thought or feeling when the individual's α function is deficient (Bion, 1962, pp. 13–14). The person who denies the importance of an emotional experience

---

3 For example, all humans reach a stage of development where the task of finding a mate presents itself and Jung postulated that inborn archetypes or pre-conceptions guide cultures in the forms they evolve to assist individuals in that task.

could be someone who is using the defense mechanism of denial to defend against conscious knowledge of an experience that *is* being processed unconsciously. If that is the case, a night-time dream might help the person to acknowledge her pain. But the verbal denial may also be a way of discharging the painful experience because she is unable to process it. These are different problems and while the therapist's optimal handling of them might look similar, understanding the deficit she is addressing will change her posture and her tone and therefore the atmosphere of the room. As I will describe at the end of this chapter, Gertrude, my patient with severely deficient α function, discharged massive quantities of distress with a brilliant and inappropriate smile that confused and disoriented me until Bion's work helped me to understand its function.

As I mentioned above, when it functions optimally, the psyche produces a constant stream of α elements to image the emotional experience of the moment. α function makes experience thinkable by creating a steady flow of α elements that unite the bodily and emotional aspects of each moment and create a self that is distinct from and related to outer objects. α elements are symbols. In night-time dreams or in the waking dreaming that we can follow by listening to the unconscious communication embedded in ordinary con-versations,[4] these symbols are combined with each other and elaborated into larger symbolic units. In the above example, the child's emotionally distorted image of her father's car or of the feral cat who slinks around it will be collated with α elements formed at other moments – images imbued with emotions that deepen or extend the immediate somatic–emotional experi-ence into the exact one the dreamer's psyche wants to convey at this precise moment of her history. Dreams, whether waking or night-time, string these developed symbols into a narrative form. When α function works adequately, this story-making process produces a more or less constant foundation of unconscious dreaming. The unconscious waking dream works over the emotional demands of the moment and enables the conscious individual to function without being overwhelmed by an avalanche of sensory and emotional experience that would otherwise inundate her (Bion, 1962).

Jung also describes the activity of waking dreaming, the continual emo-tional work that the psyche does to remain related to present reality, both outer and inner. The unconscious, he says, "is never quiescent . . . but is ceaselessly engaged in grouping and regrouping its contents. This activity [is normally] co-coordinated with the conscious mind in a compensatory relationship" (1953, para 204).

This unending activity produces the dreams and fantasies that give our lives depth and substance. Sometimes the background dream can "break through the inhibitions imposed by our daytime consciousness" (Jung, ibid.,

---

4 The analysis of an hour with Gertrude at the end of this chapter provides a detailed example of how to follow the waking dream being imaged in an ordinary conversation.

para 273) and disturb conscious attempts to maintain an appropriate persona. When consciousness begins to dim, often as the individual moves toward sleep but occasionally in other states, perhaps as a result of stress, we get glimmers of these usually unconscious waking dreams that image the underlying thoughts and feelings of the moment (Jung, 1984).

In this theory, dreaming is a continuous process and the difference between waking and sleeping life relates to the degree to which dreams are observable. It is even possible that the only time we are *not* dreaming is during non-REM sleep. Dream work depends on α function; α function is the initial stage of thinking (where "thinking" includes "feeling"). Bion's first major book about psychoanalysis (1962) explored how we accomplish "emotional growth" by learning from our experiences, a process that depends on α function. α function is the primary transforming function of the psyche, using the experiences of life to build a self that is related to that life.

Grotstein (2007) suggests that α actually precedes β – that the individual has the unbearable experience, or senses it as a possibility, and rejects it, dissociating from it by turning it into β. This is similar to Ferro's (e.g. 2006) concept of "balpha elements" as the building blocks of psychotic thought. There has been considerable work in the literature on how people may attack their own α function in order to not-experience their envy or jealousy, for example. This kind of self-attack is one example of the attacks on linking that Bion (1959) wrote about. These developments of Bion's ideas are interesting, especially because they each describe the injurious effect of anti-related energies, but for the therapist or even analyst who works primarily with reasonably functioning people, these various distinctions seem peripheral. What is core is the distinction between experiences the person possesses and those that possess her, between emotions that she can feel and emotions that she can only discharge.

The contact barrier

As α function transforms the sense impressions of emotional experience into α elements, what Bion calls a "contact barrier" is in the process of continual formation. The contact barrier is a sort of screen that "marks the point of contact and separation between conscious and unconscious elements" (Bion, 1962, p. 17). It is a permeable membrane keeping the unconscious unconscious and the conscious conscious while allowing elements to pass back and forth between them. The term "contact barrier" speaks to the *contact* between the finite "I" and the infinite unconscious that the screen enables as well as the *barrier* the screen establishes to protect that bounded "I" from being flooded by the endless unconscious. The waking or sleeping dream that is always being created combines α elements into symbols and then into stories that keep consciousness and the unconscious separate while operating harmoniously together.

When one can turn emotional experiences into α elements, the experiences can be used by the unconscious in its creative capacity. Thus a child who is "having the emotional experience called learning to walk" can allow his conscious efforts to become unconscious so that he can walk "without any longer being conscious of any of it" (Bion, 1962, p. 8). α function thus makes conscious thinking possible by relegating a repetitive aspect of thinking to the unconscious. We call this process "learning a skill." In a different vein,

> a man talking to a friend converts the sense impressions of this emotional experience into α elements, thus becoming capable of dream thoughts and therefore of undisturbed consciousness of the facts whether the facts are the events in which he participates or his feelings about those events or both. He is able to remain 'asleep' or unconscious of certain elements that cannot penetrate the barrier presented by his 'dream'. Thanks to the "dream" he can continue uninterruptedly to be awake . . . to the fact that he is talking to his friend, but asleep to elements which, if they could penetrate the barrier of his 'dreams', would lead to domination of his mind by what are ordinarily unconscious ideas and emotions. The dream makes a barrier against mental phenomena which might overwhelm the patient's awareness that he is talking to a friend, and, at the same time, makes it impossible for awareness that he is talking to a friend to overwhelm his phantasies.
>
> (Bion, 1962, p. 15)

Thus the individual can unconsciously feel, for example, his homosexual love for his friend while talking about politics. The fact that the fantasy continues to evolve in the person's psyche gives the interchange between the two men depth and resonance because the contact barrier *is* in some sense permeable; the fact that the fantasy can remain unconscious protects both men from the anxiety that would accompany a full conscious realization of the elemental fantasies unrolling in the primal layers of the psyche. It also allows the political discussion to continue in a meaningful way. Noticing life, paying attention to it, relating to it, remembering all depend on α function.

A patient I will call Sally had the following dream:

There's a large cave behind our house. The floor slopes downward from the entrance and is made of sand. I'm afraid that if I go in I'll slip down and be unable to climb out. I can see that after going down a fair way the floor of the cave levels out. It seems to go back for a long way. At the point on the flat part where the light from the outer world ends, a screen is set up for movies. The screen goes from one side of the cave to the other, but one could get past it by slipping under or around it. Chairs are set up on both sides of the screen. Apparently the movies are projected from both the outer world and from deep inside the cave. I can see that the problem is to coordinate the two projections so that the images from inside and from outside match each other perfectly.

The screen is an image of the contact barrier that stands between consciousness (where "the light from the outer world ends") and unconsciousness (the dark depths of the cave). Sally felt that the cave, which she associated to Plato's cave, stretched back forever. It is a symbol of the depths of her psyche, connecting to the outer world while hidden from it. At that point in Sally's development, the dream was speaking to her fear of the unconscious processes unfolding inside her (her fear of falling in and being unable to get out).

But the dream also demonstrates a fundamental problem in human thinking. As she reflected on her dream, Sally realized that there was no way for the images projected from the outer world to accurately match the images projected from the depths of the cave because the outer pictures had to hit the screen at an oblique angle while the inner projection would contact the screen at a right angle. Some distortion was inevitable. The archetypal expectations of the psyche can never be matched by real experiences in the outer world. One's flesh-and-blood mother will never perfectly coincide with the good mother the newborn yearns for or with the wicked witch he fears, and his experiences with his real mother are distorted by his anticipations – his preconceptions. The "movie" that the people in the cave see will be more like images in the mirrors of a fun house than accurate reflections of the reality of either the inner or outer world. In Plato's cave, the individual took the distorted shadows of outer reality for the real thing; Sally's dream explains that the disjunction between expectation and experience and the emotional distress occasioned by that disjunction are the causes of the distortion.

The concept of the contact barrier is related to Edinger's ego-Self axis but Bion's barrier focuses more on the separation between what Jung called the personal unconscious and the "I" than it does on the active relationship between the "I" and the Self or O. The contact barrier seems to be a passive connection and separation rather than the active relationship that Edinger hypothesizes. This difference must be a function of the fact that Jung's idea of the Self imagines an unconscious that is actively interested in the "I" and purposefully working to relate to it, while Bion's contact barrier, like O, has no intentionality attached to it.

Both Bion and Jung conceived of the dream as the fundamental mental activity needed to process experience. Jung focused on night-time dreams and came to see them as compensatory to consciousness, facilitating the individual's development by balancing her one-sided view of life with the many neglected, overlooked or unwanted possibilities that exist in the unconscious. These potentials will expand the person's self and life if they can be included in her consciousness. Bion suggests that the capacity to dream is the bedrock of sanity and that all psychopathology begins with an inability to dream, an inability based in deficiencies in α function. α function allows a person to be asleep or awake and in its absence one can be neither conscious nor unconscious. "The sleeping patient is panicked; because he cannot have a nightmare he cannot wake up or go to sleep; he has had mental indigestion ever since" (Bion, 1962, p. 8). This is the psychotic state, where trauma cannot be worked through because the dreaming apparatus does not exist.

The development of α function

As mentioned above, Jung did not explore the origin of the psyche's dreaming capacity, apparently imagining it as an inborn given. Bion believed that the fetus and infant begin to learn the capacity to dream and continue to develop that capacity throughout the life span. This is not a process, like breathing or digesting, that the individual organism jump-starts on its own. A more developed person, whether a parent, an analyst, a friend or a spouse, is needed to (unconsciously) teach one to alphabetize experience and then to use α elements in dreaming, thinking and feeling. In Bion's theory, the mind is "meaning and emotions in search of mental representations" (Andrade de Azevedo, 2000, p. 85) rather than meaning and emotions that must be unearthed after having been repressed. α function, the source of "mental representations," develops in interaction with the mind of another person, someone whose α function operates (perhaps only at this moment) more robustly than one's own. Rather than making the unconscious conscious, the clinical task is to facilitate two psyches working together to make experience thinkable. In this model, the analyst *dreams* the patient (and herself) into existence in the same way that the infant's mother, in a state of reverie, dreams her baby into existence by growing his emotional capacities through her "hold." Let us look at how that works.

The infant operates as though he believes his mind is a muscle that can expel painful stimuli in the same way that an arm can throw a ball. Klein describes this process as a phantasy. We do not understand its mechanism but the word "phantasy" (or "fantasy" for most non-Kleinians in the United States) does not tell the whole story: the painful experience that the baby (or adult) "imagines" he is expelling is constellated, in actual outer reality, in the psyche of his partner, whether that partner is the infant's mother, the patient's analyst, or the person's spouse, friend or child.

To begin with, the mother (unconsciously) grows the infant's α function through containing his projective identifications and returning them to him in a manageable form. "There, there," she croons as she picks up the distressed infant. "You're afraid you're dying, but you're only hungry. I'm here to feed you and isn't it wonderful that you want to live." The mother holds the suffering that the baby cannot hold; she takes it into herself and experiences the baby's terror, probably as anxiety and tension. She thinks about it – a process that is *not* primarily intellectual – and transforms the unbearable pain (fear of dying) into something manageable (hunger). She can then return the transformed projection to the infant through the music of her voice, the quality of her hold, the electrical valence of her skin, and perhaps in ways we do not yet understand. This kind of interaction is the foundation of the infant's developing capacity for relatedness as well as his growing ability to process his own feelings.

The crucial phrase "she thinks about it" is shorthand for the mother's state of reverie. Reverie is the open state of mind, permeated with love, that seeks to receive from the infant whatever he is projecting, be it good or bad. It is the basis of relatedness and is an aspect of the mother's α function. Much of the thinking that occurs in this state is unconscious, and all of it is imbued with what Jung called feeling as well as thinking. The mother's α function takes the sensory–emotional experience of her infant's distress and transforms it into α elements inside her, enabling her to process what is happening rather than simply reacting to it.

♀ ♂

What Bion called "thinking" involves two core processes, for which he used the concepts of "container/contained" (he used the symbol ♀ ♂ to represent this) and "PS ↔ D." The "apparatus for thinking thoughts" consists of these processes. The above example of the infant's projective identification being received by the mother as a communication demonstrates the operation of both. Let us look first at ♀ ♂ (Bion, 1962, 1963, 1970): imagine a painful emotional experience (here, fear of dying) that the infant cannot bear; ideally, the mother takes in (contains) the baby's distress, experiences it emotionally and transforms it. Ordinarily, the mother will be unable to hold *all* of the baby's distress. A human being can orient to the other only up to some given point (a point that varies enormously from person to person); after that point, the person's narcissism kicks in and all she can see is her *own* needs. What the mother cannot bear, she will block out. It is a rare parent indeed who can have a conscious, empathic sense that her infant is terrified that he is dying. In good-enough situations, she will feel enough of his distress to think of him as "ravenous" or "furious" and to respond urgently to his urgency. In less optimal scenarios, she may decide that her baby is exercising his lungs or that it will foster his independence to let him cry himself to sleep. In extreme cases she could respond by shaking or otherwise abusing the baby. The mother blinds and deafens herself emotionally to that part of the infant's distress that is beyond her capacity to hold, but ordinarily she is open to enough of it to support some formation of α function. There is no end to the ways in which a mother or an analyst can avoid containing – suffering – the full extent of the other's pain, but in adequate circumstances she can hold enough to foster the development of a growing α function in the other.

The language here – blocking out or taking in – reflects the notion of a container. We talk of "digesting," "absorbing," or "processing" experiences.

All of these words suggest a model of the thinking process based on the processes of nutrition. Bion suggests that the ability to think about our experiences is evolutionarily a new one for our species and that the apparatus for the task is in an early stage of development. He believes that the thinking apparatus has developed from an inborn psychological capacity that deals with the sensations of eating, digesting and eliminating (1962, p. 57).

Recently, eating breakfast in a café, I was seated beside a group of six or eight people with a newborn baby. The proud parents were passing the infant about from grandparent to uncle to cousin. The infant's eyes were tightly shut, its face was sealed and its body tensely compacted. It is now thought that the unborn infant absorbs a rudimentary α function from its mother's α capacity so that the neonate begins with some ability to think about its experiences (and therefore to learn from them), an ability that presumably varies from infant to infant depending on how robust its mother's α function is and on the baby's innate talents. But the α function present at birth is necessarily minimal, and this newborn, to my eyes, was in shock, flooded by the avalanche of stimulation to which it was exposed. The adults' intentions were obviously loving but they were busy with their own emotions concerning the baby; they were not attempting to imagine – to take in – the newborn's emotions. The infant was not protesting; he seemed to have retreated into a state of suspended animation. His experience was more than he could process on his own and because no one was helping him with it, it remained in β form. It is not enough to say that in this experience the infant is not developing the capacity to process his emotions. He is learning that emotions are best sealed out – his parents and relations are demonstrating how to do this in their ability to not take in his emotions. He is introjecting as his own the paradigm to which he is exposed.

In Chapter 4 we will explore how the narcissistic emotions of envy, greed and jealousy throw the developing person into an inability to think, into a state where she is subject to possession by the emotional states she cannot bear to hold. In the example of the baby in the café, we can hypothesize that these frightening emotions are being constellated inside the infant. His true state is utterly vulnerable and no one (at this moment) offers an empathic auxiliary ego to support him. To whatever extent he is able to be conscious of the giants who hold him in their power while blinding themselves to his emotional need, he cannot fail to envy their presumed omnipotence for it contrasts so dramatically with his subjective state of utter vulnerability and aloneness. To the extent that he can feel how these giants relate to *each other* while ignoring *his* emotional experience, jealousy will be born, and with it a desperate greed for what they have that he lacks. These liquefying emotions[5]

5 We will explore this concept more deeply in Chapter 4. These emotions (envy, greed and jealousy), fueled with the energy of infantile omnipotence, liquefy the person inside so that we see the phenomenon of the patient who feels as though he's a jelly inside, just bits and pieces floating incoherently in a liquid. Penny, who I present in Chapter 4, described this as "not having any shape."

are fueled by omnipotent rage, an inflating emotion that protects one from primary terrors by making someone of any age big rather than little; we will explore these difficult emotional states, which throw the individual out of relationship to any inner or outer other, more fully in the next two chapters.

When a mother, struggling with her baby's experience in the atmosphere of her love for him, manages to abstract something from the mass of emotions and sensations flooding into her, she emerges with some understanding of what he is going through. One person (the infant) has put his unthinkable emotional state into the other (the mother) and that second person has been able to hold and think about it. Both mother and baby grow from this mutual activity because it *is* mutual and related and this is the basis of emotional health. Bion suggests that this process, which is originally shared by two people, is "introjected by the infant so that the container-contained apparatus becomes installed in the infant as part of the apparatus of α function" (1962, p. 91). The emotion (the mother's love in this example) and the connection are both crucial. When two people are disconnected, no containment occurs; stripped of emotion, the container loses its vitality. "Hospitalism," the wasting disease of infants who are cared for perfectly on a physical level while being seriously deprived of emotional human contact, illustrates the potency of the human need for emotional relatedness.

While the pattern of ♀ ♂ begins with a few "undifferentiated preconceptions probably related to feeding, breathing and excretion," (Bion, 1962, p. 93) it develops increasing complexity over time.

> Learning depends on the capacity [of the growing internal container] to remain integrated and yet lose rigidity. This is the foundation of the state of mind of the individual who can retain his knowledge and experience and yet be prepared to reconstrue past experiences in a manner that enables him to be receptive of a new idea.
>
> (ibid.)

In other words, the container's ability to change emotions determines how receptive it can be. Can the person who was hurt by something someone did let go of his angry pain when the other person apologizes? This internal relationship between container and contained is one basis of creativity, something that we hope will develop increasing strength inside an individual throughout the life cycle. When psychoanalysts talk about the primal scene, they are using a particular image to symbolize the nature of the person's inner ♀ ♂ process. Does the contained violently force its way into the container in a kind of rape or is the interaction considerate and mutual? Does the container receive the contained lovingly or hatefully? Over and over we come back to inner and outer relatedness as the core foundation for a healthy human life. The ♀ ♂ process is one image through which we can measure relatedness, whether between two people or between someone and his own not-I parts. The nature of this process determines the quality of thinking that a couple or an individual can accomplish.

When the mother receives a projective identification from her infant, processes it and returns it in detoxified form, she is demonstrating a method for taking a pre-conception (the infant's expectation of a nourishing breast, for example) and matching it up with what Bion called a "realization" – a concrete experience in the outer world that provides an image for the pre-conception. The infant's pre-conception mates with an experience and from that union a conception is born, in this example the conception of a good breast. Remembering Sally's dream, we can say that the mother tries to offer the baby an experience that will match its inborn expectations well enough to create an adequately harmonious and comprehensible picture. Jung talked of "the material of conscious experience" filling in the empty archetypal given (1938, para 155). If the mother can meet the inborn expectation well enough, the empty archetype will be modulated into images of "mother" that would strike us as reasonable; if a severe disjunction between the infant's anticipation and his reality exists, his developing images of "mother" will split more violently into wicked witches and fairy godmothers with no approachable human beings to be seen. When the exchange of projective identifications goes well, both people grow, meaning that both mother's and baby's ability to be aware of experiences – both their own and the other's – and to integrate them expands.

PS ↔ D

The second aspect of the thinking apparatus is what Bion calls "PS ↔ D." This describes the mother/analyst's process of reverie. Bion's language reflects his Kleinian heritage: PS stands for the paranoid schizoid stage of mental development, where the opposites are split and experience is in fragments rather than wholes. D refers to the depressive position, an emotional experience that holds the opposites together so that one feels the wholeness of life. Instead of a good breast that feeds and a bad breast that deprives, the baby recognizes that the two are aspects of the same breast that is neither good nor bad but both. Instead of good Jungians and bad Freudians (or vice versa) there are imperfect analysts each of whom brings strengths and weaknesses to their work. But this description makes PS sound inferior to D and while Klein and the early Kleinians talked about "achieving" the depressive position as though it was a place to be reached and rested in, we now realize that each kind of emotional experience has its strengths and weaknesses. In D one has a more balanced and "accurate" picture of the world's coherence than one does in PS, but the static quality of this picture contrasts with the creative dynamism possible in PS's off-kilter world.

Even though Bion talks of a "non-persecutory" state of PS, his language is problematic because it comes from a theory of pathology rather than of healthy development. In his later work, he describes PS as a state of "patience" and D as an experience of "security" (1970, p. 124), but the letters PS and D cannot help but retain a flavor of their original reference. The Jungian analyst Michael Fordham (1978) has described an oscillation between integration and deintegration that occurs throughout the life cycle (see Chapter 2, p. 60). I think of these states as a stage of bits and pieces followed by a stage of wholeness and integration. These terms are more useful than the pathologizing PS ↔ D, and they refer to the same movement between chaos and order, but since Bion's terms are in such wide use, I will mostly use his.

The PS state of taking in the world in bits (and therefore of experiencing oneself in something akin to fragments) is crucial for the thinking process. The patient speaks first about an experience the previous day with his spouse, then of a memory from his childhood, and then he tells a dream to which he associates something he believes the analyst said, although the analyst is silently certain that she could never have said such a thing. "What is going on here?" the analyst wonders, hopefully managing to be patient with her confusion. But the question may easily be tinged with a persecutory feeling for it is painful to be lost in a chaotic mass of data. Now it is ten minutes before the end of the hour (or the week or the month) and the patient throws in one more story. Suddenly the analyst thinks, "Oh! He's talking about such-and-such:" greed or loneliness or the danger of hope. Perhaps she will make an interpretation out of what she has suddenly come to understand. This is the state of D, where the fragments have come together to form a whole, and the thinker gives a sigh of relief: *Now* I understand what is going on; finally I feel secure.

It is easily seen that this process of resting in a state of not-knowing while gathering data until coherence emerges must underlie the attempt to make scientific sense of the world and our place in it from any perspective, be it physics, philosophy or psychology. Certainly the good-enough mother of the crying infant must go through the experience of unknowing: is her baby wet, or cold, or hungry, or is it gas? Until a successful understanding of his state emerges inside her, she may well feel persecuted by the infant's cries.

Bion calls the element that brings a sense of the whole "a selected fact." This language comes from the French mathematician and theoretical physicist Poincaré, who describes it as something that

> must unite elements long since known, but till then scattered and seemingly foreign to each other, and suddenly introduce order where the appearance of disorder reigned. Then it enables us to see at a glance each of those elements in the place it occupies in the whole. . . . The new fact . . . gives a value to the old facts it unites.
>
> (quoted in Bion, 1992, p. 2)

A selected fact is *an emotional experience*. "Obtrusion of the selected fact is accompanied by an emotion such as is experienced in regarding the object in reversible perspective [i.e. like the image of the vase that becomes an image of two profiles facing each other when the viewer shifts his perspective]" (Bion, 1962, p. 87). It leads to the discovery of coherence where none had been seen before. The gestalt revealed by a selected fact is not held together by logic; like the color of someone's eyes or the destruction wrought by a hurricane, it simply *is*. The swirling bits have come together to make a particular picture at a precise moment in time just as the pieces of a jigsaw puzzle make one image rather than another.

With this understanding of how α function develops from experiences of containment by individuals capable of holding the PS ↔ D tension for as long as is needed, let us recall for a moment the weeping camel. As we reflect on her story, the transformative impact of containment is vivid. Not only is the camel's trauma healed through the containment that her caretaker expresses with her touch and her voice; the caretaker herself is able to do this because she is contained by the visiting musician's cello playing and by the myth behind the ceremony that he and she perform together for the camel. The authentic human condition can never be independent; the woman needs the musician's containment if she is to be capable of containing the camel.

The family's process in reaching the decision to send for the musician illustrates the PS ↔ D sequence nicely. The family members in the movie talk very little. There is none of the extended discussion a psychologically minded Westerner might engage in: what is wrong with the mother, why is she rejecting her colt? What will happen to us if we lose the colt? We were counting on this addition to our herds; how will we manage if he dies? Instead, the family seems to reach decisions by a non-verbal consensus that the Western viewer can understand no better than he or she can the camel. First they try one religious ceremony that fails to include the camel; when it fails they gradually – and largely non-verbally – decide to send for the musician. The atmosphere of their process is permeated with patience and with what Keats called "Negative Capability," meaning the ability to remain in unknowing for as long as is needed without irritably reaching for a premature closure. The Mongolian family does not know why the camel behaves as she does or how to help her, but they hold their unknowing patiently, waiting for clarity to emerge in its own time. They demonstrate a felicitous PS ↔ D sequence for us.

These two processes, container/contained and PS ↔ D, describe some of the nuts and bolts of relatedness but Bion's language is as unrelated and mechanistic as one can imagine. He is looking at the "apparatus for thinking thoughts." His text (1962) is filled with mathematical signs and even equations. He refers to his infamous "Grid,"[6] the form of which seems to be

6 In Bion's Grid, the vertical columns represent the different *uses* of a statement. This would include to define something, or to call attention to it, or using a statement to *do* something and effect a change. The horizontal rows each represent a kind of thought, such as an α element or a pre-conception or a concept. His idea was that every statement made by either patient or analyst could be categorized as belonging in one of these intersecting boxes, and that thinking

modeled on the periodic table of the elements. He is a brilliant thinker who has dissected the elements of human relatedness, but it seems as though he is afraid to be simply human in his description of it. He focuses on the individual's growing ability to *think* – something that sounds as though it could be a one-person activity – rather than on his growing ability to include the other in his understanding of his situation. This latter capacity is actually crucial for thinking, something that he alludes to in his exploration of the need for binocular vision and in his discussion of the opposites "narcissism" and "social-ism [i.e. relatedness]." But the dearth of assistance he offers his readers makes his writing itself quite unrelated. Perhaps he is trapped in the British culture's historical tendency to idealize schizoid defences.

α function in the analytic situation

A number of Bionian authors have suggested that all psychopathology can be understood as a function of the robustness of the patient's α function and of his thinking apparatus. James Grotstein expresses in Bionian language Jung's (1937) idea that neurosis is the avoidance of legitimate suffering:

> It is the purpose of dreaming/phantasying [dreaming occurring during waking] to effect a mental transformation from the cosmic indifference of "O" to an acceptance of one's own personal, emotional, subjective response to "O" and to accept this response [this suffering] as one's legitimate portion of circumstance. All psychopathology . . . represents unprocessed (undreamed) "O".
>
> (Grotstein, 2004a, p. 102)

Antonino Ferro describes pathological patterns in Bionian terminology: panic attacks reflect a terror of being flooded with β elements; hypochondriacal problems image the danger that a barely adequate α function will be overwhelmed by "emotional fevers;" the blood tests or X-rays demanded by the patient are "an inquiry into the proximity and dangerousness of this other emotional scene;" obsessional syndromes are attempts to magically reinforce the dam that holds the threatening β mass at bay; phobias are externalizations of that unmanageable mass of β, that store of unthinkable, unfeelable anguish that the individual believes will destroy him if he comes in contact with it (Ferro, 2006, pp. 3–4).

From this perspective, the therapeutic/analytic situation offers the patient a new experience in which the analyst's mind can function for him in the same way that a parent's mind functions for an infant, taking in and processing

about a session from this point of view (after the patient has left) would help the analyst to understand more deeply what had happened in the hour. (See also Chapter 5, p. 193 for further discussion of the Grid.)

β elements that the patient cannot process and then returning them in alphabetized form. In this understanding,

> the 'disease' borne by the patient must *infect the field*: the field must . . . contract the very disease from which the patient is suffering, which thus becomes a disease of the field, and the field must then be transformed by itself undergoing a healing process. Once this has taken place, the healing can be introjected by the patient into his internal world and reaccomodated in his history – which will in a way be a new history.
>
> (ibid., p. 4)

Jung, describing the analytic situation phenomenologically, says that "it is inevitable that the doctor should be influenced to a certain extent and even that his nervous health should suffer. He quite literally 'takes over' the sufferings of his patient and shares them with him" (Jung, 1946, para 358). This is the state that Ferro refers to as the patient's "disease" infecting the field.

Remember that the theory of α function begins with the idea that at every moment we are working to make our experience psychologically meaningful by transforming the raw experience into α elements, the building blocks of symbols. To the extent that an individual is not working on a task (planning an event, adding up numbers, teaching a class), the constant stream of α elements that is in the process of forming the contact barrier will determine the course of his waking thoughts. His ongoing associations will consist of stories that derive from the flow of unconscious α elements being formed.

There is an ancient alchemical saying, "Make the fixed volatile and the volatile fixed." This speaks first to the psyche's constant attempt to take the concrete outer world and transform it, via α function, into something volatile, into symbolic images imbued with personal, spiritual meaning. The symbols that emerge may image objective realities, but they are quite different from the outer object(s). A symbol pulses with meaning and implications that cannot be pinned down. A sign means one thing: "STOP" says the sign and you stop the car. A symbol is vibrating and alive. The symbolic image says "STOP" and I wonder: what does it mean? Does it mean that my savage superego has risen to punish me or that my driven search for financial security is undermining the quality of my life or that my omnipotence is leading me astray? And if I take it one way, will some other implication emerge next week?

Second, the alchemical saying asks that we make the volatile fixed. We must recognize the *reality* of the psyche, for this is also the need of the intangible psyche, to be known as fixed, symbolically "concrete." The psyche – something much greater than the "mind" – wants to exist in the material world and to turn that sensual world into part of its nonmaterial self. In the previous chapter we saw how both Jung and Bion analyze the Christian myth as an image of turning the intangible Self into an embodied self, of making fixed what is volatile.

In the therapeutic situation the patient's first job is to associate while the analyst's is to receive those associations in a state of reverie. Because he is trying to let his psyche lead and to report whatever spontaneously comes up inside him, the patient's communication, *in addition* to its manifest content, also describes his constantly forming waking dream. The patient is unconsciously picturing in symbolic form his immediate experience of the analytic field at this present moment, including (but not limited to) the emotional stresses operating between the two people and the unconscious transference fantasies of the day. This ongoing narration of its state is the psyche's way of pressing toward existence in the world. It is sending a moment-by-moment bulletin about its experience to both the patient's conscious mind and to the listening analyst. The analyst must, of course, stay empathically connected to the manifest content of the patient's communications. He really *is* talking about his childhood, his marriage, his work. But he is *also* talking about the present moment. The patient is unconsciously telling his analyst all the time about the unconscious emotional experience he is having and, via projective identification or other forms of discharge, about the experiences he needs help to have.

The manifest content of the patient's communication has value. The theoretical orientation that focuses *exclusively* on transference interpretations, as though observing and speaking to patterns in other sectors of the patient's life can have *no* value, simply makes no sense. We all know that we have been helped at times when others, including our analysts, have pointed out repetitive patterns we are caught in with our spouses, parents, children or work. But any interchange has two aspects. A discussion of extra-analytic or intrapsychic problems helps the patient to know something about himself; at the same time, like every interaction with another person, the discussion generates an emotional experience.

Psychic healing depends more on emotional experiences than on cognitive understandings. When a discussion of her marriage culminates in some new piece of insight for the patient, she has the opportunity to take that insight home and to use it to generate new kinds of emotional experiences with her spouse. The new experiences will heal or wound in a way that the insight alone cannot. The emotional experience that was generated in the discussion with her analyst that led to the insight will also be healing or wounding in a way that her new knowledge about herself cannot be. This is why some analysts go overboard and orient *only* to the therapeutic relationship – to the transference. It provides the biggest bang for your buck. It is the fundamental thing going on all the time, supporting and potentiating all other levels of the interaction. But there are other levels of the interaction and sometimes it is valuable to pay attention to these, too.

The analyst tries to make room for the patient's emotional upheavals, for the most disturbed and disturbing projective identifications that are constellated inside her by the interaction of the patient's suffering with her own.

Acting out, on either person's part, is symptomatic of a disturbance in the α function of *the field*. The *couple's* α function, based on both the analyst's and the patient's α functions, has broken down and the mass of β elements pressing for transformation has overwhelmed the couple's ability to dream. The distress is therefore being discharged in action. This action could present as typical acting out by the patient – lateness, forgetting to pay the bill, pressures to reschedule hours and the like. But it could also present as the analyst's acting out, subtly or egregiously. Premature interpretations, a hostile tone of voice, forgetting to give the patient his bill, or neglecting to consider raising his fee when the therapist is raising other people's fees – the enactment can look "loving" as easily as "hateful." When the analyst's responses are unthinking and reactive rather than mindful, he or she is expressing a failure of the field's α function.

Since it is ultimately the analyst's job to process what the patient cannot, either person's enactment must be understood, at least partly, as reflecting a way that the analyst's mind is functioning less robustly than is needed by the existing analytic situation. If her mind were working optimally all the time she would hear the signals present in the patient's unconscious commentary and adjust herself accordingly. Usually such awareness will prevent the disturbing elements from bursting into behavior. (At times, of course, the patient's difficulties are too severe to be held inside the limited analytic situation, requiring instead an inpatient setting.)

But human minds rarely function optimally. They all break down at some point in response to emotional pressure. It is difficult but also important for the analyst to find a way to hold the idea that her mind is not functioning adequately without feeling ashamed. She must hold the fact of her "failure" in a way that fosters curiosity about it rather than excessive distress. Thomas Ogden speaks to the acrobatics needed to accomplish this as "the effort to transform my experience of 'I-ness' (myself as unselfconscious subject) into an experience of 'me-ness' (myself as object of analytic scrutiny)" (2001, p. 19). This is a crucial stance that conflicts at a primary level with the complex of omnipotence that we shall explore in the next chapter. It is difficult to find this attitude because it requires that the therapist feel comfortable in the PS state of unknowing and lostness when what she does not know is how she herself is lacking. She must patiently settle into her smallness, often in charged situations that feel personally threatening and even objectively dangerous. It is a capacity we work toward for our entire professional lives rather than an ability we can develop and take for granted.

If we begin with the idea that constrictions in the ability to have life experiences lie at the root of all psychopathology, then we will try to receive the undigested aspects of the patient to begin the process of transforming them into thinkable α elements. By receiving the patient's β elements the analyst functions as a container, and the more flexible and enduring the container she provides, the more functional the patient's introjected container will be. In centering herself in her reverie, the well-functioning analyst moves fluidly between states of integration and deintegration (PS ↔ D); her ability to do so will gradually be introjected by the patient, building the strength of *his* thinking apparatus.

In the emotional atmosphere created by the patient's stories, held symbolically, the analyst finds an unconscious description of the unthinkable and unrepresentable world of the present moment. If the therapist can receive the story at this deeper level as well as at its surface level, she can imagine the experience the patient is currently trying to have with her. This hard-won understanding will then determine her response, whether a verbal interpretation or not. Most of the time the therapist will stay within the patient's metaphor: when he talks about his wife, his father, his work, the therapist will respond at that same level. But if she is *thinking* about the meaning of the patient's stories for the present moment, it will greatly affect her response. When the patient describes his wish to leave his wife without discussing it because she is so overwhelmingly hateful, the therapist may feel simply supportive if she is thinking only about the borderline wife; if she is aware of the immediate implications of the patient's communication, she may instead focus on the intensity of his fear of the wife, implicitly imagining that it could be different. When the clinician hears the derivative meaning of the patient's stories, the patient's pulsing mass of β is slowly transformed inside her. Gradually, she can offer it up for him to take back in. In this new, digested form, the patient can use his experience for the dreaming process that brings him into being. His experience becomes his own; he possesses it rather than being possessed by it.

All the difficulties that arise between an infant or growing child and his parents can emerge in the therapeutic situation between patient and analyst. Just as parents can project their anxieties into their children rather than receiving their children's anxieties for processing, analysts can project their concerns into their patients. After taking a week off following my father's death, I returned to work in a fragile state. Penny, whom I will describe in the next chapter, talked about her reaction to my week's absence in a way that led me to suggest that she was afraid to be angry at me because she knew of my bereavement. No, she said, she didn't think she was feeling that. Fifteen or twenty minutes later, my hearing of her material led me to make the same interpretation again. No, Penny said. And what was wrong with me, anyway, she wondered, bringing this up for the second time. Maybe I *was* afraid of her being angry at me. And probably I was.

Analysts, like parents, can project their concerns into a patient or be unable to receive and process the patient's anxieties. Of course the process is not a one-way street; patients can almost compel therapists to project into them if doing so fits with the shape of the patient's characterological complexes. A patient may be so unconsciously destructive that the (possibly disguised) emotional attacks that bombard his therapist could not be contained even by very developed practitioners. But it is never fair to blame the patient for his pathology. Even an involuntary patient has a part of himself that tries to grow. It is the analyst/therapist's responsibility to handle the dyad's emotional experience well enough even if it is virtually impossible to discharge that responsibility adequately. Therapists project rather than receive; they block out the patient's missiles rather than absorbing the communication. Each of these analyst "failures" occurs regularly. The analyst's capacities may simply be limited – she needs to grow to serve a particular patient at a particular time – or these capacities may be weakened by personal experiences of stress. I put the word "failures" in quotations because working with therapist errors is one basic aspect of therapeutic work: the patient is working to have his experience and become himself by expanding his dreaming capacity; the analyst's task is exactly parallel. Her "failures" are the basic material she works with to become more of *her*self and to expand her dreaming capacity. As she progresses in this work, she unconsciously teaches her skills to the patient. Each person's developing ability to process his own emotional life expands the dyad's capacity to have the experiences they are generating together.

Optimally, the analyst listens to the stream of the patient's associations both at the literal and symbolic levels at once. The therapist makes a comment and the patient responds by telling a story about the tummy ache that kept his daughter home from school. The therapist understands that her comment was indigestible for the patient. It is not relevant whether her comment was "true" or not. As we shall see when we look at the issue of truth versus falsehood in Chapter 5, truth is not a fixed entity that can be *known*; it is always partial, relative and shifting. In this example, the important truth is that the analyst's interpretation was persecutory, very possibly because it overtaxed the patient's thinking apparatus. It is

> essential to respect the patient's threshold of tolerability . . . on the assumption that persecution feelings in the session are substantially a signal of excessive stress: the α function, $♀ ♂$ and $PS \leftrightarrow D$ emit a *signal* when they are overtaxed. If this signal goes unheeded, 'thoughts' (or β elements) are evacuated . . ., giving rise to 'waking-dream snapshots', or to acting out, to basic assumption behavior[7] and to psychosomatic

7 "Basic assumption behavior" refers to Bion's work on groups. He suggested that under stress primitive unconscious fantasies take over the group as a whole, determining the behavior of the individuals and making it impossible for any one of them to think objectively about his interactions. Bion describes a number of primitive basic assumptions that a group may have. The analytic dyad is a kind of group; some basic assumptions that are easy to imagine for the therapeutic couple would be the belief that the analyst is a savior who will rescue the suffering, victimized patient, or a belief that outside their dyadic group, patient and analyst are surrounded by hostile others who envy their perfect union.

manifestations in the patient's body or in that of the setting (arriving late for sessions, or skipping them altogether).

(Ferro, 2006, p. 18)

Should the analyst fail to recognize the story of the tummy ache as a response to her intervention, she will not hear the patient's experience of persecution and it will remain in β form. Having missed the patient's response, the therapist is apt to repeat her problematic behavior until sudden unexpected emotions burst onto the scene for no comprehensible reason. To the extent that the therapist can take in the patient's communications, she will be transforming β into α inside herself, a process that will gradually make unthinkable emotional distress thinkable for the patient.

In this theory, the effective action of analysis does not lie in making unconscious contents conscious. We could even say that it lies in making unthinkable elements capable of *being* unconscious, though this is only half the story. Healing also increases the analytic couple's ability to produce new conscious thoughts. Ferro (2006; see also Ogden, 2001) suggests that the activity of joining the patient in constructing a narrative, a kind of dreaming-together, is the core healing activity. Joining in, keeping company, sharing the patient's experience: over and over we come back to relatedness as the most basic issue in the work. Interpretations become valuable for their containing aspect more than for the way they inform the patient about something she did not previously know. They are a way the therapist communicates her understanding of the patient's experience, and if her understanding is good enough they function to hold the patient in that experience.

Winnicott speaks to this process in different terminology. He talks, for example, about a clinical situation in which he refrains from offering an interpretation "because the patient is essentially at a stage of discovering things for herself, and premature interpretation in such circumstances annihilates the creativity of the patient . . ." (1971, p. 117). The patient's "creativity" in this sentence is closely related to her dreaming capacity, although since his work basically predates Bion's, Winnicott does not articulate what he clearly knows intuitively about the way his holding (containing) the patient fosters the unfolding of her dreaming process. Instead of telling the patient what is going on, Winnicott is joining in with her in an emerging story that images the self being constructed by the ongoing dream narration.

Ferro describes the analyst and patient as "together constructing a dream" and suggests that neither member of the couple has an inherently clearer connection to the truth of the moment. "Within this mode of proceeding . . . *transformational co-narration* takes the place of interpretation" (2006, p. 1, emphasis in original). The analyst, being more interested in how the patient might elaborate, revise or develop the ideas she offers than in giving him insight, will proffer tentative hunches more often than definitive interpretations. The goal is a stream of transformations occurring in the session, transformations that create the patient as he speaks (dreams). The field is not something that needs "analyzing"; it is

> the 'medium' that permits operations of transformation. . . . It is precisely the field which, in proportion as it is explored, constantly expands (Bion 1970), becoming the matrix of possible stories, many of which are left 'in store' pending the possibility of development.
>
> (op. cit., p. 13)

The hope is to stimulate the creation of new meanings, to foster the unfolding of the patient's dream, not to nail it down. Trying to alphabetize the unthinkable store of β elements that is disturbing the peace of the field is the opposite of decoding the patient's communications. When the analyst has alphabetized something of the patient's experience for him, she may be able to say something new, in the patient's own dialect, something that facilitates his creativity by furthering his ability to hold his emotional state. This will be very different from interpretive behavior that consists of translating the patient's story into the analyst's language. This latter behavior is more apt to attack the patient's creativity – his dreaming function – than it is to support it.

Thinking about the session in this way harkens back to Winnicott's work on play, something that occurs in the transitional space between analyst and patient. Play is the intermediary between the inner world and external reality, the means of communicating unconscious fantasies to oneself and to others. Narration is the adult's form of the child's play. Where the child may act out a game of escaping the clutches of a wicked witch, the adult will tell stories of encounters with domineering women bosses or of television shows about harsh matrons. The important thing is that the analyst join the patient in his play, fostering its development and expansion rather than disrupting the ongoing dream's formation with translations of its "meaning."

If the analyst's joining in with the patient in the unfolding of his dreaming capacity is the crucial healing activity, it would help to explain why analysts from very different schools of thought, who offer very different interpretations of the patient's dynamics, all seem to have reasonable levels of success in their work. The Kleinian who talks to her patient about his wish to nurse at her breast, the Jungian who speaks about his need for her to embody the Good Mother and the interpersonalist who suggests that the patient worries about whether or not she is keeping him in her mind, each connect with the patient in psychoanalytic language (although the interpersonalist's is the least arcane). Speaking in the patient's language would always be preferable; in the real world, patients make do with what they can find and they learn the language of their therapist well enough to manage.

Freud urged the analyst to listen to the patient in a state of evenly suspended attention, neither taking notes nor attempting to concentrate on anything.

> For as soon as anyone deliberately concentrates his attention to a certain degree, he begins to select from the material before him; . . . and in making this selection he will be following his expectations or inclinations. . . . [H]e is in danger of never finding anything but what he already knows; . . . he will certainly falsify what he may perceive. . . . [H]e must turn his unconscious like a receptive organ toward the transmitting unconscious of the patient.
>
> (Freud, 1912, pp. 112–15)

Freud describes the way the analyst opens herself to her own ongoing dream work, to her reverie, in order to receive the dream that constantly forms inside the patient. Bollas (2006) suggests that when the analyst turns her unconscious toward the patient's, she fertilizes his unconscious creativity. This unconscious creativity is the work that the patient does to heal his wounds. Let us turn now to the case of Gertrude, a woman whose α function was severely compromised at the beginning of our work.

Gertrude[8]

I first saw Gertrude when she was seventy-seven. She had had over thirty years of classically oriented Jungian therapy before coming to me. One area that I want to explore involves the contrast between what happened for her in that previous work and what happened for her with me, a more developmentally oriented Jungian. Gertrude functioned adequately in the world: she cared for herself capably, paid her bills, stayed in touch with her family. She had never done anything that would be called "crazy." Her associations came in complete sentences and paragraphs. But I experienced her as incomprehensible and in her presence my capacity to think was virtually destroyed. As we shall see, this was the result of her violent attacks on linking – on building relatedness. She could not bear to experience her emotional life and she protected herself from her emotions by destroying any attempt to connect her experiences with her subjective reactions to them. When I began working with her I was unfamiliar with Bion's work but seven years after I first met her I came across a passage that describes the elderly woman I began seeing in 1994:

> [The patient's associations are] characterized by a peculiar lack of 'resonance.' What he says clearly and in articulated speech is one dimensional. It has no overtones or undertones of meaning. It makes the

---

8 The case study of Gertrude was originally published in Sullivan, Barbara Stevens (2007) "Alphabetizing in Old Age", *The Journal of Analytical Psychology,* 52:1–16. Journal published by Wiley-Blackwell and © The Society of Analytical Psychology.

listener inclined to say 'so what?' It has no capacity to evoke a train of thought.

(Bion, 1962, pp. 15–16)

By the time I discovered Bion's work, Gertrude's capacity to hold her emotional experience and communicate it had greatly developed despite the fact I had not had an adequate theoretical container to understand the nature of her problems. So one question we might ask is, what proved to be so healing in our interaction? If, for most of the work, I had as little understanding of her difficulty as it seems to me I had, what did I manage to do that helped her as much as it seems I did? As we shall see, Gertrude's α function greatly expanded and solidified in our work even though I did not understand my job to be helping her to grow the capacity to experience her life. I was caught in an old paradigm, where I imagined that my job was to help her to know about the experiences she was denying, repressing and projecting. But despite the fact that I did not have the concepts that would have enabled me to focus on how she was *attacking* her already limited α function because she did not have the inner container she would have needed to process her very painful affects, something about the way I was with her proved deeply healing. I want to look at her work with me and at her thirty-odd years with Dr. X, each of which was to some degree helpful, offering some thoughts about how the analytic process fosters development.

When our patients' communications are imbued with α function, they are (relatively) easy to remember. We do not have to memorize the "facts" of a patient's life. The facts are threads, woven into a fabric that is a person; the patient's associations bring other aspects of his or her self (dreams, experiences, bits of history) to the listening analyst's mind. When α function is missing, the sensory data of experience remain in their state of thing-ness, not woven into the person but just-as-it-is "facts" that, because they are not integrated with the emotional reality of a self, have no meaning and no capacity to call up other aspects of the self that is (not) experiencing them.

In the analytic situation the patient's associations bring to the analyst's mind memories, images and affects that her own α function has stored. As early as 1946 Jung understood something the interpersonal psychoanalysts have more recently developed: patient and analyst create a "third," an "us," a "field" that is neither patient nor analyst (Jung, 1946, paras 358, 364; Ogden, 1997; Barranger *et al.*, 1983; Ferro, 2002, 2005, 2006). Recognizing this "us" allows the analyst to use her apparently personal associations to inform herself about the patient's immediate unconscious experience, for the analyst's silent associations are constellated by the emotional experience she is trying to digest in the moment.

In our initial phone contact, Gertrude told me that she had read my book, *Psychotherapy Grounded in the Feminine Principle* (1989), and that she wanted to discuss it with me. Gertrude's overwhelming fragmentation prevented me from having the obvious thought that she might be interested in working with me. Though she was not a therapist, she had been in Jungian-oriented psychotherapy for nearly thirty-five years (ending one year before our first hour), and my understanding was that this quasi-professional patient wanted to think about the ideas presented in that book. I could not, however, understand most of what transpired in the hour.

From my point of view, Gertrude unleashed a torrent of chaotic ideas heavily peppered with Jungian terms such as animus, shadow and individuation. Although I knew "the" meaning of these words, I had no idea what *she* meant by them. Thinking that we were having an "intellectual" consultation, I did my best to respond intellectually to whatever concept I could grab hold of from the deluge of words inundating me. At the end of the hour I asked something neutral about how we should wrap this up and was amazed to hear that Gertrude wanted to come back on a weekly basis. The barrage of β elements in that hour had made me unable to think the obvious thought: she was looking for a therapeutic relationship.

We set up a schedule of weekly visits. After I had accepted her in this way, she told me she "knew" I would prefer to work with a young person rather than an old woman with no future. I got no glimpse of any emotion surrounding this "knowledge." I felt a further confused surprise since I was consciously interested in an intimate relationship with an elderly person. (Although I did feel dismay about my inability to comprehend Gertrude.)

Gertrude went on to explain that she had suffered from severe depression through much of her life. While her previous therapy had greatly helped, she still had "bad days." "Wouldn't it be dreadful if death came on a bad day?" she asked, smiling brightly. Despite the confusing smile, my heart flipped over with empathic anxiety, grief and hope. For the only time in that first hour, Gertrude offered me a felt connection to her self, a connection that was over as suddenly as it appeared. But any reluctance that I felt to see her disappeared. She was looking to save her soul.

Gertrude, the second-born child, was the only girl in a wealthy Midwestern family of seven children. In addition to the children, the household consisted of the father – a businessman who had greatly increased the wealth he inherited – a cold, bitter mother, and a large number of servants, none of whom Gertrude remembered with fondness. A baby appeared every year or two and after each birth, perhaps to cope with postpartum depressions, the parents went on extended trips, leaving the new baby and the older children with maids. When Gertrude was four, a baby died at birth. Several months before that birth, Gertrude became ill and was sent to live at her grandmother's house in a nearby part of town. She lived there for four months, underwent two surgeries and came close to dying. Her mother visited only once, her father not at all. We can perhaps imagine that she survived that degree of abandonment because she did experience her grandmother as loving.

Gertrude felt her mother hated her. Once, for example, when the mother was knitting Gertrude a sweater, the child asked when the mother thought it would be ready. The mother answered that Gertrude was such a cow it would surely take a long time. As I heard the stories, I imagined that Gertrude's mother identified with her as the only girl, and that the mother's self-loathing and her envy of the child's youth and aliveness led her to hate her. The father relied on manic defenses. He largely ignored the children and was blind to his wife's grim unhappiness. In addition to working long hours, he left the family for long stretches on hunting trips with male friends. In this atmosphere of non-attachment, he could easily be off on a hunting trip while his wife gave birth to one of his children. Gertrude's primary emotional models thus offered two adaptations: a hate-filled depression or an apparently lively manic flight.

In due course, Gertrude married a man whose work took them to a number of large cities before they settled in San Francisco with their three daughters. In her early thirties, while living in a city on the East Coast of the US, she sought help for the first time and was told by a Freudian analyst that she was "too old." In San Francisco, in her middle forties, she found a Jungian-oriented therapist and began to work with him after another Freudian had rejected her as "too depressed."[9] She worked with Dr. X for fifteen years, and then with a woman he referred her to for about five, returning to him for another fifteen years. Her reports of these therapies described a classical Jungian approach in which she presented dreams and her therapists interpreted them.

Her main therapist, the man, sounded intellectual, decent and kind – but cool. I met him once at a social event and the atmosphere of being with him struck me as congruent with Gertrude's descriptions of him. Gertrude said no one before me had ever talked to her about feelings. It is certainly clear that she had never *heard* her therapists discuss feelings, and it does seem that feelings were neglected, at least in the thirty-year therapy's ending: she presented a dream which they mutually took to mean that the therapy was not working. The therapist ended the hour (after fifty minutes) saying he guessed that was it. And that was it. When she first told me of that final hour, my shock led her to insist that their ending had been the only reasonable approach: the work wasn't working, the dream said so. Seven years later, when I finally "got" her feeling, I said, "But you wanted him to say, 'How can we make it work?' " Gertrude came as close to crying as she ever did; I had articulated her wordless emotion.

My hunches about Gertrude's previous analytic work must be held with

9 I am in no way suggesting that the rejecting analysts' failure was a function of their theoretical perspective. In any case, I strongly doubt that the reasons for the rejections were her age or her mood. Her dauntingly incomprehensible mode of communication made her very ungratifying to work with for a long time.

warnings. First, it was what she was able to experience and should not be taken to imply that it was all Dr. X offered. Second, the work with him began in the 1960s, a long time ago for such a young field; we know much more about the psyche now than we did then, and forty years from now we will undoubtedly look back on our present work with some dismay. Third, Gertrude's frozen emotional state compelled the construction of an emotionally frozen field. No therapist could have created a feelingful field with the Gertrude of the 60s, 70s or 80s. She and I had a rough time of it in the 90s and early 2000s.

After six months Gertrude increased the frequency of her visits to twice a week, a move that surprised me as much as her initial interest in working with me had. But even with the more frequent contact, I typically felt lost in her hours for the first two or three years, an experience I'm sure Dr. X knew a great deal about. She talked *at* me in a way that felt like a machine gun barrage of words. There was never a moment's silence. Topics changed abruptly for no reason that I could imagine, and virtually all of the topics seemed disconnected from meaning. Why was Gertrude talking about an unnamed cousin or a book she had read years ago? Even when a subject had obvious emotional implications, such as what approach parents should take to teaching a child manners, the subject was emphatically not about her childhood, her experiences as a mother, or – so crazy an idea that I mentioned it rarely – about her relationship with me. When I wondered how her material related to one of those areas, Gertrude answered briskly that she wanted to understand this theoretically or philosophically, not personally.

Let me quote Bion's description of Gertrude's difficulty: "The attempt to evade the experience of contact with live objects by destroying α function leaves the personality unable to have a relationship with any aspect of itself that does not resemble an automaton" (1962, p. 13). I did not think of her as an automaton, but I often felt unable to find a *person* other than myself in the room. Even after nearly five years of work, Gertrude dreamed of me as an enormous hospital building. A connection with a living person, whether an inner image or an outer individual, was too threatening at that stage to be tolerated. Whenever I began to feel oriented – to have some sense of a connection to meaning in Gertrude's associations – the topic would abruptly change and we would be off on a roller coaster of ideas completely disconnected from her, me, or us.

As I reread her dreams to write up our work, I was amazed to discover that they often seemed clear. Feelings that were not available in the hours came through years later; I could follow the line of her development. But at the time, her dreams, associations and stories made almost no sense to me. For the first four to six years of the work, Gertrude insisted that her inner life (i.e. her dreams) had no relationship to her outer life. She had certainly absorbed the Jungian idea that everything she needed for her healing would come from within herself. Her need to prevent anyone from breaching her rigidly fortified bunker had unfortunately perverted this good idea into an insistence that nothing from outside (a thought of mine, for example) should be allowed in. She refused to entertain the notion that a dream could relate to something that had happened between us, or that a dream figure could refer to a way she experienced me (or any other outer figure). She refused to consider the possibility that her mood swings from terrible depression to manic excitement related to anything in her life, certainly not to her hours with me. Besides, she was unable to remember anything that had happened in her life or in a previous hour. These rather thorough attacks on all connections, especially on the link between herself and me, protected her from linking (connecting, relating) with the grief and rage that lurked inside her, needing to be experienced; it also left me feeling fragmented. In retrospect, I think that her attacks on linking (Bion, 1959) constellated my fear of connections and my primitive self's capacity to attack links. With both of us attacking any connection that swam into sight, it's not surprising that her dreams were incomprehensible to me.

Certainly there was no way she could work on the ordinary task of old age, weighing the gains and grieving the deficits and losses of one's life. Gertrude was so fragmented as to belie the very concept of a self. She could hardly concern herself with the meaning the approaching end of her life held for this not-yet-born self.

In any case, she explained that she could not hope to contact herself in my presence. The years passed and she began to be more reachable; I could sometimes ask how she felt about something I had said or done. She would promise to think about it at home. Could she think about it now? No. She could not have emotional responses with anyone because in the presence of another her fear of being taken over made her unable to contact herself. For the most part, this distressing feeling of disconnection from herself kept her from attending any collective event. When she was not alone, she armored herself with a "normal" persona that felt profoundly not-her. A collective event that asked Gertrude to sit still and be an audience deprived her of her pressured stream of talk. Without this safety valve, the strain of maintaining her false self became so painful that she feared losing control (something that had never happened). If she was truly herself Gertrude imagined she would pee on my sofa and shout obscenities. The "real" Gertrude would run naked in the streets. For the first five or six years of our work, she rarely felt safe enough to peek out of her thick false-self casing long enough to have a feeling that she was seeing and being seen by me.

Again, a passage from Bion's work offers a way to think about Gertrude's situation:

> Only β elements are available for whatever activity takes the place of thinking and β elements are suitable for evacuation only. ... These β elements are dealt with by an evacuatory procedure similar to the

> movements of musculature, changes of mien, etc. ... [A] muscular movement, for example, a smile, must have a different interpretation from the smile of the non-psychotic personality. ... A smile or a verbal statement must be interpreted as an evacuatory muscular movement and not as a communication of feeling.
>
> (Bion, 1962, pp. 13–14)

Gertrude's words discharged the indigestible mass of her emotional experience. Her smile functioned in the same way. Years into the work, as this discharge mechanism receded, I finally came to understand it: her face lit up when she felt sadness, grief, rage, but hardly ever in response to pleasure. Gertrude could not bear situations where she had to dam up these central outlets. A healthier person transforms the accumulating mass of emotionally charged sensory bits produced by a collective situation into α elements that form the unconscious waking dream that protects him from being overwhelmed. Lacking α function, Gertrude could only evacuate emotions; she could not bear to experience emotions because she could not process them.

In those first years I often felt that I was metaphorically grabbing a frail old woman by the shoulders and shaking her. "Gertrude!" I felt. "Look at me, talk to me, I'm here, I'm a person," undoubtedly experiencing (silently) the feelings the child Gertrude had (silently) felt toward her mother. Gertrude maintained that our relationship was a purely business one, and when I was able to persuade her to talk about it in any way, she associated immediately to examples of clerks in stores or dental assistants. The closest she got to a positive image of our relationship was to acknowledge that if a man has thirty horses in a stable, she was sure he would care for all of them equally well. She seemed autistic rather than schizoid, and my violent image of shaking her speaks to how desperate I felt, sealed out of any human contact.

But centimeter by centimeter, our dyad's α function was growing. In the fourth and fifth years of our work, Gertrude began to express an interest in her feelings despite her fear that they would swamp her. She occasionally associated dream images to me or wondered if something she felt could be related to the previous hour. She began to express mild feelings of abandonment around vacations.

A new image arose in me. I became able to track pieces of time and instead of shaking her I began to feel myself reaching for her. Often I would reach until we made a brief connection, only to have Gertrude break it with an abrupt change of subject. I would gather my energy and try to make another connection, stretching across a vast expanse of emptiness. Again the connection would be brief. After two or three experiences I would give up, exhausted, and let the meaningless flow of disconnected topics carry me along, stupefied. I imagine that my reaching so strenuously to connect and having her repeatedly break the connection until I gave up in despair captured Gertrude's infantile experience with her mother. But the field between us was so fragmenting that I was unable to think of talking to her about my idea. Still, islands of connection emerged and grew.

At the end of a Monday hour, five and a half years into the work, Gertrude, talking as she walked across the room to the door, expressed a wish to see me sooner than her next hour. I did not understand what she was saying until she was in the hall, still talking. I asked her to come back in and closed the door. Was she saying she wanted to see me before Thursday? I asked. Oh, she knew I wouldn't have time and I shouldn't worry about it. I told her I could see her on Wednesday. In that Wednesday hour, she acknowledged that she would like to see me more frequently, although she would not be troubled by the fact that, of course, I would not have time. I told her I would be glad to see her more often but I didn't see why we should meet three times a week. "Why not five times a week?" I asked. Gertrude leaped at the chance and over time our new schedule made a dramatic difference.

In the five and a half years of five-times-a-week work that remained before Gertrude's death, a fundamental shift occurred in her psyche. A core sense of self emerged, along with a qualitative leap in her capacity for relatedness.[10] Underlying this change was a substantial enlargement of the potency of her α function.

What happened in our intensive analytic work to cause this? I believe one event, stretching over many months, was central in Gertrude's transformation. It began a little less than five years into the work, while we were still meeting twice a week. I had written a novel about my mother's death by assisted suicide. A tiny number of books had been published by a small press and in my neighborhood bookstore one book remained, sitting on a high shelf gathering dust. Gertrude, who "never" went into bookstores, found this book, bought it and read it.

I had the usual narcissistic investment in my book, compounded by the fact that it was autobiographical, dealing with my relationship with my mother and my helping her to die. Gertrude seemed not to realize that I would have feelings about my book, perhaps because she was unaware that she had feelings about it. Certainly, when I tried to explore the kinds of interactions I am about to describe, she responded by adamantly insisting that she had no feelings of any kind about the book and its subject. Treating it as an intellectual matter, Gertrude maintained I had not described my emotional experience of my mother's death because I had not described the anguishing doubts that had assailed me about the rightness of what I did. Unable to arouse her curiosity about her own feelings or concerns, I would eventually respond that I had not had anguishing doubts about that. I had had other feelings that were described in the book. She insisted I must have felt the

10 These two conceptions are two sides of one coin, as Jung (1946) indicates: "The unrelated human being lacks wholeness, for he can achieve wholeness only through the soul, and the soul cannot exist without its other side, which is always found in a 'You.' " (para 454)

doubts she described at great length. She set out arguments proving I had felt various things I had not felt, arguments that she presented many times. A response was demanded. For reasons I could not understand, my book would suddenly become the topic and I would be assailed with what felt like battering attacks on my sense of myself.

I now see that in this interchange, Gertrude gave me a taste of her experience of life: an endless sense of annihilation in which her/my sense of self was continually attacked as wrong. Doubtless she often felt this with me: maybe when I suggested she felt something in response to some event between us. What I intended as a gentle question, she might take as a frontal attack on who she was. But this insight was unavailable to me in those middle years of our work.

Another way I now think about our impasse is that we were asking the wrong question. Instead of "What did Barbara feel when she helped her mother die?" it should have been, "How does Gertrude feel about the image of Barbara the book gave her?" But Gertrude was trying to handle her feelings with denial. Because her denial was so important to her – because the image of me "murdering" my aged mother was so intolerable for her – I was unconsciously infected by the terror behind her denial, and I could not ask the question that needed to be asked. And then, of course, the issue was so intensely charged for me that I was about as far from neutrality as I could be.

Ten months after she read the book and two months after beginning daily visits, she was pursuing this same topic, and I exploded in what Neville Symington (1983) has called an "analyst's act of freedom." I burst out with an interpretation I had not known I had. "You always want to talk about my feelings," I said. "We never get to talk about your feelings. We never talk about the fact you're the same age as my mother, and I'm the same age as your daughters and you're afraid I want to kill you." There was a stunned silence. Gertrude laughed nervously and said she had never had such a thought.

On the next day (Friday) Gertrude told me that she was quitting her analysis. The idea I had presented was psychotic, something that might come to one in the middle of the night, not the sort of thing one would say or think in the light of day. Our work had become irrevocably unsafe. In this quiet hour, I felt how dangerous I had become. I told her I was sad to think our work would end in this way. She shook her head, perhaps in sympathy for my sadness. I said I would hold her hours for a few weeks in case she changed her mind. She did not want me to do that, worrying I would charge for the hours. I assured her I would not charge her, I would just hold them. The hour ended with her quietly maintaining her sense that I had become too dangerous.

On Saturday a message reinstated her hours, and on Monday she said she realized she needed to ask herself why my insane thought had upset her so much. Her question explicitly sought connection: what had my comment touched inside her? If she developed any thoughts about her question, I did not hear them, but the experience connected us powerfully.

In this incident Gertrude attempted to end her work with me in the same way her previous analytic work had ended. In both cases, we see how her father's manic flight from difficulties orchestrated an enactment. With Dr. X the enactment was carried by the analyst, but Gertrude's manic defenses must have contributed. I was less cooperative than Dr. X and Gertrude had grown to a place where she could interrupt her flight.

One year after this pivotal enactment, as Gertrude talked about her persistent depression, I was able to offer a greatly detoxified version of my interpretation. I said she might be afraid I would support the parts of her that wanted to die. Gertrude first insisted I always supported the parts of her that wanted to live, and then said that if she imagined me supporting her death wishes, she would instantly flee. She felt she hung by a thin thread over a deep well. I held the thread. If I decided she was hopeless, I could cut the thread, even by accidentally turning away my attention. "Oh well," she concluded, dismissing the topic, "I don't think your husband lives in fear of your killing him! Why he could even want to kill you!"

This brief vignette shows how far we had come, only one year into our intensive work. I had become able to attune myself to her much more than in the past and she had become able to talk about her emotional experience in complicated symbolic ways. She spontaneously created an image (hanging over the well) to convey her terror; she entertained possibilities (what "would happen if I cut the thread") without being overcome by the omnipotent fear that imagining this scenario would make it happen. And her creative trickster orchestrated a delightful escape from this dangerous topic with another image, one implying that Gertrude (my husband) could have murderous wishes toward me, and that we could safely contain these primitive instinctual energies.

But this was not the end of this interchange. The next week Gertrude fell on her way to her hour, breaking her arm. The fall initiated a severe decline lasting over two months: Gertrude contracted pneumonia and spent six weeks in a nursing home. I was able to go to the nursing home for three hours each week, and her daughter brought her to my office for a fourth. The question of which side I was on, life or death, overwhelmed her, presumably because it constellated both her mother's unconscious attempts to annihilate her and her fragile inner balance between life- and death-impulses. I have no reason to imagine that Gertrude consciously thought my nursing home visits represented particular devotion, but perhaps she unconsciously noticed the contrast between the committed analyst and the mother who visited once in four months. Whatever mixed feelings I had, in this brush with death I worked mightily to support her connection to life.

After ten and a half years of work, Gertrude received news of a large, aggressive cancer. She dreamed she had to go away for a month. She told a gardener what had to be done in her absence. Sheets of tissue paper lay about in the yard, the kind you use to wrap fragile things, and there was a large ceramic bowl that (in the dream) she had recently ordered.

Gertrude felt the dream was hopeful: a month was a length of time you could get through. I was enthusiastic about both the gardener and the bowl. "You have a helper man inside you," I said, "who will support you in this ordeal." The bowl, Gertrude said, was something she could keep things in, like fruit. Or she could put earth in it and plant something. I said it was wonderful she had a new container to hold things. Gertrude liked this idea, but she especially liked the gardener as a helper. That was a very good idea, she said several times in the next weeks. The dangerous male pursuers of her dreams had faded away in the earlier years of our work, and she had at last come to a positive masculine figure.

From a state of severely limited α function, Gertrude had moved to an alliance with a positive inner figure who could tend the garden of her soul. She had acquired a container to process her emotional experiences in, to hold the thoughts and feelings growing inside her. For the last few years, Gertrude's inappropriate, brilliant smile, and rapid-fire speech had largely disappeared. She could talk for long stretches about grief, remorse and other painful emotions, with a congruent expression on her face; periods of quiet reflection and silence were common. Even when I could not track her associations – a situation that was becoming uncommon – I no longer felt barraged. Our time together felt companionable and warm, rarely chaotic or fragmenting.

She had made considerable progress in holding and expressing deep feelings of connection with me. When I went away, instead of feeling only relief at her freed-up schedule, she would acknowledge that this freeing up amounted to a hiatus in her life that consisted largely of her analytic work. She talked directly about how much she missed me. After my last vacation, only six weeks before her death, she was especially heartfelt in her relief at my return. She said she had been able to write in her journal during my absence, but it was only in my presence that she could find her self and sort out the confusion in her head. Her ability to recognize her dependence on and love for another person represented stunning progress for a woman who, in the first years of the work, talked about her inability to know that she loved even her children; when she was angry at them or felt burdened by their needs, she lost connection to her love.

In her outer life, her relationships with her children were most strikingly transformed. The youngest is mildly retarded and Gertrude had felt frustrated and bored with her, causing her to avoid contact. In the last few years of her life, Gertrude became patient and loving with this daughter and held the younger woman's feelings in ways that were clearly introjected from how she experienced me. In the last years of Gertrude's life, various strains between her and her two older daughters were worked out so that in the months of Gertrude's illness, they provided devoted and tireless support.

When she died, her daughters and her granddaughter, herself a woman approaching middle age, were with her. The atmosphere in the house was one of loving kindness among them all. Death did not come for her in the dreadful form she had feared, on a "bad" day. A self had been born inside her. In some sense, we had saved her soul.

Discussion

Before trying to understand what happened between us to facilitate Gertrude's dramatic development, I want to offer my hunch about what happened in her previous therapeutic work. My point of view is skewed: I am eternally outside that therapy; my knowledge comes only from the patient, who was no longer in the experience, and whose point of view was distorted by the interpersonal demands, both conscious and unconscious, that she experienced in relationship to a new therapist (me). But I think that by imagining what the curative factors in that therapy might have been, and combining that perspective with a sense of how I might have helped her, we may be able to suggest something about the curative elements in analytic work.

Gertrude told me that she initially described herself to Dr. X as not understanding how he could tell that she was a woman and not a man. I take this to mean that when she met him, she felt confused about who she was at the most fundamental level. In our work, even when she went through a period of six or nine months of great anger at him, she remembered and repeated that he had "saved her life." She had gotten her gender sorted out; "the mess inside her head" had been somewhat cleared up. Her immobilizing depression had lifted a good deal. These improvements were major successes.

An important focus of her work with Dr. X was "the animus" (meaning the masculine side her psyche). Dr. X had apparently told her, in the first period of their work, that women should be receptive and should let men lead. Without knowing the details, he seems to have taught her old-fashioned ideas (ideas Jung encouraged) about how women are "supposed to be." After about fifteen years, she left Dr. X and spent five years in what she experienced as a failed therapy with a woman. She returned to Dr. X enraged at the indoctrination she had received from him.[11] Dr. X responded by telling her he had been wrong before and had learned a lot about women and men in the years of their separation. He told her he was sorry.

Telling a powerful authority figure that he was wrong had to be an enormous experience for Gertrude, who had certainly never talked back to her parents. And that he would own his shadow, apologize and change! The transformative power of this event is shown by the curative experience

---

11 A development which, parenthetically, should give us pause about dismissing her work with the woman as utterly failed.

Gertrude repeatedly pointed to: in the second round of their work, Dr. X supported her through her "big operation," a hysterectomy. She would always feel grateful to him for that. This experience of his "support" symbolized his helping her to ground a sense of self in her gender as it was authentically expressed in her rather than as it "should" be. Their work established that foundation on so solid a basis that losing her female organs did not disrupt it.

But as is obvious from my report, something fundamental about Gertrude's capacity for relatedness seems to have been untouched in that work. When we met, a strongly autistic streak dominated her ability to relate. Her stories of interactions with others frequently displayed an inability to imagine the other's experience, certainly the other's experience of her. While a comfortable identification with her gender indicates a substantial growth in her sense of self – from having nothing, Gertrude moved to having something, an infinitely large step – her sense of self was still woefully lacking. Her psyche was projected everywhere; the smallest sliver of it was consciously owned. She frequently "lost her ego:" meaning, I believe, that she experienced serious episodes of depersonalization and derealization.

Gertrude had a profound engagement with Dr. X. While their last hour is certainly disturbing, his professional devotion to her over thirty years had to be very healing. His interest in her not very coherent monologue began the process of forming a self, something her mother's lack of interest in her infant's emotional experience had not encouraged. I suspect Dr. X's reliable attention was the major factor leading Gertrude to attach so strongly to him. (The fact that the two Freudians she had consulted rejected her indicates, I think, the reaction that many people would have had to this chaotic woman. Dr. X's listening to her as attentively as he was able to was surely a new and amazing experience for her.)

But, as far as I could see, he did not focus on the meaning of her engagement with him. They talked about Gertrude, not Gertrude-and-Dr. X. In a therapeutic venture with someone as incoherent and primitive as Gertrude, it may not be important to talk about anything except in so far as the topic functions as a vehicle for mirroring back to the patient her own emotional experience. This is the reflection of self the infant finds on its mother's face. This is the privation on which Gertrude's psyche was built: her mother did not reflect back Gertrude's self, she barely saw her infant for the projections she was herself discharging. Thus Gertrude appeared in Dr. X's waiting room lacking the most elemental sense of who she was. His interest, attention and concern fostered the formation of Gertrude's self. His continuing attempts to talk to her about her animus, her ego, or any aspect of her self as though it was an element of her inner self that she could be separate from and analyze, disrupted that development. These discussions could not have made any sense to the fragmented, chaotic "self" inside Gertrude. An intellectual false self was engaged and shored up by the conversation.

A caricature of a classical Jungian approach has the patient and the analyst allied in an attempt to study the patient's psyche, especially as imaged in dreams. To the extent that patient and analyst are related people, with grounded "I"s, this approach can be effective. But the unrelated, primitive parts of any patient, the autistic, schizoid, uncohered aspects of the self, cannot participate in such a discussion. Deeply unrelated, Gertrude's "I" was only a costume. Imagining her as a separate person whom she and Dr. X could study functioned to reinforce her depersonalized defenses and her fantasy that a self was something constructed by one's intellect rather than an emotional entity, alive and growing. Dr. X's compassionate concern expressed itself through this activity of trying to understand Gertrude, and his own growing nature had to shine through that activity. These elements – his attachment to her, his openness to her attachment to him, his own open, developing condition – supported her development. But one activity through which these factors were conveyed – trying to parse Gertrude as a self-contained organism – could only have blocked her growth. What she needed, a self-connected-to-another, could be born only through attachment.

While the analyst need not necessarily talk about it, it is valuable if he or she thinks about the interpersonal experience of the moment. Even without Bion's invaluable understanding of the dreaming process, orienting toward the emotional interaction occurring in the analytic dyad functions to support that dreaming process. But no matter how one tries to stay in that present, symbolic perspective, one is frequently pulled into the patient's content. Nurturing experiences occur while the analyst is thinking about the patient's outer relationships, her history, her dream as an X-ray of her psyche. But the mutative place is the present moment, a highly charged emotional relationship involving both people. Developments in the *reality* of that relationship affect the patient more strongly than anything else. Developments in his *knowledge* about anything, including the relationship, are peripheral.

In considering the healing factors in Gertrude's work with me, I think first of what my work and Dr. X's had in common: reliable attention to and interest in her material. All the ordinary ways that I held her material and processed it functioned to create a container that she gradually introjected (as the image of the bowl indicates). But why did her work with Dr. X not constellate more of an internal container?

One memory she related several times offers a clue: she dreamed someone had delivered a bouquet of flowers to her home and someone else had stolen it off the porch. She reported Dr. X as interpreting, "Someone hurt your feelings." Gertrude felt chided for her "oversensitivity." I doubt Dr. X intended any critique of her sensitivity, but I could hear that his response had hurt her feelings and apparently he never asked if anything he had done triggered the dream. "Someone" hurt her feelings. In Gertrude's memory, no one seemed disposed to wonder who that someone might have been.

When the field allowed me to do it, I took the emergence of this memory as a sign that I had wounded her. If I could imagine how that might have happened, I asked her about it. But the atmosphere of non-connection often left me unable to think symbolically; I could "forget" that her association reflected something in the present, something that involved me. This vignette highlights the barrier to any therapist imagining what had hurt her: I'm sure Dr. X neither intended to chide her for "oversensitivity" nor knew that she felt criticized. I could discover months or years after the fact that she had felt criticized by something I said. I believe, however, that when I was able to hold a silent question – how is Gertrude's material reflecting her immediate experience with me? – it created an interpersonal atmosphere that fostered relatedness. The analyst's silent listening and the understandings he develops are absorbed by the patient just as the infant takes in his mother's inner state. When I could hold it, an interpersonal focus impacted Gertrude positively.

While Gertrude talked, I tried to understand who was speaking to me by listening to the content and manner of her presentation and, through deduction, by listening to the states she evoked in me. I used my hunches to suggest possible ideas about her immediate experience for her to consider. My normally silent focus was on her-and-me as a couple rather than on her as a separate person, although her strong autistic defenses could certainly knock me into a less related orientation. I tried to function as a container for her immediate experience in the same way a mother works to contain and transform her infant's immediate emotional experiences. Over time the infant/ patient introjects that container and uses it to process her experience.

Where Dr. X's attention helped that inner container develop, his lack of focus on the immediate emotional experience limited how far that development could go. To a large extent, the problem in their work reflected a lack of understanding throughout the depth therapeutic world. When Gertrude started with Dr. X in the mid 60s, analysts focused on insight into the unconscious as the curative factor. Jung's (1946) prescient insight into the intersubjective nature of the therapeutic relationship had not been understood even in Jungian circles. It was not until the 80s and 90s that intersubjective understandings of the analytic process flowered. Gertrude came into my office carrying the gains she had made with Dr. X at a time in history when new perspectives on analytic work existed for us to use productively.

If an intersubjective orientation formed the water in which Gertrude and I swam, it was greatly heightened by the dramatic interpersonal tangle that erupted over my novel. The uncontained quality of my behavior, in startling contrast to my normal "professional" manner, offered a shocking contradiction to her defensive belief that we had no personal connection. The atmosphere became saturated with the fact that we mattered to each other. I was not simply "an analyst," and she was not simply "a patient." Where she had once imaged me as "Kaiser hospital," her dreams of the last four or five years presented me as a doctor, a nurse, a teacher, etc. She and I had become the unique couple we were. "Gertrude" had come into treatment with "Barbara" and because I clearly saw her as a person, her personhood took shape inside.

The hour as a dream

I have talked about the way that each person's α function works to create an ongoing unconscious dream at all times. Let us now look at a particular hour's work in Gertrude's analysis and see if we can track the dream that she-and-I as a couple were constructing together. The interaction of the hour is presented in ordinary type and my retrospective thinking is in italics. This is a Friday hour from a point in the work where my experience of being persecuted by Gertrude's barrage of words had passed but before I had developed an understanding of my need to hold and mirror her experience rather than trying to help her to see the ways her experience was "distorted" – an unconscious attempt on my part to make her experience more congruent with *my* understanding of "reality."

Gertrude begins the session by telling me that she's carrying a baby around all the time on her left arm – while she stirs a pot, whatever she does. Gertrude says it seems to be a boy, about one year old.

She talks of feelings of intense anxiety, all the time: is she spending her time constructively? This is a constant worry.

She says she's thinking that she wants to sort out her photos and organize them. They're in big shopping bags.

Her youngest daughter, L, had a retarded friend who died. All three of her children are urging her to sign the sympathy card that L is sending the woman's parents but Gertrude fears that the dead woman's mother could call her (Gertrude) and invite her to tea. Gertrude wouldn't want to go, the woman is boring. Gertrude's middle daughter, Z, says she could just say no if the mother did that, but that is very hard for Gertrude to do. When she's been with the woman, she gets bored and then she's deadened and has nothing to say. Maybe she herself is boring.

There's a silence. It's a wonderful feeling to have this baby on her shoulder. It feels loving and warm. But it's *not* good to think of this baby as Jesus. The Christianity of her childhood did not feel protective. It came through her mother. It must be wonderful for those people who received comfort from Christianity.

This represents the first ten to fifteen minutes of the session. I have not said anything yet so I want to pause and wonder, in hindsight, what we might imagine she is trying to tell me. My inner emotional reaction in this segment is largely focused on the baby. I feel excited and very pleased to hear that she is carrying around a baby. Babies are good, positive images, I feel. What a wonderful development! I am not asking myself what this new birth is. Gertrude, perhaps intuiting unconsciously that I am not well-related to this particular baby, tries to help me a bit: this baby is not Jesus – it's not a savior. Perhaps she is trying to say to me, "Don't be so excited about the baby yet. You don't understand his nature."

The fundamental theme of the hour is announced in the material about the dead retarded woman. Gertrude is resisting the impulse to relate to this sad event. She does not want to express (feel) sympathy for the mother's loss. This is rationalized as being related to the mother's deadness (boringness). The mother's deadness deadens Gertrude. Deadness, deadness, deadness. Gertrude expects that attempts to be with her sadness will fail; it is too much to be borne and she will respond with deadness. She does not yet know much about mourning. She cannot bear to be with her sad deadness, perhaps because she has still been unable to sort out her photos (her history, her life, her self) and organize them. When you don't yet have a self, mourning is not yet possible and experiencing your deadness is intolerable.

As we shall see, the deadness also appears in this hour in that neither Gertrude nor I ever relate in any way to the fact that the week we are in is dying today. We are jointly dead to that immanent loss.

At this point I come in:

I say how sad it is that Gertrude isn't one of the people who received comfort from Christianity.

Although I have no conscious idea of what Gertrude is talking about, I have gotten her feeling right. The baby, as I think will become clear, is not the happy new birth that I am imagining it to be. This baby is a new birth, and it does hold the hopeful seed of her development, but this is a very sad baby. It holds all the terrible grief that the baby Gertrude was unable to process because no one was available to hold her through it, and in this condition the sad dream baby promises to help Gertrude to develop the capacity to mourn, a capacity that she lacks. In so far as the baby is our baby, it speaks to our need as a couple to develop the ability to mourn. On this day, we are unable to mourn the sadness of our coming parting for the weekend.

Gertrude responds to me by saying that the Lutheran Church she was raised in believed you would be resurrected in your body. They said you could have conversations with those you loved, that you could work everything out. That's a comforting thought, she feels.

In the unconscious dance occurring between us, Gertrude is telling me that my understanding her sad feeling is a hopeful and comforting occurrence, virtually a miracle.

Gertrude goes on to say that when her granddaughter couldn't think of anything to do, Gertrude used to tell her that they could sit down and cry. It's good to sit and think about where you are. Gertrude fears getting stuck and thinking nothing new. She's afraid of feeling/being dead. [This is clearly not meant literally.] Even a little action like washing the dishes can bring something new. She's always been afraid of sinking into gray deadness with nothing new to happen.

I say that if she is carrying a baby new things have to happen.

I am almost directly saying that I cannot bear the deadness and sadness she is trying to tell me about. My inner response to the story about sitting down and crying with her granddaughter was completely concrete: I did not think about the image in symbolic terms at all. I was filled with a sense of distress at the idea of saying such a thing to a little girl who is asking for help finding meaning in life. I insist on my image of the happy baby rather than making space for Gertrude's attempt to bring in her deep sadness and despair. I seem to be afraid of sitting down and crying with Gertrude.

Yes, Gertrude responds, but it's a new relationship she has with this baby.

You don't understand who this baby is yet, she is telling me.

When she first learned about Jung, she continues, she had a dream in which her grandmother was very angry at her. Why would that be? Her grandmother was always loving to Gertrude.

Perhaps she feels angry at my refusal to understand what she is trying to tell me. Perhaps she feels that I am angry at her for bringing in these dark, difficult emotions. Can't I remember how to be loving?

Perhaps, she says, the grandmother was angry because Gertrude was always in a rush.

I ask if she might be rushing so fast because she is running from deadness.

At this moment it is not Gertrude who is rushing away from deadness, it is me, her analyst. But, I easily accept that the role of "patient" belongs to the designated patient, perhaps especially because the designated patient in this situation is sufficiently wounded for me to unreflectively distance myself from her, imagining that she is disturbed while I am sane.

Gertrude says that she thinks that is true. Maybe she's also running from lots of guilt and shame.

Which is indeed an aspect of what I feel as I study this hour!

Gertrude says that there was one tree in her grandmother's garden that she and her friends were not allowed to take fruit from. The only time she remembers her grandmother getting mad at her was a time she took a plum from that tree.

I say that sounds like the Garden of Eden.

She laughs. "But this really happened!" she says (thus dismissing any meaning to my association).

The association to the Garden of Eden is obvious and surely relevant, but I have not linked it in any way to Gertrude personally or to the interaction that she and I are involved in. If I had understood the meaning of what she and I were talking about, I might have thought that Gertrude felt as though she had committed a primal sin in disagreeing with me and in feeling (unconsciously) angry at my lack of attunement. God is angry in the Eden myth because humankind has developed the ability to understand good and evil. In the current situation, that ability would allow her and me to see how I am sealing out her darkness and unconsciously refusing to join her in mourning the enormous griefs of her life. This association tells us that there seems to be a taboo today against understanding what is happening – that I will be angry at her if she eats of the tree of knowledge, that I am refusing to take a bite from that fruit. But, perhaps to reassure us both that I am not typically so far off, she goes on to describe

the ways her grandmother functioned as a good mother to her.

I say that she didn't want to make her grandmother mad, and that it seems that reading Jung and being independent made her mad.

Again, without understanding the meaning of our interaction, I have unconsciously understood her feeling well enough. Gertrude is trying to be independent in this hour, to lead me down the path she needs to walk rather than staying in an elated, manic denial of the grief of her life and of this particular day.

Gertrude says she can almost imagine that. She had a dream once where her father-in-law died. Her previous therapist said that these old figures have to die.

There is an old problem in our relationship, perhaps, that we need to let go of. Perhaps the problem relates to the tenacity of the manic defenses that I am carrying with such fervor today; perhaps it is an old attitude that I, as a therapist, have toward the work. Even though by this point in my professional development I no longer think that I have a greater handle on "reality" or "sanity" than my patient does, in my relationship with the quite eccentric Gertrude, I am still caught up in preconsciously imagining that I am going to help her to see the world more accurately.

It's not fun for her to be the oldest [i.e. the oldest remaining person in her extended family]. People look at her and think that she'll die soon. They don't want to see her, people don't want to be with old people.

She feels the ways that I do not respect, or even see, her today.

I say that when we first met she feared I wouldn't want to see an old woman.

Although I do not understand the problem she is trying to tell me about, my basic relatedness brings this memory to my mind. I am unconsciously saying that I can bear her having negative feelings about me and also that I do want to see her even if I am having a rough time of doing so today.

She says she feared that even with Dr. X and she was only forty-eight when she started with him. He said that her growth in consciousness would ripple out into the world. That was such a nice image.

She is hopeful that my wish to see her may lead to a growth in my consciousness that will ripple out to inform all of our work. This hope now emboldens her to talk about very bad feelings regarding how she mothered her children. She feels there could have been much more love from her and from them, too, if she had been able to do a better job. Gertrude talks about this for five to ten minutes and I just listen.

This is a complex association on Gertrude's part. On one level, she is talking about my having been insufficiently loving in this hour. My running away from her despair and grief can reasonably be conceptualized as unloving – I have been unwilling to take on that much suffering for her.

But, this association is also a true expression of her considerable grief and remorse. It is an expression of her being fully in the depressive position at this moment in the hour. She expresses the sadness that she has been trying to tell me about all hour, and I am sitting still and listening.

I say that now she's holding her baby, the love that she's feeling for her baby can ripple out to her children, her grandchildren and even her great-grandchildren.

The hour is coming toward an end and the weekend – which we have studiously not mentioned – is looming. I cannot let the hour end on the authentic sad note she expresses; I bring back the manic energy I've been caught in all hour.

Gertrude is very happy with that idea. It would be like her spirit affecting her descendants. That would be like the holy spirit. This is the end of the hour.

In this hour I carry the intense manic energy that Gertrude more commonly expresses. It does not matter that manic defenses are not my most common. In this hour, the couple Gertrude-and-Barbara are highly dependent on manic defenses and I am the person expressing them. They are neither hers nor mine, they are ours.

The Monday hour that followed this was deeply sad in nature. Gertrude talked about having fallen into "gray, blank deadness" for most of the weekend, and I was able to stay simply attuned to her feeling without trying to brighten it up or to magically disappear her grief. She felt at the end of the Monday hour that she was still immersed in the deadness of the weekend, and at the end of the hour she expressed disappointment in it. I was able to say, "How sad. This is our first hour of the week, and it hasn't really worked for you, has it?" No, she agreed, and we were both able to leave it at that (which seems to me to express the fact that the hour actually *had* worked). It is apparently the separation of the weekend that she-and-I were unable to face on Friday; it is certainly striking that neither one of us mentioned the weekend on either Friday or Monday.

I did not function very well in the hour I have presented, and the reader may wonder at my displaying such a flawed piece of work. But I think that we can see in the unconscious interaction between Gertrude and myself a way that both of us are chewing on the depth of her grief and despair. Because I carry the fear of it, she concentrates on trying to get me better oriented to it, and some small progress in that direction seems to me to have occurred in the course of the hour. The fact that we were able to sit with considerably more of her dark feelings on Monday is partly because the weekend was past rather than looming, but it was also because we had taken this tiny, halting step on Friday.

Almost all therapeutic hours are seriously "flawed." This is how therapy or analysis works. The therapist is listening to extremely charged material. Even if the manifest content of the hour seems empty and dead, it covers over highly emotional areas that bleed into raw archetypal levels of wounding and pain. The patient's undigested agonies call up the primal griefs that the analyst has not yet been able to experience. Envy, jealousy and greed – the whole range of human destructiveness that lurks inside us, waiting to be triggered by the existential terrors that our infantile selves fall into – are invariably hovering in the background of the therapeutic situation. The idea that a therapist *could* do an hour without some flaws is based in the narcissistic complex of pathology that we will explore in the next chapter. Bion (1979/2000) says that when two personalities come together, an "emotional storm" is unleashed. Surely it is an omnipotent fantasy to imagine that the work we do on the deck of a ship caught in a hurricane is going to be centered and competent, lacking serious slips. Bion comments that the turbulence unleashed by the meeting of patient and analyst is unlikely to be felt as an improvement on either person's previous situation. There will always be unconscious currents in the therapist as well as in the patient that push the work hither and yon.

Since patient and analyst *have* come together, Bion suggests that they may try to " 'make the best of a bad job' " (ibid.). The naïve point of view suggests that the patient should not have to grapple with the therapist's pathological complexes, but the reality is that the person that fills the job of analyst (or mother) is only human and that human beings are all profoundly wounded. Healing actually flows from the couple working on the damage arising out of the therapist's tangles and missteps rather than from her flawless functioning. Winnicott (1971) suggests that the therapist will inevitably fail the patient in the specific way that the patient needs to be failed, meaning in a new version of the way his environment originally failed him. It is the working through of this new failure that enables the patient to work through his old undigested pain. In this hour, Gertrude and I are caught in complexes that are more centrally hers than mine even though I express them in the hour. (Of course, I am only able to express them because I *do* share them.) As we follow the hour, we see the current of our approaching her pain constructively and then falling away, via manic defenses, into avoidance, blindness, denial. This back-and-forth motion occurs several times in the hour. The small bits of constructive work that are done help to bring us to a slightly stronger place on Monday and over the years these kinds of difficult hours (along with a fair number of not-so-remarkable good-enough hours, of course) did produce very significant healing.

Chapter 4

The structure of psychopathology[1]

Relatedness is the basis of health but it also exposes us to interpersonal wounding. We protect ourselves from being hurt by calling up anti-related energies: by denigrating the other in our minds, by erasing him through not-seeing his need, by forgetting his wishes when those wishes would cause us distress. All the pathological tendencies in the psyche push us toward an anti-related approach. Anti-related energies underlie the American culture's predilection for an extraverted manic "friendliness" that precludes real relatedness because its goal is to make everyone into a friend, bypassing the much more substantial issue of finding the individual(s) with whom one has a real heart connection. Similarly, these anti-linking forces create the British culture's reliance on schizoid defences. In Chapters 2 and 3 we have explored the basic structure and operation of the growing psyche: the nature of the unconscious and the fundamental work it is always engaged in, turning the onslaught of life into thinkable and feel-able symbols. In this chapter we will look at the structure of our anti-relational aspects, of the parts of ourselves that value stability over development, safety over creativity. In the next chapter, we will explore the dynamic interplay between the energies that pull us to grow and the energies that resist new ways of being.

The theoretical perspectives we explored in the previous two chapters are archetypal: they describe elements of our inborn emotional nature rather than elements that may or may not arise depending on the individual's personal experiences. We have been thinking about the nature of the unconscious psyche and its development into the world of lived experience; about the fundamental processes that enable people to be conscious and to reflect, to orient toward people and the world as they are rather than as we wish they would be; about the inherent tension – torment would be a more accurate word – that colors the human condition, pulling us into relatedness by facing openly into the moment and pushing us against relatedness by evading the

---

1 Much of the manuscript in this chapter was originally published in *Jung Journal* (www.ucpressjournals.com). Reproduced with kind permission.

pain of that openness, a tension that was imaged in the religion that swept the Western world as a crucifixion.

In this chapter, I turn to the internal structure that organizes our anti-relatedness tendencies, the structure that underlies psychopathology. Although the particular form in which we know this complex is at least partly shaped by our Western culture, the basic configuration is archetypal because the fundamental need for relationship is part of human nature, as is the vulnerability that relationship brings and the consequent terror of submitting to it. Cultures can elaborate our need for relatedness in many ways, but its primacy in grounding emotional health cannot be changed. The structure we will explore here is a kind of ur-complex that determines the shapes that emotional woundedness can take in our contemporary Western world. Much of what this ur-complex organizes is so deeply ingrained and widespread in our world that only a limited perspective is possible regarding it; we cannot say how the same human difficulties that shape this template in our world might play out in a traditional culture that values the group rather than the individual, for example. Some elements are universal and some are culturally determined and the deeply entrenched nature of the pattern makes it impossible to say what the proportions of these two elements might be. But the organizing template I will describe in this chapter is, I believe, a central one in all our Western psyches and in the inner worlds of our patients, friends and relations. Whatever perspective on it we can gain will be valuable.

Anti-related energy is narcissistic energy, where "narcissism" carries its colloquial (and mythic) meaning of an egocentric over-valuation of the self. Relatedness and narcissism are the two poles between which human beings are inherently torn. What Freud called the pleasure principle and the reality principle can be understood as the wish to magically or omnipotently arrange the world in the way that I would most like it to be versus relating to the facts of reality, including, especially, the facts of other people who have wishes and needs just as I do. This acceptance of reality does not mean that the individual ceases to try to find ways to meet his needs. Rather, it means that in that attempt he is respectful of the needs of others, too. It does not mean that he will never put himself first, but it does mean that he will not *always* put himself first. Sometimes, his awareness of reality will lead him to think that although he wants one thing, the needs of others or of a given other are strong enough for him to willingly support the other's need instead of his own. The perspective that brings us to relatedness is a point of view that includes the "I" as a member of a group, whether that group is one's nuclear family, one's inner society or the family of man. From this vantage point, one tries to be fair rather than triumphant. Contemporarily, there is considerable academic research into altruism, one of the many words describing relatedness, and it is now clear that many animals, certainly including human beings, have strong inborn tendencies toward concern for their loved ones.

This description of related and anti-related energies applies to the inner world in an exactly parallel fashion. To the degree that the individual is trapped in a narcissistic orientation to the world, she is trapped in a narcissistic orientation to herself. She is caught in the defense of triumph, wanting to dominate her deeper self, even to annihilate it so that her "I" can be the hero, conquering and subduing all the other energies of her soul. Perhaps the reader can feel the seductive lure of this erasure of weakness and neediness, of all the helpless, lost, confused aspects of the self, but the loss of these vulnerable parts means the loss of the new life that is trying to be born. These dependent aspects of the self that need help and that therefore pull us into relationships with other people are the parts of us that can grow, that can learn new ways of looking at the world, that can be creative. It may be more comfortable to amputate them, but, oh, what a loss!

Freud assumed that the selfish attitude is primary and that it is only through painful experiences in the world that the infant learns to orient to others, but the infant research of the last few decades has definitively disproved this assumption. Neonates seek interpersonal connection from the first hours of their waking life. They focus intensely on human faces rather than random images; they know their parents' voices from their intrauterine existence and are soothed by these familiar people more easily than by strangers; they quickly learn the odor of their mother and of her milk and demonstrate a strong preference for her over strangers. There is considerable evidence that when the mother is hurt or frightened by the infant's aggression or by its difficulties with feeding, the baby responds, perhaps by truncating its protests, perhaps with depression or even despair that can manifest biologically in illnesses or emotionally with limpness or timidity or in some other way. Depth therapists find overwhelming evidence of patients' fears of hurting those they love, whether the loved ones are parents or spouses or the therapist herself. Our need for relatedness is a major organizer of our behavior at least from birth on.

But relatedness is a terrible source of suffering in addition to being the wellspring of love and joy, for a related stance is inherently vulnerable. In this chapter, we turn to the characterological organization that supports the human flight from the reality of interdependence to a "reality" where the "I" is the most important – or perhaps the only important – person in the world (both inner and outer).

As I describe this complex of psychopathology,[2] we must remember that I speak of something that cannot exist in the form I am describing. Winnicott commented that there is no such thing as an infant. At this point in the

---

2 Technically speaking, what I am describing is not a complex *per se*. Each person will fill in this structure, this ur-complex, with his or her personal images and with dynamics that are shaped partly by the particular familial and social patterns to which he or she was exposed when growing up. What I am describing is the underlying organizing structure *before* it is filled in with the "material of conscious experience" (Jung, 1938, para 155).

development of depth psychology, we could say in exactly the same spirit that there is no such thing as an individual. The self, no matter how selfish it is attempting to be, exists only in relationship. Whether the relationship is with an outer person or with an inner figure, the "individual" is never an isolated unit that can be studied on its own. Thus, we meet this universal pattern when sitting across from someone else, whether in a business meeting, a social inter-action, or in the consulting room. The other's complex of psychopathology will constellate my own. My ability to tease out what is going on between me and the other depends as much on self observation as it does on my ability to perceive him. The contours of his complex are determined partly by the contours of mine. If one member of the dyad can keep his footing outside the complex, the other's relationship to his complex will be dramatically affected. If one person's complex is too powerful at this moment, both people will be pulled into the orbit of narcissism, even if only one of them is acting out the complex. Whether or not a person acknowledges the web of human relation-ships within which he lives does not change the fact that he cannot exist as an isolated unit. However, in this chapter I will describe the pattern as though it existed inside an individual because understanding its basic shape can enable the therapist or analyst to notice its operation inside herself as well as in the patient.

As I described in Chapter 3, Jungians think about the psyche as organized into complexes. These are interactive patterns of emotional relatedness that the individual has been unable to digest and integrate, leaving him vulnerable to unconscious enactments when a given complex is triggered. Most therap-ists are familiar with Freud's Oedipal complex. Like parental complexes or inferiority complexes or divine child complexes, the Oedipal complex is one form that the universal pattern I will describe in this chapter can take. We are looking here at the foundational skeleton of any complex, even though the shape of my complex may appear at first glance very different from yours.

Neville Symington, a British Middle School psychoanalyst who has been deeply influenced by Bion, describes this universal complex in *A Pattern of Madness* (2002) and a large part of this chapter is my translation and interpretation of his very original and creative idea. His work has been underappreciated because it is painful to see this complex. It is easy to think of narcissism as a pathology that touches *some* people but not *me*; it becomes painful when we recognize the way narcissism and relatedness are at war in each of our psyches. Symington's perspective challenges many of our basic assumptions about the nature of a healthy emotional orientation. Truly look-ing at this structure pulls the reader up short and confronts her with her own selfish and destructive tendencies. To the extent that the reader is able to emotionally absorb the ideas I will present in this chapter, she is apt to suffer. Suffering is one basic ingredient for growth, but it is also, of course, painful. Our instinctual natures pull us into resisting our legitimate suffering regard-less of our conscious beliefs. This template that organizes our pathological aspects is also difficult to understand because it is a very deep layer of the psyche. It is hard to find solid ground to stand on outside it because the pattern is shared to some extent by all of us.

The narcissistic complex

As I have mentioned, one polarity that Bion notices from time to time (e.g. 1962, 1970) is narcissism versus social-ism. Bion offers no substantial definitions of his terms, but they relate to the balance between a selfish orientation to the "I" as contrasted with awareness of and concern for others, including the not-I others who personify the unconscious parts of the self. His invention of the term "social-ism" is symptomatic of the lack of relatedness within the psychoanalytic field. The opposite of narcissism is relatedness, but instead of using that word, Bion invents this new one. (As we shall see, narcissism leads the person to want to be the greatly admired expert who is *right*. I believe that Bion's inability to use the very ordinary English words, related and relationship, reflects unconscious narcissistic pressures inside him that he is consciously struggling with in this theory.)

Bion does not develop his notion that whether someone is growing or deteriorating psychologically depends on the immediate balance between social-istic and narcissistic currents in the psyche. Symington, perhaps intrigued by Bion's blanket statement, has developed a theory that all psychopathology can be understood as a form of narcissism, where "narcissism" implies arrogance, selfishness and an inability to love. In this approach, narcissism may look very different from the popular image of someone who thinks himself superior to the ordinary run of people. Indeed, the individual may consciously feel inferior. But regardless of the presenting symptomatology, the person's focus is on him*self* rather than on himself *and* the group. The narcissist may even seem compassionate in his behavior, but if his secret focus is on how virtuous and loving he is being and on the "credits" he is racking up in heaven or in the eyes of the world for his kindness, the orientation is narcissistic rather than related.

What is at issue is the person's underlying psychological organization – the unconscious complex that structures the person's perceptions, judgments and relationships. This complex exists in all of us and we shall see how individuals who seem anything but "narcissistic" can be seriously dominated by it. But the reader must try to let go of the pejorative tinge that the word carries: first, because it is the nature of the psyche to be torn between this narcissistic complex, which we shall explore in this chapter, and the healthy growth complex organized by the Self that we explored in Chapter 2; and second, because in this complex of pathology the individual is so captivated by terror that he forgets his connections with others and behaves, secretly if not flagrantly, in a completely selfish manner. That selfishness injures his own self at least as drastically as it hurts the others around him. The point is not the selfishness.

The point is panic about survival, whether literal survival or annihilation by levels of pain that the person feels unable to bear. The individual who is possessed by this orientation deserves compassion, not blame.

Symington (2002) describes madness as "a pattern of interlocking elements that distort perception, damage the self, and prevent emotional freedom" (p. 79). In this definition, anything that destroys self-fulfillment and wholeness is "mad." Following Bion, Symington imagines that each of us contains a psychotic part and a sane part. When fundamental anxieties are triggered, psychotic defenses are constellated and while the person's behavior and words may seem quite ordinary, the thinking behind that behavior contradicts consensual reality in dramatic ways. For example, when people try the same thing over and over, unable to learn that their approach isn't working, their "thinking" is actually an inability to think and we can appropriately call it "mad" even if it is common. The quotidian experience of imagining that one's personal failings are seen, remembered and discussed by large numbers of people is similarly unrealistic, as is the fantasy that one can thoroughly hide one's personal failings by refusing to know about them. The defense of putting one's disowned aspects into other people – of projective identification – is both mad and universal. We do not call the young patient "psychotic" when he tells us that his childhood was perfect, although we know that his belief can rest only on a severely distorted pattern of seeing and remembering. Much of the ordinary behavior of well-functioning people falls into this category, for madness encompasses anything self-damaging, and the psyche is eternally torn between healthy growing currents and destructive ones.

The original self-deceptive and self-destructive act is the rejection of parts of the self, something that we all engage in, no matter how developed we may be. Rejecting aspects of the self is the opposite of relating to them. Jung called these rejected parts of the self "the shadow," and as we have discussed, the concept includes positive aspects of the person as well as negative. Symington calls the energy that expels these unwanted elements "the intensifiers:" envy, jealousy and greed, fueled by the terror that stokes the omnipotent defenses of infancy.[3] As we shall see, these emotions "intensify" the rigid armor the individual constructs to protect him from authentic contact with others. They "intensify" the violence with which the person projects his unwanted elements into others, projections that liquefy his inner self, leaving him with the feeling that he is just a jelly inside, lacking spine, perhaps lacking even a self.

Let us look at how this might work, focusing on a positive element of the self that has been denied, because the rejection of one's positive capacities is

---

3 Symington is specific: the emotions involved are envy, jealousy and greed, not emotions *such as* envy, jealousy and greed. I held back for a long time, imagining that the later formulation was surely more realistic, but I cannot actually imagine a destructive emotion that does not emerge from these three, so I have capitulated.

harder to understand intuitively than the rejection of something negative. Carol's mother hid her destructive envy of her daughter by completely devoting herself to Carol. She led Carol's Girl Scout troupe, she assisted in her classroom, and when Carol became a cheerleader, her mother became the cheerleaders' parent liaison, scheduling and coordinating their practices, performances and trips, choosing and arranging their uniforms and generally making herself indispensable to every aspect of their existence. Even when Carol became the lead cheerleader, she felt overshadowed by her mother. As an adult, Carol felt terribly inadequate compared with everyone else. She became a biochemist, worked for a large medical research company, and was promoted to a responsible position that involved giving a major presentation to important people. Although the presentation went well – she was able to persuade the relevant people of the value of her project – she felt overwhelming shame and self-loathing about her performance, even though she could not say what she felt ashamed about. Certain that people felt scorn and pity for her "failure," she discounted their praise as insincere and motivated by pity. She tried to go on as the leader of her project but felt so exposed and so certain that colleagues considered her wanting that she left her job several months later and took a less responsible and less interesting position elsewhere for a reduced salary.

By consistently diminishing herself, Carol protected herself from her own rage and from her inner mother's envy as well as from everyone else's envy. At the same time, she truncated her ambition, a potentially constructive derivative of envy, and instead loathed herself for the corrosive envy she felt toward all the people who didn't have to destroy their capacities as she did. Rather than feeling her envy and using it to compete constructively, she turned it on herself and ate herself up inside. The intolerable envy that had permeated her childhood relationship with her mother and that continued to saturate her inner world was kept at bay by diminishing herself in such dramatic ways. She rejected her competence to avoid being exposed to the suffering that would have arisen had she recognized her mother's envy, felt the severity of the injury it dealt her, and taken up the struggle with her own envy.

We need a loving inner or outer other to provide enough safety and protection to make an experience of vulnerability bearable. When we lack a nurturing presence, the intensifiers – emotions which tend to come together with one or the other of them becoming dominant – rush up to protect us. Instead of feeling the terror of lost helplessness, envy, jealousy or greed, powered by omnipotence, make the frightened individual feel larger than life. *The Incredible Hulk*, a 2008 Hollywood movie, describes this mechanism in a comic book-level story. Under emotional stress, physicist Bruce Banner turns into a giant green monster. (The writers' instinctive choice of green, the color of jealousy, one of the intensifiers, is interesting.) Instead of feeling little, rage puffs up a person. She becomes huge. Unable to hold a feeling of weakness, envy of the apparently centered other takes over and the individual feels enraged and gigantic. Or greed roars in, demanding all the attention, security and comfort available. Or perhaps jealousy fills the space with the fantasy that if she can be the only person into whom the other pours his love, then she will have enough. In fantasy, the no-longer-weak individual violently murders her rivals. The omnipotent rage that envelops the little one caught in an unsafe situation fuels these destructive emotions and allows the frightened person to look big instead of little, both to herself and to others. The "I" is all powerful, not small and helpless; it is the vehicle of a towering rage. Those parts of the self that feel weak and vulnerable are amputated. "All the better," the puffed-up and no-longer-frightened individual feels. But the sensibility, the energy, the potential of the expelled parts of the self are lost to the "I;" they go underground and live on, pushing the person into compulsive behavior that deprives her of opportunities to grow.

When parts of the self are rejected, they are projected, often violently, into others or into the body, distorting perception, damaging relationships, causing emotional and/or physical pain, sometimes even serious bodily illness. Total sanity would require the acceptance of all parts of the self. The act of acceptance, of holding each aspect within the self's wholeness, transforms the negative elements. It is only from the conscious experience of fear that one can forge courage, for example, for courage is formed from the raw energy that first manifests as fear. A lack of fear in a dangerous situation is not brave, it is foolish. The act of acceptance is the integrative act. Sanity and madness are thus both rooted in what Symington calls inner (unconscious) "choices" that lead the person either to an attitude of relatedness that accepts all the parts of the self that emerge or to an attitude of condemnation toward whatever arises inside him or her that looks strange or weak. Since we treat others as we treat our inner selves, these same "choices" will manifest in outer behavior and in some cases (but by no means all) will make the individual look "narcissistic" – vain, inflated and selfish.

"Choice" is a problematic word for unconscious decisions. As we have explored, Bion believed that the ability to bear frustration – the frustration of not understanding, of lostness, helplessness, dependency, vulnerability – determines an individual's capacity to take up the healthy attitude of acceptance toward herself. The strength and flexibility of the individual's inner ♀ ♂ as well as her capacity to comfortably navigate the PS ↔ D sequence that reflection requires, depends on the degree to which empathic primary attachment figures supported the little one in her vulnerability and bore the pain she could not bear, thus fostering the development of her ability to think. At every stage of life, the person needs assistance if she is to tolerate and process frightening experiences of helplessness and need. Factors outside the person's control decide whether she can respond thoughtfully rather than reactively to her vulnerability.

In practice, the conscious attitude is the only psychological element that one may choose, and even that choice is limited. One's attitude can respond to conscious attempts to moderate it, but because attitudes have deep unconscious roots, they, too, shift slowly. They differ in degree, however, from something like perception, which is completely controlled by the unconscious. This means, for example, that conscious attempts to take up an attitude of interest in what one really feels and to bear it can help the person to find her authentic self. But even when the person is trying to know the truth of her experience, her defenses – her unconscious "choices" – can easily trip her up. The choice to react automatically rather than thoughtfully is typically made by someone who feels unbearably endangered by inner or outer forces, someone who does not possess the psychological structures she would need to consciously hold these terrifying experiences and to reflect on them rather than reacting. The "I" sitting or lying in the consulting room may have been completely shut out of the decision-making process behind the choice. We will come back to this question of choice later.

Symington maps an extremely deep structure of the psyche. Imagine that at a macro-level the entire psyche is comprised of two interpenetrating complexes. There is a relational complex that is healthy and growing, actively working to find the path of individuation by meeting and listening to all the disparate parts of the self. Then there is another complex, which brings around one great table all the parts of the person – all the mini-complexes – that are pathological: the tendencies that urge the individual to space out in front of the tube or to lose himself in substance abuse, that undermine his wish for a close loving relationship by leading him to approach those he loves in a hateful, suspicious manner. These are the parts of the person that subvert individuation, the negative thrusts in the psyche that have been labeled aspects of "the death instinct," or the root of "negative therapeutic reactions." Herein lies the psychic energy that leads someone to come late after a particularly good analytic hour; that prompts the parent to remove his child from therapy just as the work is beginning to gel; that sends me out for a donut because some unhappiness is rumbling around in the background and I'd do anything rather than sit still and feel it. This is the energy that fears the vulnerability of love and that fosters the substitution of a power drive for eros, for when I feel my need for love I am weak and must rely on the unpredictable impulses of others. But if I center myself in the power drive, an illusory experience of control and potency arises. Anti-related energy fuels the emotional connection that Bion called "H," the hate-link that we will look at in the next chapter, the negative attachment to an inner or outer other that rejects growth for the safety of stasis. Caught in this self-destructive complex, the individual has no freedom: he reacts blindly, lacking the space to think. This pathological constellation includes the complex that Donald Kalsched (1996) describes as the Protector, and it is related to Herbert Rosenfeld's (1987) Omnipotent Narcissistic Object Relations Structure. I will look at the way Rosenfeld's ideas connect with Symington's later in this chapter, but the latter's construct is broader and more encompassing than either

Kalsched's or Rosenfeld's. Symington is trying to describe the fundamental template that structures all psychopathology.

God and worm

A complex is a drama occurring within the psyche, a stuck drama where the same pattern repeats endlessly in different costumes and with different actors but always telling the same story, with the same basic characters, and having the same outcome. Complexes structure our relationships with others as well as our attitudes, our perceptions and our judgments – all elements that we have seen to be highly subject to distortion, all of the time, by everyone. The drama we are looking at here is a basic template. The individual's personal experiences, especially within his family, build the specific ways that this person's complex will express itself. Symington's structure underlies the unique way a given person's psychopathology will appear in the world.

The drama that Symington describes is a two-person play, a tragedy starring god and worm. In fact, god and worm are really only one person in two incarnations, but even they know nothing about their secret reality. Around god and worm swirl great storms of energy in terrifying patterns that a depth psychologist might label envy, greed and jealousy. If the cardboard-cut-out creatures god and worm could imagine anything, they would imagine the energy patterns as fixed – that envy is envy and always shall be. But in fact they are simply patterns, and as Jung (1956) describes, in the right circumstances, energy can transform from envy to admiration, from greed to generosity and from jealousy to comradery. Worm's panic in this dangerous atmosphere of uncontained destructive energy is rooted in his sense of his insides: faced with the dangers of life, he feels as if he is all bits and fragments jiggling about in a jelly. A thick crust surrounds the jelly so that no one can penetrate and know him, but though he may look like a medieval knight in armor who has to be hoisted onto his horse with a system of pulleys, he unconsciously feels that he has no bones, no shape, no definition.

And so, with all his might, worm gloms onto god. God knows everything and in her omnipotence she solves all problems instantly, magically dispersing emotional pain and zapping terrifying internal energies into outer others. She is a puffed-up hot air balloon. Painful emotions may be present – grief, for example, or shame or guilt. But neither god nor worm need ever feel them because they never have to reflect. They react immediately to any difficulty, most frequently disguising frightening emotions of smallness behind something big like certainty or rage, certainly never thinking a personal thought that might leave them vulnerable to making mistakes! Worm will consciously feel oh-so-inferior and will worship the omniscient god he has chosen to pair himself with, but appearances can be deceiving. His true inadequacies are denied and a global sense of inferiority is presented as a cover for exploring the complexities of his strengths and weaknesses. By adopting a stance of blanket inferiority that makes it impossible for him ever to come up against his real limitations, worm avoids the impossible attempt to find his authentic size in the community of human beings, a lifelong process that depends on the continuing emergence of more and more aspects of the true self. And by modeling his thoughts and choices on god's instructions, he knows he is thinking and doing everything perfectly.

God demands absolute obedience and outlaws individual thinking. God, who wants only to be worshipped by everyone at all times, is so busy inflating herself like the little man behind the curtain in *The Wizard of Oz*, that she also never thinks, but simply seizes a system of thought that someone has told her is It and swallows it down greedily. The system can be analytical psychology or psychoanalysis just as easily as it can be Christianity, fascism, constitutional law, homeopathy or cutting-edge scientific medicine. The important thing is simply never to think outside the boundaries of whatever box has been chosen.

As I noted above, it is uncomfortable to recognize the ubiquitous nature of this complex. The history of psychoanalysis and analytical psychology is rife with examples of it. One example is the notion that a failure to use the couch or that twice-a-week work cannot possible qualify as "analysis" because the experts (another word for "gods") laid down other rules. This protects the therapist/analyst from the much more insecure state of not knowing if his work with a given patient is reaching an adequate depth. The idea touted by a shrinking number of classical Jungians that psychoanalysts have nothing to offer them, that Jung's understanding of analytic technique represents the last word on the subject, is equally mad and equally revelatory of this god–worm paradigm that imagines the Possession of a Truth, thus solving the problem of insecurity for all time. If this complex were not powerful inside of us, we would not have to struggle with drive theory, for drive theory as a fundamental explanatory model of the psyche is recommended only by the thinking of a highly idealized person who formulated his ideas more than a hundred years ago. It would not have been such a slow and uphill battle to let go of Freud's ideas about infancy when the data of infant observation so dramatically contradict them. When a writer justifies her own point of view by citing obscure footnotes of her preferred analytic genius (Freud, Klein, Jung, etc.), the underlying pattern is revealed.

So here is the pattern, and when a human being falls into it, he falls into the experience of either god or worm with the other half in the unconscious and projected out onto people in his environment. When a person is identified with god, we see some form of what is colloquially called "narcissism." When he is identified with worm, we may see something that looks like the opposite; what is important is that the inner structure that organizes the person's being-in-the-world is the same.

People tend to easily identify with worm. Individuals who look narcissistic in the ordinary sense of the term are often as responsive to the image of worm as are people who look timid and self-effacing. Inside, it seems that even highly supercilious individuals know what it is like to feel inferior to virtually everyone else. On the other hand, so-called normal people do not imagine themselves to be god. They may feel quite sure they know how to cope with more or less any crisis; in quotidian behavior they may convey to colleagues that they know all the answers or at least so many of them that they can dismiss others' uncertainty with a wave of the hand; they may quite madly maintain, for example, that they are "never frightened" – or express some other omnipotent fantasy of invulnerability. They know cognitively that they are not omnipotent or omniscient, but they behave unconsciously as though they were. Unconsciously they are identified with god and projecting worm into friends or colleagues who are aware of their anxious, insecure selves. But because everyone knows it is mad to imagine oneself to be god, and that it is frowned upon to think one knows all the answers, the arrogant narcissist hides his own unconscious assumptions from himself.

Unlike Klein or Bion, who would see innate envy as the source of this complex of psychopathology, Symington sees childhood trauma as its root. His formulation acknowledges the determinative role played by how related one's original attachment figures were. He suggests that the intensity of the complex parallels the severity of the infantile trauma. There is an interaction between a given infant/child's innate capacity to experience emotional distress – to bear frustration – and his parenting figures' ability to relate to his needs. This interaction determines the degree to which an adult can tolerate a conscious recognition of his smallness. It leaves each of us with a specific inner container for the processing of suffering; the adequacy of that container depends on the particular mix of innate and environmental factors. Envy, jealousy and greed are the archetypal responses to feelings of endangerment that emerge when (as always) this interaction leaves the person with some exposure to experiences she cannot process. Destructive energies are innate in the sense that they are pre-programmed responses to unbearable experiences of danger, but the infant does not meet the parent's love with envy. She begins by meeting love with love; the intensifiers develop in response to experiences of not being held and cherished. They protect the baby from her pain and are related to the inner figure that Kalsched (op. cit.) calls the Protector: a domineering bully who berates the person inside whom he lives for any weakness or vulnerability. This "protects" him or her from taking up their suffering and working with it. This tormentor also frightens away anyone the individual might turn to for nurturance, thus protecting the battered individual from the experience of being taken care of, an experience that must bring up feelings of smallness.

The traumas of infancy and childhood flow from the failure of big people to empathize compassionately with little ones, failures that vary a great deal in magnitude but that are universal. Looked at from a structural perspective, these failures leave the child unable to empathize with himself in a compassionate and related way, the *sine qua non* of processing emotional experiences. To whatever extent this is the case, the result is catastrophic for the little one, who grows up with deficits in the apparatus that he needs to function in the world. Envy, rather than being innate, is a result of an unbearable inner hole that the person unconsciously knows about. Symington's very hopeful formulation suggests that the coloration of an individual's complex of pathology is the infantile trauma transformed. The complex is the replacement for the creative spirit that the trauma broke. It is the "fossilized presence of the catastrophe" (Symington, 2002, p. 133). Thus, the complex offers us the possibility of exhuming the ancient disaster and integrating it into our wholeness.

Why does Symington label all this "narcissistic?" He defines narcissism in the colloquial way as self-centeredness and "I"-ism, an orientation that worm would certainly imagine as alien to himself. Let us see. Drawing on extensive philosophical reading, Symington describes the world as divided into two layers, the contingent and the necessary, a division that is comparable to the Eastern religions' distinction between the illusory, ever-changing world of our senses and the Ground of Being or the Absolute. Freud was aware of the contingent layer when he suggested that human motivation is founded on the pleasure principle, the compulsion to evade pain. Caught in the ever-changing world of the senses, I want what feels best to ME at this moment, and only because it furthers my immediate self-interest do I learn to accommodate to others.

As we have explored, both Jung and Bion rejected the pleasure principle as the fundamental human motivation, substituting a search for wholeness[4] or for truth as the core dynamism of the psyche. This desire for *all* of one's authentic self is a relational drive that, in health, trumps the selfish desire for pleasure. This drive comes from the necessary layer of existence, from the realm of Ultimate Truth and the Absolute. It is a search for who the person really is, rather than an attempt to feed the transient hungers of any passing moment. Instead of trying to be the person she wants to be, in the necessary layer, the individual is looking for her true self. Both Jung and Bion believed that the core human impulse is not to feed the "I" with luxuries or untruths that will silence inner voices of distress. In health, the individual strives to hear those painful inner voices and to engage with her personal suffering, for this is how she will find herself. Obviously, this orientation can easily conflict with the search for pleasure. Symington maintains that the pathological complex that leads the person to look for pleasure and its transient, self-indulgent soothings (including such pacifiers as money, power and fame) is the root cause of all human "madness," from the greed and corruption of a dictator

---

4 Remember Symington's formulation that madness consists of rejecting parts of the self and that sanity depends on welcoming all of them.

to the murderousness of the serial killer, from the coldness of the unempathic mother to such physical ills as back pain, cancer and heart disease.

In the contingent layer, ruled by Freud's pleasure principle, we are trapped in reactive, instinctual behavior and are unable to reflect. Consciousness is impossible. Only by holding both the contingent and the necessary layers do we have choices. (Again: a choice requires holding two points of view at once.) For example, if someone taunts me, my (defensive) instinct is either to lash out or to flee, to save myself without regard for anyone else. If, instead of reacting, I am able to remember my values, my personal sense of good and evil, my ideas about the meaning of my life and of the current situation (all elements of the necessary rather than the contingent layer, for these are aspects of who I am, not of how I am feeling at this moment), then I will have a choice. I will be able to think. I may respond angrily, I may retreat, but the response will include an awareness both of the taunter as a human being and of my connections to the other aspects of myself and the other people who will be affected by my response. In the instinctual response of fight or flight, the person values only his conscious "I." This response is "mad" (i.e. destructive of freedom) for it has not been chosen, it has taken him over. In Jungian language, he has become possessed by a complex. The chosen response is the essence of freedom.

One way to understand the differentiation between the necessary and contingent layers of the self is to pay attention to what people are easily able to talk about and what they consider private. The contingent layer is freely shared. Movies, recipes, the ups and downs of the children's encounters on the soccer field, even the way one's spouse leaves his or her detritus lying about: these are all contingent elements. The individual has feelings about these things, but the feelings belong to today, not to eternity. Thus, the man who fears and denies his own homosexual impulses may describe *Brokeback Mountain*, the 2005 movie that explores two men's homosexual love for each other, as "not interesting." The idea that it frightens him will be a secret, probably from himself. His fear reflects a deep truth about who he is (although the contours of that truth could shift if he allowed himself to engage with his unacceptable impulses). Similarly, my distress at my son not qualifying for the A-list soccer team is something I can talk about at a cocktail party; but my shameful sense that I love him less wholeheartedly than I love his more athletic little brother is something I will not mention, not even to myself. The "insufficient" concern that I carry for my athletically clumsy boy reflects an injury deep inside me; it reflects something central about who I am. My wounded ability to love exposes the necessary layer.

Symington suggests that a thoughtful response will always be based in love rather than power. A free response will embody relatedness. We can see the truth of this when we remember that the way we treat the other is always the way we treat our inner selves. The "choice" of the complex-possessed person to disregard others is compulsive behavior that reflects his disregard of his own deeper self. It is rooted in an inability to bear some kind of suffering. This inability leads the person to latch onto envy, jealousy or greed as an escape from the unbearable vulnerability that has welled up inside him. These emotions (the intensifiers) are anti-relational in nature. Caught up in envy, jealousy or greed, the other is of no account, he is hated and feared rather than respected. His value lies only in what he can do for *me*.

Suffering is the sine qua non of development. We need loving experiences of support and cherishment as a foundation that enables us to bear the suffering, but it is only through bearing suffering that one can think or create. The instinctually programmed but pathological behavior that avoids emotional pain may look free, but it is actually the opposite. The person is impelled by inadequately robust inner structures to flee from her authentic responses; she has no real choice. Returning here to worm, the reader can perhaps see that worm's responses to life, based on an axiomatic belief in his own inferiority, turn out to be fundamentally self-centered. He gloms onto god, attempting to Know Everything and to always be Right because he is so frightened by the insecurity of life. He is unable to hold much authentic concern for others no matter how much he may want to because he is so caught up in his terror. His "solution" to the terror leaves him prey to violent, destructive passions – envy, jealousy and greed – passions that he cannot process. Dominated by a belief in his fundamental inferiority, he is certainly not looking for his authentic self. He wants to be different from who he really is, not to find himself. Unconsciously he knows that his inner capacities to deal with the emotional demands of life are inadequate. He cannot imagine that working with his inadequacy could change it.

The result is a deep selfishness. In the case of worm, the selfishness will be cloaked in a deferential and humble manner, in requests for guidance and advice that (of course) he will typically find to be not quite right. In the case of god, her behavior will look overtly narcissistic, but it is important to remember that god, too, is caught in a belief in her inner inferiority. Her conscious sense is that she is extremely capable but in her complex she does not feel safe enough to think a truly personal thought. She subscribes to a philosophy that she knows is Right, even if this philosophy is a very unusual one representing a tiny splinter group of the larger society. The important thing is the terror that has led her to cling to a worldview that will protect her, and that prevents her from actually thinking about what makes sense to her. Like worm, god cannot listen to another person's unique point of view and think about it. The result is a fundamental self-centeredness of which she is completely unaware.

In our culture this is a universal pathology. It is commonplace to suggest that narcissism is the leading unconsciousness of our age. The influence of this constellation penetrates into every therapist's work for we are all unconscious carriers of the complex and the world we live in reinforces and fosters it. Theories of psychopathology and therapeutic treatment are thus often distorted by the theorist's personal version of the universal complex. The unfortunate psychoanalytic use of the word "object" to mean "person" as well as parts of people or inanimate objects is an example of our collective imprisonment in this distorted worldview. The influence of this pathological orientation is revealed in the way "object relations" are so often talked about when the subject being discussed is actually "relationships." There are, of course, people who treat others as objects, but they are seriously narcissistically wounded rather than more-or-less healthy individuals. Therapists cling to this kind of language because its arcane quality reminds us that we belong to a secret fraternity that knows about deep truths that are hidden from merely ordinary people; we are gods. The common "therapeutic" behavior of translating the patient's language for him into the language we learned in our training (as though "penis-as-a-link" is a truer or deeper symbol than "spine," for example) is narcissistic, imagining as it does that *my* metaphor is better than yours. This language protects us from experiencing our emotional dependence on the human beings we so expertly dissect ("analyze") in our papers and case conferences. The standard psychological approach of sorting people into various psychiatric categories based on their outer symptoms is also a fundamentally pathological approach: it obscures real understanding, which must be based on inner processes, not surface symptoms, and it fosters, for the psychiatric sorter, the illusion that *they* are disturbed and *I* am sane.

The common therapeutic focus on helping people to get or accomplish what they "want" frequently supports our secret, underlying narcissism. There is an unexamined implication that being thin, or "taking care of oneself" by buying luxuries, or striving for fame and power is "healthy." Sometimes seeking things of this nature can be important in compensating for a complex-based attitude that masochistically deprives the self but frequently supporting the patient's desire for a Lexus to replace his Corolla simply feeds an empty inner culture based on greed, an inner world cut off from the interpersonal love that would meet the person's deeper need for nourishment.

This narcissistic complex distorts psychotherapeutic thinking in an even more fundamental and destructive way. The literature can often sound as though the therapist, if she works hard enough, can achieve perfection. Successful cases are typically presented without meaningful descriptions of the extreme problems that emerged for the analyst in the work. If we study run-of-the-mill hours in therapies that can be shown to be extremely effective, we will see many startling "errors" on the therapist's part. In the previous chapter I described my work with Gertrude, an analysis that proved deeply transformative for her, and I presented a process record of a vividly flawed hour taken from the last third of the work. In this hour we saw my inability to hold the depths of her despair and our unconscious dance as she-and-I-together worked on my limitations, hoping to help me enough to enable me to do my job. Tracking the unconscious communications back and forth through the hour shows me making small but noticeable progress in this direction. It is unusual for therapists to present their less-than-adequate hours for public scrutiny. This is true even when the writer's focus is on the way that errors and their working through are the nourishing meat and potatoes of the work. Patrick Casement (1991), who offers blow-by-blow descriptions of his ordinary (and therefore terribly flawed) work, is a notable exception to the profession-wide avoidance of analysis or therapy as it really exists. His very flawed work is actually very good.

The therapist/analyst who understands the many levels of interaction occurring at any given moment, who remains solidly grounded through the emotional tempest of the work, who is not pulled into the patient's complexes and does not discharge her own, and who can produce the transformative interpretation at the moment it is needed, does not exist. The more we recognize the infinite depths of the psyche and the intensity of the turmoil that both individuals must struggle with at every moment of a clinical hour, the more we must acknowledge that the widespread fantasy of "getting it right" is a fantasy of omnipotence. The fantasy is selfish as well as arrogant. It is rooted in the therapist's need to be perfect even if on the surface it looks as though the issue is her wish to help the patient.

And this omnipotent fantasy can lead to chilling work in which the analyst's theoretical beliefs trump her human empathy and kindness. In one egregious example, a holocaust survivor brought his analyst a journal entry in which he described some of his experiences in the camps. He felt unable to speak about the torments he had been subjected to. The analyst let the pages sit on a table in the room and did not respond verbally to the patient's wish that she read his story. After the patient left, the analyst's receptionist called to tell the patient that he had "forgotten" something in the office and that she was mailing it back to him. The analysis continued to its conclusion without patient or analyst ever again mentioning either this incident or his experiences in the camps. Both patient and analyst considered this analysis successful.

I had a personal experience of the power of this omnipotent energy at a conference once. The case presenter was a Bionian analyst and he presented two hours from his work. The patient, in opposition to her analyst's wish, was sitting up rather than lying down. The analyst was taking notes and the patient was noisily protesting about this note-taking. The unperturbed analyst did not respond in any way. At the end of the presentation, the analyst announced with an unmistakable note of triumph that in the next hour the patient had returned to the couch. In a rather lengthy discussion period, no one raised any question about the analyst's non-responsiveness to the patient's distress about the note-taking. No one seemed to doubt that the patient's return to the couch demonstrated the efficacy of the analyst's stance. And "no one" included me. In the atmosphere of the conference's group mind, I felt very impressed by the analyst's ability to remain true to his inner compass and to not be swayed by the patient's distress. Only in hindsight could I notice how terribly unrelated the analyst had been and to remember that relatedness is the most crucial and central element needed in the clinical situation. What was the patient learning here about rigidity and the possibility of being vulnerable? Surely the analyst could have tried letting go of his notepad. If he found himself unable to function without it, he could always have brought that up and begun to use it again.

The pathological fantasy of perfection, control and knowing leads analysts to imagine that this or that perspective is the correct one. So the analyst makes only transference interpretations, ignoring the patient's attempts to understand his relationship with his spouse, perhaps; or she focuses only on his defenses, never on content; she never reveals any fact about herself, or never laughs at a joke, or never provides a sympathetic cluck-cluck.[5] All of this ignores the fact that patients consistently believe that the feeling of being cherished and understood is the transformative ingredient in the work; they never focus on brilliant interpretations and they certainly never talk about their therapist's perfection as the key to their healing. They may appreciate the analyst's solidity or reliability, but to the extent that the analyst is perceived as perfect, the ur-complex of pathology that we are discussing is constellated in the patient: he is small, inadequate and needy; he envies his therapist's omniscience; he is jealous of the self-sufficient union with herself from which he is excluded; his terrible state of lacking exposes him to attacks of greed.

The pathological complex of perfection is something we all need to become more conscious of. In this orientation, the individual is possessed by a self-centered quest for invulnerability that seeks to transcend the ubiquitous insecurity of mortality. As in a Greek tragedy, the safety-seeking person who buys a Hummer will find himself slipping on a metaphorical banana peel as he exits his car. Is a desperate search for omnipotence the root of all pathology? Or is the idea that we could identify one basis for all emotional disturbance itself a manifestation of our search for perfection? Does it seem that when someone "falls into a complex," it is always structured by god and worm and their relationship with each other? I would invite the reader to play with this idea in his or her consulting room to see if it makes sense.

The structure of pathology imaged in a dream

Let me bring this complex alive with a dream that images its operation in the psyche of a middle-aged woman who was relatively ordinary – "normal," as it were – in the level of disturbance she was coping with:

5 This kind of technically rigid behavior is much less common contemporarily than it once was, and even analysts who are attempting to be rigid will sometimes be pulled into responses in which their humanity trumps their theories.

I'm with my father and my husband. We've been outside, an urban scene, with panicky people rushing about: we're preparing for the onslaught of a terrible hurricane. We've taken refuge in my father's apartment, a dream place that's on the ground floor, though it also has a spiral staircase leading to an upper level. The ground level has cement floors and no real door. The door is maybe one of those huge sliding things a stable might have, and it's open. I'm panicked, and X [the patient's older brother] comes rushing through. He's bringing up the end of a group of five or eight people who are following a ship captain who is promising them safety from the coming hurricane on his ship. It's a sort of Noah's Ark feeling, though in reality you don't seek refuge from a hurricane on a ship, you hunker down or flee inland. But in the dream X is doing this so I just react without thinking and know I'll be safest if I do what X is doing. I find out that the captain will take us, too, and turn to my father and husband and say commandingly, "Let's go!"

My father dithers about in his defensively stupid way, asking the captain repeatedly if he thinks this is really the best way to go. The captain says yes the first two times, but the third time he asks my father if he wants to come and my father says no. I'm amazed but before I can feel very much the captain asks my husband if he wants to come. My husband makes the face he's making when he's in his "you're-not-the-boss-of-me" mood and he says no. I'm stunned. I feel utterly betrayed and abandoned. It feels as though going with this group is a life or death necessity and I have to decide in a moment because the group is going on, so I go along with it. But in just a few blocks we reach a supermarket and are inside it. Structurally it is almost exactly like my father's house but somehow this building seems extremely safe. I want to stop and call my husband and father and tell them about the strong structures that can hold us if they come on this trip. Again, if I do that the group is going to go on without me.

This time I let the group go and spend time at a pay phone trying to call. I have all the kinds of problems you have in dreams and can't make the connection. I don't get through to them and I fall into a very sound sleep – really deep unconsciousness – apparently on the supermarket floor.

When I wake up the hurricane no longer seems to be an issue. I go back to my father's house, missing my husband in the most terrible way. I feel such an awful rift with him, and I so want to mend it, but I'm hurt and so caught in my wounded pride that I can't bear the pain of making the first move. So I half-sneak in. They're talking at the bathroom door. I think my father is shaving and my husband is talking to him and they don't notice me. I skulk around in the background until I finally make my presence known. My husband looks at me without any particular welcome. He's not exactly hostile to me, but he's involved in his relationship with my father and it's feeling good without me. I am so upset I go into a violent rage and attack him physically. But the image is of my attacking a woman with a bouffant

hairdo, pulling and messing up her hair. I'm yelling, "fuck you, fuck you!"
and wake myself.

Let us begin by looking at the problem the dreamer faces. A terrible hurricane is in the offing: an overwhelming flood of grief (a deluge of tears) and rage (a raging storm) threatens her. The dream gives no particular hints about the nature of the grief/rage, but the dreamer felt that it was a primal grief about the way her narcissistic mother could never have molded to her needs, not even in earliest infancy when she would have needed it the most. The dreamer fills in her association with her particular history but at an archetypal level she is threatened with the elemental grief of the human condition. At least some of the quotidian slights of an ordinary childhood are experienced as catastrophic by the little one who cannot comprehend them. The universal catastrophe of childhood grounds our infinite griefs. Each person has his or her specific story, but the suffering of life is universal because along with the joys on offer come all the woes – the shame of not being the favorite or the guilt of being favored, the distress that accompanies being the oldest or the youngest or the middle one, the hardships of poverty or sickness or of emotional neglect disguised by material privilege: every life situation includes considerable pain. When the pain can be held in awareness and endured with respect for its legitimate place in the natural order of life, it becomes suffering instead of meaningless pain and the experience is of grief. The dreamer's raging storm points toward Harold Searles' (1979) belief that analysis is all about the griefs the patient has been unable to grieve. As we shall explore more fully in the next chapter, the rage is secondary to the grief, for rage is a defensive emotion that functions to hide one's terrified vulnerability from oneself.

The archetypal problem that the dream presents is how to deal with this universal grief and the awesome rage that flows from it. As psychologists we know that the constructive answer is, "experience it consciously." This is because the person's authentic self *is* filled with grief and the question is not whether or not to have it; the question is whether or not to be aware of it, whether to suffer it or to evade it. When we avoid consciousness of an emotional experience, we do so by splitting off the part of ourselves that is caught in that emotional reality, and we consequently lose the contribution of that part to our conscious, choice-making selves. The rejected part of the self sinks into the unconscious, where it lives on in a complex, pushing us into reactive (as opposed to thoughtful) behavior. This saps our potency and creativity; we are left with less of ourselves.

The ability to think and choose rather than reacting blindly is the fundamental ingredient of highly developed levels of creativity. Symington, following Bion, suggests that the prototypical creative act is the creation of a personal thought. We are far before the emergence of a poem or a painting or an essay. We are instead looking at the degree to which the individual can wriggle out of the constricting role of god or worm to have his or her unique idea. Like the little boy in "The Emperor's New Clothes," can someone see something to which the rest of the world is blind? We are talking about the psychological capacity that enables a constructive relationship with an other (one of the most creative "things" one can fashion). This is the ability to pause and reflect, to have the experience that one is beset with, to absorb it and to have a thought about it, to react thoughtfully rather than instinctively. Only to the extent that this ability develops can one have a real relationship, because it is only to that extent that one exists as a person rather than a copy of a stereotype. Symington calls the pseudo-individuals who are deeply trapped in this complex "corporate entities."

In actual life, it seems reasonable to assume that even the most fragmented psychotic has not split off all of himself – he feels pain and sometimes suffers. And no matter how capable and mature a person may seem, all human beings lack parts of themselves. Indeed, Winnicott defines primary agonies as universal experiences that are so unbearable that once the infant has caught a whiff of them, he will try any possible psychological contortion to avoid the full experience. The theory I am presenting here suggests that an uprush of the intensifiers is the archetypal human response to elemental agonies and their derivatives, but that with development it is possible for the person to be aware of, rather than possessed by, the omnipotent envy, jealousy and greed offering to "protect" him from his terror. At every moment (more or less) the developing infant/child/adult is confronted with two alternatives: can I bear the pain of the present moment (and consequently also its joy) or must I evade the legitimate suffering of life by splitting off the part of me that feels the pain?

Symington, like Jung, Klein and Bion, emphasizes the aspect of choice. The choice is forced rather than free when the person lacks the inner tools to process her terror, but when it is possible to choose a thoughtful response instead of a reactive one, the experience of choosing is clear. It is hard to think instead of discharging, it is not the easy alternative. It is even possible for a more developed person to "choose" to snap angrily rather than doing the work of thinking about his reaction and holding it in some more constructive fashion. From the point of view of the person who does have a choice, it may look as though the undeveloped person is choosing to discharge, but from the point of view of the individual caught in his complex, discharging is the only possible alternative. To the extent the individual is possessed by this primary complex of pathology, the "I" does not have a choice; the larger psyche chooses for it.

As the individual becomes more conscious, moment-by-moment choices emerge. A woman discusses her situation with a therapist whose compassionate attention calls up her compassionate attention to an inner experience that would have overwhelmed her on her own. In the consulting room, where the overwhelming emotional reality is reconstellated in a supportive atmosphere of reflecting rather than acting, the patient notices elements that were missed before. She becomes aware of factors belonging to the necessary layer of existence that her panicked flight into the contingent survival layer led her to neglect. She may realize that she can choose, for example, to apologize to someone she wronged or take some other kind of constructive action that is humbling/humiliating but which she actually desires. She may become aware of other kinds of personal sacrifices she wants to make, rather than fleeing. It is possible that she will act on the basis of these kinds of considerations only to discover that elements of her chosen behavior were also compelled rather than truly chosen. But elements can be chosen. We cannot freely choose something as enormous as a marriage – although it may be possible to freely choose not to make a foolish marriage. Choices can be made in day-to-day areas that may seem relatively minor, but each such choice is a brick that begins to build new characterological structures.

The larger psyche makes unconscious choices – unconscious in the sense that the "I" has had no say in these decisions. The person is responsible for these choices although this responsibility has nothing to do with blame. It is similar to the fact that I am responsible for cleaning up after my dog. The praise/blame dimension comes up around whether or not I take up my responsibility, not around whether or not my dog defecates on the parking strip. When unconscious anxiety impels someone into behavior that slights someone outside of the anxious person's awareness, the question is how she will respond if the mistreated individual speaks up. Will she justify herself by somehow blaming the victim or will she absorb the fact that she hurt someone and try to make amends? To the extent that she can take up her failing, she can grow from it; to the extent that her vulnerability is too great to allow that, she is stuck.

The therapist must attend to the ways in which the patient feels wounded by others (parents, spouses, bosses, analysts), but ultimately the focus must turn to how the patient stokes her own suffering. She is not typically more of a victim than anyone else. Her psyche, impelled by its nature and its nurture, has been unconsciously forced into one choice after another and these "choices" have built up a character structure that determines much of her suffering. When her supervisor or her husband is rudely demanding, for example, she can respond by ratcheting up the rudeness or by trying a thoughtful response that has the potential to defuse the situation. To the extent that the therapist can stay centered in the necessary layer of existence rather than the contingent, he will view himself, suffering humanity, and therefore his patient, with compassion. Rather than thinking of these choices in a moralistic sense, the analyst's goal is to open the patient's eyes to the fact that alternatives exist. The conscious person in the consulting room is trapped in her unconscious reactivity and must be met with empathy and concern rather than criticism or judgment. But she also needs to be met with the expectation that she can be an agent in her life rather than a victim.

The therapist must help the patient to develop the ability to experience her suffering rather than discharging it. Empathy and mirroring are useful, but without attempts to understand the way the patient maintains her suffering through her own forced choices, empathic mirroring will not lead to fundamental character shifts. In practice, empathic mirroring tends to create a holding environment within which most patients will begin to explore themselves and to take increasing responsibility for their inner choices, without the analyst's pointing this out. Through the process of self-reflection, which we hope is heightened in the analytic/therapeutic situation, the patient, supported by the therapist/analyst's compassion, will become aware of some of the ways in which she reacts rather than thinks. She may become able to recognize the emotional triggers that cause her to go blind and behave instinctively and thoughtlessly. She may begin to become aware in the moment itself of the possibility of a different choice. When her development has proceeded to the point where she is able to make the choices that help her to grow, she can begin to see the alternatives to which she was blind.

So, to return to our dreamer, she is presented in the dream with a fundamental choice point: can she bear to experience the grief, rage and terror of her emotions? Her dream "I" responds by running away from the experience as fast as it can. In the symbolic image of the life-threatening hurricane, we see the assessment of her infantile psyche living on into her present adult life: experiencing this grief and rage will kill her. Unconsciously, she does not feel like the grown-up person she actually is, with an "I" that is now strong enough to begin to bear this suffering, especially with her therapist's support. Because she is caught in the complex formed in infancy, when the grieving/rageful person was first split off, she is caught in the reactivity that was the infant's only viable choice. Outside her awareness, she feels as though she is a helpless baby. Panic envelops her and makes her unable to think; she has no freedom in the dream; she is behaving in a reactive way rather than thoughtfully. This is a core characteristic of the complex of pathology: it smothers the individual's freedom and his creativity. If the prototypical creative act is thinking a thought of one's own, the complex-ridden person's panic – "Oh, oh, I will die if I have to suffer" – obliterates the space for thinking.

The dreamer is caught in the contingent layer's pleasure principle. She has lost touch with the part of her psyche that is seeking self-fulfillment, as opposed to gratification. She has forgotten that she was on an individuation journey searching for her authentic self. The concerns of the moment have swept her away. Taking the space to understand the situation and to have a personal thought about how best to deal with it would reveal the dreamer's inner self (to herself as well as others) and would thus further her individuation. Contemplating the imagery of the dream, the dreamer's waking "I" immediately sees that the choice that her panicked dream "I" is making (to follow her brother's lead in seeking refuge from the storm on a ship) is not the choice that she "herself" would make. The dream "I"'s infantile, instinctual reaction serves to obscure the dreamer's individuality and to sweep her away into an amorphous crowd of non-individuals. So her fear that the coming inundation of grief is life-threatening is paradoxically true about her fear of her grief: she does lose herself when she panics. Her panic obliterates her individuality.

Panic is the fundamental emotion that drives the complex-possessed individual, but the person who is caught in this complex is no more conscious of her panic than she is of anything else. (Hence the panic's appearance in the dream, for the dreamer's psyche is trying to bring her attention to the disowned parts of herself.) When the person can feel her panic, she is paradoxically coming out of its grip. I will return to this panic later when I talk about how, in this complex, the individual's center is nothing but a jelly. Here we can simply note that the panic is a natural concomitant of the fact that the threatening grief/rage has thrown the individual back into an infantile place – into a complex: a piece of his character structure that began to coalesce in the first weeks of life. In the center of the complex he experiences himself as an infant, without inner resources, and is naturally panicked about the onslaught of strong emotions.

It is easy to lose track of why the reactivity imaged in the dream is "narcissistic." It may seem to be simply self-preservative, surely a healthy impulse. But we must not extrapolate sloppily from Darwin's insight that the survival of the species is a fundamental drive of life. The species' quest for survival does not mean that survival of the individual is the core impulse of a human being. Jung describes individuation as a process that struggles against nature. We are part of nature, but our nature pits us against our own nature. We wish to remain alive but we also wish to grow toward wholeness: to retain our integrity, to follow the promptings of our personal sense of right and wrong. We want to be "good" though the raw human psyche obviously contains a great deal of "not-good." These two fundamental human needs, to survive and to be whole, may conflict. When they do, simply to fall into the self-preservation pole and abandon the individuation drive is pathological (even if it is universal). The healthy attitude is to hold the opposites (even if it is never possible to hold them without dropping one or the other from time to time).

One of the hallmarks of the pathological constellation is the fact of being swept into the self-preservative pole of our inner tension. This is the level of experience that the Eastern religions call "illusory" and that Symington calls "contingent". It is the ever-changing aspect of life as opposed to the ground of being from whence we come and where we find our essential nature. It is by seeking that eternal and unchanging substrate that I will find who I really am and will take my true place in relation to others. This is the level that Bion called O, that mystics call THAT or the Truth and that Jung referred to with his concept of the Self.

The discovery of who I really am can only come as a blow to my narcissism. In my narcissism I want to be someone who is not-me, a perfect person (or at least a better person), someone extraordinary (or at least not ordinary).

The dreamer's panicked belief that experiencing her grief/rage will kill her reflects the fact that experiencing it will, indeed, destroy her inflated self-image. She will not know the best way to proceed; she will feel her smallness, her vulnerability, her ordinariness. Paradoxically, that deflated experience brings her true substance and potency by opening out her real uniqueness, her particular shape. The "shrunk" person is "as singular as a daisy," in the poet Mary Oliver's formulation. Taking on one's suffering means sacrificing the wish to be in charge of one's life and of one's self, for this universal wish is a denial of the true nature of the psyche and of life. The fact that the attempt to be in charge is universal speaks to the fact that Freud's pleasure principle is instinctual and is always in conflict with the truth drive (Grotstein, 2004b), which is also innate. When the search for pleasure pushes relatedness and the search for truth out of the picture, we are in the world of emotional illness. In health, both of these fundamental needs will be given their due.

Another way to think about this is to recognize that in her panic the dreamer is caught in valuing her physical survival above her emotional integrity. The most important thing has become the instinctual drive to stay alive: I am the most important person in the universe, at all costs I must survive. The dream pictures this in the contemptuous way she treats her father and husband. She does not relate to them in the crisis that threatens the three of them; she decides unilaterally what is best for them and expects the others to follow her commands. She seems to think that she is the queen of their world and they are her subjects. Seeing herself behave in this way toward the two men is distressing for her waking self. She is ashamed of her behavior. In the dream, panic about her survival leads her to sacrifice her relatedness, her integrity.

When the two men assert their independence and function separately from the dreamer, she forgets her connection to them and impulsively rushes off to join her brother in his solution to the crisis. She makes this "choice" because she is caught up in her panicked over-valuation of her immediate survival (the pleasure principle) rather than remembering her quest to find her self. If she were not caught in the complex that takes as axiomatic that she (since she identifies with god rather than with worm) always knows best, she would have the space at least to ask her husband and father why they don't want to go along with her idea. She would be able to imagine a perspective other than her own and, in fact, this perspective would enrich her. But to do this she would have to be able to tolerate separation – the recognition that her husband (or father) is an independent person with his own mind rather than the worm that completes her and makes her whole. She would be an ordinary fallible person with a partner who, although fallible, could enrich her with different ideas, with a new point of view. She might, however, have to watch her "other half" interact with someone else (her father, say) and she might have to tolerate the feeling of being second (at a given moment) rather than first. In the complex of pathology, an outraged jealousy protects her from the pain of separateness; in health, the pain is suffered.

The judgment the dreamer makes in her panic is foolish, as her waking "I" immediately notices. A boat is not a good place to take refuge in a hurricane; one should head inland or hunker down, which is what the husband/father does. But in the dream she is swept into following her older brother. Why is that?

Here we must turn to personal information about the dreamer that we must then disentangle from its archetypal core (as I did above regarding her personal understanding of her grief and the way that that same grief is a manifestation of a universal emotional state). The dreamer has a twinship relationship with her brother. They are very close in age and traveled through childhood as two allies in the relative coldness of their mother's gaze. The parents, trapped in the pleasure principle, had little space outside this fundamental complex; the mother was the queen, and the father, a lowly courtier, worshipped her. The mother was the most beautiful, most intelligent and most creative person and the father's value came from her having chosen him. The children were the mother's and were therefore the most beautiful/handsome, most intelligent and most creative children. The family (including the father) denigrated the father. One parent played god and the other, worm.

In the face of the coming hurricane the dreamer finds herself in a foursome, a common dream image of an individual's wholeness (although it more typically appears with three people of the dreamer's own sex and one of the opposite sex, while here we see the female dreamer with three men). She and her brother, heirs of her mother the queen, are gods, extraordinary people. But in reality we are all just people, ordinary people regardless of the (even extraordinary) talents we may have. Consequently one can be god only by being paired with worm, because when one is identified with the god side of the polarity, the worm side is in the unconscious and must be located someplace in the outer world if it is not to threaten overtaking the person herself. So the dreamer faces the assault of her grief/rage in a foursome that represents the fragmented wholeness of her wounded self: a pair of gods and a pair of worms.

A person possessed by this complex swings between positive and negative inflations. As clinicians we know that when the patient is inflated, she is comparably deflated in her unconscious; when the patient is caught in a negative inflation, experiencing herself as the lowliest creature ever, in her unconscious lies a grandiose superhuman "true" self. One or the other generally predominates, and it is the person who identifies with god and projects worm whom we commonly call narcissistic, but the psychological pattern is the same in the individual who identifies with worm and projects god. Regardless of which orientation is "up," the person is trapped in reactive behavior that will not, ultimately, serve her own best interests. In this complex our dreamer turns arrogant and her husband effaces himself, but neither of them has any real choice regarding their behavior. (Although in this dream the husband and father have begun to free themselves from the complex. They are imaged as having a choice rather than simply reacting. The remnants of the complex are displayed in the self-effacing ways they express their choices.)

The dreamer, identified with the god side of the polarity, manages, in her reactivity, to stay unconscious of the shame that envelopes her waking self when she sees her dream behavior. Shame is the ur-complex's central emotion. When the individual can stay identified with god, the shame is held at bay, but torn out of that identification it washes over him, perhaps in flooding proportions. Worm accomplishes the same feat of evading his shame by emotionally merging with an outer god whose infinite power and insight assures him of his own righteousness.

Shame can be thought about from at least two angles. An awareness of being alive begins to coalesce at some point in the prenatal experience. Even as a newborn the organism is extremely fragile and needs great external support to stay alive. As an un-self-conscious awareness of aliveness begins to turn the fragile collection of developing cells into a person, a fundamental terror of annihilation awakens. This is the terror that Winnicott (1963) referred to with the concept of primitive agonies – fears of falling forever, of breaking into pieces, and so on. Out of this vulnerability comes a drive to bigness. The terrible danger of aliveness constellates a violent rejection of helplessness, one manifestation of which is shame about one's smallness. Powerful people are proud of their power, although it may reflect nothing more personal than a meaningless accident of birth. Impoverished people feel "less than," although their social weakness may again indicate nothing about their essential natures. So one aspect of the shame that permeates this complex is simply a reflection of the underlying awareness of our essential smallness in the face of mortality.

When the individual can hold the fear of annihilation that aliveness involves and can suffer it in the ways I describe in this book, the objectively small person gradually develops a limited but authentic strength. It is not the imagined omnipotence of the big people who surrounded the helpless infant, but a real capacity to interact successfully enough with the dangers of aliveness. To the extent that a person is caught in the pathological complex, he has failed to develop true potency. Symington suggests that the shame of the complex stems from an unconscious awareness of the fact that the person is not doing the emotional work that individuation demands. The "solution" of denying one's grief, projecting one's shadow and clinging to god is self-damaging. When a person finds a poisonous bit – of envy, say – inside himself, identifies it and holds it, he is no longer simply inundated by it. He becomes able to initiate action rather than simply reacting. That piece of poison no longer must be projected; it can take its place within the wholeness of his self and its energy becomes available to the individual rather than possessing him. The envy becomes a signal to the envious person, pointing him toward what he lacks and stimulating him to develop it. Ultimately, envy may be transformed into admiration. "The human personality is . . . a 'possibility' that can become a personality through a creative act [of containing and suffering the negative emotions]. Guilt occurs when that creative act is refused. Shame is the emotional consequence of this damaged state" (Symington, 2002, p. 175). These self-damaging choices may have been the infant's only option, but as the possibility of other choices develops and is "refused" – as the individual grows – unconscious guilt and shame develop.

In looking at my patient's dream I am suggesting that it pictures the dreamer's relation to her version of this universal complex. There are, of course, many personal elements in the dream's images, such as the fact that it opens in the father's apartment, and since these personal elements are not relevant to understanding the essential complex, I ignore them. In this dreamer's psyche we see that the inner father/husband, the worm side of the dreamer's complex, has gone further in extricating itself from the self-destructive constellation than the dreamer's "I" has. The two men are able to stand separate from god's commanding voice and to make thoughtful decisions regarding the coming hurricane, whether we see god in the person of the dream "I" or in the authority figure of the ship captain. It is the dreamer who is immersed in her complex. It is as though her psyche is telling her to re-evaluate these men vis-à-vis herself. She thinks of them as "less than," but in the father's apartment there is an "upper level" that is reached via a spiral staircase, a common symbol of the individuation process that circles round and round, addressing the same issues at levels of increasing complexity. It is by working with her inner worm that the dreamer can become a whole person rather than a two-dimensional caricature of an omniscient deity. From a clinical perspective, the fact that the two worms are separating out from the dreamer's reactivity indicates that while this root complex is pictured in an extensive way, the dream is also telling me/us that that structure is in the process of being deconstructed from within itself. To whatever extent one is individuating, the complex of reactive self-involvement is in the process of dissolving.

In her complex the dreamer assumes that her father/husband will obey her commanding voice and come along. She has no idea that the husband/father could have a different thought from hers. When he/they do have a different idea, the dreamer, enacting her projection of worm onto him/them, does not listen to their ideas, instead rushing off after her over-valued brother. But as soon as she realizes that her other half, the husband–worm, is separate from her, thinking thoughts of his own, she is devastated. Like the ancient God of the early Hebrew Bible, she cannot be god unless worm abases himself before her. She feels betrayed and abandoned. We see here the quality of her attachment to the husband/father: it is a glue-like attachment, a merger rather than a real relationship. We can think about this merger in a number of ways.

Symington focuses primarily on the fact that when one is in this complex, one's center feels jelly-like, as though the person is filled with a mess of bits, the jumbled fragments of what could become a strong self. Unconsciously aware of a disastrous inner situation, the individual glues himself to others. He cannot truly connect with someone because real relatedness requires an experience of our separateness and whether worm or god, in this complex the person feels too vulnerable to bear that. As long as he is merged with another, painful and dangerous emotions are evaded. He need never feel lonely, he is always together with someone; living inside a loving cocoon, he need never experience his hatred and destructiveness; he is always safe, never threatened, always big, never small. The narcissistic person's jelly-like core is both the result and the cause of his rejecting his violent inner emotions: envy, greed and jealousy. Terrified by the unconscious knowledge of the profound vulnerability that his lack of development implies, the individual is gripped by intense, hateful states that make him feel consciously big and powerful rather than little and helpless, even though these hateful states unconsciously reinforce his terror of the dangerous universe in which he lives.

Envy leads the person to project his own goodness into someone else – someone who has some goodness of her own, but not all the goodness in the couple. The individual fears the envy of others and unconsciously recognizes that if he holds his goodness, reality will produce some painful experience. After all, every previous time joy lifted him up, something happened that brought him down! So he gives away his positive potentials and swallows all the other's badness to add to his own. Then, resenting the resulting impoverishment of himself, the person projects all the bad stuff back into the same (now hated) person and tries to spoil or steal back the good stuff.

Greed swallows all the goodness, obliterating the boundary between the self and the other, and crushing the self through its violence. It is like the bulimic patient who consumes two large pizzas, four burritos and a quart of ice cream before throwing it up. Just as the body is stretched to the point of injury in this behavior, the psyche's metaphorical skin is stretched or even torn when the individual grabs all the credit, when she fills her emptiness either with dozens of expensive shoes and handbags or with a life-consuming quest for fame and power.

Jealousy supports envy and greed by wiping out the third and thus destroying the space within which the person would be able to find other points of view. It is like the only child raised in a single-parent home: sometimes the child becomes the parent's clone, seeing the world exclusively through the adult's eyes. In the more ordinary triangle of two parents and a child, two points of view compete for the little one's allegiance, leaving him space to construct a perspective that is different from either example. If you and I both accept without question the idea that the point of life is the security of wealth, only by letting in a third person's viewpoint might we question that notion and begin to wonder what place love might hold.

These dreaded emotions – envy, jealousy and greed – ally with the god-energy of the psyche, to become Symington's "intensifiers." They liquefy the person's inner self into a jelly and petrify his outer self into a rigid crust.

As the liquefiers, they dissolve the grief of the early trauma, and leave passivity and depression in its wake. Consciously accepting these terrible emotions and struggling with them is what builds character. Accepting and holding my envy teaches me what I yearn for and spurs me toward attempts to get it. This constructive attempt allows me to admire the quality when I see it in others. My greed, infused with the moderation that flows from recognizing the size of my true hunger, generates the wish to share rather than to hoard. My jealousy can provide me with an inner third, Archimedes' point to rest his lever on, a capacity to imagine points of view other than my own. But when someone hates his emotions, he chops them into bits inside and violently projects them out, leaving the core of the psyche a formless mass. It is this formless mass that leads a person to feel like a worm (a mess inside, lacking spine) and this self-experience in turn leads to a greedy swallowing of god's pronouncements rather than attempts to consider and integrate new ideas. The conscious "I" may identify with god as our dreamer does, but we see in her reactive appropriation of her brother's (foolish) idea that whether arrogant or excessively humble, the individual caught in the ur-complex of pathology cannot think for herself; she buys god's pronouncements wholesale.

Where does this god come from, and what can we say about its nature? More staid psychoanalytic discourse talks in experience-distant terms of "omnipotent defenses." When we call the person who is caught up in his omnipotence "god," the personal and interpersonal experience of omnipotence comes alive. The term makes vivid the irrational inner contortions involved. This false god is an energy in the psyche that magically changes realities. It expels pain, jealousy and anger into whomever or whatever is handy. This god is not a spiritual reality and it is, unfortunately, very similar to the standard-issue god of Judaism, Christianity and Islam: a being that commands us not to think for ourselves and who hates our envy, greed and jealousy. The Western God has many authentic spiritual qualities expressed by the Hebrew prophets, by Jesus, by Mohammad. But, as Bion put it, "The Christians got him [god] in the end; from his messianic prison house he never escaped till every vestige of meaning had been squeezed out of him" (quoted in Symington and Symington, 1996, p. 57). Organized religion presents us primarily with a false god who wants to amputate our pathology rather than hold and transform it.

The person gripped by his pathological complex gloms onto this god and hangs on for dear life. A part of the self was wounded in infancy by a god (an adult). The little creative self was crushed, causing it to feel like worm and to identify either with worm or with god, worm's secret other face. The baby/ child's inability to tolerate the pain of thinking about and living his experience has led him to evade it and to surrender to the instinctual urge to seize an attitude that will protect him from a repetition of his pain. The wound is really an accident – of birth perhaps, of one's parents' wounds. The traumatizing adult is not personal in the mistreatment he or she metes out; the parent is simply behaving reactively (i.e. unthinkingly) and treating the child in a way that is unconsciously determined by past injuries that have distorted the adult's own capacity to perceive the world and to think about what he or she sees. But the anguish of the experience throws the little one into the contingent layer of the psyche. In this layer, he cannot bear being accidentally shattered. It is better to feel like the object of an angry god than the anonymous victim of a meaningless accident, both because an angry god can be placated and because at least one counts if the attack was personal. If the pain is personal, the child can prevent its repetition by revising her behavior. The little one fashions god as a short-term solution to the disaster, a "solution" only in the contingent layer, for it refuses the growth-producing suffering of a painful reality.

The false god is very different from conscience. This god prevents growth, for when the individual errs in some way, it says, "You messed up, you're worthless," rather than, "You made a mistake, let's see how we can learn from it and repair it." God demands, conscience invites. It is only as the voice of god diminishes that conscience can begin to develop. Conscience is the voice of the Self. It is the presence of the necessary in this contingent world. Following the voice of one's conscience is a creative act that calls the person to combat the life-destroying tendencies created by the activity of the intensifiers within himself. The true god, conscience, produces original thoughts that may be startlingly different from the received wisdom.

An unconscious awareness of his jelly-like inner self leads the person caught in the complex of pathology to glom onto god with a glue-like merger. She can glom on as worm or through being god and finding someone else to play worm. In her weakness, something the individual knows about unconsciously, the fact of her lostness in the universe is unbearable. As we have explored, we have little firm data regarding who we are, where we are, or what is going on, either inside or outside. The universal fantasy that arises in this situation is that it is possible to know reality and truth in a way that goes far beyond anything we blind and groping human beings can reasonably hope for. The little one, viewing the big people who can so effortlessly bring into being light or darkness, nurturance or neglect, imagines that these giants are *in charge*. If he simply listens to their pronouncements and thinks the right thoughts, he, too, can be secure in what is really an infinitely insecure universe, reliable only in its constant flux. God – having mindlessly selected a system of thought to rely on – can feed him the correct understanding of every dangerous current swirling around. Of course he seizes the offered system and hangs on for dear life.

To return to our dream, when the dreamer sees that her husband/father, the worm whose attachment confirms her god-like status, is a separate person who is not functioning as a worm, she is thrust from her throne and cast out into a world where she, too, is just a person, no longer a god. This throws her into her jelly-like core. The dreamer is devastated, thrust back into an infantile experience of abandonment, with no access to the capable adult parts of herself that could go a separate way. She tries to merge with the god–brother, but that cannot work. How can one be god if the worm population is not worshipping one? (We see this repeatedly in the Hebrew Bible, where a jealous God demands endless adoration and sacrifice from humanity. His narcissistic rage at any neglect shows His secret weakness: His desperate need for a thoughtlessly adoring other to sustain Him and keep Him from falling into His jelly-like core. The ancient people who developed this myth were unconsciously projecting onto this god-image the archetypal reality they sensed inside themselves.) Without the husband/father to carry the worm part of the psyche, the intensifiers and the chaos overwhelm the dreamer from within.

So we can think of the merger that characterizes the pathological constellation as growing out of two related elements: god needs worm to exist as god; and the jelly-like worm must be part of god in order to survive.

Continuing with our dream, let us look at the ship captain with his anonymous five or eight followers. The captain is not a person; he is a "corporate entity," submerged in his role. To the extent that one is caught in one's pathological complex, one does not see individuals; one sees stereotypes: doctors are wise healers, men are unfeeling (or reliable), women are vain (or nurturing), Jews are greedy (or smart), African-Americans are lazy (or rhythmically talented), and so on. Here, ship captains know how to manage hurricanes and therefore embody god when one strikes. Attaching to corporate entities – glomming onto gods – turns the person into a non-individual, one of a group of anonymous followers. The dream pictures the dreamer's deteriorated capacity by describing her as unable to tell how many followers the captain has: five perhaps, or might it be eight? They are so indistinct and undifferentiated in terms of anything we might call individuality that we cannot even say how many of them there are.

The father and the husband, exhibiting their identifications with worm, are self-effacing in the ways in which they decline to side with the dreamer in joining the ship captain–god. The father is evasive and passive, afraid to simply state his opinion and having to pay homage to the authority/god before he can speak his own idea. The husband makes a face that the dreamer identifies as indicating that he is asserting his independence from her in a complex-ridden way rather than a comfortable one. But as I suggested above, these figures are asserting their separateness from the reactivity of the complex and thinking for themselves, indicating that the dreamer's pathological complex is beginning to break down.

We see that breakdown again in the fact that the dreamer is not swept up for long in her reactivity. Only a few blocks from the father's apartment, she begins to realize that there are structures here strong enough to weather the hurricane in. Again she has to choose between her relationship to her father/

husband – to her beloved – and her clinging to god in his incarnation as a ship captain. But this time she chooses eros rather than power. She is not able, however, to make the (telephone) connection with her loved one, presumably because the narcissistic constellation is still too strong. Because she cannot make that connection, she is unable to find her center and from it experience the hurricane of her emotions. (Or, because she cannot find her center, she cannot make the connection.) We see the linkage of making the connection and finding her center in the dream sentence: "So I don't get through and I fall into a very sound sleep." The two elements are equal clauses in the same sentence and imply that if she could have gotten through she would not have needed to sink into unconsciousness; she could have experienced the storm.

The last element in the dream is the jealousy that grips the dreamer when she sees her husband's relationship with her father. "He's not exactly hostile to me, but he's involved in his relationship with my father and it's feeling good without me," the dreamer says. His "crime" is independence and separateness. In her jealous rage the dreamer attacks him physically, but "the image is of [her] attacking a woman with a bouffant hairdo, pulling and messing up her hair." The dreamer associated the attack to an experience she had in high school, when she starred in the senior class play as a character who wore a bouffant hairdo. The dreamer is thus associating this image with an inherently narcissistic activity (being the star of the play), and the bouffant hairdo itself images the fear of smallness that leads the person to inflate her size (by teasing her hair into a puffed-up "beehive" shape, where queens rule). In the dream she attacks her pathological complex, but she does so with the unhealthy energy of hatred and rage rather than embracing it with the loving acceptance of the self-complex that would, paradoxically, welcome the dreamer's pathological constellation into the wholeness of her self.

For this complex is a universal fact of human existence in our world. It is pathological, but the healthy perspective must include the psyche's pathology as part of the necessary given, the element of the Absolute that brings pathos to life (Hillman, 1975). Delineating this ur-complex may allow the reader to see it everywhere. People are frequently involved in being Right and in evading the facts of human not-knowing; we strive to dominate uncertainty in ways that are easily shown to be irrational in the fantasy of potency that lies behind them; we tend to imagine that others are aware of us in ways that are surely unrealistic. Not everyone is focused all of the time on the pimple on my forehead; people are actually agonizing about their own pimples, not mine. Recognizing the ubiquitous nature of this complex must make us recognize that therapists and analysts are caught up in it just as surely as patients are. The aim of analysis, Symington says, is

the transformation of the 'narcissistic constellation' wherever it may

> be most in evidence. Sometimes the evidence will be that it is manifesting in the patient: that is the place to which the clinician's psychic attention needs to be directed. Sometimes it will be manifesting itself in the clinician: that, then is the place to which the clinician's psychic attention will be directed. . . . What will be crucial . . . is the clinician's own level of emotional functioning and the degree to which he is aware of the 'narcissistic constellation' within himself.
>
> (Symington, 2002, p. 213)

The reader can hear in this statement Jung's insistence that it is the person of the analyst, rather than her intellectual mastery of analytic theory, that is the decisive factor in this work.

Symington suggests that the "central problem [of analysis] . . . is to bring about the transition from hatred of the liquefiers [envy, jealousy and greed] to acceptance of them" (ibid., p. 198). The activity of the patient's liquefiers/intensifiers constellates in the analyst his own intensifiers, causing pressure, often great pressure, to either reassure the patient or to lash out at him. The analyst's core job is to contain his own inner pressure, to accept the presence of the intensifiers and of the ur-complex of pathology inside himself. The therapist must notice the urge to reassure or condemn and must hold it until he understands what it is about and can formulate a related (i.e. accepting) interpretation of what is going on. The long-term effort is to center oneself in the necessary layer, in the Absolute rather than in the transient elements of embodied life, and to help the patient to find a footing there as well. Keeping the contours of this complex in mind can orient the therapist in fundamental ways. At this time in the psychological evolution of our species, it is this reactive layer of the psyche that lies waiting for the light of consciousness. It is our job as analysts to begin to unpack it, to explore it, to get to know it – to become conscious of it so that we can stop enacting it ourselves and begin to help our patients to become aware of it in themselves.

Rosenfeld's narcissistic omnipotent character structure

Herbert Rosenfeld was a British Kleinian who died in the late 1980s. In his last work, *Impasse and Interpretation* (1987), he presents a clinically detailed exploration of one highly destructive way that the anti-relational complex we have been looking at functions in the consulting room. Rosenfeld's "narcissistic omnipotent character structure" describes the narcissistic complex from a point of view that will enlarge our understanding of it.

Like Symington or Bion, he thinks about a sane part and a psychotic part of each of us – in my language, a related part and an anti-related part. Rosenfeld suggests that the center of the person's sane part is her dependent, infantile aspect because it is here that she can grow. This is another way of saying that the baby-inside is the undeveloped, new life waiting to unfold. This childish, needy side of the person is the side that seeks relationships with others, including the connections between apparently independent adults. The independence of the adults consists in their ability to maintain themselves as separate individuals who can *connect*, in contrast to psychologically undeveloped adults who can only merge. To the extent that a relationship is centered in love (as opposed to power), it is ultimately a connection between the two people's vulnerable selves. Relationships are the experiences in which people find the emotional nourishment of life; they are therefore also the experiences in which people get hurt. Rosenfeld's perspective emphasizes the interrelationship between these two elements: to receive and absorb nourishment, one needs to be incomplete, needy, undefended; opening oneself at this level means being vulnerable to emotional pain.

Rosenfeld considers primarily envy as he describes the destructive impact of narcissism on clinical work. In clinical work, we typically find that the conscious patient devalues the baby inside herself (perhaps breathtakingly so). She may, apparently wholeheartedly, express the wish to get rid of it or to kill it. She wants to be a strong adult unencumbered by needy, dependent elements. The baby is not seen as the carrier of the person's new life and unrealized potential; he is seen only as the vulnerability that exposes the person to rejection, abandonment, pain. It is so easy to forget that we develop only through dependent and interdependent relationships. The apparently strong adult who disowns her neediness and imagines herself sufficient unto herself has nowhere to go. She has arrived. She may look stuck, but this is an illusion. The psyche is always in motion, growing or deteriorating, and to the extent that someone refuses her incompleteness, her weakness and need, she will not stand still. She will rigidify and decline.

The psychotic part of the person is described in different terminology, but in Rosenfeld's understanding it is easy to see Symington's underlying pattern. Rosenfeld focuses first on the omnipotence of the god–worm dyad, whether that omnipotence is consciously imagined to be part of the self or of the person onto whom god has been projected and with whom the self is merged; and secondly on the envy that overwhelms the patient[6] when she recognizes that the therapist/analyst has goodness that she needs and lacks. In the pathological part of the personality, the fact that the therapist offers valuable and

---

6 Rosenfeld does not emphasize the fact that "patient" should always be understood to refer to the patient inside the therapist as well as to the designated patient, just as a "therapist" part exists inside the official patient. If we listen to the unconscious commentary in the analyst–patient dyad it is not rare to hear ways that the therapist, feeling threatened by what the patient has to offer, enviously attacks it. I believe that this dynamic underlies the very frequent analytic attempt to put the patient's understanding of himself into the analyst's technical language rather than respecting the creativity of the patient's formulation. This constellation reflects the ways the therapist/analyst is dependent on the patient to whom she is attached.

needed help constellates envy rather than gratitude, because this aspect of the self hates whatever incompleteness and need exists inside, wanting to be self-sufficient and invulnerable. In her omnipotence, the patient believes that she can magically solve all her problems instantaneously. This belief is seductive. Instead of struggling along with all the suffering this implies, seeking help from others and taking one small, stumbling step after another, this part of the self believes it can attain immediate perfection and the safety that implies.

Rosenfeld describes omnipotence as a force inside the patient that "prevents him from thinking and observing what is going on" (Rosenfeld, 1987, p. 90). This is the force behind the seemingly endless patterns that block people, as they repeat over and over the same attempt that failed over and over before, perhaps trying to "just do it," to resolve self-destructive behavioral patterns by a conscious act of will. The main goal of the supposedly all-powerful force that Symington personifies as "god" is to keep intact the patient's delusional reliance on his omnipotence rather than on outside assistance. The omnipotent force consequently attacks and belittles any developing ability to depend on the analyst or to turn to her for help. Kalsched (1996) calls this omnipotent force the "Protector." Each time the patient feels the therapist helping him, this Protector urges him to devalue both her and the help, for in his omnipotence the patient needs to feel that he is self-sufficient. The devaluation is most destructive when it is direct, for in this case the patient will shred the progress he has made – by forgetting what happened, by attacking his own capacity to think, by destroying the positive image of the analyst inside his psyche.

Less catastrophically, the patient, in his omnipotence, may preserve the progress he is making by imagining that he develops his own insights and navigates his growth on his own, without any contribution from the therapist. In this situation, if the therapist can prevent her own narcissism from intruding with a demand for her rightful credit, progress may be made without directly confronting the patient's omnipotent narcissism. In either case, the pattern may be subtle and difficult to detect, or it may be violent and obvious. The attack, which is most centrally directed against the patient's own infantile, dependent self, often appears to be an attack on the analyst's potency because it is the analyst to whom the inner baby is drawn. The person's hidden weak and needy part knows that the analyst has capacities that he lacks and that could help him to develop. But the omnipotent energy that the patient has depended on is jealous and greedy, unwilling to relinquish its absolute status as the place to turn for help.

These attacks on the therapy and the therapist are impelled by envy. The patient's narcissism has shielded her from awareness of her destructiveness. If she is omnipotent, she need not deal with weakness or frustration or with the envy that rushes up to prevent experiences of smallness. As the patient begins to connect with her baby self, the raw envy of the infant is mobilized against the contemporary incarnation of the good, full breast. As she begins to take in the goodness that the analyst offers, she is overwhelmed with envy and wants to "steal the food and rob the person who is feeding [her]" (Rosenfeld, 1987, p. 68). Behind the patient's omnipotent stance lurks a murderous envy of anyone who dares to challenge it. The patient confirms her superiority through her scornful withholding of the needy inner one who wants the therapist's assistance.

I do believe that Kleinian technique can constellate a good deal of the envy that it finds. Because they see envy as innate, Kleinians sometimes seem blind to the way experiences of smallness terrify the patient and constellate envy. They do not seem to recognize the way their supposedly "perfect" interpretations assume that only they have insights to share, while the patient provides only the raw mess that needs interpreting. There is a basic (narcissistic) attitude in much of the analytic literature that imagines the patient bringing only associations; this attitude ignores the ways that the patient also creates meaning from his associations, finding interpretations of his own when he is contained simply by the analyst's presence. If the therapist can hold the patient and support him in finding his own understandings, instead of telling him everything he needs to know, much of the envy and hate that Rosenfeld writes about can be avoided.

But not all, because even an awareness of the therapist's constructive function as a sympathetic and compassionate support threatens the omnipotent structures we are talking about. The patient's envy may attack the work not only through directly devaluing the analyst; it may be subtle and express itself in "persistent indifference, [or] tricky repetitive behavior" (ibid., p. 109). To the extent that envy is a significant impediment to the patient's development, a gentle approach to him will not be able to avoid its constellation. Anything that might make him aware of his inner weakness will be "criticized, belittled, devalued, and distorted" (ibid., p. 87) as will the needy inner self he glimpses.

In his case examples, Rosenfeld presents many dreams that image the omnipotent complex actively opposing the patient's development. In one of these dreams,

> *a small boy was in a comatose condition, dying from some kind of poisoning. He was lying on a bed in a courtyard and was endangered by the hot midday sun which was beginning to shine on him. [The patient] was standing near to the boy but did nothing to move or protect him. He only felt critical and superior to the doctor treating the child, since it was he who should have seen that the child was moved into the shade.*
>
> (ibid., p. 110)

The child, of course, represented the patient's undeveloped self, someone in need of help. The patient's icy lack of concern describes the posture that fits the popular image of narcissism, and the constellation of the dream shows us the way destructive omnipotence keeps the young inner person in a "constant dead or dying condition" (ibid., p. 110). Rosenfeld does not explore who poisoned the boy or what the poison was. He does not ask what it might have felt like being roasted by a hot midday sun. Could we imagine that the brilliantly penetrating interpretations he describes might feel like a potentially deadly exposure to too much heat?

The more a person tries to turn away from his frozen state of perfection and toward the vulnerability of aliveness, the more threatened and therefore threatening his omnipotent organization becomes. Usually, the inner god that we have been discussing appears in dream images as benevolent and helpful in her promise of instantaneous solutions for his difficulties, but as the infantile self reaches out to the analyst and turns away from the domineering inner structure, god grows angry and threatens the self with destruction if the patient does not obey her dictates. Kalsched (1996) sees this angry god as the Protector who shields the vulnerable self from the dangers of its vulnerability; Rosenfeld sees this angry god as defending her own pre-eminent role in the psyche. Both perspectives have value.

In another dream reported by Rosenfeld, the patient realizes that he has no milk in his house and his neighbor tells him about a store that is open on Sundays. They go to the store together and the patient takes his place in the long line of customers waiting to be served, but the neighbor, instead of waiting his turn,

> quickly approached the cash-register, and exchanged [a] small coin for a large bundle of ten pound notes. ... [The patient] thought at first of informing the two women [who owned the store] about this ruthless arrogant theft but then he remembered that his responsibility was primarily to protect himself and not to interfere or intrude upon the milkmaids' business ...; but the real reason was that he was afraid for his life. He thought that the women in the shop would not be able to protect him against the ruthless man, who, once [the patient] was outside the shop, would doubtlessly retaliate. Why should he endanger his life because of such a theft and because of the fact that the women did not care for their money ...?
>
> (Rosenfeld, 1987, pp. 121–22)

In subsequent scenes of the dream, the patient pictures himself as down-and-out, the lowest of the low, gripped by despair and helplessness at what he now experiences as his own cowardly ruthlessness. The cruel neighbor, someone who lives right beside the dreamer, is a shadow figure who is very close to consciousness. The narcissistic structure we are talking about comes out of the shadows in this dream because of the good analytic work the patient has been doing with Rosenfeld. That structure is turning ugly and threatening rather than disguising itself as a helpful, reliable person who will protect the patient's inner worm. The dreamer fears for his life if he opposes this inner incarnation of god.

We see vividly in the dream the way the person caught in the archetypal complex of pathology moves back and forth in his identifications with god and worm. Rosenfeld tells us that the dreamer easily became "dogmatic, superior, and arrogant" (ibid., p. 120) but in the dream he clearly identifies with worm. As I noted above, everyone seems to know what it feels like to be worm; it is a rare narcissist indeed who is so thoroughly identified with god as to be unaware of the inner experience of inferiority and helplessness. Sometimes at least, when the patient behaves in a "dogmatic, superior and arrogant" manner he must be feeling arrogant and quite sure he knows exactly the right way to approach the situation in question. But sometimes he feels frightened and insecure, with no awareness of his superior and arrogant appearance. When the patient is not possessed by the god part of his psyche, he knows what feelings of inadequacy are.

Sometimes the omnipotent god appears in the form of a delinquent gang or the mafia. In this case its destructive nature is directly stated. But sometimes the gang is disguised in benevolent terms. In one case, after a particularly fruitful session, the patient of one of my supervisees came in with no recall of what had happened earlier in the week. She reported a dream about a group of construction workers who arrived at her home. They were young and full of life, healthy and strong. As she associated to them she realized they were immersed in an attitude of triumph, certain that they could do anything required and that they needed help from no one. The therapist reminded the patient of the very real help she had received from him in the last session, and the patient spontaneously commented that the group in her dream would mock her for needing help. They would never believe that a therapist, who uses only words, could have anything of value to offer.

Penny

Penny almost died when she was six weeks old. Her parents took the sleeping baby with them when they went out to a club and left her in her basket in the cloakroom. Unfortunately, they forgot all about her when the time came to leave and only realized their mistake when they woke up sober the next morning. They rushed back to the club, which was closed. It took several hours to alert the police, who located the owner. Soaking wet with urine, feces and vomit, the unheard infant had exhausted herself and was virtually unconscious. The story that the parents retained of this incident had been told to the growing child as a sort of joke, since the baby had been "fine" once they cleaned her up and fed her. Until she met me, Penny had been unable to recognize the full extent of neglect that this event captured.

Penny's central wound was a response to the frozen capacity for concern that her parents demonstrated in this incident. As I describe the organization of her psyche and the way in which she and I worked to transform her wound, we will see how virulent this cold unrelatedness was and how it lived on, infecting Penny, myself and even the people to whom I turned for help in my work with her. In our work, relatedness, the foundation of emotional health, developed from our facing and experiencing frightening levels of *un*relatedness in each of our psyches. While the story of her abandonment at the club was the worst incident of neglect that Penny knew of, several other potentially life-threatening events occurred during her first year. Both parents, but most destructively the mother, scorned anything small and needy, feeling something closer to revulsion for the helpless infant Penny than the more common maternal wish to nurture a vulnerable creature, especially a baby.

In the early years of my work with Penny, I had an experience that I later understood to be diagnostically significant. I found myself, not infrequently, feeling intensely cold toward her as she talked about what looked to be great emotional pain. I presented her in a consultation group, bringing in especially my concern about these feelings of my own. As I tried to describe the way I would find myself eyeing her from a frigid, cruel distance, the group pulled away from me and seemed to imply that I was a monstrously unempathic therapist. They were unable to help me become curious about these emotional responses, simply joining me in horror. For years I held this experience with enough shame to prevent me from exploring it. As I will describe below, I came to understand that my frozen feelings of separation from Penny, of non-concern about and distaste for her emotional self, reflected the extreme disfigurement that dominated Penny's mother's psyche. Her mother's coldness reflected a self-loathing that went well beyond the ordinary neurotic levels we typically encounter. It lived on in Penny's attitude toward herself and it infected me in the countertransference, calling up my own capacity for harsh indifference and loathing. The emotional responses that had so appalled the consultation group (while also infecting them!) were actually a glimpse of Penny's central wound.

When Penny was seven, her mother gave birth to twins, a boy and a girl. A constellation was thus established in which her siblings were close to each other and Penny was left out. Being so much older, she aligned more with the parents than with her younger siblings and felt superior to them. The parents, however, were immersed in a narcissistic bubble that excluded all of the children. They made a great show, throughout Penny's childhood, of their intensely passionate sexual bond, dramatically disappearing into their bedroom on weekend mornings. Once or twice a year they would go off on grand vacations that excluded the children, leaving them with maids. Mother and Father made it clear that their immature offspring were irrelevant and inferior, certainly not people they missed while they were away. Penny was starved for the loving relationship that ordinarily develops from a parent's relatedness vis-à-vis his or her infant; at the same time her parents' dramatic displays of their supposedly loving relationship tormented her with their lack of related-ness toward her.[7]

Penny responded to her situation by sharing her mother's disdain for her neediness. Her life was dominated from a very early age by the desire to attain self-sufficiency and perfection. She was effectively alone, with the twins on one side and her parents on the other, and her unsuccessful attempt was to be so good – perfect – that the parents would welcome her into their union and the twins would recognize her greatly superior status. Despite the fact that her attempt had never succeeded, the fifty-year-old Penny who came into therapy still believed that if she could only work out this perfection business, her life would work. As I described above, Penny was caught in the endlessly repeti-tive behavior that stems from the god energy of the psyche, the complex of omnipotence that Rosenfeld (1987) calls the omnipotent character structure and that Kalsched (1996) describes as the Protector. She could not think about her situation; she had her plan for how to succeed in life – a plan she had adopted from her inflated parents. The fact that the plan had never worked could not overcome her omnipotent belief that if she could only do it properly, it would work.

Penny experienced any personal imperfection as disastrous and felt con-sciously inferior if she was not clearly superior. Like her parents, she believed it imperative to be far beyond the "ordinary run of people" and the infinite elements of ordinariness that come up – the dirt, the mistakes, the wrong turnings of human life – immersed her in painful experiences of shame. Her authentic emotions seemed despicable to her. She hated the baby self she experienced as filling her and hid it assiduously, stuffing her needy, greedy hungers into as small a box as she could find. She could not bear to feel her yearnings for all the impossible things people can desire because yearning plunged her into her central wound, where she had received so little warmth or affection. In her yearnings, Penny was abandoned in the cloakroom all over again. Her cries, muffled by the coats around her, were lost in the night-club's din of music and talk. She considered vulnerable feelings shameful and inferior. She feared that opening the door to the grief that she felt about her life would cause her to drown, to cry forever. When feelings of distress came up, often in intrinsically upsetting situations, Penny felt great shame. Unlike herself, a valuable person would transcend and manage any difficulty. In one dream, shortly after she learned that her mother was dying, her feelings were imaged as a Neanderthal man who towered above her in a menacing posture. The ordinary feelings of fear and loss that filled her seemed ugly and weird.

---

7 I describe their relationship in these terms because it was a merger rather than a real relation-ship. A relationship can only develop to the degree that the two people involved have developed the capacity to be separate and therefore to come together or to connect. Penny's descriptions of her parents were vivid images of god (the mother) and worm (the father) glomming onto each other and becoming one person.

By the time I met her, Penny had become a person of considerable substance in the outer world. In her work, where her role shielded her from deep levels of vulnerability, she was highly related, skillful and compassionate, but Penny felt that only her ravenous infantile self, immersed in its envy, jealousy and greed was "real." Experiencing the intensifiers is painful when one is conscious of it, and the simple process of saying out loud what came to her mind confronted her with her destructive feelings in very painful ways. Anger, rage, aggrievement, indignation would roar in and push away her unbearable envy and jealousy. A friend of Penny's seemed to feel that she (the friend) had to live with her suffering; Penny could not imagine that perspective. "How can this be happening to me?" she would demand, even as she "knew" her outrage made no sense. She experienced a repetitive fury that she had to feel painful feelings in order to "get" me to hold and nurture her. Why could she not get the comfort and love she sought without being vulnerable? Penny's inability to suffer her distress by accepting it as her legitimate portion of fate left her in an extremely painful cycle. Because she was in such anguish, it looked to the observer as though she was suffering but mostly it was raw pain that could not take her anywhere new because she could not submit to its transformative power by respecting it – by suffering it.

Although she devoted a great deal of energy to her quest for perfection, she also placed the highest value on relatedness. Consequently, much of her search for perfection focused on her attempt to be perfectly attentive and loving in her interactions with others. She *looked* related, but her secret focus was dominated by what grade she was getting in her attempt to be perfectly attuned. Penny was a prisoner of her desperate need to be right and to be in control at all times, to dominate herself rather than to know herself, to erase any weakness, need, uncertainty, dependency. She wanted so much to care about others, but a terror of nonexistence hung over her and forced her into violent experiences of envy for anyone who received admiration and of jealousy toward anyone who received attention. This apparently substantial woman felt almost nonexistent and these symptoms were all responses to her terror of annihilation. It was far too dangerous to imagine exposing her "disgusting" neediness or yearning or vulnerability to another's gaze, so Penny's hunger for closeness and connection was constantly blocked by the impermeable armor of her wound. She felt that her self was formless, that she had no floor and was falling forever. In fact, she felt she had no self at all.

Penny directed her energy toward trying to be different from the self she sensed inside. She wanted to feel important and valuable and so she held off the insecure feelings that plagued her and searched for praise, even in trivial situations. Underneath, she felt so rejected and unwanted that she exhausted herself trying to be the most special, most delightful, most amusing person in every situation. Only if she were recognized as the best person in the world and therefore received all the love and respect that existed, could she imagine feeling good enough. When I first met Penny, her attempts to think and feel the way an "admirable" person would had totally confused her. Every time an emotional message from her self tried to contact her, she fled from it, searching for exemplary feelings instead of the "wrong" ones that kept trying to get her attention. Naturally, she felt empty, as though she had no self.

Penny felt that she needed to be the queen of the world to balance her core experience of being worthless, empty and lacking. Instead of feeling abandoned by the ends of hours, the weekends or the vacation breaks, Penny felt like disposable trash when I left her or when it became clear that people other than herself mattered to me.

The experience of not-knowing was terrifying for her, a matter that came up most destructively in relation to her own emotional responses. The unpredictable nature of spontaneous feelings seemed extremely dangerous. Her need to be in control led her into negative distortions of her emotional truth. In fact, she was a deeply compassionate and concerned individual and worried terribly about the ways her selfishness might hurt others, but fearing the confusion that would be generated by recognizing the clash between her selfish wishes and her concern for others, she split off her concern. When her sister-in-law, who had just adopted a baby from India, broke her ankle, Penny felt distressed and took considerable time off work to help her, insisting that she was doing this because it was the "admirable" thing to do. She *was* doing it in order to be an admirable person, but she was *also* doing it because her sister-in-law's dilemma touched Penny's out-of-control, unpredictable heart. She needed to deny her fear and concern, for it opened her to terrifying experiences of her helplessness in the face of life's uncontrollable ebb and flow.

Anger at me remained relatively secret for many years. She felt that expressing real anger at me was equivalent to saying that she would come with me to the nightclub and see if I was going to stick her in the cloakroom at the same time as she raged at me. Although terrified, she did know that until she expressed the fullness of her anger she would never know if I would consider the "real" Penny disposable. Until she tried it, she would continue to feel that I acted as though I cherished her because I did not know who she really was.

When we began our work, the self-imprisoning nature of her secrecy about her "shameful" feelings manifested especially in relation to her husband. She did not tell him the true vulnerable feelings that arose because she "knew" he would condemn her for them. As we explored the pattern, she began tentatively to speak the truth, and he consistently surprised her by responding with loving concern. She began to realize that she had constructed a terrible fantasy of who he was. This fantasy of him as a terrifying protector (Kalsched, 1996) who kept the danger of vulnerability at bay by forbidding its expression kept her secret anger simmering all the time, making her feel big (with rage) instead of little (with need). It was also safer for Penny to "know" that her husband (with whom she was merged) would condemn her than to open herself up to the uncertainty of not knowing what his response was going to be. His true responses were out of her control. And, of course, sometimes he did disagree with her or express a mildly negative judgment. Inside Penny, her husband was a condemning god who echoed her mother's opinions. Painful though this inner situation was, it had the further advantage of supporting the maintenance of her infantile tie to the mother she consciously wanted so desperately to escape from. Her husband's imaginary condemnation helped Penny hang onto her painful, self-wounding adaptation.

Working through Penny's complex

Penny worked with me for nearly ten years, most of it three times a week. I cannot hope to detail all those years of unpacking and reworking her fundamental complex, but I would like to describe an especially fruitful period of several months that preceded her cutting back from three to two times a week. As she turned around and moved from deepening her union with me toward disengaging, all of the issues that I described above became intensely heightened at the same time as they began to resolve at a deeper level than had been possible before.

About four months before the date she had set to give up her third hour, Penny talked about her inability to imagine that someone could hold pain and digest it rather than fleeing from it. Over the years we had talked about this from time to time, but the stance of welcoming her suffering as legitimate continued to elude her. This was partly because her pain was so sharp, partly because no one in her life had ever modeled such a stance, and partly because she simply felt too small and weak to bear it. As she talked about her distress at giving up an hour, she slipped and said that she would always be someone who drowns in grief because she was a "glass-half-full" sort of person. When I pointed out her slip she was astounded, for her sense of herself as an "inferior" glass-half-empty person was so central to her self-image. Semi-dismissing her unconscious comment, she said that this must be related to "my" belief that if one holds pain and suffers it, more space opens up inside them so that they possess their grief rather than being possessed by it. She went on to say that she had had experiences like this in the years we had worked together, but insisted that "she" did not believe in this. If she were sufficiently "evolved," Penny said, giving up an hour would be painless. She was clinging to the fantasy that pain did not have to be a part of life at the same time as she was unconsciously beginning to suffer the pain that would fill her up and give her substance.

But at the same time as Penny's omnipotent stance was softening and transforming, it also reared up in a last-ditch attempt to hold onto its dominant place in her psyche and violent demands that I disappear her distress arose. She wanted me to see her for free so that she would never need to give up an hour; she wanted me to allow *her* to end the session rather than obeying the movement of the clock. The intensity of her coercive requests frightened me and drove me into a variation of my coldness, the exact feeling she feared. Protecting me from awareness of my anxiety, critical and distancing feelings grabbed me by the throat and threw me out of a related attitude of openness and curiosity into a narcissistic stance that was superior and condemning even if it was couched in supposedly neutral psychoanalytic language. "How had I failed for so long to notice the malignant nature of her regression?" I asked myself anxiously, unable to remember that complexes intensify in a last gasp as one works them through. In one incident, three months before she cut down her hours, I found myself confronting her in a harsh way. The next day she began by speaking of her cruelty and after a few minutes I suggested that she might have experienced me as cruel the previous day. Penny danced around this possibility for a short while before she took it up and allowed herself to feel the distress I had caused with my own complex-ridden behavior. She wanted me to apologize and I did.

A month later, when I again fell into the role of a condemning god in relation to her loathsome worm, she began to speak for the first time about ways that she found me cold. It had been many years since my horrifyingly frigid distance sent me into my consultation group looking for help. I no longer felt consciously frozen in my emotional responses. I am sure that my having passed through the worst of it was what enabled Penny to now bring up this complaint, which had been present but denied for years. She felt panic. Penny said that she needed more warmth than I offered and fell almost immediately into the idea that she should see someone else. On the surface, she felt so frightened and small that her omnipotent entitlement took over: it seemed imperative that she get what she wanted right now. But beneath that selfish demand lay a terror that either she would injure me with her criticism or that I would destroy her with my retaliatory rage. Over the years we had chipped away at her idealization of me, but now she saw a real limitation in my behavior. Horrified, she talked about her inability to imagine that I could be good enough if I were not perfect. Slowly, the rage that she had always worked so hard to protect me from emerged in all its intensity. She was angry, many years after the fact, about the slow pace at which I had managed to free up the late afternoon hours she wanted. "For some reason," she declared angrily, I had not wanted to push people out of their hours to accommodate her. Her jealousy rapidly expanded. She did not see how I could care for her if anyone else mattered to me. No one counted for her except herself, she insisted. Penny began by experiencing the parents' coldness that permeated our field as located inside of me, but its virulent nature (as we saw in the case of the consultation group that caught it) infected everyone it touched, and as she became angry at me for participating in it, she fell into it, too.

The selfishness of her attitude did frighten me, but in this hour I was able to keep my footing and when she asked me why I was being so silent I told her that I was trying to imagine what she must feel in this mood. I wondered if it might feel lonely. Penny talked about how dangerous it seemed to actually take others into account. She felt that she would lose something if she thought that the intense deprivation she experienced in relation to me could not be attributed to my having other people in my life. Together we realized that accepting that fact would open the door to her sense that her deprivation could never be expunged, stemming as it did partly from my authentic limitations. She tried to say that she couldn't bear to imagine me as flawed because she felt so defective herself that she needed someone perfect to help her. But she stumbled repeatedly over the words and realized that they were no longer true. She did not really feel defective any more, she said, although she did feel wounded. She remembered a movie she had seen in which impoverished Indian children had been forced to hide in a latrine, immersed in shit. I suggested that her desperate need to be so special as to be the only one was her shit and that when she felt I saw her as an ordinary person, bringing her down to the muddy ground with all the other ordinary people – who might even include me – she felt that she was being thrown into her shit. As this theme of specialness wove its way through the months that preceded her cutting down, she gradually acknowledged her authentic compassion for others. Her terror, she saw, had led her to harden her heart against her concern.

Within the human psyche, attitudes based in love and relatedness struggle against the narcissistic greed for power that is called up by a terror of annihilation. Another way to say this is to note that the vulnerability of warmth struggles with the safety of coldness in each of our souls. Although some mixture of love and power almost always drives us, the extent to which one is present precludes the other. The narcissistic complex of pathology that we have been talking about, fueled by a sense of weakness that emanates from the jelly-like core, is an expression of the power drive. We each fall into some version of the god-worm relationship under stress. Penny's need to be number one, the only valuable person in the world, would have brought up vastly superior feelings had she not protected herself by demeaning herself inside. Her perfectionism, in addition to its other meanings, led to vicious attacks on herself for her various failings. This constellated the superior, omnipotent god inside me and in this period where her complexes were greatly heightened by the looming approach of her loss of an hour with me, my tendency to turn to ice inside caused me considerable shame when she or I recognized it.

Penny's mother, who lived nearby, began to decline sharply in these months and there were endless crises around her care. (Her father had died before I knew her.) Penny became the target for her sister's distress and the sister, living almost a thousand miles away, fired off endless scathing emails that criticized Penny's handling of their mother's care. As we talked about her sister, she realized that she felt the same kind of criticism and judgment from me as she did from her sister. I commented that since the judge seemed to be in the room, it would make more sense for us to work with that critical energy here than at a distance. She talked about her feeling that if she did not suspend her life and devote herself full time to her mother, thus shielding her mother from suffering, I would condemn her as a selfish daughter. Together we were able to see that Penny wanted me to suspend my life to protect her from suffering, but that her fear of the demand she felt led her to turn the criticism on herself. Gradually she saw that if she attacked me/herself for not providing infinite nurturance, she was protected from blaming me for various comments that she had realistically experienced as cold or critical just as she was shielded from struggling with her own real imperfections. We did not have to grapple with our true failings if we focused on the ways either one of us was not superhuman. With trepidation, she allowed herself to criticize my realistic difficulties and to stick with ways she experienced me as cold and harsh.

She became overtly angry with both her sister and with me, allowing herself to be not-so-perfect, to be down in the muck with everyone else. She felt unlovable in her anger and was sure that I hated her (when I was actually relieved, for we were no longer caught in a frozen dance of perfection). Penny felt terrible about her fury, recognizing that it meant she would not win the competition for the-most-perfect-person. She was comforted, however, by my pointing out that she felt so needy and empty and vulnerable that she became desperate and wild like a cornered animal. Penny became noticeably more authentic in her relationship with her husband and with one of her daughters, who lived nearby. She dreamed that she was shrinking. She was giving up her inflation and making nourishing connections with people. She dreamed of an interracial couple she knew; in the dream, the white person had become darker and the brown person had become lighter. Life was turning mixed and confusing instead of black and white.

In these months we talked a lot about the loss and fear she felt around giving up her third hour. She felt that I was abandoning her by allowing her to give up an hour and at times her distress led her to feel furious about it. I was sticking her in the cloakroom all over again. But she also realized that she was not rejecting her baby part as she previously had. Instead of being crammed into a tiny box, she now could often feel the baby's presence, and she admitted that she had become able to hold it on her lap when I was not available. Penny was warming up. She allowed herself to know how much money she was making and to take on some of her authentic bigness and substance, a change that made it more possible to accept her smallness and vulnerability.

Interspersed with the upsurge in her complex's activity were many themes of progress. When threatening material presented itself, sometimes because the weekend loomed, Penny could frighten me with the violent force of her complex; at other times, she amazed me with her growing self-possession and maturity. She dreamed twice in this period of sleeping in her own bed rather than sharing one with her husband. She felt funny about it; she worried she might hurt his feelings; but it felt good to have her own space. The dream reflected her growing ability to see both him and me in more realistic ways and to believe in the validity of her own point of view. She was no longer merged with him (or me); she was more and more separate and related rather than attached with glue. Although Penny felt that it was very hard to give up her third hour, she also thought she could do it. She could bear this suffering.

One week after a long weekend that left her with only two hours, Penny felt a clinging need for me. Rather than falling into self-attacks, she commented that her desperation looked like backsliding to the linear, non-psychological part of herself, but she could see that it was progress to be able to notice and feel her need rather than denying it and falling into envy or jealousy to cope with it. When her wish to get an A+ in analysis came up, she was able to recognize it as an attempt to protect herself from her insecurity and to let it go. She felt jealous of my other patients when confronted in one way or another with proof of their existence, but as we mutually worked through the permafrost her infantile experience had created in her (and thus in me), Penny (and I) began to feel the depth of my love for her and the importance of these invisible other patients receded. She read a psychology book by Masterson that a friend recommended and thought that he acted superior to his patients; she was surprised to find herself thinking that she and I were partners in the work and that we were holding hands as we faced the truth together. It seemed to be good enough and it was solid, not like dancing around trying not to see distressing things. She imaged me in a dream as a woman she had known years ago who had adopted an Eastern European child with serious attachment problems. The adopting mother had "completely" cured her child, who developed a healthy attachment to her new mother.

Envy, jealousy and greed continued to erupt in stark and shocking ways but in this period I worked through my fear of their strength and became more able to hold the condemning responses they constellated in me. Instead of being a prisoner of my harsh coldness, I became able to hold the coldness and remain separate from it. Remember that Penny quoted me above (p 160) as saying that if one can suffer his distress rather than fleeing from it, he becomes the possessor of his pain instead of being possessed by it. As we worked together on Penny's complex in this pivotal period of the work, its mirror image in my psyche was getting worked on, too. Neither my working this tangle out inside me nor her working it out inside her came first. The field we lived in together was worked on by both of us, and as the field shifted we were each freed, inch by inch, from its grasp. The ice-queen-mother was being redeemed inside each of our psyches.

As I became more able to view myself with compassion, I became able to hold her increasingly sympathetically. In turn, this enabled Penny to hold her vulnerability more and this helped her to hold and recognize her shadow more often, too. Envy, jealousy, greed: instead of terrifying demons, these emotions became simply painful human failings to hold and work with. She cried about her fear that I would lose interest in her when she cut down, that she would be replaced by someone else who would do the "intensive" work that I seemed to value. But the next day she told me that she could feel my commitment to her and knew I would not stop cherishing her when we began to meet only twice a week. When she felt I had particularly helped her, her envy could certainly erupt, but in one experience of this she remembered how jealous and excluded her mother always felt when the children formed positive alliances. Everything had been about triumph in her family, and Penny now saw how imbued with triumph her connection with me had been. One of us had to be good and superior and the other had to be bad and inferior. One of us triumphed and the other failed. It was safer for me to be strong and her to be weak, but she also wanted to tear me down from my pedestal. As she opened her eyes and allowed herself to see me as fallible and to criticize me for my failings, she became increasingly able to imagine us as two limited creatures, limping along together and doing our work well enough.

As she overcame the coldness of her perfectionism by expressing her "irrational" or "excessive" anger at my coldness, she expressed the belief that I had changed and become warmer. Subjectively, I had always liked her a lot. Her desperate need to be "good" had twisted her psyche into terrible knots, but behind that lay the fact that she really did try to be good in ways that almost anyone would admire, for she placed the highest value on being a loving and concerned person. Her crippling wish to be "good" also led her to work very hard in her analysis, to take up as much of her suffering as she could possibly manage – even when taking up her suffering took the deceptive form of the intensely (but overtly) expressed wish to not take off her protective armor. I did not feel that my basic feeling had changed, but I was certainly aware that the cruel emotions that had frightened me so much were modulating as I recognized Penny more and more as a peer, struggling with injuries in her psyche just as I struggled with the wounds in mine.

As her mother's health failed and Penny worked through basic levels of this primary complex, love and concern arose for the mother Penny had once held as all bad. She remembered times her mother had been nurturing with her and the mother's weakened condition constellated pity and understanding. Deep reservoirs of grief emerged. Instead of defending against her grief with rage, she swam in it. She began to let go of believing that the only way to be an admirable daughter was to sacrifice herself completely because she was developing the capacity to hold the suffering that an inner conflict arouses. She felt crucified between her wish to ease her mother's pain and her own life's demands and needs. She struggled successfully against the inner judge who insisted that if she would only do the job of caring for her mother properly, the mother would not have to suffer. More and more, Penny recognized suffering as an intrinsic part of life rather than something to be avoided. Paradoxically, she became less internally sensitive to her sister's criticisms as she became able to lash out angrily when the sister found Penny's efforts wanting. And the sister, connecting with a real person with needs instead of a pretend saint, became less critical and more compassionate regarding the difficult situation Penny was coping with.

People change slowly and development circles around and around rather than proceeding in a straight line. Each time Penny's complex intensified inside her in its attempt to hang onto dominance, I was pulled into my version of the mother's frozen heartlessness. But each time, slightly less so. By talking actively about my coldness, something that she had never done before, Penny became my ally in noticing it, becoming curious about it, and transforming it. Certainly, I could still become frightened and distance myself by (silently) diagnosing her in some critical way. It was hard, in the moment, to remember that the intensification of symptoms is part of their resolution and we *were* dealing with a frightening injury to the capacity for concern. But as we faced into it together, it softened and modified dramatically.

Penny's progress in this period was stunning. She became much less subject to the dominance of the intensifiers because her awareness of them grew; she took up her true potency as she gave up her omnipotent defenses; her need to diminish herself eased as she realized that she could contain the cold hate that lurked behind it; she took long strides in authenticity with everyone in her life, including me, and found the ensuing intimacy nourishing enough to compensate for the relinquished role of perfect-person. Her husband and I were emphatically demoted from gods to mortals as she came to believe in the value of her own point of view. The next years were spent consolidating and widening these gains until she felt able to give up her remaining hours. She felt real, she felt strong, and she felt rich in nourishing relationships when she eventually terminated the therapy. The partly inauthentic concern that had been so tangled up with her wish to be a *perfectly* concerned person slowly transformed into the real warmth and concern that were such a central element of her true nature.

Chapter 5

Truth and lies

Whether to see life as it is will give us much consolation, I know not; but the consolation which is drawn from truth, if any there be, is solid and durable; that which may be derived from errour must be, like its original, fallacious and fugitive.

(Dr. Johnson's letter to Bennet Langton, quoted in Bion, 1970, p. 7)

Relatedness depends on the attempt to see and bear the truth. When the truth is feared, the "I" seals itself into a solipsistic bubble that shuts out other points of view, whether the perspectives of other people or the perspectives of other parts of himself. The person who fears the truth of this moment is not trying to think about his point of view or to imagine others' perspectives. He is trying *not* to be aware of something that he unconsciously believes to be present, something that some part of him has decided is too threatening. As the story of the blind men and the elephant makes clear,[1] searching for truth depends on the ability to hold multiple points of view. One perspective offers only a flat picture that easily deceives. When I can see a situation from the point of view of my "I" and from the point of view of *your* "I" as well, elements that I was originally blind to become plain. In the previous chapter, we explored the internal structure of narcissism. In this chapter, we turn to an examination of the dynamic interplay in the psyche between related and anti-related energies, between the parts of ourselves that seek the truth versus the parts that fear it.

One strand of Bion's thinking circles around truth and lies. Many people resist the stark moralism of his terms but, as always, Bion is talking about currents that exist in all people. He is not sorting people into truth tellers and liars. He is trying to explore a fundamental paradox of the human condition: we need to face into the truth in order to be related and therefore in order to grow but we have to lie to ourselves both to titrate emotional pain that we

---

1 Each blind man feels one part of the elephant with his hands so that the one at the tail thinks it a skinny, snake-like creature, one at a leg imagines a tree-like creature, and so on.

cannot bear and to maintain our stability as ongoing, familiar selves in a reliable world. In using the moralistically tinged words "truth" and "lies," Bion follows the Kleinian tradition of holding the individual responsible for the unconscious emotional choices that he makes – in this case either facing into the truth or avoiding it. It is as though Bion is saying, "Don't call it a *defense*; call it by its real name, a *lie*." The words force the reader to acknowledge the pervasive nature of the distortions by which we live.

The psychoanalyst's commitment to truth has been a bedrock of our profession. As early as 1914 Freud noted that

> [p]sycho-analytic treatment is founded on truthfulness. In this fact lies a great part of its educative effect and its ethical value. . . . Anyone who has become saturated in the analytic technique will no longer be able to make use of the lies and pretences which a doctor normally finds unavoidable. . . . Since we demand strict truthfulness from our patients, we jeopardize our whole authority if we let ourselves be caught out by them in a departure from the truth.
>
> (Freud, 1914, p. 164)

Truth is the analytically oriented practitioner's North Star. She seeks not to help the patient become "healthy" or "well adapted;" rather, the goal is to help the patient become himself. The analytic attitude hopes that both members of the couple will be open and curious, first about the patient but then about the therapist, too. Analysts believe that open curiosity will enable the patient to process (alphabetize) emotional aspects of his experience that he could not dream before. As he introjects the container that his therapist's receptivity inside the consulting room has fostered, the patient's inner container and his ability to sit with unknowingness grows stronger. His α function becomes more reliable and capable. He is able to gather more of himself into his conscious experience and knowledge of himself. He will have choices about his behavior and his life that were not present before. It is certainly possible that the patient will choose a "healthier" approach to his life as he becomes more of himself, but it is also quite possible that his choices will be eccentric and may *not* conform to society's rules for "appropriate" behavior. If the history of depth psychotherapy and psychoanalysis is a story of one split after another, one factor that no dissenters have yet disputed is the therapist's fundamental stance toward unearthing the truth of the patient. And, as a sort of bonus, the truth of the therapist and of the therapeutic interaction as well.

Freud initially believed that the central human motivation is the "pleasure principle:" a search for pleasure and an avoidance of unpleasure, where "pleasure" means a quiescent state of non-stimulation. One strand of the psyche seeks nirvana, the extinction of desire and passion, a state beyond the suffering of embodied existence. Although Freud called this the "pleasure principle," it does not refer to what most of us call "pleasure:" sensual gratification, excitement or fun. Life is painful and all living organisms try to avoid pain. To the extent that this basic drive away from pain and toward peace and quiet is operating, the individual tries *not* to have her full life experience. She does not want to notice the way her mother's tone of voice is envious or scornful; she tries not to be aware of conflictual feelings about her loved ones; she blinds herself to signs of her aging or her weakness or her potency. The "pleasure drive" leads to the defense mechanisms that shield us from large aspects of our aliveness in order to protect us from destabilizing experiences. We are afraid to see ourselves and our loved ones from new and different perspectives, for that would throw our relationships and worldviews into question. Seeing the formerly unseen may trigger more emotional pain than we can bear.

Many theorists since Freud have challenged the primacy of the pleasure principle and have suggested, using a broad variety of terms, that while one strand of human motivation is certainly the avoidance of pain, a quest for the truth is also inborn. We are afraid to see, but we are also driven to see. Indeed, since our species, in the eons of our existence, has managed to amass considerable (relative) truth, much of which humanity initially experienced as emotionally disturbing,[2] we might think that the search for truth is at least slightly more powerful than the quest for not-pain.

Freud hypothesized that the truth-seeking drive was an *ego* instinct (i.e. a desire that arises in response to the individual's development) and that it expressed the "reality principle." When the breast is not immediately present, the infant, gripped by the pleasure principle, attempts to hallucinate it as a way to avoid the pain of its absence. But the hallucination does not satisfy and the baby is forced to accommodate to the reality of his dependence, helplessness and need. For Freud, the reality principle is avoided when possible, but life experience softens this. In reasonable circumstances, the infant learns that feeling his distress and expressing it by crying will bring greater satisfaction than will avoiding his distress and hallucinating. Reality begins to appeal. But there is no innate search for truth. Despite the fact that he himself turned up every rock inside the psyche, examining every frightful creature he could find in the inner world, Freud considered his own search a secondary, learned adaptation rather than an inborn drive rivaling the quest for pleasure.

Both Jung and Bion believed that truth is the basic material of emotional growth. They each hypothesized that the search for the truth is as implicit in the organism as is the genetic drive toward biological maturity. Bion states repeatedly that the psyche's relation to truth parallels the body's relation to food: it is the basic sustenance without which the soul shrivels and deteriorates. Jung, using the metaphor of infection instead of starvation, takes a similar position:

---

2 As with the heliocentric image of the solar system or the theory of evolution.

Suppose a very disagreeable thing has happened to me and I don't admit it, perhaps an awful lie. . . . The lie is there objectively, either in the conscious or in the unconscious. If I don't admit it . . . it becomes a strange body and will form an abscess in the unconscious, and the same process of suppuration begins, psychologically, as goes on in the physical body.

(Jung, 1984, p. 20)

Bion postulates as axiomatic the theory that a truth drive (Grotstein, 2004b) is stronger than the pleasure principle. But he admits that he "cannot support this conviction by evidence regarded as scientific. It may be that the formulation belongs to the domain of Aesthetic" (Bion, 1965, p. 38). While truth may be the nourishment of the soul, lies (or defenses, as most lies are more commonly known) are also universal, a fact that would seem to imply that to survive, the psyche also depends on lies. "I think it is 'better' to know the truth about one's self and the universe. . . . But I do not wish to imply that it is 'nicer' or 'pleasanter.' Whether it is 'better' is a matter of opinion" (Bion, 1970, p. 4). These two drives – a truth drive that wants to see and a stability drive that blinds us – compete endlessly in the human psyche.

The individuation drive

Jung's thinking about the truth drive is described in his work on individuation. He was the first psychoanalyst to imagine an inborn urge toward truth and to place it at the center of human motivation. He postulated that the core human drive is to become the individual one innately is, as opposed to the person society or the family or the "I" wants one to be. He called this instinctual process "individuation" and he first began to develop his ideas about it in the aftermath of his devastating break with Freud in 1912. The energy fueling this process comes from the Self.

As we explored in Chapter 2, the unconscious psyche always aims to create a balance that will replace the one-sided perspective of consciousness with an appreciation of the vast depths surrounding it. This is the psyche's attempt to live the truth of its nature. The truth drive opposes the impulse to avoid emotional pain and to maintain the status quo because it explicitly seeks to know about the conflicting impulses that tear apart the person and destabilize him. The individual wants and doesn't want to see the unappealing aspects of himself as well as the desired ones. (I would hope that the reader would keep in mind the fact that aspects of the person that *he* considers unappealing can often be qualities that the world at large considers positive; it is threatening for someone to own his generosity or compassion, for example, when these qualities conflict with the image of himself that his primary attachment figures fostered. And it is frightening for most people to fully own their strength, for recognizing one's potency means recognizing one's capacity to do harm.

If the person is strong, by implication he is responsible to some extent for the state of his life.)

The Self presses to be actualized in the specific form that expresses the individual's nature. But like Truth, that actualization can never be complete. Typically, the young person identifies with her persona: with the role, the title, the function she performs. But the persona is a secondary phenomenon for the individual, often shaped more by outer forces than by her own nature. Rather than being identified with the mask with which we meet the outer world, people are called by inner necessity to live the truth of their natures. Although Jung was much less focused on the healing capacity of the analytic relationship than is the case with contemporary thinkers, he was always quite clear that a radical encounter with oneself can occur only in the context of an intimate relationship. The most a solitary individual can hope for, he said, is a "general and merely academic 'insight into one's mistakes' " (1946, para 503). But rather than *focusing* on the interpenetration of analyst and patient that he mapped so brilliantly in *The Psychology of the Transference* (1946), Jung concentrated on the way analysis provides a special container within which the patient, imagined as a separate, self-contained being, begins to explore the unconscious self pressing to exist in the outer world.[3] He believed that the analytic container supports the search for this self by helping the patient to look inward to her unconscious depths at the same time as she grapples with the demands of conscious life. The puny "I" the person lives in is pummeled by conflicting energies from within and without. By struggling consciously with these forces, the individual is gradually differentiated.

The state of being torn is a basic reality of human life that can never be overcome: "the psyche is at cross purposes with itself," Jung commented (ibid., para 523). One sharp difference between human beings and other animals is the fact that our nature is to be at war with our nature. How the "I" will harmonize the conflicting energies that toss it about cannot be predicted. At the same time as the individual tries to protect her security and comfort by not-knowing about her conflictual impulses, an inner force pushes her toward a recognition of who she is – neither this nor that but both – and in the specific proportions that create her singularity.

Most contemporary analysts, including a large percentage of Jungians, look primarily to the ways the patient's conflicts express themselves within the transference relationship, believing that exploring the patient's conflicts in the analytic situation will enable the patient gradually to work on them and to make some progress toward holding the opposites inside herself. Jung's rift with Freud left him needing to clearly articulate his differences with his

---

3 We see in this example of Jung's theories how frightening relatedness is. It is the basic fabric of emotional health, but it brings with it deep experiences of vulnerability. Analytic thinkers take refuge in fantasies of relatively autonomous *individuals* with *individual* psychologies instead of staying with the overwhelming interdependence of the human condition.

old mentor. This led, in 1916, to the first version of what was ultimately revised as *Two Essays on Analytical Psychology* (1953). The second section of the second essay is called "Individuation" and, caught in the worldview held by our profession in the first half of the previous century, it focuses on the individual as a closed system. Jung looks at the way the patient can work on her inner conflicts inside the container that analysis provides. Although we would not see this work today as an adequate basis for analytic technique, Jung's ideas provide valuable insight into the way the truth drive and the stability drive pull the person in opposing directions, toward growth or toward safety.

Jung suggested that in this non-rational life process of individuation, the person's psyche creates symbolic images that bring her to a new level of integration. Jung's exceptional talent for intuitively grasping the meaning of the patient's symbolic images led him to focus on the ways her dreams and fantasies describe the unfolding of her differentiating self. From her own images, he believed, new attitudes will emerge to guide her to her unique path.[4] Against the desire of the "I" to be one unified entity, the person must be fair to the myriad demands of the inner and outer worlds and must submit to the meaning that emerges from this struggle. Otherwise, she will fall back into a state of inner disunion. Ongoing work with opposing inner and outer energies brings the person toward her center, toward the Self.

But no matter how much work one does, individuation is never "attained." One exploding conflict between the warring impulses of the deeper psyche, the demands of the outer world, and the narcissistic strivings of the "I," is gradually resolved through a new attitude. A period of relative peace and harmony then emerges, based on the expansion of the connection between the "I" and the Self – on the strengthening of the ego-Self axis. But the unconscious, always in motion, churns up new material to challenge one's complacency.

> If the unconscious is not allowed to express itself through word and deed, through worry and suffering, through our consideration of its claims and resistance to them, then the earlier, divided state will return. . . . We are always in doubt: there is a pro to be rejected and a contra to be accepted. All of us would like to escape from this admittedly

---

4 The focus on images is one way that people grow. It was Jung's personal way and was reinforced because the interpersonal experience of a personal analysis was never available to him. For some people, the dreams and fantasy images that emerge from the unconscious are a natural form of discourse in which they can engage with their unconscious. In Jung's early work with psychotic people at the Burghölzli, it was possible to follow a conversation between him and the patient's unconscious that occurred through his interpretation of the patient's dreams. He would speak to the meaning of the dream, and the patient would return with a new dream that imaged her unconscious response to Jung's comment on the first dream.

uncomfortable situation, but we do so only to discover that what we left behind us was ourselves.

(Jung, 1946, para 522)

Through one painful struggle after another, the Self begins to incarnate as the self. The unique person gradually taking shape in the material world combines the universal human qualities in her own way, emphasizing and weaving these qualities into a novel tapestry. Far from becoming selfish as this process unfolds, the person becomes herself, something vastly different from egotism, something, in fact, that her selfishness will not welcome. As we explored in the previous chapter, the "I" always wants to be a "better" person than the true self emerging continually from this struggle.

The drama that pummels the "I" from all directions is pictured in *The Book of Job* as a wager between God (the Self) and the fallen angel whom the Hebrew Bible calls "the Adversary." Psychologically, this "Adversary" is known as the shadow or the repressed unconscious. In the individuation journey's quest for wholeness, this dark spirit brings us face to face with who we *are*, separate from who we might wish to be or from how we appear, either to ourselves or to the world. All of the tendencies and desires that we do *not* want included in ourselves push us to recognize them. This is "a stark encounter with reality, with no false veils or adornments. . . . What was hidden under the mask of conventional adaptation" is revealed (Jung, ibid., para 452).

Using the various defense mechanisms that enable us to not know about our experiences, we push aside awareness of the shadow. The truths on which the person turns his back are

> integral components of the personality . . . and their loss to conscious-ness produces an inferiority . . . a lack which gives rise to a feeling of moral resentment. . . . The moral inferiority [comes] from the conflict with one's own self which, for reasons of psychic equilibrium, demands that the deficit be redressed.
>
> (Jung, 1953, para 218)

When someone is blind to her hate, for example, she not only enacts it destructively. She is also *less* of herself than she should be and while the "I" may feel pleased with what a kind and generous person she imagines herself to be, she will also feel bitter and envious of more substantial people who know about their hate and who, by containing it constructively, have its emotional energy at their disposal instead of being possessed by out-of-control emotional turmoil. On some level, the person who turns his back on his self feels resentful and bitter, ashamed and guilty, unable to establish an intimate (i.e. true or authentic) relationship with another because he has evaded an intimate relationship with himself.

Analysis is effective partly because the patient works consciously with the products of his unconscious, but simply confessing his secrets also helps the patient to approach his own true nature. Secrets, disguises, concealment – lies – protect the person from pain and confusion but they isolate him from others and because a person's relationship with himself mirrors his relationship with others, secrets isolate a person from himself. The Church, the premodern container for people's attempts to manage their emotional upheavals, created the sacrament of confession as a prelude to communion. This ritual held sway over the Western world for so long because it embodies a fundamental truth about human psychology: confession of secrets brings one out of narcissistic isolation and into the community of human relationships. The confidential therapeutic process expresses the same fact of our natures. Depth psychological treatment, a contemporary container for development, has inherited and (greatly) reworked Catholic confession.

The alchemists consistently advise the seeker to begin with something unappealing: the menstruum of a whore, the diadem buried in filth. We must "take truth, goodness, and beauty where we find them," says Jung. "Often they are hidden in the dirt" (Jung, 1946, para 384). The stone that the builders rejected will become the cornerstone, says Jesus (Mark 12:10), quoting Psalm 118. As early as 1914, Freud noted that a central task for the patient is to turn toward the neurotic symptom, rather than scorning its value and trying to suppress it. The symptom, he said, "has solid ground for its existence" and from it will come "things of value for his future life" (Freud, 1914, p. 152). "*In the intensity of the emotional disturbance itself lies the value, the energy which [the patient] should have at his disposal in order to remedy the state of reduced adaptation,*" said Jung (1916, para 166, emphasis in original). Edward Edinger suggests that

> every neurotic symptom, every compulsion, every addiction, every primitive affect . . . [contains] within it . . . the precious stone of the Self. . . . [T]he secret that is taught in the analytic process [is] that in the course of dealing with one's smallest, most despicable, most apparently insignificant psychic matters, one discovers the [Self] and makes a connection to it.
>
> (Edinger, 1996, pp. 112–14)

Though we recoil instinctively from pain and lie to ourselves to evade it, pain is inherent in life. To the extent that we succeed in ridding ourselves of suffering and in protecting our "security," we turn away from growth, away from the full vibrancy of our potential aliveness. Pain is not something to be gotten rid of, it is something to learn to work with. Distress, unhappiness, grief – "negative" emotions of all kinds – are ordinary elements of the life cycle rather than shameful failures or symptoms of inferiority. In fact, analytic thinkers tell us from one perspective after another that working with these despised and avoided experiences brings a sense of wholeness and meaning to life.

As we explored in Chapter 2, Bion and Jung, like many other analytic thinkers, explicitly reject the idea of a "complete" analysis. Contemporary thinkers do not use the word "cure" often, but it does appear from time to time and "healing" is quite often talked about. Patients typically seek a "cure" for their wounds, their anxiety, their obsessions and addictions. Jung denies that "perfection" – which may be thought of as a synonym for "cure" – is possible. My own experience, on both sides of the couch, suggests that even "healing" may be a problematic word. In some sense, a person *is* her wounds. A sapling, planted beside a supportive stake that the gardener neglects to remove, will grow around the stake. The stake's presence will injure the growing tree; the tree will adapt by distorting its "natural" shape to accommodate the stake. But the mature tree will *be* the shape it has taken; it cannot be "cured" of the injury, the injury is an intrinsic aspect of its nature.

Human beings develop similarly. For example, the adult who comes into the therapeutic container may be someone who rushes through her feelings, evading a real experience of them by moving so fast that their acknowledgment is never absorbed. Such behavior is symptomatic of how the stresses of her childhood environment interacted with her inborn temperament and talents. After many years of therapeutic work, we hope that the symptom will be modified. We would like to see the patient develop the ability to slow down, to hold and therefore to experience more of her emotional life. Perhaps she will become able to experience *much* more of her truth than was the case at the beginning of the work. But the person is not going to turn into someone else. Under stress, she will always become somewhat speedy; she will always have a tendency to skim the surface and fear the depths. She may become aware of how her symptom interferes with intimate relationships; she may become able to notice interference early on and to adapt by backtracking or shifting her behavior. But difficult patterns will not *completely* disappear.

Sometimes, the patient's worst symptoms can almost dissolve. Colin came into therapy because he was unable to succeed in his work as an attorney. As we unpacked his difficulty over eleven years of work, he came to see how his mother had demanded that he share her vulnerability and weakness. His father, apparently threatened by his growing son, had also unconsciously pushed him to be weak and ineffectual and had punished him emotionally on the rare occasions that Colin tried to test his developing manhood against his father's. In the transference relationship, I, unlike his mother, sincerely and consistently celebrated his developing strength and competence. Energized by my faith in his potential strength and by the insights he developed in his exploration of himself, Colin's income nearly tripled in the course of our work. His core *symptom* – an inability to be strong in his work – relaxed so dramatically that we could say it was "cured." But, under stress, he could still fall into avoiding interpersonally challenging situations or become anxious about standing up to them. He still disowned enough of his aggression and rage to fear hostile responses from others, even when objectively there was no evidence to indicate a potentially hostile response. Although he was not a *new* person, Colin had become much more of himself and that enabled him to become successful in his work. But an ingrained basic timidity could still trip him up.

We come back to our basic complexes over and over throughout the life cycle, hopefully reworking them at deeper and deeper levels. What we *can* expect from a successful piece of therapeutic work is that the person will find solid ground to stand on *outside* his central complexes. He should be able to know when a complex is triggered and to extricate himself from it sooner rather than later or not at all. "I'm feeling intimidated again," Colin might think to himself. "What's going on? What's frightening me? I know so and so is trying to bully me into accepting an inadequate settlement. I don't *have* to roll over and play dead!" Coming to this place meant that Colin had stuck with his analysis through many painful times, bowing down to the fury of his complexes and suffering them rather than evading them. Although both Jung and Bion say repeatedly that truth is the nourishment of the psyche, the food that enables us to grow, people vary a great deal regarding how much truth they can bear, how much suffering they need to evade; the deep shifts in Colin's psychological attitudes that allowed him to work through so much of his complex at so profound a level came at the cost of facing a great deal of pain. It is unusual for someone to be *as* available to grow as he was.

The most hopeful result of analysis finds the patient suffering *more* of his pain than he was able to manage before. More of his pain is held in conscious awareness instead of being discharged into behavior that jumbles up his life, injuring his relationships or his work. A successful therapeutic venture leaves the patient's outer life improved, perhaps dramatically. Ideally, the patient will find more satisfaction and pleasure than before. But instead of being tormented by meaningless pain, he will suffer pain constructively. Pain is always part of life, and the wounds that have molded the person into exactly this or that shape will continue to channel his responses to pain in his unique ways.

All the "negative" qualities of our selves – neediness, dependency, driven sexual urges, self-loathing, terrors – demand recognition and push their way into the analytic relationship. It becomes "the hiding place for all the most secret, painful, intense, delicate, shamefaced, timorous, grotesque, unmoral" feelings known to humanity. But at the same time, and in the same place, are found "the most sacred feelings" possible. This whole confused mass of energy "twine[s itself] invisibly round . . . doctor and patient" in the transference experience (Jung, 1946, para 371). Far from being the problematic complication that Freud and Breuer initially took the unavoidable development of the transference relationship to be, we now know that this basic mechanism, whereby the patient projects her unconscious psyche into the analytic relationship in one way or another, is the fundamental condition for healing even though it also creates a confused mass of data that can never be fully sorted out. The mutual projections that saturate the analytic container cause both people to lose track of what belongs to each one of them, but the lengthy project of owning distortions and untangling confusions that then takes place *is* the healing work. The no-longer conventional person "is in very truth reborn from this psychological relationship" (ibid., para 420).

> The individuation process pulls the "I" into relationship with the Self and reveals our relationship to that inner friend of the soul into whom Nature herself would like to change us – that other person who we also are and yet can never attain to completely. . . . We should prefer to be always "I" and nothing else. But we are confronted with that inner friend or foe, and whether he is our friend or foe depends on ourselves.
>
> (Jung, 1950c, para 235)

At first this "inner friend" appears as a foe because the unconscious turns the same face toward the "I" that the "I" turns toward it. Objectively frightening energies like envy or rage or greed that developed in response to the unthinkable terrors of infancy and childhood have been disowned and possess the person unconsciously. He imagines that the not-"I" parts of himself – the "inner friend" – will be powered partly by these fearsome drives that he *knows* are lurking somewhere. And then, too, any not-I element of an individual upsets the person's established sense of himself and confronts the "I" with what Bion (1963) called "catastrophic change[5]." Of course "we should prefer to be always 'I' and nothing else" (Jung, op. cit., para 235). To actually *experience* one's unfamiliar aspects is painful and confusing, even when those elements turn out to be objectively positive. But as the individuation process becomes established and the person begins to recognize the objective reality of the larger psyche and of the Self, he may be able to reach the place where he can join more wholeheartedly in this search for his true nature. When the "I" can approach the unknown self in a friendly spirit, the unconscious reciprocates and appears as an ally.

The first few years of Kathy's analysis were marked by a repeating dream image in which she was a prisoner of or pursued by the Nazis. In terror, she fled these demonic foes who had been born from her own horrifyingly unacceptable (to her) hatred and rage. For several years I supported her growing interest in the figures produced by her psyche and encouraged her to get to know them by extending her dream images in waking imagination. On a number of occasions, images less centrally threatening than the Nazis (such as a dark homeless man) surprised her by displaying a positive side in

---

5 In Chapter 12 of *Attention and Interpretation* (1970) ("Container and Contained Transformed"), Bion develops this idea at length.

her spontaneous fantasies. The dark stranger *was* filled with anger, but Kathy connected with his suffering and empathized with it; his hatred was comprehensible rather than something simply to be condemned. Three years after she first entered analysis, the following dream marked a fundamental transformation of her attitude:

> In one scene after another, I am fleeing from the Nazis again. I come to a beach and am running along the shoreline. But then I come to a cliff – the ocean is on one side and the cliff is ahead of me. There is no place left to run. I turn and face my pursuers. Now I am wearing only a poncho to cover up my nakedness. As the first tank begins to come over the sand dunes toward me, I kneel down in the sand and spread my arms outward in the shape of a cross. The turret of the tank comes over the rise and instead of a Nazi there's an American GI sitting on top of it. A soldier with light brown hair and green eyes, just like mine.

Kathy had submitted to the demands of the Self, which was orchestrating an individuation process inside her. Her submission, imaged in kneeling down and offering herself up for crucifixion, represented not simply intellectual acceptance of my repeated statement that the unconscious turns toward us the face that we turn toward it. She had given in – or given up or given over – and found that the supposed Nazi pursuing her was actually a fraternal twin who sought the inner union with herself that would rescue her from her state of alienation.

This example images another aspect of the turning toward the Self/self that individuation promotes and requires. Ideally, as the person ages, she moves toward identifying with the Self rather than with her ego. Power concerns (like Kathy's attempt to flee her fate), the province of the "I," recede and are recognized as secondary to the core issues of human life. Instead of power, love toward outer and inner others becomes the goal. The quest for truth rather than for security grows stronger to the degree that the individual is able to center herself in the Self rather than in the "I." Analysis supports this development because the patient projects the Self onto the analyst, just as the infant projects the Self onto the parent. The small child's parent is seen as godlike in his or her potency and perfection; in the ordinary experience of a positive transference, this is repeated with the therapist or analyst. The love and gratitude that the patient feels for the therapist who is *realistically* experienced as helpful and concerned (even though other currents must exist, too) fosters the patient's developing capacity to orient toward others in open and loving ways.

It is the "I" that craves security and comfort, not the Self. As the process of identifying with the Self gains strength, the individual's connection with humanity begins to modify his concern with his position vis-à-vis others – for the Self, in addition to its personal meaning, exists in us all. It is universal in the same way as is the thumb, and orienting toward the Self helps a person recognize the shared humanity that permeates his uniqueness. An expanded and expanding "I" that moves in the direction of the Self is the goal, an "I" that struggles to hold the opposing demands of power and love, of selfishness and caring, narcissism and relatedness, security and truth. The experience of coming to the Self is humiliating, humbling and relieving all at once. The petty concerns of the "I" become less compelling, and it becomes more possible to orient to one's growth process instead of one's power concerns. The person begins to feel his shared humanity, and the needs of the community of humans that existed before his birth and that will exist long after his death grow more vivid and compelling. In this process, the person approaches the truth of his nature. Ultimately, this is a satisfying state that feels like sinking into something solid and reliable.

(But, of course, this description is too black and white. Catastrophic change always feels catastrophic in anticipation, even if one has had many experiences of how welcome that same change will be in retrospect. There is a tendency in the direction I have indicated, but the psychological organism never transcends the primary conflict I describe in this chapter. A fundamental tension exists between accepting the suffering that leads to growth and fleeing from the frightening developments that will ultimately prove so welcome but that initially cause so much pain by turning our character structures upside down.)

In his memoir, Jung describes a childhood experience that illustrates the intense conflict between the forces that push us to become our true selves versus those that pull us toward the safety of the known. At the age of twelve, Jung imagined a perfect, golden God sitting in the sky on a perfect, golden throne, looking down on His beautiful cathedral.

> Here came a great hole in my thoughts, and a choking sensation. I felt numbed and knew only: "Don't go on thinking now! Something terrible is coming, something I do not want to think, something I dare not even approach."
>
> (Jung, 1965, p. 36)

He believed the terrible idea pressing to be thought would be a sin against the Holy Ghost and would damn him for all eternity. After several days of this conflict, the child decided that God Himself must have put the potential thought into his mind and he allowed himself to entertain a vision of his perfect, golden God shattering the dome of His cathedral by defecating on it from above.

Winnicott (1989) and other psychoanalysts have written about the likely personal meanings that Jung ignored in working with his waking dream image. Among other things it surely speaks to Jung's relationship with his minister father. This area of thought did *not* press Jung to recognize it. This reflects something about the personal emotional limitations he could not work through, especially because he lacked an analysis of his own. But his experience after allowing his fantasy to be born is still instructive. He felt "an enormous . . . indescribable relief. Instead of the expected damnation, grace had come upon me and with it an unutterable bliss" (Jung, op. cit., p. 40). He took his experience to mean that God had tested his courage by pushing him to think a forbidden thought, and that by acceding to God's demand he had been accorded grace, something that his father had never felt because he had been so careful to think only acceptable thoughts. He realized that "one must be utterly abandoned to God" (ibid., p. 40) and that one crucial test of this is the willingness to think the collectively unacceptable thoughts that arise in our uncensored minds – to be ourselves.

Jung deliberately omitted his memoir from his *Collected Works*. When he talks of "grace" and of "God" he is speaking off the record. Throughout the *Collected Works* he describes "God" as a projection of the life energy that animates and organizes our psyches, the energy that forms the dynamic aspect of the Self. In *Psychology and Religion* (1937) he recounts a patient's experience that was similar to his childhood struggle. He describes the resolution of this struggle as the patient coming to himself, accepting himself, and therefore becoming reconciled to painful circumstances and events. He comments that this is akin to what religious thinkers call "making one's peace with God." This is a state of union with oneself, an experience of wholeness and inner peace that ultimately emerges from an acceptance of one's inner truth in relation to one's authentic life circumstances: a submission to thinking the real thoughts that press to be thought and to feeling the real emotions that press to be felt. This is the basis of an authentic relationship with oneself.

If we strip Jung's experience of the religious terminology in which it is cloaked, we have a case example of intense resistance to facing one's personal emotional truth, and also a testament to the way that overcoming this resistance nourishes the psyche and allows it to continue developing. The image of God defecating on His cathedral contains an emotional truth that the child Jung was unable to consciously recognize. Jung focused on the way the image expressed feelings he had about the organized religion that his father was attempting to pass on to him. He also thought of this fantasy as imaging his personal sense of the nature of God. This level seems to me to have validity, but Jung was blind to the way in which the image also said to his father, "I shit on your cherished ideas, I shit on you." We do not know if Jung was ever able to think his hate in a direct, unvarnished form, but allowing himself to have the fantasy that implicitly expressed that hate brought him to a union with himself that moved him closer to becoming who he truly was by forcing him to recognize some of what he really thought.

As the individuation process takes hold, the person is less apt to struggle futilely against his or her own nature.

[T]he [Self] is our life's goal, for it is the completest expression of that fateful combination we call individuality. . . . Sensing the [Self] as something irrational . . . to which the ego is neither opposed nor subjected, but merely attached, and about which it revolves very much as the earth revolves round the sun – thus we come to the goal of individuation. . . . The ego is the only content of the [Self] that we do know. The individuated ego senses itself as the object of an unknown and supraordinate subject.

(Jung, 1953, paras 404–5)

While only conscious reality can be known, Jung is saying that there is a subjective sense of being a part of a living entity much greater than the "I." Contemporary relational analysts explore this experience in their work on the analytic "third" (Ogden, 1994) or the "field" (Baranger et al., 1983), the larger-than-either-of-us energy that so dramatically permeates depth therapeutic work. Knowing intuitively that she is part of an aliveness that is larger than her little self, the developing patient tries to orient toward the greater Self and to bring as much of it into consciousness as possible. At the same time, as we explored in Chapter 2, the Self wants to be known, producing dreams and symptoms that reflect elements of the Self that have not yet been recognized. The goal of development is to relativize the position of the "I" in the psyche. It is never possible to know the Self, but the process of working toward a conscious connection with the Self is what matters. Jung considered it the central goal of life.

The nature of truth

We have been talking about the lifelong conflict between facing into our interdependent, related nature versus evading the terrible vulnerability of that nature by seeking refuge in narcissism. As we have noted, this conflict can also be described as acknowledging the truth of ourselves versus lying about who we are. But this truth of our inherent relatedness is global; can we say something about the moment-by-moment truth that we seek? Just as there are some interpretations ("You have mixed feelings about your mother") that are universally true and therefore not terribly relevant most of the time, the danger of our interdependence is too global to mean much at any given moment. What about the truth of this particular instant, a truth that is unique to exactly now?

O, the realm of "darkness and formlessness" (Bion, 1970, p. 26), is Absolute Truth about Ultimate Reality (among other things); it is unknown and unknowable, though it is possible to have a direct experience of it, to *become* the O of this moment. We can never know the truth; we can experience it but any attempt to articulate its wholeness will necessarily be inadequate. The fundamental truth that psychoanalysts of any school aim for is emotional truth, for it is here that the person begins to know who she is. Awareness of emotional truth is a precondition for the investigation of *any* truth, because, as we explored in the previous chapter, all human perception is filtered through the psyche's emotionally laden preconceptions. As we shall see, the fact that it is never possible to be fully aware of one's emotional truth is *the* factor that severely limits our ability to say anything definitive about the nature of reality.

Bion suggests that all thinking "depends on emotions suffusing the psyche because these emotions are the connective" in which one's awareness of reality, both outer and inner, exists (Bion, 1962, p. 94). Remember that the "container" each person needs to process her experience – to alphabetize it – must be flexibly permeated with emotions. The emotions that color the container must be capable of shifting in response to life's developments if the person is to process new experiences and learn from them. The attempt to be objective and rational in thinking about something can be approached by becoming aware of one's emotions; it is neither possible nor desirable to get rid of them. To be human means to swim in an uninterrupted stream of emotions at all times; all sensory input comes to us embedded in that turbulent stream. No "fact" can be thought of as conflict-free or without emotional valence. Thinking emerges only from this stream of affective experience.

When it is not integrated with the emotional fabric of a person, "thinking" becomes a barrage of β elements, as I described in the case of Gertrude (see Chapter 3). There is no meaning because no one is present to do the thinking. Neville Symington (2006) has suggested that emotions are *the* agents of interpersonal communication, more primary than any words that may be spoken. The omnipresence of projective identification supports the idea that complex thoughts relying on words rest on a foundation of emotional communication. What emotions are animating me at this precise moment? What is the leading transference anxiety (Ogden, 1997)? What is the leading countertransference anxiety? "There is a need for awareness of an emotional experience," Bion says, "because lack of such awareness implies a deprivation of truth and truth seems to be essential for psychic health" (Bion, 1962, p. 56). So here is one definition of "truth:" the authentic emotional experience of any given moment is the truth.

Emotional truth is the basis on which other thinking rests. Personal complexes that distort a biologist's capacity to recognize his emotional reality will also distort his ability to study the life cycle of the flea. Competitive and envious strivings vis-à-vis other scientists may lead him to reject data that would push him to confirm rather than deny their findings. Greed for advancement may cause him to "see" data that are not present, or to miss data that are. Familial complexes or religious beliefs that are unconsciously projected onto the objects of study will distort perception to some extent. The modern scientific demand that results be replicated before they are

accepted acts as a control for these personal pitfalls (although not for culturally shared blindnesses), but for the individual thinker these difficulties can be
addressed only by knowing his emotional truth. Within this discussion a
second definition of "truth" is embedded: the infinite arrangements of
reality – the facts of the outer universe – are also part of the truth. There is an
inner truth – the emotional truth of the moment or of the person – and an
outer truth. However, our access to outer reality comes only through awareness of our responses to it, responses that necessarily include an emotional
dimension. Thus, because of the limitations of our species, perception of
objective truth depends on knowing one's emotional truth, something that
can never be pinned down with certainty. Michael Eigen suggests that analysts
must have faith in the reality of emotional truth, and that while that truth
"may be unknown and unknowable . . . nothing can be more important than
learning to attend to it. This is paradoxical: an unknowable is to be the focus
of our attention" (Eigen, 1981, p. 423). For Eigen, emotional truth carries the
numinosity of the Self: it is the foundation and engine of development.

Truth, whether inner or outer, is constantly shifting, always obscure in
its totality. Searching for truth requires us to "throw away everything that
[we have] thought before" (Jung, 1984, p. 443). Our task is to try to approach
the truth of the moment unencumbered by preconceived notions that would
blind us to the uniqueness of this person, this therapeutic couple, this particular instant. When Bion says that it is possible to *become* O, he means that
one can have an emotional *experience* of the present moment's truth, which
one can then struggle to articulate, but the human thought that emerges can
never capture the full experience that has been sensed. And in any case, by the
time it can be articulated, that truth has shifted. A human thought must mix
some untruth with Truth. The emotional experience of O that leads to an
attempt to describe a glimpsed truth is the "selected fact" that I explored in
Chapter 3: the feeling that suddenly makes the bits and pieces of whatever
one is studying cohere into a whole. The person "gets it."

When the therapist traverses such an experience, she may use her new
overview to say something to the patient. Sometimes the statement – an
interpretation – will resonate for the patient. The therapist's comment
expresses a cognitive deduction that has emerged from the subjective experience of her own emotional state. The patient's projective identifications in the
hour have taken root in the complex organization of the therapist's character
structure, and her ability to be aware of her own emotional experience has
combined with whatever conscious, cognitive thinking she can muster regarding the patient's spoken associations and her own silent reverie. The human
thinking process is inherently fuzzy and can help us only to *approach* the
truth; we can never get there. This fuzziness is related to the fact that so much
of our thinking is unconscious. As we explored in Chapter 2, the largely
unconscious Self is creatively engaged in attempts to understand the truth of
any given moment or situation and to communicate its understanding to the

"I" whose awareness of the whole is so limited. Much of our emotional reality is always outside our awareness.

Truth is intertwined with "realness," a quality that is equally elusive and hard to define. Being "true" or "real" implies that one is being the person one is rather than imitating another or living a role. Winnicott (1960) developed this idea with his concepts of true and false selves. Bringing in "real" as a partner of "true" leads us to an interesting paradox. An individual believes that a suicide attack that attempts to murder a large number of people who deny his particular religious ideas will cause his immediate elevation to heaven. This thought not only exists, it colors the person's behavior and informs his choices. The thought is real, as real as the bomb he carries in his backpack. Unless the people around him relate to the very true fact of his belief, many people may die, and in that sense his belief is frighteningly "true." Most of the people reading this paragraph, however, will not believe that his belief is objectively true.

Jung worked with this difficulty because one of his central interests was the psyche's religious instinct. Traditional psychoanalysts (until relatively recently) turned their back on religion, considering religion mere superstition and imagining that if someone underwent a "successful" analysis, religious ideas would lose their hold on his psyche. This expectation has not proved to be true. Beliefs that are logically impossible – miracles – are cherished by many analyzed and educated people. They acknowledge the logical impossibility of their idea and calmly maintain that an omnipotent God can do impossible things. The irrational notions of mythology typically play a central function in the human soul even when the "I" consciously rejects them. Jung says,

> One of the greatest obstacles to psychological understanding is the inquisitive desire to know whether the psychological factor adduced is 'true'. . . . If the description of it is not erroneous or false, then the factor is valid in itself and proved its validity by its existence. One might just as well ask if the duck-billed platypus is a 'true' or 'correct' invention of the Creator's will. Equally childish is the prejudice against the role which mythological assumptions play in the life of the psyche. Since they are not 'true,' it is argued, they have no place in a scientific explanation. But mythologems *exist*, even though their statement do not coincide with our incommensurable idea of 'truth.'
>
> (Jung, 1916, para 192)

All human beings carry unconscious assumptions that reflect archetypal mythologems. Conscious "religious" beliefs, in the sense of emotionally cherished and objectively inadequate ideas that individuals fervently cling to, may inform the most anti-religious people. These may be beliefs in the decency of the American government, the curative power of psychoanalysis, or the reliability of science as much as in the resurrection, the Divine origin of the

Quran, or the world-creating power of Brahma. Each of these beliefs can easily be shown to ignore large quantities of data.

But Jung's thinking fudges the question of truth. His point of view is crucial when working with a patient whose narrow insistence on rationality is being used in the service of excluding emotional factors that "make no sense." His interest in the way similar mythologems emerged in unrelated human cultures all over the globe is important in helping us to investigate the apparently innate irrational factors that vividly distort human thinking. His theory of mythological systems as projections of the universal *inner* world onto outer reality is brilliant and, in my opinion, highly effective in explaining the staying power of deeply irrational images. But his emotional idealization of the constructive psychological function played by organized religious institutions, especially the Catholic Church, greatly confuses his argument. His point of view speaks to the fact that religious systems express truths in the same way that dreams do, as symbolic images of psychic reality. But Jung's perspective ignores the fact that the vast majority of religious beliefs cannot reflect an objective truth of the universe, if only because religious systems contradict each other so extensively; it also ignores the way religious dogmas frequently injure people psychologically. Even if the objective truth of reality is more similar to Heisenberg's probability clouds than to a Newtonian rock,[6] we hold the existence of objective truth, fundamentally unknowable though it may be, as axiomatic.

Bion's O, the realm of Absolute Truth that presses to be known, is the world of objective truth, both inner and outer. Although it includes the terrorist's *belief* in suicide bombing as a route to heaven, I do not believe that suicide bombing is in truth a route to heaven, and I think the distinction matters. The pressure from O for recognition is attested to by the curious historical fact that many important scientific ideas – like the theories of relativity or of evolution, or the mathematical development of the calculus – seem to press against humanity as though they were looking for someone to think them at certain points in history. Intimations of each of these world-shaking concepts came to a number of unrelated thinkers at roughly the same

6 In the seventeenth century, Isaac Newton formulated basic laws of physics that describe the world as we experience it. In Newtonian physics, a rock is a solid object made of solidly packed atoms which are imagined (following the Greeks) to be the smallest possible unit of matter. In the twentieth century, W. Heisenberg was one of a number of physicists who radically revised Newton's understanding of the universe as a result of Einstein's dramatic new vision of reality. We now know that atoms are not the smallest particle, but are composed of a number of other particles. In Heisenberg's understanding of matter, electrons, one of the elementary particles atoms are made of, are *not* thought of as solid particles of matter. Instead they are fields of energy and their precise location can never be known. There is a probability field or cloud that suggests where they are more likely or less likely to be found. Heisenberg's universe is fundamentally uncertain and unknowable, whereas Newton's universe was fixed and, at least in principle, *knowable*.

time. One person got there first, although often only by days or weeks, and that person – Newton rather than Leibniz in the example of the calculus – gets the credit. But if that person had not worked out his theory, someone else would have. Mathematics is called the Queen of the Sciences because it *does* capture unchanging truths, but non-mathematical ideas, no matter how revolutionary, are eventually shown to *approximate* Ultimate Reality rather than to *capture* it. And though they bring us closer to The Truth than had been the case before their birth, we can never arrive at Truth. Just as emotions can be ripe for emergence in an individual, the collective world of human understanding seems to bring up extremely complex thoughts – theories – that have gestated in O long enough to seek a conscious mind or minds available to receive them. Our definition of truth must be two-pronged, so that it includes emotional truths that may be as strange as a belief in the sanctity of suicide bombings as well as objective truth about the nature of reality, both inner and outer, something that can never be known.

Against truth

Although truth may be the nourishment of the psyche, and lies may cause infections of the soul that fester and spread, there is a strong human resistance to the truth. Just as an inner drive forces us to recognize distressing truths about ourselves, our situations and our loved ones, an instinctual energy pushes us toward self-deception and lies. Emotional experiences, no matter how positive they may be, always include a painful aspect. An experience of being cherished brings up the ways the person felt unloved in important past relationships. The fullness of that old pain was either something the person *could not* experience or something he consciously avoided; the appearance of a positive listener who welcomes him and his emotions rather than sealing him out calls up a painful contrast with at least some aspect of the past. Beginning with Freud, all depth psychological thinkers explore the ways that people work to not-know about the painful aspects of existence.

The basic mechanism that enables us to know about the truth by alphabetizing our experience rather than discharging it in one way or another depends on our being held in the container of a loving relationship. Virtually all schools of depth psychology recognize this fact (using their own terminology, or course). This is the container that the mother's reverie provides for the infant and that he gradually introjects as a way to process the ongoing experiences of his life. Ultimately, an individual's inner container depends not only on the mother's initial holding, but also on the ways that others provide compassionate attention to the growing person's distress (where "growing" is understood to continue throughout the life cycle). To the extent that he introjects a loving container, a person will be able to see the ways that even his mother failed to love him without reserve.

But there are many levels of emotional life that any individual's primary caretakers will be unable to recognize and hold. The early attachment figures, like the individual whose inner world is being formed in interaction with them, can bear only so much pain. When an adult's pain threshold is reached, he will resort to one evasion or another and slip into unconscious lies that distort the facts of his emotional situation partly by distorting his ability to recognize the emotional state of the infant/child/adolescent he is involved with. The growing person's inner container will be limited by two universal childhood experiences: his parents' inability to see some of his painful emotional experiences and his introjecting/identifying with his attachment figures' capacity to distort and to lie to themselves.

Denial can be a potent force. It would seem that as the hard facts of reality present themselves over and over, the individual will eventually succumb and recognize them, but frequently this is not the case. An interpersonal pattern that repeats itself for many years, with one romantic figure after another, is doggedly attributed to not having met the right person. An entrenched inability to complete any creative task is attributed to "laziness," something one *could* control if only she would try harder, rather than something *outside* her control that humiliates by revealing her true limitations. An idealized belief in the analyst's ability to effect a magical cure or in the spouse or child's extraordinary talent is maintained in the face of repeating evidence that challenges this certainty. And yet the truth presses to be known. People do come to painful insights; they extricate themselves from destructive or limiting situations, sometimes on their own, sometimes with the help of friends or family, and sometimes by calling a therapist for help. In addition to the obvious wish to avoid pain, people also seek a connection to the truth.

There have been as many ways to think about the forces that push people toward lies as there have been analytic thinkers. Many myths describe the human search for truth as taboo. The Hebrew Bible presents eating the fruit of the tree of knowledge of good and evil as the primal sin,

> as though knowledge meant that a sacrosanct barrier had been impiously overstepped. . . . Every step towards greater consciousness is a kind of Promethean guilt: through knowledge, the gods are . . . robbed of their fire, . . . something that was the property of the unconscious powers is torn out of its natural context and subordinated to the whims of the conscious mind.
>
> (Jung, 1953, p. 156, footnote 1)

Genesis 3:6 describes Eve's sin:

> The woman saw
> that the tree was good for eating
> and that it was a delight to the eyes,
> and that the tree was desirable to contemplate.

> She took from its fruit and ate
> and gave also to her husband beside her,
> and he ate.
>
> (Fox, 1983)

Eve's sin is looking at the objective facts and thinking her own original thoughts about what she sees instead of simply accepting the Authority's statement that the tree is *not* good for eating. The Tower of Babel, a human attempt to reach ultimate knowledge of the truth, is destroyed when God decides to sow confusion among men; Prometheus' quest for fire – enlightenment – is punished by the gods in a Greek version of Dante's hell: Prometheus is chained to a rock and eagles tear at his liver for all eternity. But what truth about human nature do these taboos reflect? Historically, the incest taboo has been thought about in concrete, external ways. If we think about incest *symbolically* (one of the first requirements for any depth perspective), the taboo tells us *not* to seek a union with our unconscious selves, not to search for our own personal truth.

Jung (1953) focuses on three main ideas about the taboo against knowing: the pressures that emerge from society's need for a cooperative mass; the inherent narcissism of the "I" that wishes to be ideal; and the individual's limited energies, which can do only so much in opposing inner and outer forces. Society's need for order and coherence pushes us toward the "normal" adaptation – meaning toward conformity. Thou shalt not know thy own disruptive thoughts. But the needs of society can be met only because human nature supports them, at least to some extent. We are herd animals and we find safety by blending into the crowd. Rather than thinking for ourselves, we feel safer when we accept the collective beliefs of the mass, when we submit to the social demands that press us toward the norm, toward mediocrity.

The pull toward fitting in is supported by the "I" 's desire for perfection – its narcissism.

> You see, the Self is such a disagreeable thing . . . because it is what you really are, not what you want to be or imagine you ought to be; and that reality is so poor, sometimes dangerous, and even disgusting, that you will quite naturally make every effort not to be yourself.
>
> (from Jung's Zarathustra seminar, quoted by Ulanov, 1997, p. 122)

Most people, Jung maintained, are not honest in their attempts to know themselves. While supposedly struggling to find their true selves, their energy actually works harder to escape that encounter than to reach it. "The honest attempt is the worst danger. . . . It is a risk, one dies by living" (Jung, 1984, p. 619). Bion (1966) called this same danger catastrophic change: when a person encounters her true self, her illusions about herself are shattered. The known world turns upside down; the "I" is someone the "I" has never met before. An encounter with her true self deepens the person; she becomes substantial rather than transparent, complex and multidimensional rather than one-sided; but the initial experience tears the veil from her positively or negatively inflated self-deceptions and being "shrunk" to her true size initially feels life-threatening. Behind the fear lies a terror of mortality, for in some sense the individual's self-deceptions must die if her true self is to be born. And we all identify to some extent with whatever self-deceptions block our continuing development.

Bion talks of two opposing forces – a social, related force and a narcissistic one – that contend within the human soul. Related energies, which carry concern for others as well as the self, must orient toward the truth by attempting to be fair to the conflicting demands of many different individuals; narcissistic impulses require that the person blind himself to the needs of inner and outer others in order to protect his search for the safety and comfort of his "I." These two forces meet the individual's capacity for suffering and the result is a compromise between truth and lies. Being part of the mass is so much easier than struggling endlessly to become oneself. People fall into imitation of admired others, bypassing the much greater strain of finding their own personal ways, the unique thoughts and feelings that, by separating them from everyone else, make them lonely.

One core issue that Bion explores in his attempt to understand the interplay of truth-seeking versus lying is the person's ability to engage with frustration, meaning emotional pain. Can the individual bear to experience (suffer) his pain, a necessary prelude to work on modifying it; or must he flee from distress and discharge it by lying to himself in one way or another? As we saw in Chapter 3, relatedness, like the ability to think – to seek the truth – is founded on the $♀$ $♂$ and PS $\leftrightarrow$ D apparatus the individual develops, first in his experiences with his primary caretakers and then in later experiences with emotional helpers. The process of expanding one's "apparatus for thinking" continues throughout the lifespan. The more solid and substantial the "apparatus" becomes, the greater the person's ability to sit with frustration and think about it instead of discharging it. "Frustration" – meaning pain – is always involved in being emotionally present with another person just as it is in being emotionally present with oneself. The ability to relate to others is simply the other side of the ability to relate to oneself.

Bion suggests that there is an inborn aspect of a person's temperament that affects the capacity to tolerate frustration.

An infant endowed with marked capacity for toleration of frustrations might survive the ordeal of a mother incapable of reverie and therefore incapable of supplying its mental needs. At the other extreme an infant markedly incapable of tolerating frustration cannot survive without breakdown even the experience of projective identification with a

> mother capable of reverie; nothing less than unceasing breast feeding would serve.
>
> (Bion, 1962, p. 37)

The great variation in patients' ability to use the therapeutic container constructively is mysterious. Although it is related to the degree of emotional wounding the individual has experienced, it is clear that this is not the only important variable. All analysts have experiences with patients who seem relatively healthy but who do not use the analytic situation effectively for growth, as well as with seriously wounded patients who grab hold of the therapist's inevitably limited capacities and wrest every grain of possible assistance from him. Bion's notion of an innate variation in the ability to bear emotional pain helps to explain this puzzling phenomenon.

As we explored in Chapter 3, if he is to think, the baby has to develop something akin to a word – a symbol or image – for whatever he needs to think about, say "the breast." The proto-word or image the baby needs will be developed only in the absence of the literal breast. The experience of frustration or pain, of something lacking, is required to stimulate the formation of the symbols that are prerequisites to thinking.

Any thought or statement implies, "this exists and therefore that does not." To the extent that a person cannot bear frustration, he will focus on "that does not" because the absence or lack comes first. First the infant is weaned and suffers the pain of losing the breast; then he discovers that the loss greatly expands his gastronomic pleasure as well as bringing other freedoms. First the toddler loses the safety and security of his mother's constant presence; then he discovers that preschool is filled with wonderful adventures of friendship and learning. He may "know" cognitively that school has much to offer, but it is only when he has worked through the pain of separation from Mother that he can begin to experience the pleasure of school. To get from the loss to the gain requires submission to the suffering of aliveness. Bion talks about people who, because they are unable to bear distress, "feel the pain but will not suffer it. . . . The patient who will not suffer pain fails to 'suffer' pleasure" (Bion, 1970, p. 9). When someone flees the emotional distress of life, he rejects an authentic experience of his existence and loses the good along with the bad.

Whatever is missing, the lack tantalizes the frustrated baby or adult. It hurts. The pain stimulates an instinctual attempt to modify or evade it. As we explored above, one way the individual can change his pain is by suffering it: "thinking" about it and discovering some way to improve his situation. In order to do this, he must have some sense that pain is an inherent part of life rather than a symptom of a way that life is not working. When pain is seen as a symptom of failure and therefore something to be fled from, the person can discharge the pain in any of the ways we explored earlier.

Adam could not bear to think about the fact that his aged mother was dying. He had made an unconscious decision that his grief about the coming loss and its implications were unbearable. If he truly thought about his mother's coming death, he would have to think about the fact that he was about to become the oldest person in the family and that he, too, was destined to die. His wife, his friends – everyone was mortal! Of course Adam knew this, but an *emotional* awareness of it had to be evaded. Adam became focused on insisting that his mother go into a retirement community with attached assisted living and nursing care facilities. Although he would never have said something so clearly irrational (not even to himself), he operated on an unconscious belief that if his mother would just move into a facility designed to take care of any physical needs that might develop, Adam's emotional distress would also be handled by the retirement facility.

This quotidian example is a beautiful illustration of the interdependence of the ability to process emotional distress (to "think") and the ability to relate to another. Caught in his inability to bear his distress, Adam had absolutely no space to respect his mother's wish to remain independent for as long as was possible. He *raged* (in my office) about her total selfishness, unable to recognize that *he* was being selfish in wanting his mother to live her life so as to spare him distress.

Adam had concretized his pain; his "name" for his distress was not a symbol. He had collapsed the difficulty into the fact that his mother was going to need physical care. If the mother continued to live on her own, Adam would endure many stresses in arranging that physical care. If the mother moved sooner, before she needed the care, everything would be taken care of and Adam could imagine that his mother's coming decline would not distress him. He was working to evade the pain of sitting with his mother's aging, partly because it called up the inconceivable fact of his own mortality and the immeasurable grief of the approaching losses inherent in the older stage of life that Adam himself was entering. He (unconsciously) felt overwhelmed by the prospect of accompanying his mother on her last painful journey to death. So far, Adam had been unable to think about his real difficulty and had been unable to submit to the suffering ("working through") that would relieve it. He had been unable to develop an α element as a "name" for his problem – a word like "mortality" or "loss" that, if imbued with its authentic feeling, would facilitate his suffering and help him to grow emotionally. The ability to think is an attempt to seek the truth; the search can succeed only to the extent that one can bear the frustrations of incarnate existence. Caught in the "pleasure" principle, the individual must flee the truth, for truth will always bring some pain with it.

But it would be a serious distortion to imagine that the person who is unable to suffer pain avoids distress. In the example of Adam, while he successfully avoided an experience of his mortality and his grief, he was beside himself with impotent fury regarding his mother's "grossly unreasonable" refusal to move. Adam could hardly believe that he was not going to be able to pressure his mother to make the choice that he considered correct. After many weeks of an intensely frustrating and disappointing struggle, Adam let go of his driven demands and futile attempts at persuasion. As his mother's decline continued, presenting Adam with all the problems he had foreseen regarding her care, he gradually submitted to the situation instead of fighting it. His grief at the coming loss of his second parent began to emerge. The thought that he was about to enter "the older generation" presented itself and he allowed it in. He began to suffer his pain. The suffering hurt more than the evasion, but the hurt felt significant and potentially constructive rather than being a meaningless battering. *This* pain deepened him. Adam missed the triumphant experience of prevailing over his mother, but as he softened and opened himself to his impending loss, he began to feel his love for his mother and to receive her love for him. Gradually facing the truth of his situation clearly provided Adam with the raw material for growth.

This case vignette images another aspect of the struggle for truth versus the collapse into the safety of lies. In Adam's frantic attempts to force his mother into the course he considered desirable, the main emotion he experienced was rage. Bion comments that rage is a flight from the painful experience of an unfulfilled desire, and he suggests that its "fundamental function is [the] denial of another emotion" (Bion, 1970, p. 20). Rage, in other words, is a lie. We are trained as therapists to think of the patient's anger as something precious to be invited in and welcomed, something important to "get in touch with" and "express." And I do not think that anyone could fail to recognize that many people, some of whom become patients, disown their anger – they lie to themselves and the world, pretending that they are not angry people when, in fact, plenty of anger is roiling about inside them. No view of history could fail to notice that human rage on a grand scale has caused extraordinary levels of destruction and suffering for our species and that the destructive nature of rage is made possible partly by remaining unconscious of its existence. But rage and lesser forms of anger are responses to threat or pain. When people feel endangered, either physically or emotionally, anger is one virtually inevitable response even if it is not the leading one.

Bion suggests that the underlying hurt, fear and shame are more primary than the angry reaction. Rage, the strongest form of anger, is especially suspect. It is frequently maintained tenaciously, not simply as an immediate reaction to a threatening situation but in a longer-term fashion, too, because it protects the person from experiencing his vulnerability and helplessness in the face of whatever he labels "outrageous." Adam consciously considered his mother's "stubborn" insistence on independent living outrageous, but hidden behind his judgment lurked his outrage at the facts of mortality: the inevitable loss of loved ones, the facts of bodily decay and failure, the helplessness of needs that cannot be met, the random unfairness of aliveness. Bion often focuses on unknowing, on tolerating confusion, on thinking one's authentic thoughts even though some of them will be wild, none of them will reflect Absolute Truth, and many of them will not endear the thinker to others. A truthful position for a member of our species, he suggests, is humble, vulnerable, unsure, the very opposite of outraged. And so we come to another paradox: rage or anger are secondary emotions designed to defend ourselves from experiencing our smallness and vulnerability; people are often not aware of their anger, and one aspect of the analyst's job is to help them to expand their awareness of it. But this level is always secondary, always laid down *over* a more basic terror that lies closer to the truth than does the anger.

(I do want to emphasize that anger and rage are different animals from assertion. The individual's self-assertion, which may not involve the humble, vulnerable unsureness that an accurate assessment of his understanding and knowledge would constellate, need not be defensive. "I want," is a different emotion from, "Your wishes enrage me." Of course, when the other's wishes conflict with one's own, "I want" can shade into anger, but the anger is still something of a lie. Behind it will lurk vulnerable feelings that are more fundamental and true: "I am threatened by this conflict; I am afraid I will not get what I want; I will feel diminished if I compromise," and so on.)

Bion devised his "Grid" (1963) (see Chapter 3, p. 87) in an attempt to understand thought: how does thinking develop and what is the functional purpose of any given thought? The vertical columns of the grid describe the use that the speaker is making of speech: is he using speech to communicate, as best he can, something that is true for him or is he using speech as an action, whose purpose is the effect it will cause? Might the speaker's comment belong in Column 2, the column Bion named "ψ," the column that applies when the purpose of speech is to conceal and evade threatening emotions that loom in the background? An innocuous example would be a guest who compliments his hostess on the dinner: is he communicating an authentic appreciation of the food, or is he trying to make his friend happy by complimenting her? A more meaningful example might be the promiscuous male patient who, in talking to his female therapist about his sexual "problem," is (unconsciously) trying to arouse and seduce her, not to untangle his difficulty.

When bringing these elements into analysis, Bion asks, is the patient's association

> the most direct and informative instrument he can employ, obscure though it may appear? Is its obscurity due to the difficulty of the matter of the problem for which he seeks help or is it due to his need to conceal? . . .
> It is necessary to determine whether [the patient's association] is characterized primarily by the need to conceal O or by the need to give as direct a representation of O as possible in view of its obscurity to him.
>
> (Bion, 1965, p. 22)

Bion asks the listening analyst to wonder about the function of the patient's communications. If he is "fabricating" his stories or his feelings, what emotional experiences is he trying to cover up (1970)? Does his association express his emotional response to O as it evolves into his consciousness or is his comment an attempt to evoke an emotional response in his listener (1965)? Bion urges us to remember that

> sometimes the function of speech is to communicate experience to another; sometimes it is to miscommunicate experience to another. . . . Speech . . . has been elaborated as much for the purpose of concealing thought by dissimulation and lying as for the purpose of elucidating or communicating thought.
>
> (Bion, 1970, pp. 1–3)

Regardless of its survival value in the larger world, for the depth psychotherapist or analyst, as well as for the patient, the universal retreat from the terrors of truth to the "safe" world of lies impedes the work. In the therapeutic situation, the rapid responses that a lie such as rage facilitates are undesirable. What is called for is the containment of stress so that the person – whether analyst or patient – can think about it, where "thinking about it" means submitting to suffering the fullness of her emotional experience. By holding that painful experience inside, the thinker will have *choices* regarding her response. The ability to not respond to stress actively, to hold the flight-or-fight impulses that arise rather than being dominated by them, is needed if the stress is to lead to emotional growth instead of a flight into stasis.

When Bion talks about the learner who cannot tolerate (suffer) frustration as opposed to the learner who can, he is describing two energies present in every person, although different people will contain the opposing qualities in different proportions. No one can bear the full experience of his ignorance and the vulnerability it implies. Consider: if someone contemplates the quantity of "things" he knows, he might, even if he is not an expert of some sort, puff up with pride in the vastness of his knowledge. But were the person to reflect on the full expanse of his ignorance, his knowledge would be dwarfed into insignificance. This is why Einstein consistently spoke with deep sincerity of how little he knew (Clark, 1971).

–K and K

One of the ways that Bion explores the area of truth and lies is in his study of links. He suggests that any interaction with another, whether outer or inner, can be described as dominated by one of six links: L, H or K or their negatives, –L, –H and –K. These letters are symbols rather than signs, requiring us to circle around them rather than looking to *define* them, but the words they come from are hints regarding their meaning: love, hate and knowing. A link is an *active* connection rather than a static state. It is not that Mary loves Bob as a fixed fact. It is rather that Mary, at a given time, lives an experience imbued with actively loving Bob and Bob lives an experience imbued with actively receiving love from Mary. Although Mary may "love" Bob in some consistent way over time, at any given moment the quality of her link with him might be colored by one of the other signs as easily as by L. −L, Bion emphasizes, is not the same as H. −L is the state of actively refusing the potentially loving experience that is unfolding, and −H is the state of actively refusing to experience the hate that is present. The negative links all speak to anti-truth attitudes. H is also a destructive link, but it is not destructive by virtue of its untrue nature. H is destructive because it is the primary anti-relatedness link that we explored in the last chapter. In H, the person is *not* open to the other, to himself, to the world; he would destroy the truth if he could, he hates it. Any one of these six links could be imagined to color any person's relationship to the world or to the other in any given interaction.

The K link is the one Bion explores at length, partly because this is the link that governs the task of learning from experience that I described in Chapter 3 and partly because he considers it the only appropriate link for the analyst. (The patient, of course, will use whatever link arises naturally inside him.) Bion's assessment of K as the "only" appropriate link for the depth therapist reflects his own difficulties with relatedness. Aspects of the work must be imbued with an L link on the analyst's part if the work is to be effective. Bion himself says in his *Clinical Seminars* that "it may be very important to show [the patient] . . . that there exists some capacity for affection, sympathy, understanding . . . not just analytic jargon, but interest in the person" (Bion, 2000, p. 18). I do not think that it is important for the therapist to "show" the patient his capacity for concern; rather I would agree with Jung that unless love is constellated between the two members of the analytic couple, the work cannot work. The K link does not imply affection, and without the analyst's liking, the work cannot work. At times, the analyst must link with the patient via L if the work is to succeed.

But depth therapeutic work clearly depends on K as well. Most therapists go into the field out of a conscious desire to "help" people. Outside the young therapist's awareness, this desire reflects a yearning to be helped. "If I can put all the woundedness I sense in the room into the patient, and if I can fix it in him, I will be fixed, too," the naïve practitioner imagines unconsciously. But if the therapist tries to help the patient, she will inadvertently support one side of his inner conflict. The symptom "has solid ground for its existence" (Freud, 1914, p. 152). It expresses a part of the patient and the naïve wish to amputate the symptom results in the patient being impoverished. When the therapist tries to help someone, she is approaching unknown aspects of his deeper self via the H link, hating his pathology instead of accepting it into the scheme of the whole. This is why any depth orientation must seek the truth of the patient from a neutral perspective. The patient's "I" wants X and some element of his unknown self wants Y. The therapist must not take sides in the *conflict*, though it is important for her to take the side of the patient in his entirety, for – again – analysis is a process in which love plays a decisive role. As we explore K and its negative shadow, –K, I think it will be clear that the therapist will optimally have at least one foot rooted in K at all times.

K is the world of knowing, although "knowing" is not about facts. K points to the only partially conceivable state of opening oneself to the truth of the moment, something that can be known only imperfectly.

> If the learner is intolerant of the essential frustration [i.e. pain] of learning he indulges phantasies of omniscience and a belief in a state where things are known. Knowing something consists in 'having' some 'piece of' knowledge and not in what I have called K.
>
> (Bion, 1962, p. 65)

The K link, like all links, is a process one is engaged in rather than a goal one has achieved.

> x K y [meaning x is linked via the K link with y] does not convey a sense of finality . . . a meaning that x is in possession of a piece of knowledge called y but rather that x is in the state of getting to know y and y is in a state of getting to be known by x. . . .
>
> (ibid., p. 47)

Although this experience is not *only* painful – open curiosity may lead to joy at times – it will still be inherently difficult and frustrating because the situation of Knowing something or someone, a state that would be pleasurable and safe, is never possible. Rather we are condemned to a life of endlessly seeking truth without ever reaching our goal.

To the extent that someone can tolerate a relationship with the world that is dominated by K, she will be immersed in not-knowing, in uncertainty, and, paradoxically, she will become increasingly wise as a result. The PS ↔ D sequence described in Chapter 3, an oscillation that is absolutely necessary for learning, is one manifestation of the K link. It requires one to sit with the chaos and confusion of disjointed bits and pieces for as long as is needed. Nina Coltart (1982) reports about a psychoanalysis in which the patient, after considerable improvement, turned utterly silent, filling the room (and the analyst) with a black despair of psychotic intensity. After months of working with this increasingly distressing situation, Coltart had an outburst and

> bawled [the patient] out for his prolonged lethal attack on me and on the analysis. I wasn't going to stand for it a second longer, I shouted, without the remotest idea *at that moment* of what alternative I was proposing! . . . It was only in the subsequent interpretive understanding of . . . my outburst . . . that we came to see how much . . . this man had needed to live

out, and have *experienced and endured by another person without retaliation*, his primary hatred of a genuinely powerful mother.

(Coltart, 1982, pp. 194–5, emphasis in original)

Coltart's rage was a –K moment. She was fleeing from a situation that was so painful she could no longer endure it, but in this vignette (which is similar to my outburst at Gertrude, described in Chapter 3) we can see how complicated the subject is. Coltart's capacity to endure the "frustration" – meaning, in this case, terror – of her work with this man had reached its limit and she exploded in an *un*thinking protest against the constricting straightjacket she found herself in. Coltart's unborn thought had been suffocated by the patient's tyrannical inner mother and her act of freedom (Symington, 1983) was needed to disrupt the crushing status quo. Coltart's –K discharge became a crucial piece of data for her subsequent ability to link with the analytic situation via K and to come to an understanding of the trap from which she had extricated both her patient and herself with her rage. To my mind, her outburst was also a retaliation against the patient, but the limited nature of her retaliation probably reassured him that indiscriminate revenge was not in the offing. The –K link, filled with active hostility to knowing about the truth of this moment's situation, serves the individual truth-seeker badly in many ways, but like the hero's errors in fairy tales, it has its place in the grand scheme.

The patient says, "I don't *want* to understand what my mother is feeling! I don't *want* a mother like her!" On the face of it, one might imagine this statement to reflect –K, for the patient actively says that he does *not* want to know about an extensive and highly relevant area. But the statement, expressed violently and emphatically, is filled with true emotion. Because the patient is able to be curious about his furious exclamation, it *functions* in the hour more as a K statement than a –K one, for it rips away an inauthentic facade of curiosity and exposes an underlying intransigence *against* knowing. It also, despite its manifest content, expresses the intense hatred that the patient is gradually allowing himself to experience.

In a given situation a "truth" can be used to shut off a deeper truth, functioning in a –K mode. A woman complained to her husband that their inhibitions prevented them from going dancing. The husband responded that before they had married, he used to go dancing. "That's a fact," he said. It was, indeed, a fact but in this encounter it functioned in a –K mode, protecting him from exploring the ways his inhibitions as well as hers constricted their current life.

Another patient, Ralda, who habitually came to her sessions a few minutes late, arrived ten minutes late one day. Exploring her lateness, she admitted in passing that part of her did not want to be in analysis. I said that rather than giving that part of her a chance to speak to us in the room, she had allowed it to take over by enacting her anti-analytic feelings. This led her to talk, with some affect, of how much she hated thinking about her inner life and of her wish to remain safely ensconced in the triumphant persona she had been identified with, imagining herself to be someone with no vulnerable feelings or needs. Again, we have an example in which giving honest voice to the −K side of oneself is radically different from living out the −K energy and is a most important aspect of being in K.

Bion suggests that envy is one factor that induces a −K orientation to the world. (It is the only factor that he investigates.) As we explored in the previous chapter, I consider envy a response to terror. It comes from a wound to the ability to love, an injury that develops from traumatic experiences in primary relationships. But be it innate or as a response to life's inevitable pain, envy must always be present in the mother–infant relationship. How could there exist a mother who feels no pang of envy for the infant who is receiving all the attention and concern in this very demanding relationship? How could the analyst fail to envy the patient who is consistently the central object of attention? Why is the baby/patient[7] getting all the care? Why is no one attending to the infantile longings and needs of the mother/analyst? The infant/patient, in turn, immersed in an experience of extreme vulnerability that must, at least sometimes, result in painful non-fulfillment of his needs, cannot help but envy his apparently self-sufficient and omnipotent mother/ therapist. Finally, both members of the couple must fantasize third parties who are envious and jealous of their loving relationship (focusing on the aspects of the relationship that *are* loving). In actual reality, of course, the fantasies the mother/analyst or infant/patient may have will either be fed or created by the fact that there will always *exist* third parties who *are* envious and jealous of the loving union the two enjoy, whether these individuals are the father, the spouse, siblings, grandparents or friends. It is not necessarily common for third parties to feel primarily envious or jealous, but it cannot really be imagined that these negative emotions will not be present to some extent in anyone who observes a loving mother–baby/analyst–patient pair from which he or she is excluded. Envy crops up everywhere.

Let us return to the example of the infant who fears he is dying as pangs of hunger develop in his belly. In Chapter 3 I described the optimal situation in which the mother takes the baby's fear into herself (she contains it) and processes it with her α function until she can detoxify and return it to him ("you're not dying, you're hungry and we can fix that") along with the kernel of goodness that was embedded in the original fear ("and isn't it wonderful that you want to live"). In this positive process, the mother is operating in K, opening herself to the fullness of the baby's state and taking it in.

---

7 In no way am I implying that a patient is psychologically an infant; he has a complex and extensive character structure, he is not a relatively blank slate. But no matter whom the analyst is speaking with, the infant-in-the-patient is always present in the room, and these emotions are generated in the patient's infantile layer.

What would it mean for her to be caught in −K? The mother who cannot bear the thought, for example, that in some way she cannot protect her baby from suffering, will not be able to tolerate the uncertainty that would allow her to recognize the intensity of his fear. If she cannot bear to experience the fullness of the infant's terror, she will not be able to modulate whatever levels she has been unable to bear. She will be armored against him and he will encounter the steel of her breast plate rather than a permeable and receptive psyche. Instead of being open to the baby's state, the mother may talk about his exercising his lungs or about the importance of not indulging his "excessive sensitivity" or hyper-demandingness. She may convey to him that he is making a big fuss about nothing as she proceeds to feed him or as she decides to simply let him cry for a while. For the baby, his situation, permeated with the trauma of mother's rejection of his immediately present self, is ideal for constellating the infant's potential envy of the supposedly calm, placid state she has preserved by sealing him out. Instead of receiving hope in the possibility of transforming his terror into "wanting," along with an appreciation of the valuable will to live that caused the terror in the first place, he will have his terrified state stuffed back inside him, magnified by a new development, his mother's apparent revulsion at his terror. The precious will to live will be engulfed by fear and lost. Now the baby takes in a roiling nameless dread (Bion, 1962a) along with the milk he is sucking in.

To whatever extent the maternal grandmother was unable to contain the mother's infantile terrors – to whatever extent the mother's terrors were stuffed back into her as a baby, generating nameless dread that the adult mother now carries – she may be unconsciously so filled with her own unbearable anxieties that she amplifies her baby's gathering panic with her own while she seals out his. Sensing his mother's fragility terrifies the helpless infant and may cause him to truncate his aggression, leaving him limp and passive rather than demanding. And the baby introjects a negative container, which refuses to contain, rather than a positive one. (Let me remind the reader that this absolute example does not exist in life. The container that the mother will offer will *always* have positive *and* negative elements, at least if it functions well enough to support his physical survival; the mother can no more handle a given situation perfectly than an analyst can ever hope to do a perfect hour.) Where the optimal interaction feeds the growth of an inner container-contained apparatus in which the container and the contained nourish each other, the destructive interaction, filled with envy on either member's part, leads to an inner container-contained that is envious. "It's predominant characteristic," Bion says, is " 'without-ness' " (1962, p. 97). The person sees only what he lacks; he cannot value what he has. He is filled with a partly unconscious experience of impoverishment, a feeling of emptiness, of lacking – exactly the emotional state that we described as the source of narcissism's violent emotions: envy, jealousy and greed.

Bion discusses how the container-contained that is suffused with "without-ness," leads, in the extreme, to "an envious assertion of moral superiority without any morals" (ibid., p. 97). The stripping away of meaning and good-ness that the infant experienced when his mother sealed him out now con-tinues inside his own psyche and, to whatever extent it is not mitigated by more constructive experiences, he will continue his envious stripping away of meaning and value inside himself. At its worst, the negative container-contained represents "hardly more than an empty superiority–inferiority" (ibid., p. 97).

We have all known people like this: the couple in the Congress for Racial Equality who are violently castigating other members for their inadequate commitment to nonviolence; the woman who wants to castrate all men because they are so dangerously aggressive; the male feminist who loudly condemns others for their sexism while treating the women in his immediate life like servants. This attitude protects the person from the doubt that must characterize any constructive processing of the real emotional experiences she is immersed in. Trapped in an impoverished inner container, the person does not have a real conscience, for a conscience *invites* one to constructive behavior rather than bludgeoning one with prescriptions and demands for perfection. This righteous, superior attitude expresses itself interpersonally with blame, supercilious criticism and the like. The person clings to her ability to arouse guilt in order to protect herself from the devastating impact that her demand for moral perfection would have on her if she felt it directed toward herself.

Dr. A consulted me about her patient, Kathy, a university professor. Kathy's father had been rageful and physically abusive and Kathy had responded by building up a strong inner Protector (Kalsched, 1996), who defended her from the terror of her vulnerability by causing her to approach others emotionally in the same way her father had approached her physically. Kathy had begun working with Dr. A on a once-a-week basis but had quickly added one hour after another until she was coming four times each week. Kathy had softened and allowed herself to become caught up in an idealizing transference.

But then came her therapist's first vacation. In the last minutes of her last hour before the break, Kathy asked Dr. A to accept a book that she wanted her to read during the separation. Dr. A knew much less about the book's subject than did Kathy and at that moment Dr. A was inundated with feelings of inadequacy. With no time to explore the request, caught up in feelings of inferiority, Dr. A clumsily refused the book. When Dr. A and Kathy recon-nected after the vacation, Kathy told Dr. A that she had been devastated by the refusal and that she was determined never again to experience that kind of distress. She lectured Dr. A about the fact that *she* (Kathy) knew how to treat students kindly and that Dr. A's blindness, lack of concern, coldness and so on constituted a terrible failing. Possessed by guilt, Dr. A assured

Kathy that she had no reason ever to feel so hurt again, an assurance that she repeated many times over the months ahead, not realizing until we talked about it that the assurance made no sense. Kathy's experience, while triggered by Dr. A's clumsiness, came from inside Kathy, reflecting a truth of her inner world. A determination not to be hurt again could only succeed at the expense of the truth of who Kathy was.

By the time Dr. A consulted me, the impasse between herself and her patient had solidified. Dr. A's own personal development had not proceeded far enough for her to disentangle herself from the crushing guilt that Kathy constellated in her. Although she was intellectually able to understand the consultation I offered, she had her own power issues and needs that interfered with finding a way to be separate from Kathy. She could not really be curious about her patient's emotionally violent assertions of moral superiority, because she had not yet become sufficiently aware of her own negative inner container's moralistic judgments. Dr. A could not find a way to separate herself from the condemnation and guilt that filled the consulting room.

When the therapist falls into guilt and shame over something she has done, horrified by her own imperfections and limitations rather than curious about them and about the emotional currents in the couple that led the therapist to behave the way she did, it signals that she and her patient have fallen into a −K stance. They are fleeing from some painful truth. This is usually true even when the therapist's behavior seems egregious, like forgetting to come to an hour. (Although it is not always true, of course. Sometimes therapists behave in psychopathic ways they *should* feel guilty about but usually don't.) When the therapist feels inadequately intelligent or trained or sensitive and finds herself unable to use her feelings of inadequacy as a signal – when she finds herself immersed in these feelings and taking them literally – she must at least entertain the hypothesis that an envious and rigid container-contained has pulled her into the whirlpool of *rightness* and perfection, away from the messy world of limited human beings who are all somewhat crippled, doing what they can for each other – which may turn out to be quite a bit, though never everything one might wish for.

The destructively envious interaction between an infant and Mother that we explored above creates the universal human tendency to turn away from love, the real nourishment of the soul. Instead, material satisfactions become the desired objects and the greed that comes from humankind's horrifying ability to cut off relatedness is born. Bion's thinking goes something like this: the infant receives love, understanding and comfort from the mother, along with all kinds of material comforts. But his experience with her is also tinged with envy. The violence of the envious feelings that swirl around the nursing couple – their own envies, the envy of those excluded from their union – terrifies the helpless infant, for he can feel the destructive potential of envy's hatred and malice. To protect the mother from these dreadful emotions and to protect himself from feeling his own destructive capacity, the baby splits his interest in material comforts like milk from his yearning for love and cherishment. This is the origin of the split we have been exploring, a split between narcissism and relatedness, between emotional disturbance and health.

This is different from the early splitting that protects the immature baby from the depressive anxieties that accompany holding the opposites – recognizing his mother's goodness and badness as aspects of the same person who is neither good nor bad but both. Splitting as a response to envy in the nursing couple lets the infant enjoy such material comforts as milk and warmth without recognizing that he depends on his mother for these comforts – on a fallible and complicated human being over whom he has such limited control. His love and his need for love is displaced. Now *milk* becomes the desirable object. Love – so unpredictable and unreliable – is not needed. "The craving for love remains unsatisfied and turns into overweening and misdirected greed" (Bion, 1962, p. 11). To whatever extent the infant is caught in this process, he learns to attack his own interest in truth, for the basic point of this splitting is to deny his dependence on others. The baby is trying to obliterate awareness of his vulnerability because of his terror of the impossible emotional complications that attend relationships. As this baby grows into an adult, his denial of his need for others joins up with the ways society supports his denial and his wound may be misconstrued as independence and self-reliance.

What happens to this now-grown-up baby who has split off his need for love and centered himself instead in a craving for stuff (whether material things or the stuff of power and control)? A glance at ordinary middle-class lives in the United States (certainly including those of psychoanalysts!) reveals a breathtaking dependence on the material goods that supposedly convey security. We need our snazzy cars and our i-Phones, our children *must* go to expensive private schools and wear designer jeans. *The New York Times* reported a survey of the rich and the super-rich which found that virtually every person surveyed felt he needed about twice as much money as he had. The man with ten million dollars felt he needed twenty to feel secure, the woman with twenty felt she needed forty. At a very basic level, the things a person greedily seeks can never satisfy him because what every human being actually needs is love. But to the extent that someone is caught in this split, he is forever excluded from the loving experiences that would require him to recognize his need for other people. "To observe this taking place in analysis," Bion says, "is to feel that the patient will never abandon his pursuit of a course of action which one would think he could not possibly fail to know was futile" (ibid., p. 11).

Ralda demonstrated Bion's point. She was committed to seeing her analysis as one element among many in her day. She bristled at the idea that her analytic hour would be seen as more important than, for example, a business meeting, or that it would be a "big deal" to miss an hour. Why she had an hour every day! What difference did it make if she had four hours this week instead of five? She spoke triumphantly about her determination not to allow analysis to cause upheaval in her emotionally empty life and it was only as the years rolled by without our work coming to any hopeful conclusion that she could even intellectually notice that her refusal to value her relationship with me might be relevant in explaining her inability to "get" the marriage and family she imagined she wanted.

Before one lengthy separation, Ralda said that she would miss "these conversations" over the break, meaning the conversations that she and I had in which she was the center of interest and concern. She could not imagine that she would miss *me*, however. It was a vivid example of Bion's point: Ralda had managed to imagine that "these conversations" did not depend on my presence. Her determined refusal to allow her dependent yearnings any space in our relationship mirrored her inability to be open to a potential life partner. The men she met, she said, were all so weak! Just as she could not miss lost time with me, she could not be vulnerable with a real person in the outer world.

And what about the therapist's tendencies to lie? Just as the patient is always torn between truth-seeking and truth-avoiding, the therapist, too, struggles with an inner "pervert, the psychopath, the schizophrenic [who] behave as if they believed that it were better to destroy than to create. This is the frightful fiend, the liar, the operator of H and −K" (Meltzer, 1978/1998, p. 377). When Dr. A assured Kathy that she never needed to feel her extreme vulnerability again, she was lying, both to herself and to Kathy. In the stressful situation of her patient's condemnation and rigidity, Dr. A lost her ability to think and instead *responded* with a fearful attempt to bring back the warm, positive feeling that had been present before Kathy was traumatized by Dr. A's vacation. The fearful side of each of us is larger or smaller depending on our tolerance for true change – something we all seek but whose disequilibrating nature cannot help but frighten us.

Let us look at the second vertical column of Bion's grid, the column labeled ψ: it is the only column without an English name like "notation" or "action." When a statement is labeled ψ, what is the speaker's intended use of that statement? Antonino Ferro calls it the "column of lies" (Ferro, 2006, p. 21) but it is interesting to note that Bion chose not to give it a name, as though the area of −K and lying is too complex and murky to simplify with a label. This is the column that characterizes a "thought" that is being used to protect one's security rather than to further an investigation of the truth. There is always a great temptation for the therapist to operate in Column 2 by reaching for theory or old knowledge rather than remaining in the confusion and disorientation of the emotionally charged present. It is so easy for the analyst under pressure to reach for certainty by making an old interpretation – "again, we are facing such-and-such" – because a new interpretation – "what is going on right now revises what we have understood before in this new way" – is not yet available to be thought and the tension of not understanding has become too great for the analyst to bear.

Ferro's work challenges the basic interpretive stance of psychoanalysis.[8] Rather than decoding a patient's communications and telling the patient what he is *really* saying, he generally tries to stay within the patient's metaphors and to allow the patient to come to its transference meanings himself. He calls this "interpretation *in* the transference," as opposed to "interpretation *of* the transference." "Oh, that teacher made you feel so small in relation to her!" rather than "Perhaps you're feeling small in relation to me right now." By staying within the patient's story rather than interpreting it, he is hoping to facilitate the unfolding of the patient's dreaming capacity rather than to translate the patient's experience into Ferro's psychoanalytic language, even though that sort of translation would function to make him, the analyst, feel smarter and bigger and righter than his patient. Certainly, there is no reason to decide that the patient who talks about "wishing she could develop more of a spine" is avoiding the "real" fact of envying men their penises or that the patient's "true" need is to internalize the penis-as-link (Coleman, 2005). All of these ideas are simply metaphors that the patient or therapist uses to express something about the *intangible* reality of the psyche's state. We have no words that directly describe the psyche; all we have are metaphors transplanted from the concrete outer world. Kleinian metaphors are simply one imagistic system imagined by a particular group of analysts. We cannot talk about the nature of the psyche *as such*. There is no "true" metaphor or symbol, only useful ones that resonate for a particular person.

Ferro's work rejects the simple idea that when the patient talks about his daughter's tummy ache, he is "really" talking about his inability to take in the therapist's interpretations. The association to his daughter's pain has undoubtedly been triggered by a painful experience in the present with his therapist, but what is important, Ferro indicates, is to stay empathically related to the tummy ache as an image in the patient's attempt to process (dream) the emotional experience of the present rather than to decode it. When the patient's dreaming capacity has been strengthened enough – when the dream he is trying to dream has gone far enough – the patient will be able to notice his distress at Ferro's interpretation and to talk about it directly.

But Ferro, too, gets caught in the worldview that suggests that the patient's state is *really* something other than his conscious experience and that it is possible for the therapist to deduce that reality with some degree of certainty. Thus, he presents a case vignette in which he interprets a dream in a way that disorients and frightens the patient. The next day, another dream appears and Ferro is able to interpret it as imaging the danger the patient experienced from his previous interpretation. This relieves the patient and the couple

---

8 Relational psychoanalysts like Jessica Benjamin and Stephen Mitchell also take issue with the centrality of interpretations.

comes to a different interpretation of the original dream. In discussing this sequence, Ferro says:

> On the basis of my knowledge of the patient and of the twists and turns of this analysis, I still regard my first interpretation as more *true* (K), but it elicits an . . . almost autistic defense, whereas the second, although less true, is more syntonic (in 'O') with the patient and *for that reason* more likely to bring about transformations.
>
> (Ferro, 2006, p. 65, emphasis in original)

But whatever could it mean to say that something is more "in 'O' " – the Absolute Truth about Ultimate Reality – but "less true?" In this vignette, Ferro has fallen into the stance his work is always struggling against, a stance of *knowing* rather than one of curiosity; he is conceiving of interpretations as ways to nail down the truth, rather than attempts to test imperfect hunches about the truth against the patient's sense of herself. If we imagine O as an advancing (Bion's "evolving") tide bringing Reality into lived experience, we might think that Ferro's second interpretation has been received first, and that his first interpretation may be accepted later. But would a different therapist conceive of the patient's truth in the same way that Ferro did, and if this hypothetical therapist saw things differently, might they evolve differently? There seems to be at least a tendency for patients in Kleinian analyses to produce associations amenable to Kleinian interpretations, while patients of classical Jungian analysts dream of mandalas and divine children. Psychotherapy research consistently fails to demonstrate the efficacy of any particular theoretical approach; it is the therapist's person rather than her theories that matters. The crucial issue for the depth psychotherapist would seem to be a search for truth accompanied by the recognition of its unknowability.

We can all fall into Ferro's stance – I *know* that such-and-such is true, even though the patient continues to deny it. Holding this belief is actually one way in which we fall into a –K attitude and the ubiquity of this attitude should give us warning regarding the intensity of the human resistance to uncertainty and doubt. Truth implies an *attitude* that many analysts consider necessary for emotional development and health, an investigative stance as to what is going on rather than a state of certainty. This approach corresponds to the K link if we take that link as a model for a way to face the world. But it is so easy to forget that K is an active link, a state of *seeking* knowledge, not a description of a resting place in which one has knowledge. At issue, again, is the ability to sit with unknowing, to be lost and humble, accepting a state in which one's opinion or point of view is *known* not to correspond to The Truth. Meltzer summarizes Bion's perspective by suggesting that "the ultimate factors militating against perseverance in the search for the truth [are] the fear of the unknown, the intolerance of uncertainty, its connection with impotence, awe, dependence . . . in the face of ignorance" (Meltzer, 1978/1998, p. 359).

Jung, making a similar point to Bion's or Meltzer's, says that the "goal [of wholeness] is important only as an idea; the essential thing is the *opus* which leads to the goal: *that* is the goal of a lifetime" (Jung, 1946, para 400, emphasis in original). We are trying to become whole but it is not possible to attain completion. The goal of life is the continuous attempt to reach wholeness, a wholehearted undertaking in the face of the deep knowledge that it can never succeed. One works continuously to open oneself to the truth; taking up the struggle is the goal of life. It is no more possible to "attain" individuation or wholeness or relatedness or truth than it is to be "cured." The psyche's search for the sustenance of the truth is inherently at war with consciousness's search for the security of certainty. We can struggle against Nature as we seek to face *into* anxieties rather than fleeing from them, but it is a struggle that can never be completely won.

Part II

Clinical implications

Chapter 6

The listening process

We have looked at the nature of the psyche from a number of perspectives. We have talked about the unconscious: its infinite extent, the unknowable nature of its contents, the teleological thrust that pushes us into relationship with others and with ourselves. We have studied Bion's ideas about the nature of thinking/dreaming and looked at the way his theory can structure our listening in clinical hours. The eternal human struggle between a related approach to life and to others versus an egocentric, narcissistic one has been explored from two points of view: a structural description of the universal complex that organizes our anti-related or pathological tendencies; and a dynamic description of the conflict between facing into the truth or turning toward soothing lies. Let us consider what impact all of these matters have on our clinical work.

As I have suggested, Bion's work on α function implies that the issue is not so much to help the patient *know* about aspects of experience that he has split off, repressed, or otherwise exiled from awareness; instead, the patient needs to *live* the life experiences he has been unable to bear. Even before Bion's work, some theoreticians suggested that the analyst's task is to reflect back to the patient the particular element of his inner reality that he brings into the consulting room today. Winnicott says:

> Psychotherapy is not making clever and apt interpretations; by and large it is a long-term giving the patient back what the patient brings. . . . [I]f I do this well enough the patient will find his or her own self and will be able to exist and to feel real. . . .
>
> (Winnicott, 1971, p. 117)

Winnicott believed that the central function of an interpretation was to let the patient know what he had understood of what she was bringing, not to tell the patient something *he* knew that she was ignorant of (ibid.). He suggested that the human animal can deal with only one thing at a time emotionally and that trauma consists of being flooded by more things than can be processed:

> There is nothing more important . . . than that we try to see what the *one* thing is that the patient is bringing for interpretation or for reliving in any one particular hour. A good analyst confines his interpretations and his actions to the detail exactly presented by the patient. It is bad practice to interpret whatever one feels one understands, acting according to one's own needs, thus spoiling the patient's attempt to cope by dealing with one thing at a time.
>
> (Winnicott, 1949, p. 192, emphasis in original)

Winnicott's advice is a simple formula for relatedness. He is asking the therapist to tune in to the patient's unconscious agenda and to join him or her in furthering it. One problem with "correct" interpretations that fail to touch the patient may be that they fail to speak to the particular aspect of the patient's self that he needs to connect with today. Such interpretations, Winnicott is saying, express the therapist's narcissism rather than his related capacities.

If we begin with the hypothesis that the Self in the patient – the inner spark of aliveness that organizes his emotional being and development – is asking the analyst to perceive and reflect back one previously unknown element of his psyche, the question we must address is how we might know *which* element is crucial in a given hour. It is not possible to say much about what the therapist should *do*. We can talk about the importance of transference interpretations,[1] for example, but the power of any interpretation rests on *when* it is said. To this end, the analyst's personal intuitions of the moment will be her only possible guide. But if we look at how the analyst might listen, we can say much more. How can she receive the unconscious message that telegraphs the not-yet-experienced experience that the patient is trying to have at this moment?

Remember Bion's analysis of the infant whose fear of envy leads him to split his need for milk from his need for love. To one extent or another, all human beings will construct this split in infancy. Love, cherishment and concern will be somewhat feared and avoided by any human creature for these experiences bring up our helpless need for people who are so outside of our control, so unpredictable. Instead of yearning for the mother's love, which comes and goes with her mood and her availability, the infant craves milk; as the infant grows, the "milk" morphs into toys and trips to Disneyland, and then into designer clothes and snazzy cars, money, fame, power – security – an absolutely illusory goal for a mortal human being in this unpredictable world. The love of another, our species' deepest need, is so obviously out of our control, while the aims of the power drive seem possible to grab. This

---

1 Transference interpretations are important because they attempt to remove a barrier that exists between the therapist and the patient (N. Symington, 2005). Thus, they facilitate the deepening and intensification of the analytic relationship.

basic human dilemma has created the analytic attitude that values what the analyst *does* (i.e. interpreting) rather than the environment she creates, what she *says* rather than how she understands and receives what the patient is trying to tell her.

The therapist's narcissism also supports this skewed attitude. She feels as though she is a valuable person when she offers her thought to the patient; she may feel as though she is doing nothing worthwhile when her stance is primarily receptive. Listening is at least ninety per cent of the job. When the therapist can hear the patient's communication, she will have the data she needs to think about what to say and when to say it. Hearing the patient also has the effect of making the therapist much quieter as she devotes her attention to understanding instead of telling.

Let us look at the ideas about technique that the founding fathers of analysis, Freud and Jung, put forward. As we shall see, like most analytic thinkers, they offer little advice about what to do, although they give some suggestions on what *not* to do. Freud, Jung and Bion all maintained that every analyst needs to work out the technical approach best suited to his or her personality. Freud begins his technical advice with a disclaimer:

> I am asserting . . . that this technique is the only one suited to my individuality; I do not venture to deny that a physician quite differently constituted might find himself driven to adopt a different attitude to his patients and to the task before him.
>
> (Freud, 1912, p. 111)

Although he then goes on to write a series of papers filled with suggestions that can sound like rules, I want us to pause and absorb his advice.

Bion says something similar in his seminars when a participant asks him what he thinks of an analyst including among his contacts the patient's family. Bion says that he can talk about what *he* does, but that

> [i]t is no good resorting to the method which suits somebody else. The fact that other people do differently is useful – it may give you a hint – but the fundamental point is, can you find out what suits you?
>
> (Bion, 2000, p. 265)

Jung wrote only one significant piece on analysis (as opposed to individual psychology), *The Psychology of the Transference* (1946). Because Jung maintains that "every trace of routine . . . proves to be a blind alley" (ibid., para 367) in this central work he offers no technical suggestions, instead repeating in many ways that the therapist must be deeply related to his patient by being fully involved with and affected by her, going "to the limits of his subjective possibilities" (ibid., para 400). A deep analysis, he said, challenges "not only our understanding or our sympathy, but the whole man" (ibid., para 367). He speaks to the resistance that therapists must feel to total commitment of ourselves and to the way in which we are tempted to hide behind a professional persona, relying on the "trick of knowing everything beforehand" (ibid., para 365).

> Though he may believe himself to be in possession of all the necessary knowledge . . . he will in the end come to realize that there are very many things indeed of which his academic knowledge never dreamed. Each new case that requires thorough treatment is pioneer work, and every trace of routine then proves to be a blind alley.
>
> (ibid., para 367)

His break with Freud left Jung with a wound that never fully healed. When he writes about psychotherapy, he often seems at pains to emphasize his *differences* with his old mentor. Yet in *The Psychology of the Transference*, his parsing of the mystery of the analytic venture is not far from Freud's comment that

> the most successful cases are those in which one proceeds . . . without any purpose in view, allows oneself to be taken by surprise by any new turn in them, and always meets them with an open mind, free from any presuppositions.
>
> (Freud, 1912, p. 114)

Long before the current focus on the intersubjectivity of the analytic undertaking, Jung noted that the therapist will be impacted emotionally by the patient in painful and disorienting ways.

> [T]he psychotherapist . . . should clearly understand that psychic infections . . . are . . . the predestined concomitants of his work. . . . This realization . . . gives him the right attitude to his patient. The patient then means something to him personally, and this provides the most favorable basis for treatment.
>
> (Jung, 1946, para 365)

From one angle after another, Jung talks about the fact that the truth of the analyst's whole psyche determines her impact on the patient. He notes that the transference relationship consists of six different subrelationships: between the two "I"s in the room, between each "I" and that person's unconscious as well as between the "I" and the other's unconscious, and finally between the two unconsciouses. Attempts to control one's interventions with technical guidelines in mind will impact primarily the "I" to "I" connection of the dyad; the unconscious links will be much less affected by the simple fact of following supposedly desirable procedures than they will by the truth of each person's entire being. Unconscious connections will respond to the factors *behind* the analyst's interventions, such as the rigidity versus integrity with which she holds to technical rules, or the way the procedures she uses to guide her are congruent with her true nature. Do her technical guidelines function as a flexible container that holds and nurtures her creativity or do they squash her individuality and talent in an iron suit of armor? The patient will unconsciously know the truth of his analyst's psyche because even if the two "I"s are seriously unrelated, the deeper aspects of their selves will be exquisitely tuned in to each other.

Summing up his overarching attitude, Jung says that the analyst, working to pull the disconnected elements of the patient into an integrated whole, seeks to "bind the opposites by love, for 'love is stronger than death' " (ibid., para 398). Analysis, he says, is "a human encounter where love plays the decisive part" (ibid., para 418). Jung is explicit in underlining the way that the therapist's entire being determines the course of the work. He speaks approvingly of the love that every therapist knows is constellated in an effective clinical situation, a rare and courageous attitude. He does not use the word "related" but his emphasis on love turns us in that direction.

Sometimes, Jung can sound as though he overvalues the analyst's intellectual mastery of her subject, but I think this misleads. As he describes the mutual unconsciousness and disorientation that envelopes the analyst–patient pair when real transformation is occurring, he comments that "the doctor's knowledge, like a flickering lamp, is the one dim light in the darkness" (ibid., para 399). But when he talks about the need for the analyst to hold fast to his "knowledge," what he means by "knowing" is what Bion means by "K," an attitude of openness to learning the truth rather than a belief that he possesses The Truth. Jung says that "faced with the disorientation of the patient, the doctor must hold fast to his own orientation; . . . he must know what the patient's condition means, he must understand what is of value in the dreams" (ibid., para 478). But in the same paragraph he goes on to explain his meaning:

> In other words, he must approach his task with views and ideas capable of grasping unconscious symbolism. *Intellectual or supposedly scientific theories are not adequate to the nature of the unconscious*, because they make use of a terminology which has not the slightest affinity with its pregnant symbolism. . . . The kind of approach [that is needed] must . . . be plastic and symbolical, and itself *the outcome of personal experience with unconscious contents*.
>
> (ibid., para 478, emphases added)

He is not talking about the kind of knowledge one might acquire from reading his or Freud's writing. He is talking about the kind of knowledge one gains from one's personal analytic work, a kind of knowing that grows out of an interpersonal emotional experience rather than something that emerges from the intellect.

Although Freud did not explicitly credit the unconscious with the creative power we explored in Chapter 2, his primary suggestion depends on that creativity. In Chapter 3, we saw Freud urging the analyst to listen to the patient in a state of evenly suspended attention, trying to focus on the patient's material more from his unconscious than from his "I." Although he did not have the extensive theoretical basis for this advice that analytic thinkers constructed by the end of the twentieth century, he knew intuitively that the listener will distort what he hears, for the "I" craves security and wants to find only "what he already knows" (Freud, 1912, p. 114). Freud reminds us that it is typically only after the fact that we appreciate the import of what we hear and that "thinking something over or concentrating the attention solve none of the riddles of a neurosis; that can only be done by patiently obeying the psycho-analytic rule, which enjoins the exclusion of all criticism of the unconscious . . ." (ibid., p. 119). Just as he asks the patient to associate freely, simply reporting without censorship what comes to his mind, he is advising the therapist to (silently) associate freely. He wants the therapist "not to dispute the guidance of the unconscious in establishing connecting links" (Freud, 1911, p. 94). Theoretically, Freud did not recognize the synthetic, prospective and creative capacities of the unconscious that we have explored, but in his technical advice, he relies heavily on that dimension of the infinite psyche. As we shall see, his advice meshes easily with the attitude Bion recommends.

To conclude this brief survey of the two founding psychoanalysts, I want to point out that neither Freud's nor Jung's clinical behavior was completely consistent with his theoretical beliefs. This validates Jung's idea that it is the whole person of the therapist rather than her theories that matters. What therapists *say* they do and what they actually do may diverge dramatically without the therapist having much conscious awareness of this. And of course there is always the temptation, when describing one's work, to improve it in one way or another. Many of the case examples in the literature are too good to be true, undoubtedly reflecting how writers decide to omit a few "details" as they shape the infinitely messy reality of their work into something coherent that demonstrates their point as well as their competence.

Without memory, understanding or desire

Although he was not explicit in the way that Jung was, we see in Bion's seminars an attitude that clearly considers the truth of the analyst's psyche to be the crucial factor in analytic work. He has advice for the analyst, but it is not about what to do. His advice is about how to listen. His most famous suggestion, to eschew memory, desire and understanding, is presented in what may be the shortest analytic paper ever written, "Notes on Memory and

Desire" (1967). The advice is then elaborated at length in *Attention and Interpretation* (1970).

As I have noted, Bion's work is opaque. He consistently asks the reader to do her own thinking about the areas he describes; he does not *want* to explain his meaning clearly. Rather than clarifying the writer's point of view, he suggests (1970) that a psychoanalytic paper should constellate in the reader the experience that the writer is trying to describe; thus, the reader has an opportunity to form her own sense of the problem in question. He offers very few case descriptions, asking the reader to provide her own.

In the clinical situation, Bion suggests, the task is to open oneself to the O of the moment. The absolute facts of the analytic hour can never be known. They include the outer interaction, the infinite inner reaches of each partici-pant, and the evolving O of the dyad-as-an-organism, Ogden's "analytic third" (1994). This is the O of the session, encompassing each person's O to create something greater than the sum of the two would suggest. Within that wholeness, the patient speaks, attempting either to express his O or to conceal it. What is the O of the patient? What is his reality? Or, in simpler words, what is he talking about?

By forsaking memory, desire and understanding, one hopes to *become* O – to be at one with the immediate emotional reality – and therefore to be able to articulate (perhaps only to oneself) some previously unknown truth about the patient-in-this-moment, the patient-in-the-room-with-this-analyst. Bion (1967, 1970) maintained that the analyst must shun memory, desire and understanding to accomplish the intangible task of becoming O. His prescription is severe:

> Do not remember past sessions . . . *no* crisis should be allowed to breach this rule. . . . [Avoid] desires for the approaching end of the session. . . . Desires for results, 'cure' or even understanding must not be allowed to proliferate.
>
> (Bion, 1967, p. 260, emphasis in original)

He speaks to his severity in what we might take as an empathic comment:

> For any who have been used to remembering what patients say and to desiring their welfare, it will be hard to entertain the harm to analytic intuition that is inseparable from *any* memories and *any* desires.
>
> (Bion, 1970, p. 31, emphasis in original)

I have not met any analyst who tries to follow this advice literally, something that, in any case, is surely impossible. But turning toward the stance of radical openness to the moment that Bion's advice implies has the effect of enliven-ing the hour, speeding it up and unleashing a startling flow of new and unexpected insights.

Definitions

But what does Bion mean by "memory," "desire" and "understanding?" A misunderstanding of his language has constellated much needless resistance to his ideas. Beginning with memory: two experiences are familiar to any clinician. In the first, the analyst rereads her notes from the previous session before she takes her patient into the consulting room. The patient begins to speak – about his life, a dream, a childhood experience – and the analyst stretches inside her mind, searching for related material. What were the details of the dream the patient is referring to? Who was that uncle he's talking about? Didn't he tell me something different last week?

In his description of "negative capability" – the capacity to sit patiently in unknowing, in Bion's PS or in Fordham's state of deintegration – Keats suggests that the experience I am describing, grasping for a memory *that is not presenting itself spontaneously*, expresses fear of the "uncertainties, mysteries [and] doubts" that arise (quoted in Bion, 1970, p. 70). This straining to remember is a symptom of anxiety; something is happening that troubles me and I look for something to rescue me from my lost unknowingness.

We do not normally memorize the facts that a friend, a lover, a child or a patient tells us. We come to know *a person*, something very different from the catalogue of facts that surrounds him. In ordinary life, one's basic relatedness determines the extent to which one can know someone else. There is a *feel* to who an individual is, both over time and at any given moment; intuitively, we know that our ephemeral, inchoate sense is much more central than any data. When Bion says that we should view every hour as a first hour, remembering that the patient is *not* someone we Know but someone we are trying to get to know, he goes too far. Letting go of the Facts that prevent her from sensing the unknown reaches of her patient is a most worthwhile attempt; trying to somehow shed the feeling connection that has been built by the analytic dyad is neither possible nor desirable. Working over time with distorted or problematic aspects of that feeling connection – i.e. of the relationship – typically proves to be the most important source of transformation for both members of the couple.

In the second kind of experience that most of us call "memory," the patient begins to speak and something floats *unbidden* into the listening analyst's mind: a fragment of a dream the patient told a year ago or an image from a dream of her own, a story from the patient's childhood, a scene from a movie the analyst saw last week. This second experience is the analyst's reverie. This is *not* what Bion means by "memory." *He reserves the term "memory" for "experience related to conscious attempts at recall"* (1970, p. 70, emphasis added). The analyst's reverie is highly valued, and one of the reasons that Bion asks us to turn away from *attempts* to remember is that working to remember takes away the space for reverie. The listening therapist wants to receive her own free associations, for the *unsought* images, feelings and ideas that appear of their own accord are messages from her unconscious as it responds to the patient's "transmitting unconscious." Struggling to recall an old fact destroys the inner emptiness that invites the understandings that will develop beyond her conscious mind's limited scope.

"Desire" is a similarly slippery word. The issue cannot be to split off a desire that arises because that would only be an invitation to unconsciousness. The analyst must take her wish as a piece of data, a fact of reality to be interested in; she must try to avoid identifying with the desire and giving herself over to achieving it. In this scenario, a desire for the end of the session can be noted and can lead to curiosity: what is happening here that I want to escape from? Behind the apparent boredom, is something frightening me? In a recent hour that seemed mildly dull on the surface, I found myself vaguely wishing that the patient would terminate. That desire woke me up and enabled me to realize that beneath the patient's rather monotonous tone were hints of suicidal feelings I had not known about. I could not stamp out my desire but I was able to separate myself from the wish so that I could use it to recognize my outside-of-awareness fear of my patient's death wish.

A desire to help the patient is similar: is the patient inducing in me a subjective sense of helplessness or weakness? Is he bringing up a savior complex or sadistically rubbing my nose in the "helplessness" I feel when faced with his "extraordinary" pain? In wanting to help, am I unconsciously striving to exclude some level of suffering that is trying to enter the room? The desire to help the patient will mean something slightly different every time it comes up, even with the same patient, let alone with different people. But whatever its precipitant, the desire blinds the analyst to the ways the patient needs to be seen and accepted in his wounded condition, *as is*, before he can begin to let it go (Sullivan, 1989). This desire to help is a particularly seductive one. Our patients want us to help them and most therapists entered the field out of a conscious wish to help people. But it is important to let go of the wish because, as far as we can tell, it is usually *not* helpful to try to help. Trying to understand the patient as he *is* generally loosens his character structure and begins or reinforces a growth process inside him that leads to positive ("helpful") developments in his inner world.

The understanding that is to be avoided is, again, not universal. The PS ↔ D sequence that we explored in Chapter 3 brings understanding with it, one that is unique to the moment. This kind of understanding differs from the theoretical knowledge that we arm ourselves with before entering the consulting room: the archetypal meanings of last week's dream image or the theoretical operation of infantile sexuality or the function and meaning of self–object transferences. Theoretical knowledge, when clung to, blinds the analyst to the singular meaning of the immediate moment. When theory, based on years of study and experiences on both sides of the couch, is preconsciously present as a background understanding of the psyche, it can be part of the swirling cloud of fragments that constitutes the PS state of unknowing. In that state, the theoretical ideas that arise as part of the analyst's reverie can facilitate the precipitation of a selected fact that jolts the analyst into a new under-standing. But when the "understanding" of this moment takes the shape of a cliché – "you have mixed feelings about your mother," "it is hard for you to tolerate angry feelings for someone you love" – even if the cliché is one that has been developed in the work with the particular patient, the likelihood is that it is sealing out an understanding of *now* that would in some way disrupt previous formulations.

The volatile nature of truth

When the analyst reaches for a memory – of a dream, a story, an interchange – she is treating these past experiences as though they were fixed objects. Jungians are especially vulnerable to imagining that a dream is a *fact*; many therapists fall into this attitude in relation to childhood memories or to the patient's stories of his spouse or parent. What was/is his mother/his wife *really* like? Isn't that the same dream that went on to describe a flood? Did that abuse *really* happen? When the analyst falls into this frame of mind, she is conceiving of inner reality, the world of analytic interest, as though it were outer reality, where a chair is a chair is a chair and if you don't watch your step you will stumble over it. In psychic reality, new "memories" of childhood can emerge in very old age as the individual's inner objects are repaired, damaged or brought down to size by his developmental processes; the dream that originally went on to image a flood can slip into union with another dream and they can together give birth to a "memory" that rearranges the old images and radiates out toward possibilities and implications in this moment that could not have existed when the dreams were first dreamed and reported.

When two people disagree on what happened, we can only let the conflict go. It is extraordinarily difficult to give up one's certainty regarding the story one has constructed about the past and to hold the other's story as equally valid with one's own. But accepting the unknowability of the past puts one in a more congruent relationship to reality than an attempt to discover The Truth. When patient and analyst disagree about what either one of them said or did, establishing the "truth" of the past incident is surely the least mean-ingful response. The patient's "memory" expresses something that needs to be understood *now*. The therapist's different sense of what happened yesterday or last week may be helpful in understanding what the patient is dealing with at this moment, but clinging to the *rightness* of her memory will only shore up the therapist's narcissistic self-esteem. It has no therapeutic value at all.

Certainly, the analyst needs to be sensitive to the possible ways her patient defensively distorts his images of his loved ones (and of those he hates). But to imagine that the patient's wife is *really* kind when he experiences her as cold, or that his sense of having been intrusively wounded in childhood indicates that he was *really* sexually molested implies a vision of "reality" that is fundamentally defensive. The patient's wife is not *really* anything, any more than any other human being is; she feels and behaves in many ways in different situations, and her husband's image of her, even if defensive, undoubtedly contains at least some truth. Remembering that memories of any era, certainly including childhood, may differ wildly from the memories of the others who were involved, we must reconcile ourselves to the impossibility of knowing what outer experiences the patient has symbolized with a hunch of sexual molestation. (Though I would certainly not want the reader to conclude from this that sexual molestation does not really happen, or that the question of whether a parent's intrusive behavior is verbal or sexual does not matter. Physical abuse, whether sexual or otherwise, is always more destructive than abuse that respects the growing child's bodily integrity and when the patient feels that he *remembers* sexual molestation [as opposed to *wondering* about it], I would take his memory to be as accurate as any other memory in the absence of other compelling indications.)

The *unbidden* memories that float into the therapist's mind, along with emotions (desires), thoughts (as opposed to directing thinking), bodily sensations and images, constitute the analyst's reverie. Memories that present themselves spontaneously are the voice of the receiving unconscious; memories that are grasped for come from the anxieties of the "I." As I indicated above, conscious attempts at recall are undesirable because they block the clinician's reverie. When the analyst or the patient "remembers" a past event in a state of reverie (as opposed to reaching for facts that were catalogued in the past), whether the event that presents itself was inside or outside the analysis, the "memory" is colored and shaped by the intersubjective reality of the moment. Thus, Ogden, talking about a reverie that immersed him in re-experiencing a painful time with a close friend, says:

> The experience in the session was not a repetition of anything, not a remembering of something that had already occurred; it was an experience occurring for the first time, an experience being generated freshly in the unconscious intersubjective context of the analysis. . . . The internal object relationship with . . . any . . . internal object is not a fixed entity: it is a fluid set of thoughts, feelings, and sensations that is continually in movement and always susceptible to being shaped and restructured as it is *newly* experienced in the context of each new unconscious intersubjective relationship.
>
> (Ogden, 1997, pp. 187–90, emphasis in original)

Freud urges the analyst to give maximal space to her "unconscious memory," meaning Ogden's reverie rather than Bion's memory. The personal memory that presents itself in the present moment is not irrelevant to the analytic situation as some clinicians defensively imagine; it is a fragment of the dream that the analyst's psyche is constructing to image its emotional experience in the present situation with the patient. The so-called memory is part of the psyche's constant attempt to be fixed and real; the image *masquerades* as a historical fact. When the analyst's reverie centers on the personal interactions of her past, it reflects the emotional situation of the analytic pair at the moment as well as the transformation of the analyst's relationship to her inner figure (spouse, parent, etc.) in the crucible of the analytic dyad's immediate experience. This is what Jung means when he says that analysis is not working until the patient has become a problem to the analyst (1946). *Both* members of the couple must get under each other's skin.

A long-term patient walked into my office and there arose in my mind, with marked vividness, a memory of an experience nearly forty years earlier, in which I had felt rejected and treated with contempt by my first husband. I had no idea what to make of the sudden emergence of an incident that had long since lost its sting for me and that had no relevance that I knew to anything going on in my current life. My patient began to talk of things that had no apparent similarity to my inner image. But about ten minutes into the hour, she told me about an incident from the previous evening with her husband. She had looked forward to an intimate evening with him, but he had become caught up on the phone with a colleague for most of the evening. She had wound up surfing the internet instead. The only feeling she was aware of was a faint disappointment. Using the information I had received from my "memory" enabled me to open up her much stronger feelings of abandonment, jealousy and masochistic submission to what she experienced as her husband's bad treatment of her.

My memory was not a memory; it was an image found by my unconscious, functioning as a "receptive organ," to describe what it was picking up from the patient's "transmitting unconscious." It is notable that my psyche produced this "memory" as my patient walked into the room, before any words were exchanged. After years of work, my patient and I were deep under each other's skin. Dieckmann (1976, p. 25) has described a research group in Berlin that studied process hours of analytic sessions including the analysts' "highly charged emotional thoughts as they arose [and] also subliminal ones, fantasies, feelings and psychosomatic affects arising from the unconscious" – i.e. the analysts' reveries. They found that the analyst's associations were linked *without exception* to the patient's, even in situations where the analyst came into the hour seriously shaken up by experiences of his own. They also found that the resistances that emerged tended to be carried as much by the analyst as by the patient. Despite our lengthy personal analyses, we remain ordinary human beings, subject to extensive anxieties about the unknown depths of the psyche, anxieties that propel us into behaviors whose meaning we know nothing about. These anxieties drive us toward memory and understanding, away from true *presence* in the obscurity of the moment.

Sometimes a patient will focus on whether or not the analyst remembers some particular detail that he told her. He may feel terribly wounded to learn that the childhood incident or the powerful dream to which he is referring is not coming back to his therapist. Surely this demonstrates her lack of concern! Does it? That would seem to be the first question the clinician might ask herself in this situation. If the answer is yes, her curiosity should be directed to wondering about the nature of the barrier between herself and her patient. How are they failing to construct a functioning relationship? But very possibly, her "inadequate" recall speaks to something very different from a lack of concern. Perhaps this interaction reflects a sado-masochistic dance that the patient/therapist pair is caught in. Perhaps the patient's anxiety about being forgotten needs to enter the room and be explored rather than held at bay by his therapist's perfect memory. Though the analyst's not-remembering may be painful for the patient, it reflects some element of truth that exists between the two people and, after all, analysis is designed to explore painful truths in the belief that that the pain will be worth the resulting development.

Memory is something from the past: thus-and-such occurred between so-and-so and me at such-and-such a time. Memory and desire operate through the senses. Because the senses orient to pleasure and pain rather than to truth, memory can never be reliable. We shape our memories in directions that give us "pleasure" (i.e. in ways that protect us from pain or disorientation), even if that means twisting them into shapes that are congruent with painful inner fictions that we live by. Letting go of memory and desire will not mean the person feels less pleasure or more pain. When a startling truth suddenly erupts into awareness, both members of the therapeutic dyad may feel great pleasure at the beauty of that truth. But taking a receptive stance strips away all illusions of *controlling* pleasure and pain. It acknowledges that whether life feels good or bad depends on forces outside our power. Bion suggests that the terror of making the transition away from the attempt to control pleasure and toward an undefended openness to life's experiences is one of the main roots of the universal resistance to seeing the truth. "Unity with O is in prospect fearful," he says (Bion, 1970, p. 53).

Being in the now

The practitioner's goal must be to immerse herself in the intensity of *this* moment's experience, to be open to the ways her patient is *not* the same person he was yesterday or last week, especially if she takes seriously the possibility and hope of change. A human relationship is never static. Two nonliving things can be related in a fixed pattern, but two people are always growing or deteriorating, their myriad aspects swirling around each other in ever-developing patterns like an always moving kaleidoscope. Needs shift, preferences change, hopes and fears are always in motion. But therapists cling to the ways the patient is familiar, preventing the emergence of contact with "an unknown, incoherent, formless void" (ibid., p. 52). Rather than developing knowledge about the patient, our goal must be to facilitate the emergence and integration of the denied, repressed, unavailable parts of him. We are not detectives, amassing facts in order to prove something. And truth, in any case, is not a collection of static facts. It is an infinitely shifting and inherently unmappable reality. Like "relationship," "truth" is a verb. We move toward and away from truth, seeking to know and to not-know, at the same time as the truth-as-we-know-it evolves toward new truths.

Donald Meltzer translates Bion's advice: " 'Abandon your memory, your desire and your understanding and follow me' rather than 'Thou shalt not remember, thou shalt not desire, thou shalt not understand' " (Meltzer, 1978/ 1998, p. 375). It is a positive step, not a forbidding; it does not shut something off, it opens the door to something else. The question is not the memory, desire and understanding that Bion wants to exclude; it is the space for reverie and unknowing that he wants to invite *in*. The concupiscent psyche's desire for security and its consequent attachment to its inner *knowns* (old facts and theories) fill up the analyst's mind and crowd out the space to respond creatively to the unfamiliar immediate moment.

Bion wants to divest himself of preconceptions so that the unexpected can catch his attention and ignite his curiosity. He tries to attend to the unknown and unknowable underlying truth, hoping to glimpse "the irreducible minimum that is the patient" (1970, p. 59). If we seek an expansion of consciousness, hanging on to what is already known is an irrelevance; it blinds us to the unknown aspects of the unconscious psyche that now present themselves. When the analyst imagines that she "knows" the other, she has petrified a momentary insight as though what has been seen is fixed rather than eternally volatile; she becomes a know-it-all rather than a curious participant in an infinite mystery (Richardson, 2006). Bion's advice extends Freud's suggestions regarding listening, especially as to Freud's comment that when we focus our conscious attention and attempt to logically *think* our way into clarity, we are in danger of seeing only what we already know and of blinding ourselves to unexpected elements that would disrupt the stability of old understandings.

The traditional psychodynamic focus has been to help the patient to become aware of unfamiliar elements of his inner emotional reality: to help him to develop "insight." The main thrust of this effort has been through verbal interpretations that articulate some unknown aspect of the patient's authentic being – of the O of the patient. Until the second half of the last century, the typical therapeutic model saw the patient as a separate person whom the patient and practitioner could join together to study, a model that we now know to be profoundly flawed. We can speak to some previously unknown aspect of the patient *because* therapist and patient are all mixed up together in ways that can never be fully sorted out. This is why the analyst's reverie so reliably informs her about the patient's state. O – the O of the patient, the O of the analyst, the O of the couple, the O of the universe – is *one* unified reality, inherently unknowable and inseparably intertwined; it will always be frightening because it surrounds and dominates the supposedly autonomous "I." Our fear pulls us toward the false security of the material outer world as a model for "reality" – even though the fact that we never actually have direct contact with that world makes our "knowledge" of that reality suspect, too. But no matter what the nature of the outer world, the inner world is neither solid nor fixed. What is the "truth?" We believe that the young person who imagines that his mother was "perfect" has come to a "truer" understanding as he recognizes ways she was flawed; but were that same young man to enter a second analysis in his middle age, the understanding of his mother that he developed with his first analyst will again shift, perhaps dramatically.

One axiom underlying analysis is that giving form to some aspect of the unknown self by describing it in words facilitates its integration with the "I" and helps to prevent it from propelling the person into mindless action. When an element from that inchoate level of the psyche is articulated in words, especially when the new understanding is verbalized by the patient himself, the mature aspect of the individual can enter into a dialogue with his undeveloped self. But interpretive work on any given element may take place over weeks or months or even years before the adult parts of the patient can engage with that element and begin to integrate it. And, as I noted above, unless that interpretive work is grounded in a field of relatedness and cherishment, it will never be integrated. But when a verbal understanding of an emotional complex *is* taken in, it has some constructive impact.

Now it is a truism that analysts often make interpretations that are in some sense "correct," but that have no real impact even when the patient consciously accepts them. Although Freud began by focusing on insight as the road to transformation, even in those beginning years of analysis he knew that the transformation he sought was a change in the patient's *reality* rather than a change in the patient's *knowledge* of his reality. The change in understanding that Freud and many subsequent analysts sought is desirable only because it is imagined that new insights will precipitate changes in the structure of the patient's self. But analysts can become confused and act as though increasing what the patient *knows* is the issue. This confusion translates into interpretations that describe unconscious drives, archetypal meanings, the genetic roots of complex-driven behavior, or some other theoretically informed perspective on the unconscious psyche. Interpreting the general dynamics of the patient's psyche is very different from speaking to the unique way these dynamics manifest at a specific moment in a particular dyad. When an immediately present emotional experience is interpreted, the interpretation has a reasonable hope of actually impacting the patient; when general dynamics are spoken to, they may be taken up by the patient's mind but they are unlikely to impact his being.

Returning to our central focus, listening, we must remember that the unconscious is not "inside" the person. Dreams image the *dreamer* as inside, surrounded by the universe we call "his unconscious." An individual's unconscious extends far beyond his puny "I." As Jung's description of the five unconscious links that operate at all times in the analytic container emphasizes, the psyches of the two people interpenetrate each other. I have imaged this situation by picturing the body as the "I" with the intangible force field of each person's psyche extending out around his body and mingling with the other's psyche like a liquid or a gas. This is the field from which projective identification, introjection and intuition emerge, making viable Freud's suggestion that the analyst turn her unconscious toward the patient's "transmitting unconscious" like a "receptive organ." In the therapeutic session, as in life, both members of the dyad are surrounded by and immersed in the unconscious – in O – at every moment. The unconscious psyche is not a *place* that can be explored; it is a living process that sustains and directs our conscious selves in the moments of the analytic hour as at all other moments. The analyst's hope is to glimpse the unconscious-of-*this*-moment, not to analyze the patient's unconscious as a stable constellation that can be dissected and parsed.

Recall Bion's suggestion to *become* O in order to find this moment's relevant interpretation. The analyst "becomes" O by sinking into her own experience. This turning in and down supports the action of the Self that is being constellated in the intersubjective reality of the moment. If the analyst can let go of memory, desire and understanding, she can sink into a state of mind where O evolves toward consciousness because she is not trying to pin anything down; she is trying to be open to whatever wants to come in. In this fluid atmosphere, the reality of the patient in the moment will be invited in; a hunch about today's unique twist on his complex may emerge for the analyst, enabling her to reflect it back to the patient.

Interpreting – a strange word for this tentative, always-open attempt to suggest who seems to be here today – thus flows from becoming one with O. The patient's response to his therapist's comment will revise or at least personalize the analyst's idea. Subsequent associations will image the continuing unfolding of the O of the hour, and it is hoped that they will surprise the listening clinician rather than confirm what she already knew. An interpretation should consist of something that could be said only to this patient, only at this unique moment. Memory is problematic partly because memory is all about time, while the growth process, like the unconscious, is outside of time. When the patient talks about a way he "used to be," that supposedly no-longer-existent tendency is present *now* in some form (perhaps in the *analyst's* behavior, for example). The image of long ago can be understood as describing something metaphorically far distant from the conscious self.

We can never know exactly what the patient said or did in any given hour, even though we feel strongly that there *are* absolute, objective facts transpiring in our consulting rooms. We can, however, understand the patient through our own psyche. Bion calls this act "intuition." Kohut called it "empathy." Jung might have also called it intuition (though I believe he meant something narrower by the term than Bion did) but this would have been Jung's way because he was (in his terms) an intuitive type. We each "get" the patient in our own way. Jung says:

> The patient, by bringing an activated unconscious content to bear upon the doctor, constellates the corresponding unconscious material in him, owing to the inductive effect which always emanates from projections in greater or lesser degree. Doctor and patient thus find themselves in a relationship founded on mutual unconsciousness.
>
> (Jung, 1946, para 364)

A living being is in constant flux. One is developing or deteriorating at every moment. Meltzer (1973, p. 156) notices that life inevitably uncovers more problems than it solves; I would add that just as opening oneself to the unconscious seems to expand it, "solving" a problem opens the door to more puzzles and confusions. As one very unhappy patient put it, each time we turn over one rock to find what's underneath, three more rocks that need to be investigated come into view. The analytic task is to attend to these proliferating, unsolved mysteries. This attitude forms the optimal link from analyst to patient; it precludes a state of "understanding." In this mode, although we are always *coming* to understand the other, we never arrive there. Jung expresses this idea when he says, "The goal is important only as an idea; the essential thing is the *opus* which leads to the goal: *that* is the goal of a lifetime" (1946, para 400).

Making the volatile fixed

From a state of at-oneness with the patient, the therapist can say something about what she sees, giving him a glimpse of his true self. The psyche seeks always to be seen. This is how the nonmaterial psyche becomes real. Freud commented that self-exposure oozes from every pore. The psyche produces symptoms and slips that communicate its conflicts, its needs, its unacknowledged aspects. Our ability to grow depends on this fact – our unknown selves *want* to be found. When the patient or analyst verbalizes something that was previously unconscious, the alchemists' injunction to "make the volatile fixed" is approached. The "volatile," a formless unconscious content of O, is "fixed" by describing it in words. Because the "I" is terrified of the suffering emotional self, it calls that nonmaterial entity "imaginary." Our narcissistic society emphasizes that suffering is something to snap out of, especially since it's all in our heads and we all know that *that's* not real. Against the "I" 's frightened attempt to stamp out the inner world, the soul struggles to be as real and solid as the floor beneath our feet. Winnicott's advice to find the aspect of the patient's self that is pressing to be seen is important because it supports the psyche's attempt to be recognized as real.

O "cannot be known by any human being; it can be known *about*, its presence can be recognized and felt, but it cannot be known. It is possible to be at one with it" (Bion, 1970, p. 30). Putting this in more accessible language, Bion says that "the more 'real' the psycho-analyst is the more he can be at one with the reality of the patient" (ibid., p. 28). Winnicott (1971) suggests that mirroring the patient back to himself enables him to feel real. "Feeling real is more than existing," he goes on to say. "[I]t is finding a way to exist as oneself, and to relate to objects as oneself, and to have a self into which to retreat for relaxation" (ibid., p. 117). By being "at one" with the patient's unknown inner reality, the analyst intuits the element that the patient needs to make fixed (real) in order to go on to the next bit of his evolving self. Ogden's attempt to interpret the "leading transference anxiety" is his way of speaking to the aspect of the self seeking existence at this moment in the conscious world. It emphasizes the way an intrapsychic factor in the patient becomes inter-personal in the analytic situation. All these perspectives seek the *real*, an aspect of the truth that I explored in the previous chapter.

Not-knowing

The patient brings something singular that has never before existed in the world to be seen and held today. Even when the patient seems to be droning on about the same old thing out of fear of the unknown, the unknown is pressing to be seen. The tension between truth and lies is always present. In a dead, boring hour when the lying tendency is creating a bulwark against the truth, the unknown truth is also asking for recognition. Perhaps the therapist can pick it up through her reverie. Or perhaps the patient is asking the therap-ist to experience his deadness until she can find a way to comment on it constructively. The moment's truth will never be an element that fits neatly into any depth psychological theory because no matter how universal Freud's oedipal complex or Jung's animus may be, a given individual's relationship to these universal factors will develop in a unique manner. It is his *particular* volatile inner self that the patient seeks. And the analyst can see that only by emptying her mind of expectations, of the preconceived notions that distort perceptions in order to make "reality" less frightening than it threatens to be. When the analyst turns away from the known, toward the mysterious, she opens the door to painful experiences

> that are usually excluded or screened by the conventional apparatus of 'memory' of the session, [or by] analytical theories [that are] often dis-guised desires or denials of ignorance, and [by] 'understanding' (which consists more often than not of [lies]).
>
> (Bion, 1970, p. 48)

So the first requirement is that the analyst begin in a state of not-knowing.

"Doubt is the crown of life because truth and error come together. Doubt is living, truth is sometimes death and stagnation," says Jung (1984, p. 89).

> [W]e must be very careful not to assume that we know all about the patient or that we know the way out of his difficulties. . . . It is important that the doctor admits he does not know. . . . Personal opinions are more or less arbitrary judgments and may be all wrong.
>
> (ibid., p. 3)

> Where do we get this belief . . . that we know what is good and what is bad? . . . We are all only limited human beings and we do not know in any fundamental sense what is good and bad in a given case. . . . To see through a concrete situation to the bottom is God's affair alone. . . . Therefore I say to the young psychotherapist: Learn the best, know the best – and then forget everything when you face the patient.
>
> (Jung, 1959a, paras 862, 882)

The path to wholeness, Jung says, is filled with "fateful detours and wrong turnings" (1952, para 6). Space must be preserved for the *un*reasonable, the *in*appropriate, the *un*fitting in life. At the simplest level, the therapist cannot know that the patient is making "a mistake" when he chooses to betray his wife or to break off his analysis. If the goal of life is becoming oneself, one may need to meet oneself in the most painful and humiliating ways, after making foolish or shameful choices that bring one face to face with the most disturbing aspects of oneself. We hope, of course, that a gentler path can be found, but we cannot know what any person needs to endure to find himself.

This attempt to approach the work with an attitude of not-knowing has been spoken to by many analysts besides Jung who predate Bion. Clare Winnicott describes her deceased husband, for example, as someone who

> made it his aim to enter into every situation undefended by his knowledge, so that he could be as exposed as possible to the impact of the situation itself. From his point of view this was the only way in which discovery and growth were possible, both for himself and for his patients. This approach was more than a stance; it was an essential discipline, and it added a dimension to his life as vital to him as fresh air.
>
> (Winnicott, 1989, p. 2)

Bion explored and elaborated the attitude of openness advocated by Freud, Jung, Winnicott and others. As the emotional experience of a session unfolds, both members of the dyad are transformed and to the extent that one can accept being carried along by the living process – to the extent that one can let go of trying to dominate and control it – one's ability to remember what happened is diminished. Winnicott (1949) speaks to the obverse of this when he talks about the way the individual unconsciously catalogues (memorizes) the facts of a trauma as it is happening. It is because he cannot have his experience that his psyche memorizes it, hoping that at some future time a situation will develop in which someone will contain him well enough to enable him to live his experience instead of holding it in the frozen deadness of memory. Taking off the armor of memory causes the tempo of the session to speed up. The 50 minutes are eternal and very quick, both at once. An attempt to reconstruct what happened in what order is undermined by the aliveness of the experience, an aliveness supported by the analyst's relinquishing the attempt to dominate the session through mentally recording it.

It is frightening to face the unknown and unknowable reality of our world, our selves, our intimates. Jung tells a story about Schopenhauer, lost in thought, walking through a flower bed. The distressed gardener called out,

> 'Hey! What are you doing . . .? Who are you?' 'Ah, exactly, if I only knew!' said Schopenhauer. That is why people prefer a safe persona: 'this is myself'; otherwise they don't know who they really are. The main fear of the unconscious is that we forget who we are.
>
> (Jung, 1984, p. 248)

Grotstein suggests that the universal terror of unknowable reality refers both to who one is and to the mystery of others, of our relationships, of the world at large (Culbert-Koehn, 1997, p. 26). He suggests, in fact, that "what handicaps psychoanalytic training is really our own unconscious addiction to clarity" (ibid., p. 30). Without the comforting fictions that we wrap around ourselves and call "reality," we fear that we are nothing, with no solid ground to stand on. It is rare and most distressing to truly glimpse how distorted, unreliable and shifting our perceptions and memories are.

Jung called rationalism

> an egocentric point of view – because *I* believe, *I* think, things have to behave according to this law. If a stone should defy the laws of gravity and suddenly begin to rise . . . everybody seeing it would be sent to the lunatic asylum. . . . Human experience is only three months old, and when it is six months old it may be that the stone will rise instead of fall. The recognition of the essential irrationality of the universe hasn't yet filtered through into our Western *Weltanschauung*.
>
> (Jung, 1984, p. 448)

Bion comments:

For all the laws of science there isn't any evidence that anybody or anything obeys those laws. It would be convenient if the world of reality kept
within the bounds of our comprehension – but it doesn't and there is no
reason why it should.

(Bion, 2000, p. 237)

I found both of these statements rather extreme, but then I came upon an
article in the *Science Times* section of *The New York Times* about the unknown
dark energy and matter that make up ninety-six per cent of the universe
(Overbye, 2006, p. D3). Dark energy (seventy-six per cent of the universe)
is the anti-gravity force that fuels cosmic expansion by pushing stars and
galaxies apart. "Dark energy," the journalist (Dennis Overbye) wrote, "was a
complete surprise. How often do you toss a handful of gravel into the air
and the rocks speed up as they leave your hand and disappear into the sky?"
Truly, there are more things in heaven and earth than are dreamed of in our
philosophies.

Christopher Bollas (2006), in a public lecture in San Francisco, referred to
Freud's advice to turn one's unconscious toward the patient's unconscious.
Bollas said that the field has largely moved away from this stance to one that
expects the analyst to *know* what is going on. By definition, we often cannot
know what is going on if our *un*conscious is the organ receiving and making
sense of it. Bollas described the way that demands for clarity destroy the
space for unknowing, leading the analyst to bring into the hour her pet
organizing ideas and to cling to them like a fetish that protects her from the
castration anxiety of not-knowing. The analyst imagines she is having intercourse with the patient, he said, where the actual situation is more perverse
than loving. Bollas's language – fetish, castration anxiety, perversion – of
course embodies something of what he is protesting. These are evocative
metaphors that suggest the emotional experience being described, but they
have been reified by the analytic community as though the anxiety of
unknowing is "really" anxiety about bodily integrity. Many metaphors speak
to the fear of the unknown, and the most "accurate" is not the one that spoke
to historically admired figures like Freud or Klein; it is the one that resonates
most deeply for the anxious person.

The analyst's task is to settle into the state that Keats called negative capability, a state of not-knowing, devoid of persecutory anxieties, an experience
of comfort with profound vulnerability. I do not think this is possible.
Perhaps one can approximate it. To be with one's not-knowing reverberates
into the inconceivable fact of mortality, where Death sits always on everyone's shoulder, giving no warning of when He will take His turn, snatching
away someone without whom the individual "cannot survive," suddenly destroying some unthinkably important aspect of the person's physical being,
like sight or mobility. In the clinical hour the stakes seem less severe, even if
opening the door to unknowing leaves one vulnerable to this ultimate level. In

the hour, not-knowing exposes one "only" to experiences of terrible foolishness and helplessness. It is difficult to settle into presenting oneself to the world as a highly trained expert who is entitled to a substantial fee for the ability to tolerate being lost and clueless in the face of a suffering human being.

Bion's idea is that when we can approach an empty state, we can be penetrated by the emotional flash that he called a "selected fact." This "fact" – most people would call it a "feeling" rather than a "fact," but Bion's problematic language has the advantage of reminding us that feelings *are* facts – organizes the disparate bits and pieces of material that have been swirling around the analytic couple in an apparently disconnected cloud. It precipitates a wholeness or gestalt that has been missing and leads the analyst to understand something integrative about the hour. The emergence of the selected fact is one aspect of the experience of "becoming O." But as soon as an understanding is achieved, it can become a shield that both analyst and patient cling to for protection from the infinite unknown universe that lurks just beyond this newly understood element.

In fact, the couple needs to rest in the illusion of Knowing for a bit. This provides stability and continuity for the couple and for each individual, a sense of self and pair that is defensive and illusory at the same time as it is partially true and wholly necessary. This Knowing distorts the patient's ability to let his associations flow freely and it distorts the analyst's ability to open herself to the new stretches of mystery expressing themselves in the thoughts and feelings that are emerging both from the patient and from inside the clinician. In optimal situations, the two individuals can gradually relinquish the newly won and already obsolete Knowing and return to a state of emptiness, waiting for a new selected fact to bring about a fresh view of reality that will first enlarge both people's selves and then block their further unfolding.

This is the oscillating PS ↔ D sequence that we explored in Chapter 3. Bion emphasizes that before a meaningful interpretation can be arrived at, the analyst must pass through a period of "patience" (the PS stage of fragments) and into a phase of "security" (D, where the split opposites are brought together). The experience of sitting patiently in unknowing will include some feeling of persecution; the coming into D where a gestalt pulls together the pieces of the hour or the week or the month and makes an interpretation possible will bring with it some depression over the possibilities that have been sacrificed to make room for the new wholeness. Bion suggests that the movement between "patience" and "security" is the hallmark of meaningful work (1970, pp. 123–4). The interpretation that emerges from this oscillation is framed in what he called the Language of Achievement (ibid., p. 2), emphasizing the accomplishment that emerges from the severe demand to sit with unknowing.

The transcendent function

Jung (1916) called the psychological capacity to traverse an arrhythmic sequence of disorientation-insight "the transcendent function." Writing so long ago, Jung's formulations sometimes seem primitive now. His rather unified images of "the conscious" and "the unconscious" have been displaced by the contemporary emphasis on the multiple selves that make up consciousness and the infinite unconscious aspects and possibilities that are present. Thirty years before his intersubjective masterpiece (1946) on the transference relationship, Jung still thought of the analyst and patient as separate people, each with his individual psychology. He did not appreciate the way each person in the dyad is neither fully separable from the other nor fully continuous with who he or she is in other situations. Jung speaks of *opposites* that he imagines belong to *the patient* rather than of a chaotic mass of unsorted bits emerging from neither analyst nor patient but from the couple. Despite this overly simplified perspective, his theory of a transcendent function that works to bring together elements from conflicting aspects of the self, and that helps the person come to a new attitude toward life, is similar to the process Bion describes as PS ↔ D.

Jung speaks of the generic patient as someone who cannot fit comfortably into the prefabricated shapes society has laid out for "normalcy." The person who seeks a therapist is someone who needs an individual solution for his unique problem. The problem, Jung emphasizes, cannot be solved logically. He describes the familiar experience of being caught up in an emotional conflict:

> The shuttling to and fro of arguments and affects represents the transcendent function of opposites. The confrontation of the two positions generates a tension charged with energy and creates a live, third thing – not a logical stillbirth . . . but a movement out of the suspension between opposites, a living birth that leads to a new level of being, a new situation.
> (Jung, 1916, para 189)

Jung's attitude "presupposes insights which are at least potentially present in the patient and can therefore be made conscious" (ibid., para 145). These insights cannot be found in theories or even in the wisdom accumulated by the analyst over decades of experience. Each insight is unique to one patient and must be unearthed at one particular time. Viewing the session in its singularity, with eyes uncontaminated by previous images, constellates Winnicott's area of transitional phenomena where paradoxes are accepted without question, allowing symbolic activity to develop in the psyche. The transitional area, where play holds sway, does not sound painful, while the state of being pulled or torn between the opposites certainly does, but emotional play is actually serious in nature. It is the way the child works through painful inner realities. The "play" aspect of emotional play lies in its volatility: at this moment we declare such-and-such to be the basis of our play, but at the next moment we can turn that upside down and thus-and-such will be the case. Today the plastic dinosaur is the dangerous monster who lives in the closet, but tomorrow it may be an ally who attacks Aunt Margaret for laughing at Mommy and making her cry.

Even in 1916, Jung noted that intrapsychic conflict could manifest as a struggle between analyst and patient and that the action of the transcendent function could be seen in a rapprochement between the two people, but his personal bias led him to focus on its action within the individual. Some years later, in the early 1930s, he pointed to the way that symbol formation depends on the transcendent function (1976), reinforcing the parallel that I noted above with Winnicott's (later) formulation of transitional phenomena. Jung also noted at that time that the Self both guides the transcendent function in its operation and emerges from its operation. In this context, Ulanov (1997) points to the way the transcendent function brings toward consciousness an awareness of "the mysterious presence of what lies beyond and undergirds the whole analytical enterprise" – the infinite reality of Bion's "O" or Jung's collective unconscious and the Self.

Where Jung believes that the "answer" to the impasse of the present – the insight, the wholeness, the meaning of any given situation – will lie in implicate form in the *patient's* being, Bion looks to *the analyst* for enlightenment. Where Bion focused on the need for the analyst to sit with the unknown until an emotional flash brings to his mind the missing gestalt of the moment, Jung looks more to the patient, who will find his meaning by turning inward and sitting with the personal unknown that pulls him now this way and now that. In his theory of a transcendent function, Jung proposes a model describing the therapist's central job as providing and holding the space in which the patient's inner struggle can emerge in its full intensity. The transcendent function, a natural process controlled by the unconscious rather than by the "I," does the essential work. Contemporary thinking implies that we should turn to *the couple* as the source of meaning, but what seems most important to notice here is the way that both Jung and Bion emphasized the uniqueness of the sought-for "solution," its irrational nature, and the need for patience while waiting for its arrival.

An understanding of an analytic experience or of the unfathomable inner workings of a human soul will never be deduced via logical thinking. For Bion it arrives in an emotionally charged intuition, for Jung it is "a living birth." Either formulation points to the dead end of consciousness's sterile ideas and toward the new perspective that emerges in its own good time, making something whole of previously disconnected fragments.

The frightful fiend

Remember that what is unknown is always infinitely greater than what is known and that we are seeking contact with the *un*known in an analytic session. But many parts of the analyst's self fear, even dread, contact with the unpredictable, potentially dangerous and certainly destabilizing unknown. The parts of ourselves that crave control and safety rather than a search for the infinitely ungraspable truth of our emotional psychic reality are gestured toward by Coleridge:

> Like one that on a lonesome road
> Doth walk in fear and dread;
> And having once turned round walks on,
> And turns no more his head;
> Because he knows a frightful fiend
> Doth close behind him tread.
> (quoted in Bion, 1970, p. 46)

This "frightful fiend" is duplex. It is the terrifying unknown truth from the depths that we flee from; and it is that very impulse *not* to know the truth, to wrap ourselves in lies and evasions that will not upset our equilibrium and throw us into vulnerable, out-of-control states. The fiend is the truth one fears (fiendish when seen from the perspective of fear), and it is the driven flight from that truth into lies (fiendish because lies are inherently the work of the devil). In so far as one relies on memory – on what was true *yesterday* – one blocks the possibility of learning something unknown, *today's* truth that disturbs the tidy arrangement of "facts" that we lean on to remain safe in the swirling mystery of the obscure, unfathomable universe.

The more anxious the analyst is, the more inner pressure she will feel to reach for "facts." When the patient is in crisis, the frightened analyst may search inside her memory for the "cause" of the threatening disaster, closing her mind to the current moment. But the psyche does not operate by cause and effect. If the analyst can focus on the nature of her immediate experience and open herself to her unconscious reverie instead of looking for what triggered the crisis, startling meanings emerge. For example, a patient pressured his therapist with increasingly disastrous behavior in his work life. Any sensible person would know that the way he was acting would cause him to lose his job. The therapist became more and more anxious, offering one idea after another about the genetic roots of his behavior, his fear of success, his inability to tolerate a positive self-image. She was *filled* with the desire to prevent him from losing his job and making a mess of his life. The therapist's theories were protecting her from a direct experience of the terror that permeated her patient's inner world. His self-destructive behavior had constellated his panic inside her. Her interpretations were actually attempts to discharge his tormented inner state instead of holding it. The patient's fear was Winnicott's *one* thing he was bringing to be seen, and the therapist's driven attempt to get rid of it rather than suffering it forced the patient to ratchet it up and bring it in over and over.

Faith

Bion suggests that if the analyst can shun memory, desire and understanding – all of which reflect attempts at mastery – she leaves a space into which faith can flow. By turning away from the world of sensuous reality – the outer world – the analyst can find a state of mind imbued with "faith that there is an ultimate reality and truth – the unknown, unknowable, 'formless infinite' " (Bion, 1970, p. 31). In Klein's language this would be faith in the existence of good inner objects; in Jung's poetry it is faith in the Self, in the reality of the psyche and in the transcendent function; Winnicott might call this faith in transitional space and in the psychic paradoxes that must be held and accepted rather than resolved; Ogden might point to faith in the analytic third and the psycho-analytic process. What is called for is faith in the intangible inner world that supports us in our harsh and rocky journey through the world of matter. It is faith in the meaning of suffering and the possibility of joy. Earlier ages might have called it faith in the goodness of God, or simply in God.

The basic psychoanalytic attitude is one of faith. Where memory, desire and understanding seek to control events and to dominate them, individuation – the process of becoming increasingly whole – depends on allowing experience to overtake one. In this way one encounters one's true self. But so often a person wants to create a self he can admire rather than to become the self he is. Bion suggests that the central point of any interpretation is "to help the patient to be less frightened of his own horrible self" (2000, p. 248).

Eigen (1981), describing the area of faith in Winnicott's work, contrasts the areas imbued with faith – those of transitional relating and object usage – with the area of object relating. Object relating involves splitting oneself, projecting parts of the self into the other and then introjecting parts of the other into the self. Splitting is the basis of lies. It enables the individual to not know about aspects of himself that would disturb the idealized or degraded self-image that is familiar to him. It is also a fundamentally solipsistic activity: the individual imagines that his omnipotent fantasies control other people. The other is important, but not quite real, not a subject in her own right. The splitting/projecting/introjecting activity of object relating reflects an attempt to master a situation. This projecting/introjecting activity is an aspect of memory (introjecting) and desire (the projecting that seeks to control the other) (Eisold, 2005). It seeks to eliminate the traumas of separation through the continual enactment of a fantasy of control, an (unconsciously) untruthful activity that shuts out the individual's real creativity. When the individual reaches Winnicott's version of the depressive position, the capacity for concern, the other is seen more fully, as someone who is both good and bad, and toward whom the person has both good and bad intentions. But rather than bringing the individual anything like faith, this realization creates a permanent anxiety about the way his own badness requires constant monitoring. It is as though the individual is left always worrying: are my hateful feelings polluting my behavior, is my envy leading me to devalue her, am I centered in my love or am I falling into my wish to triumph? When the individual has developed the capacity for concern, his *goal* is to be related, but as Winnicott parses the dynamics of object relating we see how it works *against* relatedness, for true relatedness demands an undefended openness to the other that must include the possibility of hurting the other as well as nurturing him.

Object usage, on the other hand, involves the destruction of the other in fantasy, followed by the startling and wonderful discovery that fantasies can *not* destroy the other. The other becomes a *real* person; the subject can believe in her; she is not an extension of himself who can be controlled by his internal mental activities. The distortions inherent in object relating are transcended. The possibility of being one's whole self without compromise is reinforced and a true relationship becomes possible: the other can be valued for her own self. A world of love begins to be created since the need for guilt is obviated. One does not need to be good to make up for one's badness, for the person has learned that the other can survive his badness; loving for its own sake becomes possible.

Object usage leads to the discovery of an outer reality that exists apart from one's self. One can have faith in the world: it is real – other people *exist* – and this truth gives the subject a more immediate sense of himself and of the realness of his inner world. The recognition of a real outer reality goes hand in hand with the discovery of a real inner reality that is safe enough to generate faith. Both worlds are essentially unknowable. As Grotstein notes, our ideas about "reality" are actually myths protecting us from the vast ignorance in which we live (Culbert-Koehn, 1997). Fully *using* another person who *survives*[2] allays the individual's terror of his own destructiveness. The attempt to dominate life can be renounced for the possibility of relationship has come into being. Our mutual realness takes center stage, enabling us to participate together in the development of our mutual aliveness.

The faith of the transitional area has a different quality from the faith of object usage. It depends less on the subject's activity in the interpersonal world and more on his experience of a kind and loving environment. The mothering person's good-enough adaptation to the baby's needs allows the baby to imagine that there is neither one person involved (as in object relating) nor are there two (as in object usage); instead there is an interpenetrating

---

2 It is important to remember that survival means continuing to function adequately in one's role (analyst, parent, etc.), not simply continuing to breathe.

field[3] that fits well enough. The baby's creative gesture is met with a responsive creative movement; faith in the goodness and safety of the world lays the groundwork for later attempts at object usage.

Bion has faith in the intangible universe of O. His faith does not seem markedly different from other kinds of spiritual faiths. He considers faith crucial for any scientific attempt to understand reality, including the attempts of the hard sciences. In analysis, faith involves opening oneself to the perceptions of the moment regardless of the way those perceptions may support or contradict the analyst's preconceived theories. Through faith the therapist "sees" or "feels" the nonsensuous activity of the patient's mind in interaction with her own. To center oneself in faith means to come forth without reservation, opening one's heart and soul fully to the unknown reality of this person and this hour. According to Bion this is the core method of psychoanalysis, far more crucial than any kind of knowledge.

Jung looks at this same area of faith in different terminology.

> If the work succeeds, [he says], it often works like a miracle, and one can understand what it was that prompted the alchemists to insert a heartfelt *Deo concedente* [God willing] in their recipes, or to allow that only if God wrought a miracle could their procedure be brought to a successful conclusion.
>
> (Jung, 1946, para 385)

Rather than faith in O, Jung is expressing faith in the purposeful energy of the Self that works both within and beyond the individual. If the person can let go of control and turn himself over to it, that energy may bring about the wholeness – the realness – he seeks by facilitating the development of his capacity for relatedness. The concept of the Self speaks to the inherent aliveness of the unconscious – of O – and to its active attempt to integrate the whole living person both inside himself and interpersonally, in the human world.

Reliance on faith maintains that resting in the unknowability of reality will lead, in time, to the emergence of coherence and integration. All human beings have parts of themselves that refuse this faith, insisting that *I* am the universe; there is no inner or outer, there is only *Me* and I am *in charge*. This is Bion's frightful fiend.

The analytic perspective

In letting go of the life preservers of memory, desire and understanding, the analyst opens herself to the ineffable reality of the psychoanalytic relationship.

---

3 In fact, this experience rather than the more adult sense of the absolute separateness of individuals seems to be closer to the truth.

In terms of the faith–mastery set of opposites that we have been exploring, the analyst, centered in faith, turns to listening and receiving rather than to knowing or formulating; she is looking for direct and undefended contact with *now* in its unique constellation. She enters into the present emotional truth of the couple that is composed of two individuals who will be different people this evening or tomorrow. When Freud tells analysts to artificially blind themselves in order to "focus all the light on one dark spot" so as to see the dark unconscious (letter to Lou Andreas-Salome, quoted in Bion, 1970, p. 43), he is describing an act of faith through which one "sees," "hears" and "feels" the nonsensual psychological truth that is present.

Therapists and even analysts often express the fear that taking this stance will result in the loss of patients. They imagine that patients must be gradually inducted into an analytic experience, that they must be educated about "how analysis works" rather than simply met with an analytic approach. It will be too disorienting and frightening for the naïve patient, they suggest. When the therapist listens deeply, trying to hear the specific element that the patient brings in today, the therapist becomes quieter and leaves more space for the patient. Deeper and more surprising material emerges. *Therapists* tend to be frightened of so much space; the fantasy that the *patient* will not be able to tolerate this generous container is a rationalization that protects the practitioner from acknowledging her own distress at experiencing her smallness and vulnerability. Partly, the analyst's driven need to *give* the patient something (an interpretation) is a function of the greed for material stuff that we have explored, for an interpretation is a kind of thing while a relational link is inherently ephemeral; her greed leads the practitioner to focus on something concrete to give the patient and to devalue the nonmaterial attention and concern that is more fundamental to healing (Sullivan, 1989).

(The patient, of course, has his own version of this greed, and it can lead him to want things – interpretations, homework – because the greed overwhelms his ability to recognize the value of the cherishment on offer. When this is the case, an "educational" response may well be called for: "I can hear how much you want me to give you something concrete to hang onto, but right now we both need to attend to listening to what comes up inside you. If you can let yourself continue to associate, we will arrive at an understanding that will make sense of your confusion." This is very different from the more impersonal sort of comment that is imagined to be educational: "Analysis works best if you will just associate; I will speak when I have something valuable to say, and that is not the case right now.")

Analysts turn toward interpretations for many unconscious reasons. Beyond the feeling that an interpretation offers something *real* lies the practitioner's narcissism. It is hard for many of us to be quiet and unobtrusive; it can feel as though we are not contributing anything when we are not receiving direct attention. And, of course, leaving the space for unexpected primitive energies to emerge is inherently dangerous. We do not know what infantile needs or demands may arise, constellating unknown aspects of our own infantile desires.

It is important to remember that being quiet is not the same as being avoidant. An *impulse* to speak (as opposed to the choice to speak) will often reflect one anxiety or another on the therapist's part. A pressured impulse should usually be resisted. A *fear* of bringing something up is a completely different animal from a choice to provide the patient with maximal space for self expression. If the practitioner can notice that she is avoiding taking something up – if she can manage not to get caught up in rationalizations that turn her avoidance into a thoughtful choice – she can use that avoidance as an orienting principle. When a subject feels too hot to talk about, it certainly means that that subject needs to be approached in some way or other. This is different from a subject that seems premature to open up, although the two experiences can easily be confused.

Writing about the distinction between avoiding something and comfortably listening in silence demonstrates the difficulty of discussing technique in the abstract. The differentiation I would like to make is real and important, but because our perceptive and judging apparatus is so deeply distorted by unconscious currents, it is extremely hard for any individual (certainly including myself) to make these differentiations without input from an independent third. Perhaps the therapist whose fear frequently leads her to avoid bringing things up can work with her fear by pushing herself simply to be more active, even if this means cutting into the space that she can offer her patients.

But most of the objections to the stance of radical openness that Bion's advice creates are projections of the therapist's fears of not knowing. The profound intimacy constellated by receptivity to the immediate moment leaves one vulnerable to the other in a way that "educating" the patient never will. While there will certainly be patients who flee the space that an unknowing approach offers, there will be others who relish it and expand to fill it up. It is both frightening and relieving suddenly to find enough room to become one's true self.

And in any case, renouncing dependence on memory, desire and understanding does not mean that the analyst cannot respond to the patient's terror of the greatly expanded container on offer. Some of the classical deprivations that psychoanalysts believe to be necessary are unconscious attempts on the analyst's part to project her own fear of the immediately present unknown into the patient. There is no reason to refuse to answer a question, even if the answer is an empathic statement about one's inability to answer. The parent of a frightened child does not need to *answer* the child's unanswerable question to comfort him with soothing words that convey the constancy of her strength and her love, even in an objectively dangerous situation. One need not comply with a patient's demand that a symptom be addressed or an answer given to respond with empathy and concern that soothes his terror:

"I can hear how frightening it is for you not to know what to talk about, but I think that if you can just continue to say out loud whatever comes to mind, even if it seems irrelevant or foolish, what we need to focus on will emerge."

"I hear how desperate you are to know what it means that you forgot that important meeting, and I wish I could just *tell* you why this happened, but my hunches are still too unformed. I feel sure that if you can bear to keep saying out loud whatever comes to mind, your psyche will take us where you need to go."

"I hear that you want me to be the expert and to tell you why you felt sexually aroused when reading to your little boy, but we will be able to find that out only by listening to what your psyche has to say. Try to keep saying what comes to mind, and we'll both try to hear what might have been expressing itself in you last night."

Everyone loses patients. No matter how "flexible" (or strict) a practitioner tries to be, there will always be people who need something she does not have. But if the therapist believes that people grow as a result of finding and connecting with the missing parts of themselves – if she believes that what matters is the *un*known – and if she has faith in the Self – faith in the psyche's knowledge of where it needs to go and how it needs to heal, there is no reason to "educate" the patient before taking an analytic stance. When some element of the clinician's behavior (or apparent non-behavior) disturbs the patient, it is helpful to explain why the analyst acts this way. I see no value in leaving the vulnerable patient terrified if the terror can be truthfully soothed. But the explanation should be personal and immediate. What is needed is not an explanation of how *analysis* (or therapy) works; what is called for is an explanation of why this particular practitioner is working this way at this precise moment. There is no reason to teach patients how the work works – especially since no one actually knows how it works. But there can easily be moments when it is important to make the therapist's apparently bizarre behavior understandable rather than disorienting and frightening. The process is the same as when a parent explains a painful medical procedure to a child as the little one endures it. Explaining the pain makes it meaningful and tolerable rather than persecutory.

We know, in fact, that the most powerful interventions are rarely planned. Just as the patient comes to know what he thinks as he speaks his associations aloud, the therapist may realize the meaning of the moment *in the act of speaking to it*. It is not her conscious memory or understanding that is operating; it is the Self, the energic force of O, bringing out a truth that may surprise both people in the room. The explosive interpretation that ultimately transformed my work with Gertrude (see Chapter 3) expressed a truth *I did not know* until I spoke it. Coltart's sudden eruption (see Chapter 5) similarly resolved a very difficult situation (perhaps more rapidly than mine did). These were acts of freedom that informed the speaker of the situation's meaning at the same time as it informed the patient.[4]

When one turns away from sensual reality and toward faith, the accompanying emotion is dread. By letting go of our armor we open the door to experiences that are painful and difficult for the patient and/or the therapist. To the extent that one needs a sense of power and control, it is too dangerous to go naked into the clinical encounter. We want to be experts who can survey a vast landscape and make sense of its essence. Jung calls this narcissistic urge the analyst's attempt to hide behind a *"persona medici"* (1946, para 365). Winnicott (1971), looking back as an older man, said that he derived far greater pleasure from watching a patient come to his own understandings than he did as a younger analyst from giving the patient interpretations.

Fear of change

Almost all human beings imagine that they want to change. Certainly, all analysts and patients consciously hope to develop, usually thinking of this as wanting to "get better," to "improve," perhaps to "be cured." But people cling to old patterns and resist change. Change is slow, "bad habits" have us in their grip. Fairbairn (1952), in a foreshadowing of attachment theory, talks about how we cling to our bad objects. Bion suggests that change is experienced as catastrophic for the personality. The word "catastrophic" turns on its head the perspective from which we view the situation. Instead of focusing on how desirable change is and hacking away at those wicked resistances that block it, we are suddenly looking at how terrifying it is and empathizing with the poor person's attempt to cling to the known and to hold off transformation. Especially since the poor person in question may well be oneself.

There is much evidence that fear of change begins at the latest with birth, the largest transformation a living creature experiences short of death. Being born is typically lengthy and fraught with strong sensations, at least some of which are probably unpleasant. And the wordless infant can have no concept of how long the process will last. From his point of view, this may as well be the new state of affairs as the beginning of a transition to a new state. Winnicott (1949) hypothesizes normal as well as traumatic birth experiences, but I am unable to imagine a birth, even a Cesarean delivery, that is not traumatic.

And while birth will bring many wonderful things, at first it can be only terrifying and incomprehensible to find oneself expelled from the safety of

---

4 As all sensible thinkers have indicated, it is impossible to offer any positive guidelines for technique. It is true that one should avoid acting on a pressured impulse to speak; it is also true that an unthinking outburst can be transformative.

the watery existence one has known into the gaseous outer world. Suddenly all the bodily systems that have been developing must kick into action, regulating the infant's temperature, digesting his food and eliminating his wastes. He must breathe, suck, cry. No one who has spent any time with a newborn can fail to notice how difficult this transition is and how much suffering the baby experiences as he traverses his first few months and settles into life, opening up to the many pleasures available in an ordinary good-enough family situation. All later change reverberates back toward his first amazing shift, bringing back the helpless infant's terror at being propelled through the narrow birth canal into the world of light.

One way that Bion explored this fear of change is in his work on the mystic and the group (1970). Drawing on his own experience in the British Psycho-Analytical Association, he wrote about the tension between an innovator, whose ideas shift familiar notions of reality in disorienting ways, and the group he belongs to that must try to preserve its integrity by maintaining the worldview that holds it together. Translating this tension into the inner world illuminates the universal intrapsychic conflict between the wish to face the truth and grow toward wholeness versus the wish to maintain the status quo that is known and secure, even if the security in question is similar to that of the prison or the grave. The inner "genius" has a new thought, a new perception that disturbs previous understandings; the inner group – the character structure, the noisy parliament of inner figures all of whom want to hold onto their power – resists the disorientation and confusion that taking in the new would entail.

Using Bion's insight in the context of the clinical relationship, we can see the anti-relational pressures inherent in the situation. A creative idea emerges from one or the other of the minds present, an idea that challenges old certainties and stabilities. The "group" – those parts of both people that fear the pain of disruption, unknowing and confusion – fights to maintain its established way of perceiving, thinking and being.

Bion's advice on listening presents us with a recipe for the establishment of a living relationship. Put aside all the protections against the other that we carry around, he is saying when he tells us to forsake memory, desire and understanding. The facts of our lives on which we have anchored our identities will change if our relationship is deeply meaningful; remembering these facts by casting them in stone will hardly facilitate this process. Our desires will surely clash to some extent with the desires of the other, and if our relationship develops, positive and negative possibilities that we could never have imagined before will emerge. Our understandings of the psyche's nature and operation will surely be reworked, perhaps radically, in the next decade or two, and what we know about people in general will always be revised in some way by any particular person's singularity. We can *never* Know a human being, neither ourselves nor another. Bion's formula for analysis is actually a formula for relatedness.

In the clinical hour we arm ourselves with psychological theories, with capacious memories containing extensive lists of things we know about the patient, with the therapeutic desires to guide or shape the patient or the hour in ways that we are certain are felicitous. We cannot help but work to defend ourselves against the helplessness of not knowing. Analysts almost always tell themselves that they are without an agenda for the patient, but I am skeptical of the possibility of attaining that perfectly pure state. At every moment the practitioner must turn away from the siren songs of memory, desire and understanding. The struggle can never be won.

And despite all I have said, it would be undesirable not to *care* about a patient and caring must bring with it a desire for his well-being. Here we have a paradox that must simply be accepted. The analyst must let go of desire, even the desire to help, at the same time as she remains involved and concerned, desiring the best for her patient.

Chapter 7

Transformation

Our hope is that the experience of analysis will facilitate the patient's transformation. We know that when this happens, transformation of the analyst
will also be involved. But can we say what we mean by "transformation?"

A patient whom I will call Sarah came for analysis. She had previously
worked for nearly ten years with a male analyst who had been extremely
helpful. She had married a man whom she loved and they had had a baby
together who was now a sturdy child. Her career was flourishing. But she had
a painful symptom that persisted: fantasies of hurting herself – by cutting,
by burning, by throwing herself in front of speeding cars or by leaping off
bridges. Her analysis had enabled her to "switch off" the fantasies when they
presented themselves. Her previous analyst had offered the image of a record
player and had suggested that when the records began to play she could pick
up the needle and put on a different disk. She could do this, she told me; the
violent images would recede into the void from which they had come. Her life
was good, but she did not want to change the record any more. She wanted
to come to a place where the record no longer presented itself to her. She
wanted a deeper transformation than what had thus far been achieved.

In Bion's terms, transformations are movements from one state to another.
His central example (1965) is a painting of a field of poppies: the vegetable
matter of the field is transformed into a picture on canvas. His concept
implies something about the stability of the self. The naïve patient approaches
psychotherapeutic work with a hope that often seems to imply that he will be
a new person when he is "cured." He will "get rid of" his insecurities or his
anger, for example. An experienced therapist, on the other hand, knows that
all aspects of the self, even the most despised, are needed for wholeness. Every
inner element is precious because each form that the self takes is an organization of energy that can potentially be transformed into something valuable.
The alchemists maintained that the gold they sought was to be found in filth
and excrement. The gospels tell us that the rejected cornerstone will be the
keystone of the desired edifice. The therapist looks to redeem, not amputate
painful and difficult aspects of the self.

Bion's overarching concept of psychological transformation means that an inchoate "something" evolves from O and, being apprehended by consciousness, takes a finite form; the inchoate "something" is transformed into a verbal statement. At first glance, it would seem that Bion and Sarah were using the word "transformation" in different ways. She wanted to get rid of the fantasies that plagued her and according to Bion the violent fantasies were already transformations: an unknown and unknowable inner reality has been changed into images. But Sarah wanted to transform her unknowable inner reality into a more constructive shape; she wanted to free up the emotional energy contained in her fantasies so that it could take a new form.

We might say that Sarah's fantasies imaged her unconscious self-loathing. Perhaps we would talk about emotional pain that she could not bear to experience directly, an anguish picturing itself as cuts, burns, the shattering of her body. A third possibility is that the fantasies represented the Self's attempt to break through some kind of inner deadness, to bring Sarah to a deeper aliveness. All these possibilities and more came together to create the scenarios that persecuted her. These interpretations make some sense of Sarah's symptom, but they reflected ideas that she had developed before she knew me; they are inchoate emotional experiences transformed into words, transformations that she and her previous analyst had effected together. These understandings – interpretations – had not led to the fundamental shift in her inner universe that would express itself in the disappearance of her symptom. Her interpretations of the symptom are what Bion calls "transformations in K," changes that he contrasts with "transformations in O." Let us look at the difference between these two kinds of development and see how they might relate to the change Sarah sought.

As I discussed in the previous chapter, the therapeutic task is to open oneself to the O of the moment by being as fully *present* as possible, hoping thereby to glimpse that not-yet-born aspect of the patient's experience that is needing to be lived today. Freud's famous maxim "where id was, there ego shall be" is an image of capturing some "thing" from the infinite and giving it a form. The fundamental goal of depth therapists has been to expand the patient's consciousness (where this includes the therapist's inner patient as well as the outer designated patient). Therapists have imagined that when the patient sees something, he will also experience it. Thus, the widespread focus on "insight" as the goal of the work. Because, in the earliest days of analytic work, it was immediately clear that intellectual insight might have very little impact on the patient, insight became defined as intellectual *and emotional* awareness of a situation. But the primary behavior that therapists had at their disposal remained verbal statements explaining something about the patient to the patient. Too often, the "insight" that the patient acquired as a result of this sort of explanation had little or even no impact on his personality.

This is especially the result when the insight is *given* to the patient in the form of an interpretation. In *Playing and Reality* (1971) Winnicott makes a case for the undirected playing around that constitutes creativity and suggests that over long periods I withhold interpretations. . . . I often relieve my mind by writing down interpretations that I actually withhold. My reward for withholding interpretations comes when the patient makes the interpretation herself, perhaps an hour or two later. My description amounts to a plea to every therapist to allow for the patient's capacity . . . to be creative in the analytic work. The patient's creativity can be only too easily stolen by a therapist who knows too much.

(Winnicott, 1971, p. 57)

Winnicott is speaking here to Bion's idea of "winning" something from the void and formless infinite. *Telling* a patient something about himself triggers a process very different from his wresting the awareness for himself from the unconscious. When an individual wins something from the void, he *has* it. When it is given to him, he may know it, but the knowing may be superficial and not touch his deeper levels. *Receiving* something often has a radically different impact from *winning* it.

Both of the constructive changes in personality that Bion describes – "transformations in K" and "transformations in O" – depend on winning rather than receiving something from O. In "transformations in K," the inchoate comes to exist in K; in "transformations in O," it is experienced in O. Let me explain.

K is the world of knowing, although, as we have explored, "knowing" is not about facts. A transformation in K is growth in conscious awareness ("knowledge") that emerges from a not-knowing stance of openness and emptiness. It is a transformation in the sense that something that existed in an unknowable form in the *un*conscious has been won by consciousness, described in words and changed in that process. Let us keep Sarah's quest in mind and turn to an experience with another patient, Penny (see Chapter 4), as a way to understand what a transformation in K is like.

Transformation in K: clinical example

Penny begins her hour talking about her sister, Pat, who has just discovered that her husband has been unfaithful for ten years, fathering a daughter with his paramour. Pat is in a towering rage. Penny talks about her driven attempts to force her sister to a modulated stance in which Pat sees both sides of the situation. Penny knows her own attitude is unreasonable – that Pat's rage is a sounder response than her "balanced" perspective – but she cannot help herself.

Penny tells me of the neglect her sister experienced as a child and then begins to talk about their mother's neglect of *her*. I hear a new story: when Penny was four months old, her scientist mother left her with a nursemaid for two months while she worked at a research institute five hours from their home. Penny once asked her mother if she had seen her in those months.

Perhaps when the father visited, she thought, he had brought the infant Penny along. Oh, no, the mother replied. Penny had been too sick to be transported.

Penny then talks of her mother's suicide gesture during Penny's adolescence. I learn that Penny and her mother were home alone when the mother locked herself in her bedroom, swallowed a large bottle of pills, and called her sister, Penny's aunt. The father rushed home. The fire department broke down the door. And the fourteen-year-old Penny cowered, unseen, in the hall.

I am filled with rage at both stories. I imagine murdering Penny's mother. Penny talks tearfully of her mother's loneliness. Suddenly the hour comes together in my mind; I say that Penny wants to modulate Pat's rage because she is afraid of her own rage at her mother. She is startled by that thought, but it makes sense to her.

My experience of the hour all at once cohering is a transformation in K.[1] It is an interesting one because the interpretation I offered, in addition to being "true," was also a −K contribution to our work: as I suddenly realized when I saw Penny in the waiting room several days later, the issue *now* was not Penny's anger at her mother, but fury with me. She was unconsciously experiencing my coming two-week vacation as a mother leaving her infant for a grossly unreasonable time. When I focused on her still-not-fully-conscious rage at her mother, I brought us closer to recognizing the immediate situation – it led to my spontaneous recognition several days later of Penny's rage at me – but in the first hour, it expanded our understanding of the moment *and* it covered over more immediately painful emotions.

In fact, *any* new piece of knowledge becomes a −K factor as soon as it is articulated. Even if I had immediately recognized the current implication of Penny's associations, my interpretation could still only speak to one aspect of our engagement. This is why Bion talks of K not as knowledge but as an attitude of openness and *not* knowing which any "piece" of knowledge undermines.[2]

Transformations in O

An experience of disconnected elements cohering into understanding does not rock one's sense of oneself. In my example, the subjective experience was somewhat pleasurable. If I had *felt* Penny's rage at *me*, I would have been frightened of its destructive power and ashamed of the heartless capacity that

---

1 As is any selected fact.
2 Bion uses "K" in contradictory ways. As his work develops and he puts more focus on the concept of O, he begins to talk more of K as though it was knowledge itself rather than an attitude of openness to knowing. His earlier emphasis (1962) seems more valuable to me than the later.

allowed me to leave her in the same way her mother had left her when she was an infant. That experience would be a transformation in O.[3]

A transformation in K means one *sees* oneself; a transformation in O is an experience of *being* oneself. When a previously formless bit of oneself, won from the unknown and infinite ocean of one's potential self, comes alive, rather than simply being known about, an old equilibrium is broken up. The individual must reconstruct a new sense of himself. Transformations in O are destabilizing. Bion calls them "catastrophic." "The emotional state of transformations in O is . . . dread" (Bion, 1970, p. 46). Parts of the self that have never been lived emerge and disturb the universe of one's being.

It has been hypothesized that one cause of resistance to transformations in K – the rejection of "correct" interpretations – stems from the fear that insight will lead to these disorienting experiences of the self. Transformations in O are catastrophic from the point of view of the old self structure being revised or destroyed to make way for something new. The new, larger, more developed structure will provide space for a larger share of the person's aliveness and will enable him to see more of the world more accurately. But leaving the safety of the known is always frightening and confusing, touching our earliest bodily memories of birth as well as all of our subsequent losses.

Referring back to Sarah's symptom of spontaneous fantasies of self-mutilation, I would suggest that her previous analytic work had facilitated the transformations in K that I described above. Those interpretations of the meaning of her symptom (whether they were first articulated by her analyst or by herself) had helped her conscious self become strong enough to turn away from the fantasies. (I am not at all suggesting that these interpretations were the main source of the strengthening of her "I"; they functioned, I believe, as tools that her "I", having been strengthened in many other ways by her analytic experience, could use.) It was even possible, she said, that the fantasies had become somewhat less violent, although she was not certain of that. Thinking of transformation in her sense of the word, the nature of her inner structure had changed in the sense that she had become stronger. But she wanted more. I would suggest that what was still lacking was an *experience* of the inner reality that the fantasies expressed. Such an experience would be a transformation in O. One can integrate an aspect of one's inner reality only by experiencing it. A cognitive awareness of its existence may

3 The example of my interaction with Penny is complicated. From the point of view of me-as-an-analyst, my experience in the hour and my interpretation are a transformation in O. I did not come to my interpretation through thinking about the different elements in Penny's associations and her psychology; I came to it through a visceral experience of her inner reality, of Penny's O. I *became* her O. But as a *person*, my understanding and interpretation were transformations in K because I did not experience a new element of *my* O, an experience that would necessarily disturb and disorient me for it would force me to revise my understanding of who I really am.

function as a guidebook or a map; one needs to actually visit the territory to transform it by digesting it.

Freud addresses this fact in his papers on technique. He talks about the possibility of a patient knowing about a repressed experience without being altered by that knowledge. This comes about, he suggests, when

> the thought lacks any connection with the place where the repressed recollection is in some way or other contained. No change is possible until the conscious thought-process has penetrated to that place and has overcome the resistances of repression there.
>
> (Freud, 1913, p. 142)

As we see, he is very much conceiving of the unconscious as a "place" and his formulation is caught in the heroic complex of triumph (where we "penetrate" and "overcome" rather than "unravel" or "submit"), but he is speaking to the same situation Bion addresses with his concept of transformations in O.

In his discussion of the phenomena of the transference, Jung talks about that point in the depths of the work where "the books ... must be ... destroyed 'lest your hearts be rent asunder.' " He is speaking, he says, to the situation where patients imagine that

> They have reached the goal of the work once the unconscious contents have been made conscious and theoretically evaluated. ... An attitude that seeks to do justice to the unconscious as well as to one's fellow human beings cannot possibly rest on knowledge alone. ... Intellectual understanding and aestheticism both produce the deceptive, treacherous sense of liberation and superiority which is liable to collapse if feeling intervenes. Feeling always binds one to the reality and meaning of symbolic contents. ... [The work demands] not only ... the reading of books, meditation and patience, but also love.
>
> (Jung, 1946, paras 486–90)

What is called for is the emotional experience of oneself in the context of a relationship permeated by love, not "knowledge" about oneself in a vacuum.

Winnicott (1960) explores this insidious overvaluation of "understanding" in his work on the True and the False Self. The person who identifies with the False Self almost always locates that self in the mind. Cut off from the True Self – the self that is rooted in the emotional life and in the body – the individual trapped in a False Self organization tries to solve the problems of living with the intellect – so much more reliable an organ than the heart, which can never be contained or even domesticated and which is so very often irrational, permanently resistant to "logic." The only difficulty is that living from the mind rather than the heart leaves the person feeling fake and rather dead. A *person*, like any other mammal, is an emotional creature first; after *having* an experience, the experience can be considered thoughtfully; thinking first in an attempt to "figure out" the experience at issue is a common and not very fruitful approach.

One of Jung's central contributions lies in his understanding of the synthetic meaning of the psyche's symptomatology. A symptom can be traced back to its origin but it also points forward to the future. It has a traumatic cause, but it also represents a constructive attempt by the Self to work through the trauma. A reductive analysis of Sarah's symptom might talk about the way her narcissistic mother fragmented Sarah's self by constantly trying to improve and correct her daughter rather than mirroring her wholeness back to her. It could focus on the way her parents unconsciously forbade any expression of her anger, forcing the emotion to turn inward, against her self. Or it could talk about how her very early awareness of her mother's fragility constellated Sarah's terror of her own aggression, again turning that aggression back upon herself. The interpretations of Sarah's symptom that I have suggested – her self-loathing, her inner deadness, her unfelt emotional pain, all begin as reductive interpretations.

But in addition to encapsulating the damage wrought by her childhood experiences, Sarah's symptom was a constructive attempt by her psyche to work out something. Her fantasy images were ways her psyche was trying to move her toward healing and toward experiencing an area of as-yet-unbearable pain. They challenged her inner deadness, trying to expand her aliveness. They expressed an attempt to reduce her to her raw material in order to reconstruct herself in a more hopeful form. I referred earlier to the fact that in the early stages of an analysis – or in the early stages of any attempt at psychological transformation of the self – dream images may appear that focus on purifying the patient. In primitive or shamanistic rituals attempting to effect a transformation of the initiate, purification is almost always one of the shaman's preparatory operations. Sarah's very painful images of self-destruction call to mind John Donne's poem, "Batter My Heart, Three-Personed God." In the contemporary opera *Doctor Atomic*, by John Adams, Robert Oppenheimer, struggling with the terrible evil he is unleashing on the world, sings this poem in a plea for purification from his involvement in this world-destroying project. One line asks God to "break, bow and burn" the poet in order to "make [him] new." At a constructive level, the fantasies that persecuted Sarah were an attempt to purge her of her evil and to make her worthy of transformation.[4] Ultimately, her fantasies represented

---

4 The reader may rebel at this formulation because he imagines Sarah an innocent victim of the bad parenting that left her with this symptom, but as we explored in Chapter 4, people respond to wounding experiences by constructing anti-relational suits of armor that are composed of "evil" elements of the power complex. Sarah must be cleansed of her reliance on power before she can be transformed.

ways the Self wanted to bring her into the experience Bion called a transformation in O. Let me describe that experience more fully before explaining how we might understand this constructive aspect of Sarah's symptom.

Jung's exploration of transformation

The analytic venture is a search for transformation in O. Insight per se (transformation in K) may lead to inner growth but it can also defend against it. Oh, yes, the patient says, he understands his lateness reflects his resistance to experiencing the analyst's importance to him. But nothing changes. He continues to show up late. The patient is resisting an experience of himself and telling him what that experience might be may be used to reinforce the resistance. "It is not knowledge of reality that is at stake . . . reality is not something which lends itself to being known. . . . Reality has to be 'been' . . ." (Bion, 1965, p. 148). Reality, in other words, must be experienced; life must be *lived*. It is good to know oneself, but the goal of analysis is to live one's life fully, to be oneself. A transformation in O means the person becomes realer. Our hope is that in the crucible of the analytic relationship each person will become bigger and take up greater responsibility for herself. If transformations in K involve knowing more *about* oneself, transformations in O involve *becoming* more of oneself. Both expand the individual, but the former expansion is potential and the latter realized.

Jung (1963) explored this two-step enlargement of consciousness in his alchemical research. Besides turning base metals into gold, alchemists wrote of trying to constellate the "coniunctio:" the marriage of the heavenly king and queen, the union of opposites. Psychologically, this means joining the conscious "I" with some aspect of the unconscious. Jungians call this "holding the opposites," an emotional experience described by Kleinians as "the depressive position." Through the operation of the transcendent function, a new birth emerges from the union of the opposites – a new attitude, a new way of being. Individuation, or emotional development, is a series of coniunctios, bringing together aspects of the "I" with the larger psyche and facilitating the continual emergence of an increasingly differentiated individual. Where Bion speaks in heroic terms that image the emotional struggle involved in growth (something is "won" from the void), Jung, following the alchemists, used the biological imagery of intercourse, conception and birth, emphasizing the helplessness of the experience, where developments "happen," insights "emerge" and new ways of being seize one against one's will.

The alchemists pictured the coniunctio as developing in three stages, only the first two of which concern us here. In the first stage – paralleling transformations in K – the head and the body are separated. Instead of being blindly carried along by the unconscious and discharging unknown emotions (via acting out, somatizing, scrambling up one's thinking and so on), the individual becomes able to think about his feelings and make conscious choices about his actions. This is "the separation of the 'understanding' from the 'great suffering and grief' which nature inflicts on the soul"[5] (Jung, 1963, para 730). It involves "an extension of consciousness and the governance of the soul's motions [i.e. attitudes] by the spirit of truth" (ibid., para 742). One gains perspective on one's complexes rather than living blindly inside a distorted view of the world, compelled to enact old relational patterns, imagining that the self-deceptions embedded in those patterns are objective perceptions of the self and others.

Accomplishment of this first stage improves the quality of one's outer life but deadens the body and the world. The individual knows about his greed, perhaps, thus enabling him to control it rather than enacting an endless quest for material or nonmaterial possessions. But this negative experience restricts rather than enlivens the self. "Now I see my greed, and having seen it I can no longer naively act it out. I am filled with 'Thou shalt not.' " The body's appetites are subjugated and contained. Remembering the distinction between soul and spirit referred to above, the soul has been separated from the body and conquered by the spirit. It is freed from its bondage to the body through the "withdrawal of the naïve projections by which we have moulded both the reality around us and the image of our own character" (ibid., para 739). The person begins to know himself and others, stripping away old comforting fantasies. Sarah's complaint would seem to indicate that in relation to her central symptom the first stage had been completed, but it had not brought her to a new level of aliveness. She knew something about herself and had developed some control over her fantasies, but she had not *really* changed.

The second stage of the coniunctio (transformation in O) reunites the head and the body at a new level. The "living birth" spoken to by the transcendent function comes forth. The soul must not merge with the body again, giving itself over unconditionally to "the world of ten thousand things." But the world of ten thousand things – material goods, ambition, sensual experiences and so on – must be included. This is the spice that gives life zest. Matter must be infused with the vision of Truth won in the first stage. Now, the *reality* of the psyche is absorbed. Where before I recognized my greed and set about containing it, now I experience its power inside me and am humbled. If one developed insight into one's complexes in the first stage, in this second stage one brings that insight into life and lives it. The demands of the complex are experienced and contained, enabling the energy of the complex to be

---

5 To understand Jung's argument, the soul must be distinguished from the spirit. The soul lives in the world of imagination, passion, fantasy. It is the seat of psychopathology and suffering. It is feminine, connected with the night, the dead, the moon. Spirit is filled with light, fire, wind. It is fast, masculine, active, oriented to clear distinctions, transcendence and purity. Where soul swims in the physical world of experience, finding a place for darkness, decay, mystery – for everything – in its universe, spirit strives to transcend the material, to wash away pathology and sin, to become perfect (Hillman, 1975).

channeled in more meaningful ways. This is the transformation that Sarah sought, a redirection into a more constructive channel of the energy that fueled her painful images.

Dividing the coniunctio into stages is artificial. The stages continually interact. A bit of insight is acquired; sliver by sliver it begins to be lived. A mini-transformation in K triggers a mini-transformation in O. I recognize something about my greed; I feel an impact in my body: Oh, my lord, I *am* being greedy! Where the simple recognition can deaden, leading to self-control but not vitalization, the second stage enlivens; energy for life rushes forth, along with the inhibition of the greedy behavior. Referring back to my experience with Penny's fear of her rage, my transformation in K in the first hour paved the way for a deeper transformation in K in the second, which opened the door to a transformation in O where I could *feel* the heartless capacity that allows me to take vacations.

A relatively new patient named Carol was a young university professor in one of the humanities; she had studied Freud, reading much of his work; she had read a little of the Jungian literature, including Jung's *Man and His Symbols* (1964). She certainly knew about the existence of the unconscious. As she talked one day of her wish to be a force for love in the world, I heard many unconscious references to other currents inside her that (most understandably) were interested in more selfish things. When I made some comment about them, she looked at me with consternation. "Does that mean I have parts of me I don't know about?" she asked with distress. Startled, I said, "Of course. Everyone does." I had never imagined that this very elemental fact was unknown to her. And, of course, it was *not* unknown to her. Nor was it actually *known* to her before this moment, and the entire tone of the hour changed after that point. This was a quiet but potent transformation in O.

But development may not proceed in this order. Sometimes a transformation in O precedes a transformation in K. The analyst appears with a small Band Aid on her cheek and the patient feels a sudden dizzying hollowness in his abdomen. He has correctly intuited that the wound is the result of a biopsy and the terror washing over him tells him that the analyst is more important to him than he knew. The physical/emotional experience of his vulnerability – a part of himself he knew less than everything about – leads to the verbal insight recording it. Again, keeping Sarah in the background of our attention, let us look at a more detailed and dramatic example of a transformation in O experienced by a woman named Susan.

Susan

Susan, a 35-year-old university professor, had recently realized that her mother had never been able to take in her anxieties. In the last few months she had talked about her sense of how this must have played out in her infancy.

These were new ideas for her, undermining the remnants of her idealization of her mother. This perspective represented a transformation in K, an insight about her mother's caretaking, not an expanded experience of her self. While she had had feelings about her mother's limitations, they had not been infantile in nature. She had not felt like a terrified infant, emotionally invisible to its mother; she had felt the compassion of an adult for that infant.

In the last of the week's three hours, Susan told a dream: she went down to the basement of her dream house. When she came up, in utter darkness, a shadowy woman told her she needed to be searched for tics. The woman turned on the lights, revealing that the front of Susan's body was "covered with a greenish-white film of wriggling larva, eggs and webbing." Susan woke in fear. Toward the end of that hour I suggested the dream imaged the extent of the problem we were unearthing. Susan nodded and seemed to feel contained by my comment. But in the first hour of the next week she said that over the weekend she remembered what I had said and felt I was triumphing over her, telling her she was inferior to me. Even as she felt this, she said, she had thought her feeling pretty crazy.

In this second week's second hour Susan told another dream: with her mother in the background, she jumped into a deep pool of water, saying, "Look at me!" She associated to her seven-year-old daughter, an only child whose best friend, Betty, also an only child, was disabled. The two children had worked out a sibling relationship for themselves, competing for each mother's attention the way sisters would. "Look at me, look at me," the children would demand, "who do you love best?" No matter how hard Susan tried to be fond of the disabled child, she failed. The rejection and hatred she felt toward the girl, whose disability repelled her, horrified her. Now, talking with considerable affect about the painful ongoing situation, Susan suddenly thought that the part of herself her mother had been unable to receive might imagine itself to be like Betty, deeply unappealing, loathsome. Talking about it, Susan cried uncontrollably. She shivered violently and covered herself with my blanket, but her teeth continued to chatter with her inner cold.

I suggested that when I abandoned her over the weekend, she felt I was sealing her out as her mother had sealed her out, and she had tied that feeling to my comment about the extent of the problem that was imaged in her dream as loathsome webbing and worms. Now Susan began to shake more violently and to talk somewhat incoherently. She said something like, "Oh, no, no, I don't feel that. I'm sure I don't feel that, I couldn't feel something like that. It's not true, I wouldn't think a thing like that, I wouldn't be able to bear thinking something like that, I know I don't." This frantic, jumbled denial went on for thirty or forty seconds. The next day she said she realized as her words tumbled out that the nature of her denial confirmed my interpretation.

This hour contained a series of two transformations in O. In the first, although insight (transformation in K) and psychological growth (transformation in O) went hand in hand, reinforcing and furthering each other, the growth seemed to trigger the insight more than the reverse. Susan's distress as she described her antipathy for Betty expressed a war between her emotions and her reason. She knew the child was simply a little girl whose physical and mental disabilities had led her to adapt as best she could. Starting life with a significant handicap, Betty "should" receive extra attention and concern. But the authentic attention Susan had to offer was negative; she didn't *have* the loving feelings the child "deserved." Susan's inner conflict was like a geological fault underlying an earthquake; it rumbled with seismic activity as she described her upset about her responses to Betty. Suddenly the inner structure swaying in this upheaval collapsed (a transformation in O); at that moment Susan realized that Betty symbolized the unseen part of herself annihilated by her mother's blindness; this insight, in turn, intensified the inner earthquake.

The second transformation, even more catastrophic in nature, clearly followed the transference interpretation that expanded Susan's insight. The ideas she had been absorbing for the past few months regarding her mother's handling of her infant self had undermined her idealized image of her mother; my interpretation now undermined her idealized image of me. These two idealizations reflected the same inner structure: a narcissistic edifice founded on splitting (a "good" part of Susan was paired with a "perfect" part of her mother/myself while the "bad" part that Betty embodied connected to an imperfect and therefore despised aspect of her mother/myself. The perfect mother/analyst is the god and the loathsome, deformed child is the worm). This narcissistic structure reflected Susan's wish to achieve perfection through her tie to a perfect other. Her yearning for perfection (and the invulnerability assumed to accompany it) both caused and reinforced the inner split, distorting her ability to perceive others or herself accurately.

After this experience, Susan found Betty less unappealing; at times fond feelings for the girl even made tentative appearances. Susan had taken in part of herself that she had split off decades earlier.

Sarah

Let me return now to Sarah and her self-destructive fantasies. In the course of an eight-year, three-times-a-week analysis, Sarah descended more deeply into herself than she had been able to do before.[6] In her work with me, Sarah unraveled into a deeply suicidal experience that lasted for about eighteen

6 I want to emphasize that I am not suggesting that I was a "better" analyst than her previous analyst had been. Any analysis will be deeper than any prior analysis because it builds on that previous work and begins with a patient who is larger than he was when he began with his previous analyst.

months. Although she continued to function in her family and in her work, her hours were filled with intense wishes to end her life. She lived across a bay from my office and had to cross a bridge to get to our appointments. She talked of impulses to stop the car and jump, impulses that arose every time she drove over the bridge. In her life, she frequently traveled a windy stretch of highway that ran along the coast, high above the ocean. Devious plans to take the family's old car rather than the newer one that she normally drove besieged Sarah as she imagined driving off the cliff. Anguish over the pain she would cause members of her family by suiciding finally led her to construct a plan to kill herself in a way that she imagined would easily be construed as accidental; she did not tell me her plan, apparently hoping (*most* unrealistically) that I, too, would imagine her death an accident. The danger to Sarah's life seemed very real and this was a terribly difficult period for me, but her lengthy immersion in the despair that lay beneath her persistent fantasies of cutting, burning or pulverizing herself wore itself out over time. Her self-destructive images faded away along with her suicidal plans. Eight years after we had ended, Sarah returned briefly to deal with a crisis; she told me then that the changes had endured. She occasionally had faint echoes of her old self-destructive imagery or of a feeling that life was not worth living. But when these emotions arose, they were neither compelling nor lasting. The transformation she had sought had occurred. Rather than imagining that Sarah "won" that transformation, I would say that she submitted to the great suffering that fueled her symptom – a suffering that could be symbolically imaged as the suffering of childbirth. Through the pain, Sarah had given birth to a fuller self; despair had been transformed into energy for life.

I suggested above that the images of self-attack that persecuted Sarah in a stuck, repetitious fashion were, among other things, constructive attempts on the part of the supraordinate Self to help Sarah to develop. They were attempts to alphabetize agglomerations of β elements lodged like foreign bodies inside her. It is now possible to bring together that notion of β with the idea of transformation in O.

β elements are the residue of experiences that are beyond the person's imagining. The individual has been unable to process them because she lacks an α function sufficiently robust to offer a large-enough inner container. If someone with greater containing capacity is available, she can use projective identification to give that larger person the unbearable experience in question. *Without necessarily engaging in interpretive activity*, by simply *bearing* the intolerable experience in question and surviving it,[7] the analyst or other helper expands the containing capacity on which alphabetizing depends, thus enabling the individual to begin to create α elements out of recalcitrant chunks of β.

---

7 Where "surviving" means continuing to function well as an analyst, not simply to continue breathing.

For Sarah, the β elements she could not transform were the residue of infantile experiences saturated with despair. During the period of her suicidal immersion, a story that she had been told about herself came up. Her sister was born just after Sarah's third birthday, and the new baby had serious colic for her first three months. The baby cried non-stop, Sarah's mother told her, for sixteen hours every day. Mercifully, the infant slept for eight hours every night, but the days were solid wailing. Sarah's mother must have been completely unavailable to Sarah in that period, intensifying the ordinary, powerful affects stirred in any child who is displaced by a new rival for its parents' attention. Additionally, Sarah, like her parents, had been forced to endure the endless hours filled with an infant's unsoothable cries.

One day Sarah's mother left her in the care of a cleaning woman and took the new baby for a walk in the carriage. When she returned, she found that Sarah had managed to climb out the bedroom window in their high-rise apartment building, where she crouched on a ledge, many stories above the sidewalk. A crowd that included two policemen had gathered to stare at the precariously positioned toddler. Sarah's terrified mother told the police which apartment to go to while she remained below, determined to catch her daughter if she "fell." The policeman did pull the little girl to safety, and her parents, like any psychologically naïve people, felt no need to ponder the emotional meaning of Sarah's behavior. But in the context of her analytic work, the incident reverberated with significance, suggesting that her despair over the value of life had roots in her earliest experiences, perhaps even before her sister's birth.

Sarah's parents had clearly loved her, as the story of her mother's delusional intent to catch her shows. But that same intention also suggests something of how limited the mother's own α function seems to have been. Faced with the terrifying sight of her daughter far above the street, the mother resorted to omnipotent plans to save the child, at least as a fallback position, in the event that the policeman's realistic intervention failed. Sarah's experience of her mother was of someone who consistently "disappeared" her children's distressing emotions, simply telling them that they did not feel whatever it was they "imagined" they felt. In this atmosphere, Sarah's doubts about the value of life could not be processed by a mother who, unable to suffer and transform her child's concerns, would erase them. As Sarah's doubts, unprocessed, were stuffed back into her infant self, they would have grown into despair about the possibility of her true self ever being seen and held. Lacking the assistance that her mother's empathic resonance would have brought, Sarah could do nothing with the despair that her mother, by sealing it out, was actually enlarging. The baby could only store her hopelessness inside her, largely in the shape of untransformed β elements.

It is not that Sarah had *no* α function available. The fantasized self-attacks can be seen as imaging a variety of elements. Sarah's mother's emotional impenetrability was supported by her (the mother's) omnipotent defenses.

Sarah must have experienced those defenses as battering attacks on who she really was. Perhaps the mother's stony-hearted condition constellated the violence of Sarah's fantasies as she attempted to penetrate her mother's armor. The murderous rage of those fantasies would be terrifying for the helpless baby and child who needed and also loved her mother. The simplest solution to this dilemma would be for Sarah to turn the images back upon herself. The fantasies in question thus represent the transformation of inchoate emotions into images; the raw emotional experience has been alphabetized at a preliminary level. But however much the images might at one time have helped Sarah to process unbearable feeling, they were now repetitive and stuck. The fantasies were not true dreams at the present time, even if once they had helped her infant self to tolerate an intolerable situation. Now, they accomplished no psychological work, blocking Sarah's development rather than opening her to life's wonders as well as to its disappointments. Before she could use the destructive images produced by her α function in dream work, her α function needed to be enlarged with someone else's assistance. Even before we had developed names for describing Sarah's despair, or the expanded narrative of its origin that we eventually came to, I shared that despair empathically to support the gradual growth in her α function that ultimately took us to the terrible eighteen-month period of a full-blown experience of the death wishes that underlay her images. That period was a lengthy transformation in O of the hopelessness behind her symptom. Sarah had already come to *know about* her despondent self; now she *lived* it.

Living her despair was a transformation in O made possible by the expanded α function that my holding facilitated; via introjection, our experience supported the growth of Sarah's α function. Transformations in O and the dreaming capacity of the psyche depend upon and nurture each other as they develop. They have what Bion calls a symbiotic relationship in that the two psychological functions, working in tandem, foster each other's growth.

Conclusion

If we hold in mind Bion's notions of the psyche's dreaming function and of transformations in O, our understanding of our role as therapists moves away from the idea that healing emerges from telling the patient something about himself. Simply making something intellectually conscious is not a meaningful activity. And our hope for what analysis can offer shifts, too. Instead of expecting the patient to become "more conscious" or "better adapted," we can hope that the patient will open to the fullness of his life experience. When the work works, the patient will become more alive, increasingly aware of the way in which so much more than we know is always happening, and increasingly able to take the terrifying step of investigating what that "more" might consist of. Instead of merely knowing more about himself and therefore having a more accurate picture of himself and the world, the quality of his experience will deepen and shift away from questions of right and wrong to questions of intensity and fullness. The patient may not be "better adapted" at all when he finishes an analysis. He may be more quirky, more independent of others' opinions; hopefully he will be walking his own unique path in time with his own unique rhythms.

The therapist, working to ground herself in unknowing and to open herself to the fullness of the immediate moment, will experience that same shift. Instead of striving to produce a "correct" interpretation, she will be trying to sink into the fullness of her own aliveness, to open herself to the patient's transmitting unconscious. Her work will quicken and become more exciting. As will her life.

Referring back to the area of Faith that can replace the world of Knowing, faith involves

> the struggle not only to know but in some way be one's true self, to take up the journey with all that one is and may become, and to encounter through oneself the ground of one's being. This is undertaken with the knowledge that we are mediate beings, that certainty is beyond certain reach, but that anything short of this attempt portends disaster and is self-crippling. The undertaking itself involves one in continuous re-creation.
>
> (Eigen, 1981, p. 425)

This is the world of transformations in O.

Bion's concept O is one aspect of his exploration of the mystery of the psyche. Winnicott also circled around that mystery in his writing. Kohut gestures toward it when he describes the indefinability of the self (1977). Jung has been violently rejected in the psychoanalytic world, partly because of his status as anti-Freud, but partly because he is straightforwardly mystical. Many psychoanalysts who recognize the value of Bion's early work on groups and psychosis shy away from the later work that delves into the realm of unknowability.

All human beings are torn between the −K wish to be certain versus curiosity regarding the truth, between the narcissistic wish for self-sufficiency and the primal yearning for interdependent relationships. The truth cannot be *known*, and this truth – the fundamental mystery of life – is bearable only briefly and only in the context of a loving relationship. We are essentially lost in the world, unable to even sort out what belongs inside us and what comes from outside, who we are and who the other is. The level of vulnerability that this implies is extraordinary, and we strenuously protect ourselves from a full experience of it. It is deeply disorienting to recognize that what modern physics teaches us about the inherent mystery of the universe's nature applies to us as well as to subatomic particles.

In the depth psychological world, narcissistic −K energy manifests in the widespread focus on insight, something that feels much less threatening than experiences that upset the ground on which patient and analyst stand. These disorienting experiences, which can emerge only in the context of a relationship – transformations in O – are the heart of the work, but even when they are experienced more vicariously than directly (more in the patient than the analyst), the out-of-control nature of a shift in the analytic couple's way of being is feared by both members of the dyad. –K energy fuels the driven quest for the "correct" interpretation (surely as illusory an object as a "complete" analysis), the over-determined use of the word "scientific" to modify the products of our field (papers, conferences, etc.), the rejection of studying the psyche's religious instinct, and, I believe, the extraordinary annihilation of Jung and his work by the psychoanalytic community.

Bion's concept of O provides a link with much of Jung's work and by holding the two men's visions in mind we arrive at a much fuller picture of our position in the world, a position of deep vulnerability. That vulnerability is experienced primarily in the context of intimate relationships. Because of personal, social and profession-wide resistances, neither Bion nor Jung was able to put our need for connection at the center of his understanding of the human animal. I believe that at this stage of our development – as a profession and as a society – it may now be possible for us to hold how fundamental the need for interpersonal relatedness is and to accept it as the basis of emotional health.

Bibliography

Andrade de Azevedo, Ana Maria (2000) "Substantive Unconscious and Adjective Unconscious: The Contribution of Wilfred Bion", in *The Journal of Analytical Psychology*, 45: 75–91.

Anonymous (1985) *Tanakh: The Holy Scriptures*, Philadelphia and Jerusalem: The Jewish Publication Society.

Bainton, Roland (1950) *Here I Stand*, New York: Abingdon-Cokesbury.

Balint, Michael (1968) *The Basic Fault: Therapeutic Aspects of Regression*, New York: Brunner/Mazel.

Baranger, M., Baranger, W. and Mom, J. (1983) "Process and Non-Process in Analytic Work", in *International Journal of Psychoanalysis*, 64: 1–15.

Bion, W. R. (1959) "Attacks on Linking", in *Second Thoughts* (1967), New York: Jason Aronson, Inc.

—— (1962) *Learning from Experience*, in *Seven Servants: Four Works by Wilfred Bion* (1977), New York: Jason Aronson, Inc.

—— (1962a) "A Theory of Thinking", in *International Journal of Psycho-Analysis*, 43.

—— (1963) *Elements of Psycho-Analysis*, in *Seven Servants: Four Works by Wilfred Bion* (1977), New York: Jason Aronson, Inc.

—— (1965) *Transformations*, in *Seven Servants: Four Works by Wilfred Bion* (1977), New York: Jason Aronson, Inc.

—— (1967) "Notes on Memory and Desire", in Robert Langs (ed.) (1981) *Classics in Psychoanalytic Technique*, New York and London: Jason Aronson, Inc., pp. 259–61.

—— (1970) *Attention and Interpretation*, in *Seven Servants: Four Works by Wilfred Bion* (1977), New York: Jason Aronson, Inc.

—— (1977) *Seven Servants: Four Works by Wilfred Bion*, New York: Jason Aronson, Inc.

—— (1979/2000) "Making the Best of a Bad Job", in Francesca Bion (ed.) *Clinical Seminars and Other Works*, London: Karnac Books.

—— (1992) *Cogitations*, London: Karnac Books.

—— (2000) Francesca Bion (ed.) *Clinical Seminars and Other Works*, London: Karnac Books.

—— (2005) Francesca Bion (ed.) *The Tavistock Seminars*, London: Karnac Books.

Blatt, Sidney J. (2007) Letter to the editor of the *New York Times*, April 11, 2007.

Bollas, Christopher (2006) "The Escape from Free Association", paper presented at Laurel Heights Conference Center in San Francisco, June 17.

Campbell, Joseph (1949) *The Hero With a Thousand Faces*, New York: Bollingen Series, Pantheon Books.

Casement, Patrick J. (1991) *Learning From the Patient*, London: Guilford Press.

Chapman, Robert L. (ed.) (1992) *Roget's International Thesaurus*, New York: Harper Collins.

Cirlot, J. E. (1962) *A Dictionary of Symbols*, New York: The Philosophical Library.

Clark, Ronald W. (1971) *Einstein: The Life and Times*, New York and Cleveland: The World Publishing Company.

Coleman, Warren (2005) "Sexual Metaphor and the Language of Unconscious Phantasy", in *The Journal of Analytical Psychology*, 50: 641–60.

Coltart, Nina E. C. (1982) " 'Slouching Towards Bethlehem . . .' or Thinking the Unthinkable in Psychoanalysis", in Gregorio Kohon (ed.) (1989) *The British School of Psychoanalysis: the independent tradition*, New Haven: Yale University Press, pp. 185–99.

Culbert-Koehn, JoAnn (1997) "Between Bion and Jung: A Talk with James Grotstein", in *The San Francisco Jung Institute Library Journal*, 15, 4: 15–33.

Dehing, J. (1993) "The Transcendent Function: A Critical Re-evaluation", in *Journal of Analytical Psychology*, 38: 221–35.

Dieckmann, H. (1972) *Ego and Archetype: Individuation and the Religious Function of the Psyche*, Baltimore: Penguin Books Inc.

—— (1976) "Transference and Countertransference: Results of a Berlin Research Group", in *Journal of Analytical Psychology*, 21, 1: 25–36.

Edinger, Edward F. (1996) *The Aion Lectures: Exploring the Self in C.G. Jung's Aion*, Deborah A. Wesley (ed.), Toronto: Inner City Books.

Eigen, Michael (1981) "The Area of Faith in Winnicott, Lacan and Bion", in *International Journal of Psycho-Analysis*, 62: 413–33.

Eisold, K. (2005) "Using Bion", in *Psychoanalytic Psychology*, 22: 357–69.

Fairbairn, W. R. D. (1952) *Psychoanalytic Studies of the Personality*, London: Tavistock Publications Limited.

Ferro, Antonino (2002) *In the Analyst's Consulting Room*, trans. Philip Slotkin, Hove, UK/New York: Routledge.

—— (2005) *Seeds of Illness, Seeds of Recovery*, trans. Philip Slotkin, Hove and New York: Brunner-Routledge.

—— (2006) *Psychoanalysis and Therapy and Storytelling*, trans. Philip Slotkin, London and New York: Routledge.

Fordham, Michael (1978) *Jungian Psychotherapy: A Study in Analytical Psychology*, Chichester, New York, Brisbane, Toronto: John Wiley & Sons.

Fox, Everett (trans.) (1983) *The Five Books of Moses: Genesis, Exodus, Leviticus, Numbers, Deuteronomy*, New York: Schocken Books.

Freud, S. (1911) "The Handling of Dream-Interpretation in Psycho-Analysis", *SE XII*, pp. 91–96, London: Hogarth Press.

—— (1912) "Recommendations to Physicians Practicing Psycho-Analysis", *SE XII*, pp. 111–20, London: Hogarth Press.

—— (1913) "On Beginning the Treatment", *SE XII*, pp. 121–44, London: Hogarth Press.

—— (1914) "Remembering, Repeating and Working Through (Further Recommendations on the Technique of Psycho-Analysis II)", *SE XII*, pp. 143–56, London: Hogarth Press.

Gay, Peter (1988) *Freud: A Life for Our Time*, New York and London: W. W. Norton & Company.

Gordon, Rosemary (1985) "Big Self and Little Self: Some Reflections", in *The Journal of Analytical Psychology*, 30: 261–71.

Gove, Philip Babcock, Ph.D., Editor in Chief and the Merriam-Webster Editorial Staff (1993) *Webster's Third New International Dictionary of the English Language Unabridged*, Springfield, MA: Merriam-Webster, Inc.

Greene, Brian (2004) *The Fabric of the Cosmos: Space, Time and the Texture of Reality*, New York: Vintage Books.

Grinberg, Leon, Dario Sor and Tabak de Bianchedi, Elizabeth (1977) *Introduction to the Work of Bion*, New York: Jason Aronson, Inc.

Grotstein, James (2004a) " 'The Light Militia of the Lower Sky': The Deeper Nature of Dreaming and Phantasying", in *Psychoanalytic Dialogues*, 14, 1: 99–118.

—— (2004b) "The Seventh Servant: The implications of a Truth Drive in Bion's Theory of 'O' ", in *International Journal of Psycho-Analysis*, 85: 1081–101.

—— (2007) *A Beam of Intense Darkness: Wilfred Bion's Legacy to Psychoanalysis*, London: Karnac Books.

Hillman, James (1975) *Re-Visioning Psychology*, New York, Evanston, San Francisco, London: Harper & Row.

Jacobi, Jolande (1959) *Complex/Archetype/Symbol in the Psychology of C. G. Jung*, Princeton, New Jersey: Princeton University Press.

Jung, C. G. (1916) "The Transcendent Function", in *CW 8*, Princeton, New Jersey: Princeton University Press.

—— (1926) "Spirit and Life", in *CW 8*, pp. 319–37, Princeton, New Jersey: Princeton University Press.

—— (1936/37) "The Concept of the Collective Unconscious", in *CW9i*, Princeton, New Jersey: Princeton University Press.

—— (1937) *Psychology and Religion, CW 11*, pp. 3–105, Princeton, New Jersey: Princeton University Press.

—— (1938) "Psychological Aspects of the Mother Archetype", in *CW 9i*, pp. 75–112, Princeton, New Jersey: Princeton University Press.

—— (1939) "Conscious, Unconscious, and Individuation", in *CW9i*, pp. 275–89, Princeton, New Jersey: Princeton University Press.

—— (1940/1954) "Transformation Symbolism in the Mass", in *CW11*, pp. 201–96, Princeton, New Jersey: Princeton University Press.

—— (1946) *The Psychology of the Transference, CW 16*, pp. 163–323, Princeton, New Jersey: Princeton University Press.

—— (1948a) "The Phenomenology of the Spirit in Fairytales", in *CW9i*, pp. 207–54, Princeton, New Jersey: Princeton University Press.

—— (1948b) "A Psychological Approach to the Dogma of the Trinity", in *CW 11*, pp. 107–200, Princeton, New Jersey: Princeton University Press.

—— (1950a) "Concerning Mandala symbolism", in *CW 9i*, pp. 355–84, Princeton, New Jersey: Princeton University Press.

—— (1950b) "A Study in the Process of Individuation", in *CW9i*, pp. 290–354, Princeton, New Jersey: Princeton University Press.

—— (1950c) "Concerning Rebirth", in *CW9i*, pp. 113–50, Princeton, New Jersey: Princeton University Press.

—— (1952) *Psychology and Alchemy, CW 12*, Princeton, New Jersey: Princeton University Press.

—— (1953) *Two Essays on Analytical Psychology, CW 7*, Princeton, New Jersey: Princeton University Press.

—— (1956) *Symbols of Transformation, CW 5*, Princeton, New Jersey: Princeton University Press.

—— (1958) "Jung and Religious Belief", in *CW 18*, Princeton, New Jersey: Princeton University Press.

—— (1959a) "Good and Evil in Analytical Psychology", in *CW 10*, Princeton, New Jersey: Princeton University Press.

—— (1959b) Letter to Valentine Brooke, November 16, 1959, in Gerhard Adler in collaboration with Aniela Jaffe (eds), trans. R. F. C. Hull (1975) *C.G. Jung: Letters*, Volume 2: 1951–61, Princeton, New Jersey: Princeton University Press.

—— (1960) *The Structure and Dynamics of the Psyche, CW 8*, Princeton, New Jersey: Princeton University Press.

—— (1963) *Mysterium Coniunctionis, CW 14*, Princeton, New Jersey: Princeton University Press.

—— (1964) *Man and His Symbols*, New York: Bantam Doubleday, Dell Publishing Group.

—— (1965) *Memories, Dreams, Reflections*, Aniela Jaffe (ed.), New York: Vintage Books, a Division of Random House.

—— (1971) *Psychological Types, CW 6*, Princeton, New Jersey: Princeton University Press.

—— (1976) *The Visions Seminars: Notes of the Seminars in Analytical Psychology, 1930–1934*, Zurich: Spring Publications.

—— (1984) *Dream Analysis: Notes of the Seminar Given in 1928–1930*, William McGuire (ed.), Princeton, New Jersey: Princeton University Press.

Kalsched, Donald (1996) *The Inner World of Trauma: Archetypal Defenses of the Personal Spirit*, London and New York: Routledge.

Klein, Melanie, Heimann, Paula and Money-Kyrle, R. E. (eds) (1955) *New Directions in Psychoanalysis*, New York: Basic Books.

Kohut, Heinz (1977) *The Restoration of the Self*, New York: International Universities Press.

Meltzer, Donald (1973) *Sexual States of Mind*, Perthshire, Scotland: Clunie Press.

Meltzer, Donald (1978/1998) *The Kleinian Development*, London: Karnac Books.

Milton, J. (1968) *Paradise Lost*, Clinton, MA: Colonial Press, Inc.

Ogden, T. H. (1994) "The Analytic Third: Working with Intersubjective Clinical Facts", in *International Journal of Psychoanalysis*, 75: 3–19.

—— (1997) *Reverie and Interpretation: Sensing Something Human*, Northvale, New Jersey and London: Jason Aronson, Inc.

—— (2001) *Conversations at the Frontier of Dreaming*, Northvale, New Jersey and London: Jason Aronson, Inc.

Overbye, Dennis (2006) "Knowing the Universe in Detail (Except for That Pesky 96 Per Cent Of It)", in *The New York Times Science Times*, October 24, p. D3.

Redfearn, J. W. T. (1983) "Ego and Self: Terminology", in *Journal of Analytical Psychology*, 28: 91–106.

Richardson, Tom (2006) Personal communication.

Rosenfeld, Herbert (1987) *Impasse and Interpretation*, Hove and New York: Brunner-Routledge.

Searles, Harold F. (1979) *Countertransference and Related Subjects*, New York: International University Press, Inc.

Siassi, Shahrzad (2007) "Forgiveness, Acceptance and the Matter of Expectation", in *International Journal of Psychoanalysis*, 88: 1423–40.

Steiner, J. (1993) *Psychic Retreats*, London: Routledge.

Sullivan, Barbara Stevens (1989) *Psychotherapy Grounded in the Feminine Principle*, Wilmette, Illinois: Chiron Publications.

Symington, Joan and Neville Symington (1996) *The Clinical Thinking of Wilfred Bion*, London and New York: Routledge.

Symington, Neville (1983) "The Analyst's Act of Freedom as Agent of Therapeutic Change", in Gregorio Kohon (ed.) (1989) *The British School of Psychoanalysis: The Independent Tradition*, New Haven: Yale University Press.

—— (2002) *A Pattern of Madness*, London: Karnac Books.

—— (2005) "Change Generated by Person to Person Contact", unpublished paper.

—— (2006) *A Healing Conversation: How Healing Happens*, London: Karnac Books.

—— (2007) "A Technique for Facilitating the Creation of Mind", in *International Journal of Psychoanalysis*, 88: 1409–22.

Ulanov, A. B. (1997) "Transference, the Transcendent Function, and Transcendence", in *The Journal of Analytical Psychology*, 42: 119–38.

Von Franz, M.-L. (1974) *Shadow and Evil in Fairytales*, Zurich: Spring Publications.

Winnicott, D. W. (1947) "Hate in the Countertransference", in D. W. Winnicott (1958) *Through Paediatrics to Psychoanalysis*, London: The Hogarth Press.

—— "Birth Memories, Birth Trauma, and Anxiety", in *Through Paediatrics to Psychoanalysis* (1975), London: Basic Books, Inc.

—— (1952) "Anxiety Associated with Insecurity", in D. W. Winnicott (1958) *Through Paediatrics to Psychoanalysis*, London: The Hogarth Press.

—— (1960) "Ego Distortion in Terms of True and False Self", in *The Maturational Processes and the Facilitating Environment* (1965), New York: International Universities Press, Inc.

—— (1963) "Fear of Breakdown", in Clare Winnicott, Ray Shepherd and Madeleine Davis (eds) (1989) *Psychoanalytic Explorations*, Cambridge, MA: Harvard University Press.

—— (1965) *The Maturational Process and the Facilitating Environment*, New York: International Universities Press, Inc.

—— (1971) *Playing and Reality*, London and New York: Tavistock Publications.

—— (1989) *Psychoanalytic Explorations*, Clare Winnicott, Ray Shepherd, and Madeleine Davis (eds), Cambridge, MA: Harvard University Press.

Index

acceptance: of people as they are 24; of terrible emotions 146, 150; by the therapist 150

acting out 72, 91, 93, 120, 250

Adams, John: *Doctor Atomic* 249

agonies 116, 137, 143

"aha" moments 40

alchemy 33, 36, 43–4, 89, 250–1

alpha (α) elements 74–8; transformation of beta elements into 71–2, 76

alpha (α) function 68, 71, 72, 74, 75–7, 78; in the analytic situation 88–96; analytic study of a patient deficient in 96–116; contact barrier and 79–81; development of 81–5; PS ↔ D sequence and 85–8

analysis: aim/goal of 1n1, 22, 31–2, 43, 149–50, 244, 250; alpha function in the analytic situation 88–96; analytic study of a patient deficient in alpha function 96–116; effective action of 3–4, 13–14, 94; the hour as a dream 111–16; monomyth and 14; nature of 22–3, 24, 211–13

analysts/therapists: analytic practitioner's development 54–5; awareness of their own clinical choices 10–11; compassionate holding of distress 24; containment by 26–7, 64; curiosity of 5, 12, 24, 44–5, 91, 168, 221, 222; inevitable and needed failure of 116; reverie of 16, 85, 90, 92, 96, 183, 216–18, 219–22, 226, 233; "taking over" of patient's suffering 89; transformative work to change self 16

analytic field 14, 18–19

analytic frame 5

analytic relationship *see* therapeutic relationship

analytic stance 19–20, 24–5; symbolic attitude 23–5, 37–8

analytic third 14–15, 26, 97, 181, 234

Andrade de Azevedo, A. M. 48, 49, 81

anti-related energy 5, 22, 78, 117, 118–19, 125

archetypes 42, 45–8

assumptions: basic assumption behavior 93; unconscious 128, 184–5

Balint, Michael 14

Baranger, M., Baranger, W. and Mom, J. 14

basic assumption behavior 93

being in the now 221–5

beta (β) elements 70–2, 76, 91, 101–2, 255–6

Bion, W. R. 9–10, 33–4, 36, 192; alpha elements 76; analytic technique 211; (β) beta elements 70–2, 76, 101–2; Christian myth 58; contact barrier 78–9, 80; container–contained process/apparatus 82–5, 199–200; dreams 48, 80–1; emotional storms in the analytic situation 116; envy 198–200, 201–2; experiencing emotional life 68–9, 182; faith 234, 236; fear of change 241; Freud and 34–5; frustration tolerance 73, 124, 189–90, 192–3, 194; α (alpha) function 68, 75–7, 78, 80–8; God 52; Grid 87–8, 193, 203; Hate (H) link 125; infinite nature of the unconscious 31; intuition 225, 232; K link 21, 195–6; –K (negative K) 198–9, 203–4; Language of Achievement 20, 230; linking attacks 78; links 194–9, 245, 246, 247; the listening process 214–18, 221–2; maternal reverie 82–8; motivation principles 129; narcissism versus social-ism/relatedness 88, 121–2, 189, 201–2; not knowing 226, 230; "O" 19, 32–3, 38–45, 47, 48, 52, 55, 65–6, 181, 183, 193–4, 215, 221, 226, 258–9; openness 227–8; pre-conception 75–6; primacy of the psyche 35–8; primordial mind 46; rage 192–3, 194; reality 229; the repressed unconscious 69; thinking 18, 34, 82–8, 182, 203–4; transformation 243–4, 245, 247; translations and varying uses of concepts 20–1; truth and lies 167–8, 169, 170, 182, 189–90, 192–4; "withoutness" in the container-contained 199–200

Bollas, Christopher 229

Printed in Great Britain
by Amazon

52801379R00156